The
Dise

**V**

# The Limits of Disenchantment

*Essays on Contemporary European Philosophy*

◆

PETER DEWS

**VERSO**

London • New York

First published by Verso 1995
© Peter Dews 1995
All rights reserved

**Verso**
UK: 6 Meard Street, London W1V 3HR
USA: 180 Varick Street, New York NY 10014–4606

Verso is the imprint of New Left Books

ISBN 1–85984–927–X
ISBN 1–85984–022–1 (pbk)

**British Library Cataloguing in Publication Data**
A catalogue record for this book is available from the British Library

**Library of Congress Cataloging-in-Publication Data**
Dews, Peter.
    The limits of disenchantment : essays on contemporary
European philosophy / Peter Dews.
        p.      cm.
    Includes bibliographical references and index.
    ISBN 1–85984–927–X. — ISBN 1–85984–022–1
(pbk.)
    1. Philosophy, European—20th century.   2.
Philosophy, Modern—20th century.   I. Title.
B804.D47 1995
190′.9′04—dc20                                    95–36286
                                                          CIP

Typeset by M Rules
Printed and bound in Great Britain by
Biddles Ltd, Guildford and King's Lynn

For Clair

# Contents

# Preface

Feelings of pleasure are invariably mixed with surprise, and a certain sense of disorientation, when one finally discovers what one has been thinking. When I came to assemble the essays for this collection, and to complete a number of projects for it which had been abandoned under the pressure of other tasks and commitments, it emerged that their common feature, however muted and refracted, was a resistance to the widespread deflationary tendency of contemporary thinking. This tendency seems to cut across traditions, from analytical philosophy and neo-pragmatism, via deconstruction, to current versions of Critical Theory. It frequently presents itself as an open-eyed acceptance, whether exuberant or sober, of the cold reality of the modern world. Apart from their scepticism about the assumptions behind this posture, the essays in this volume do not pretend to any special coherence of theme, or even to strict consistency in their conclusions. They are offered here as a record of excursions and excavations, in the hope that others will take up the invitation to argue.

I owe some rather specific debts of gratitude to individuals and institutions for helping to make this volume possible. I would like first of all to thank the Alexander von Humboldt Foundation for the Fellowship which I held at the University of Tübingen in 1991. A good number of the essays in this collection were either completed or initially drafted during this precious period of respite from everyday academic duties, and the essential research for others was carried out. To work in the library of the Philosophical Seminar at Tübingen, looking out over the Neckar, and with the school attended by Hegel, Schelling and Hölderlin just along the street, is to be movingly reminded of those historical responsibilities of reflection whose modern forgetting the three young comrades so powerfully diagnosed in later years. The University of Essex kindly provided support from its research promotion fund in the spring of 1995 to speed the completion of the project. My colleague Jay Bernstein was generous to a fault in agreeing to take over some of my administrative duties prematurely, in order to enable me to meet my deadlines, and his marginalia on

a copy of the draft of Chapter 12 proved an invaluable guide when I came
to revise it. Malcolm Imrie was a patient and encouraging editor at Verso.
Jason Gaiger provided vital editorial and practical assistance, and made
many shrewd philosophical criticisms and helpful stylistic suggestions
during the final stages of the production of the manuscript. His calm
collaboration was a genuine source of pleasure during a very busy period,
and I would like to record my special thanks here. Special thanks are due
also to Jane Hindle at Verso for all her work in turning the manuscript into
a book.

Rodolphe Gasché's lively improvised response to an early sketch of
Chapter 6, which was presented during a round-table discussion with
Simon Critchley and myself organized by the Centre for Theoretical
Studies at Essex in February 1992, encouraged my conviction that the
issues at stake were central. I hope he will take the vigour of my arguments
as a tribute to the challenge posed by his position. Chapter 12 continues a
debate with Slavoj Žižek which I have enjoyed pursuing across sporadic
encounters over the past few years.

I must also thank the following colleagues who, by inviting me to speak
or write on various occasions, have encouraged me to venture into new
areas and to look askance at my own assumptions: Maria Baghramian,
Richard Bernstein, Rüdiger Bubner, Anthony Elliott, Jürgen Habermas,
Margaret Iverson, Richard Kearney, Harry Kunneman, Lucy O'Brien,
Jacob Rogozinski, René von Schomberg, Bernard Taureck, David Wood
and Wolfgang Zierhofer. I am fortunate to work in a philosophy depart-
ment where passion and experimentation are not regarded as incompatible
with the discipline of thinking. My own thoughts have been stimulated and
corrected by the many discussions, whether formal or impromptu, I have
had with colleagues at Essex, and by a number of friends who have been
invaluable and inspiring critics and interlocutors. I must mention in particular: Jay Bernstein, Andrew Bowie, Maeve Cooke, Simon Critchley,
Alex Düttmann, Manfred Frank, Axel Honneth, Stephen Mulhall,
Michael Newman, Peter Osborne, Dagmar Reichert, Julian Roberts, Cara
Ryan, Mark Sacks, Rudi Visker and Joel Whitebook.

Back home, Maude, Jacob and Luan have continued to surprise me
with insights I am unlikely ever to find in a philosophy book. And Clair
Wills, through her love and support, her verve in discussion, and her frank
criticism, has kept me mindful that thinking only truly stays alive when it
is part of a wider and more generous pattern of commitments. The dedi-
cation of this book can give but the faintest indication of all I owe to her.

*Peter Dews*
*Essex*
*August 1995*

# Author's Note

In revising these essays for publication in the present form I have sought, wherever possible, to provide an additional reference to an English translation when the existing reference was to the original foreign language edition of a text. In these cases, despite the double reference, the translation is my own. Where only the translation is cited, any amendment on my part has been signalled.

The bibliography lists the individual articles which I have cited from a collection, as well as giving the details of the collection itself. However, where the collection was not originally published in English, I have not listed the translation of every article drawn on, but have considered it sufficient to give the details of the English version of the collection as a whole. An exception occurs, of course, when the translation of an article is not included in the English version of the relevant collection, or where the original reference was directly to the English translation.

# Introduction: The Limits
# of Disenchantment

In a passage from *The Case of Wagner*, Nietzsche affirms that 'Hegel is a *taste*. – And not merely a German but a European taste. – A taste Wagner comprehended – to which he felt equal – which he immortalized – he invented a style for himself charged with "infinite meaning" – he became the *heir of Hegel*. – Music as "idea." –'[1] Nietzsche's virtuoso attack on Wagner's music for its portentous depths and sham reconciliations – traits which he sees as inherited from Idealist metaphysics, but which here mask egoistic calculation and a manipulation of emotion which violates aesthetic form – marks the emergence of a distinctively modernist sensibility. For this new outlook, philosophical and aesthetic attempts to restore meaning to a disenchanted universe are in deep collusion with what they seem to oppose. As Charles Taylor has recently reminded us, by the late nineteenth century: 'Victorian piety and sentimentality seemed to have captured the Romantic spirit. For those who saw this whole world as spiritually hollow and flat, Romanticism could appear as integral to what they rejected as instrumentalism was. It merely offered trivialized, ersatz, or inauthentic meanings to compensate for a meaningless world.'[2] Astutely, Nietzsche suggests that 'transposed into hugeness, Wagner does not seem to have been interested in any problems except those which now occupy the little decadents in Paris. Always five steps from the hospital. All of them entirely modern, entirely *metropolitan* problems.'[3] Against such mystification, the new aesthetic of modernism strove for a coldness, remoteness and impersonality which Nietzsche already anticipates when he invokes against Wagner 'the great logic, the dance of the stars'.

Since the time of Nietzsche's polemics, this suspicion of depth and meaning – of any mode of significance which cannot be relativized to a specific practice, framework or perspective – has recurred throughout twentieth-century art and philosophy. One might have thought that the disenchantment of the world classically described by Max Weber, the collapse of belief in a cosmic order whose immanent meaning guides human endeavour, would constitute a cultural trauma of such magnitude that

1

philosophy could do little other than struggle to come to terms with it – and indeed, the shock waves of this collapse have reverberated throughout nineteenth- and twentieth-century thinking. Yet there have also been many philosophers who appear to have registered no turbulence at all. On the contrary, they are eager to drive the process of disillusionment further. Richard Rorty, for example, advocates a 'philosophical superficiality and light-mindedness' which 'helps along the disenchantment of the world' and which, he believes, will 'make the world's inhabitants more pragmatic, more tolerant, more liberal, more receptive to the appeal of instrumental rationality'.[4] It is arguable, however, that Rorty can think thus only because he assumes that we can take *seriously* meanings which we know we have created, and which flimsily veil the indifferent universe of physicalism which Rorty – for all his hermeneutic gestures – regards as the ontological bottom line. Other recent thinkers have been intolerant of even this resid-ual soft-heartedness. They have considered it their job to track down and eradicate those last traces of meaning which adhere to the human world, to dissolve any supposedly intrinsic significance of lived experience into an effect of impersonal structures and forces. The impulse here is still Promethean: for meaning, as Adorno emphasized, implies *givenness* – it is something we encounter and experience, not something we can arbitrarily posit, as Rorty and others too quickly assume. And this very givenness seems often to be regarded as an affront to human powers of self-assertion. It is for this reason, no doubt, that so much recent French thought has raised the question of whether, as Herbert Schnädelbach has put it, 'man himself has become, after God and nature, an anthropomorphism'.[5] And while contemporary Critical Theory in Germany has insisted on preserv-ing that island of human significance known as the 'lifeworld' from radical dismantling, there are serious questions, as we shall see, about how reliable the insular dykes and defences might be in holding back the tide.

The dominant paradigm of hostility to meaning in recent European philos-ophy has undoubtedly been deconstruction, which initially appeared on the scene as a radicalization of Heidegger's overcoming of metaphysics. The thought of the early Derrida is marked by a determination to go beyond Heidegger which focuses on his mentor's refusal to abandon the philosoph-ical quest for meaning, in the form of *Seinsfrage* – the question of the 'meaning of Being'. In his lectures on Nietzsche from the late 1930s and early 1940s, Heidegger argued that Nietzsche's doctrine of the 'will-to-power' represents both the culmination and the definitive exposé of the subjectivism of Western metaphysics. In its equation of 'being-ness' [*Seiendheit*] with makeability or manipulation [*Machenschaft*], it announces the 'age of completed meaninglessness' in which 'meaninglessness becomes the "meaning" of entities as a whole'.[6] But at the same time the very extremity of this experience of the collapse of meaning opens the way for a questioning of the meaning of Being as such, as opposed to that of entities, a meaning which the history of metaphysics has plunged into oblivion. Thus for Heidegger the *Seinsfrage* is a post-Nietzschean question. It is distinct from the various interpretations of the totality of beings, and of the being of entities, which a metaphysics fixated on the objectifying notion of presence has offered over the past two thousand years. These interpretations culminate in the Nietzschean doctrines of the eternal return and the will-to-power, which finally give the game away.

But, as is well known, Derrida refuses to recognize this distinction between Being [*Sein*] and beings [*Seiendes*] as Heidegger proposes it. In his earlier writings he takes Nietzsche's part against Heidegger, claiming that Nietzsche's distinctive *practice* of writing has contributed to the 'liberation of the signifier from its dependence or derivation with respect to the logos and the related concept of truth or the primary signified'.[7] This is because 'Reading, and therefore writing, the text were for Nietzsche "originary" operations . . . with regard to a sense that they do not first have to transcribe or discover, which would not therefore be a truth signified in the original element and presence of the logos.'[8] From such a standpoint Heideggerian thought could be seen as reinstating rather than destroying 'the instance of the logos and of the truth of being as "primum signatum"'.[9] Indeed, Derrida draws the conclusion that the 'meaning of Being is not a transcendental or trans-epochal signified (even if it was always dissimulated within the epoch) but already, in a truly *unheard of* sense, a determined signifying trace'.[10]

In his manifesto 'Différance', Derrida returns to the issue of how his own thought of *différance* goes beyond Heidegger's thought of the ontological difference between Being and beings: 'And yet, are not the thought of the *meaning* or *truth* of Being, the determination of *différance* as the ontico-ontological difference, difference thought within the horizon of the question of *Being*, still intrametaphysical effects of *différance*?'[11] In this function of being 'older' than the ontico-ontological difference Derrida terms *différance* the 'play of the trace', which 'no longer belongs to the horizon of Being, but whose play transports and encloses the meaning of Being: the play of the trace, or the *différance*, which has no meaning and is not'.[12]

It should be noted that Derrida's intention does not seem to be to claim, in nihilistic fashion, that there simply *is* no meaning. He merely asserts that the sense conveyed by Nietzsche's writing is not a *discovery* or *transcription* of some 'transcendental signified'. He does, however, seem to be committed to the view that a process which 'has no meaning' is logically prior to all meaning, or that the 'text as such' can generate meaning as an 'effect'.[13]

Indeed, it is clear that in his earlier writings Derrida accepts as a starting point the structuralist account of the constitution of the semantic units of language. In 'The Ends of Man', for example, he gives such an interpretation of the focus on system and structure in French thought of the 1960s. Structuralism, on his account, consists not in 'erasing or destroying meaning. Rather it is a question of determining the possibility of *meaning* on the basis of a "formal" organization which in itself has no meaning, which does not mean that it is either the non-sense or the anguishing absurdity which haunt metaphysical humanism.'[14] The implication of this approach, Derrida suggests, is that whereas phenomenology effected a 'reduction of meaning', structuralism in its 'most original and strongest aspects' involves a 'reduction *of* meaning'. Derrida does not question the possibility of such a reduction. Indeed, he again makes the point that one of its consequences would be a break with the '*hermeneutical* question of the *meaning* or the *truth* of Being', as conceived by Heidegger.

But can meaning be considered in this way as something 'already entirely constituted by a tissue of differences?'[15] Formally speaking, the structuralist assumption that the identity of the signified, or meaningful face of the sign, could be constituted in a purely differential way (the principle of 'considering every process of signification as a formal play of differences', as Derrida puts it[16]) always involved a philosophical short circuit. For since, as structuralism rightly insisted, the elements of language whose difference is supposed to determine semantic identities are conventional, not *naturally* given, these elements cannot themselves be identified independently of an awareness of the distinctions of meaning which they imply. Only because 'zap' *means* something different from 'sap', and so forth, are 's' and 'z' distinct phonemes in English. Thus, as Manfred Frank has pointed out, 'If the *marque* can be distinguished and identified as the *marque* which it is, only in so far as a meaning is – hypothetically – attributed to it . . . then we cannot employ the formula that meaning is generated out of the "marque", or out of its relation to other "marques".'[17] Frank summarizes this argument in the slogan: 'No identification without signification!'

This is not to deny, of course, that differentiality is a *necessary precondition* for the production of new meaning – merely that such a *sine qua non* is not equivalent to a cause or ground of which meaning could be an 'effect'. Long ago Paul Ricoeur made a similar criticism of Derrida when he suggested that the semiological frame of his thinking had prevented him even from reaching the level of propositional structure, which is the first level at which language appears as meaningful, in the sense of capable of opening up a world.[18] But this may be just another way of saying that an understanding of the 'meaning of Being' – in the sense of a grasp of the 'is' of predication – must already be in play for even the differential, semiological structure of signifying systems to be disclosed. Thus the thrilling recklessness of Derrida's earlier thought – the plunge into the 'bottomless chessboard on which Being is put into play', the surrender to the movement of *différance* as the 'unity of chance and necessity in calculations without end'[19] – may turn out to have been mock heroics after all.

The issue is not simply a formal one, of course. For Derrida's notion of his work as informed by a strategy without finality, and his persistent deconstruction of meaning through its objectifying equation with the *presence* of the signified, raised from the start the question of where deconstruction was heading both culturally and politically. In one sense, Derrida's appeal to Nietzsche against Heidegger was misleading, since Nietzsche's desperate sense that life can thrive only within a limited horizon of significance was no less strong than his drive to break through all boundaries in a self-affirmative emancipation from purposefulness. And as Derrida, through the 1970s, became more concerned with the ethical consequences of his own thinking, his advocacy of a dissemination without origin or aim, whose disruption could sheerly 'explode the semantic horizon',[20] required some kind of qualification. Derrida has recently claimed that 'a deconstructionist approach to the boundaries that institute the human subject (preferably and paradigmatically the adult male, rather than the woman, child or animal) as the measure of the just and the unjust, does not necessarily lead to injustice, nor to the effacement of an opposition between just and unjust'.[21] But in his earlier work, at least, no move is made which could provide a principled defence against Charles Taylor's accusation that 'for Derrida there is nothing but deconstruction, which swallows up the old hierarchical distinctions between philosophy and literature, and between men and women, but just as readily could swallow up equal/unequal, community/discord, uncoerced/constrained dialogue and the like'.[22] Unable to explain why certain oppositions survive as indispensable points of orientation, and thus as potentially emancipatory rather than repressive, even in an apparently directionless world of endless instability, Derrida preferred to display his deconstructive prowess indiscriminately – and hope for the best. This is not to imply that Derrida's work, even in its initial phases, was not driven by profound ethical impulses. It is, rather, to suggest that the very insistence of deconstruction on an intense *theoretical* self-awareness, on a reflexivity carried to the point of paradox, drove its own ethical presuppositions into a penumbra of inarticulacy. David Wood once remarked that Derrida's invocations of an 'affirmative writing', of the 'adventure of the trace', seem to convey values remarkably close to those staples of existentialism, freedom and authenticity.[23] And one could surely argue that the internal incoherence of Derrida's notion of a strategy without finality, which was ignored in the first surge of enthusiasm for his work, simply marked the limit of deconstruction's capacity to move from theoretical to ethical self-reflection – or perhaps masked a fear of discovering unwanted affinities.

In Derrida's latest writing, of course, all this has changed. Formerly Derrida had insisted that the 'general text' cannot be 'commanded by a referent in the classic sense, by a thing or by a transcendental signified which would regulate its whole movement'.[24] This raised the question of whether terms such as 'writing', 'trace' and 'general text' were themselves functioning in his work as transcendental signifiers. In response, Derrida tended to suggest that nothing remained immune to the movement of deconstruction, so that each term employed to designate this movement would have a limited shelf life – would sooner or later be sucked down into the vortex of its own dissemination. Now, however, he states emphatically that the *possibility* of deconstruction is itself 'undeconstructable'. Indeed, he writes: 'what remains as irreducible to any deconstruction as the very possibility of deconstruction is perhaps a certain emancipatory promise', or a certain 'idea of justice' which is not to be equated with any empirical edifice of law.[25]

It is important to register just how large a shift in Derrida's orientation this represents. Many commentators seem to assume that what has already come to be known as the 'ethical turn' in deconstruction represents an unproblematic extension of Derrida's earlier concerns, but in fact there is an extreme tension and torsion at work here. For example, when Derrida argues that 'an interrogation of the origin, grounds and limits of our conceptual, theoretical or normative apparatus surrounding justice is on deconstruction's part anything but a neutralization of interest in justice',[26] one would like to know *why* the signified 'justice' has been singled out for this privilege, why it has effectively been given transcendental status and exempted from the logic of supplementarity, the perpetually displaced enchainment of concepts. Why should the notion of justice in particular, a notion as deeply embedded in the discourse of metaphysics as any could be, now appear as invulnerable to deconstructive suspicion, contextualization and dismantling? Conversely, if it is possible to distinguish between justice itself and the 'conceptual, theoretical or normative apparatus' surrounding it, then why should this not also be possible in the case of other key 'metaphysical' concepts such as 'subject', 'truth' or 'reason'? How, in other words, can Derrida still be so sure that the 'experience of the effacement of the signifier in the voice' is 'the condition of the *very idea* of truth';[27] or that 'each time a question of meaning is posed, this can *only be* within the closure of metaphysics'?[28]

In fact, what Derrida's most recent thinking indicates is that earlier deconstruction was based precisely on a collapsing of the distinction between conceptual and theoretical apparatuses and the phenomena they attempt to determine and regulate. Whereas formerly Derrida denied that there could be any meaning, truth or history outside of metaphysics, his whole enterprise is now in effect an attempt to *liberate* these concepts from their metaphysical determinations. At its best, his recent thinking represents an attempt to restore a sense of ethical orientation and political possibility, to defend what he terms an 'emancipatory desire'[29] without the support of an objectivistic metaphysics; and this means: while acknowledging a permanent insecurity which prevents the 'infinite promise' of emancipation from congealing into a falsely reassuring 'meaning of Being'. To this extent, Derrida's earlier work can be said to have performed a useful propaedeutic function in dismantling inherited, reified conceptions of truth and meaning. But at the same time one should be aware that that early deconstruction will have played this path-breaking role *only* if the unconditionality its own earlier dismantling of the unconditional is clearly renounced. One cannot at one and the same time claim that 'the absence of a transcendental signified extends the field and play of signification to infinity',[30] and *also* appeal to an unconditionality which 'is independent of every determinate context, even of the determination of context in general'.[31]

Contemporary Critical Theory does not attempt or endorse a reduction of meaning of the kind which Derrida describes in 'The Ends of Man'. On the contrary, it has been engaged in a constant struggle with forms of social theory, such as those of Luhmann or Foucault, in which lived meaning is reduced to an epiphenomenon of social systems and functions. But it is no less hostile than Derrida to the idea of a transcendental signified, if by this is meant a point of existential and ethical orientation which transcends all particular cultural contexts. Derrida's argument against Heidegger was that if the 'meaning of Being' is always dislocated and disguised in a particular epoch of the 'history of Being' [*Seinsgeschichte*], then there is in fact no 'meaning of Being' except as a derivative or effect of this dislocation. Habermas similarly wants to argue that although we can explore hermeneutically the unreflected meanings which structure a particular lifeworld, we must be wary of taking this web of significance for a revelation of the meaning of being as such.

For Habermas, the idea of philosophical access to orientating truths about the world in general is no longer plausible. He allows only two complementary tasks of philosophy. One is the reconstruction of the *formal* communicative infrastructure of lifeworlds, which is presumed to be universal; the other is the hermeneutic exploration of a particular lifeworld, of the deep tacit assumptions which structure the common life of a community, from a standpoint which cannot claim general validity, since it is itself immersed in what it reflects on. The texture of such a lifeworld, in which cognitive, normative and aesthetic dimensions are inextricably inter-woven, should not, he asserts, be projected on to the world as a whole, whose structures can be known only through the methodical procedures of science. In Habermas's view: 'The interpretative knowledge of essences, which discerns patterns of meaning, bounces off an objectified nature; and the hermeneutic substitute for it is only available for that sphere of non-being in which, according to metaphysics, the ideal essentialities can-not even gain a foothold.'[32] Thus, as Charles Taylor puts it, the 'old sense of order falls between the strands' of Habermas's differentiated account of modern reason.[33] The question is: must we take it as an irreversible lesson of modernity that the ambitions of thinking have to be constrained in this way? Why does Habermas assume that philosophical thinking must take an *objectified* nature for granted – and then struggle to avoid collision with it – rather than questioning the scope and import of this process of objectification?

We have already seen that in *Sources of the Self* Charles Taylor argues that our confidence in the 'epiphanies of being' once offered by Romantic and post-Romantic art has been undermined by modernism. According to Taylor, this does not mean, however, that modern art, despite its frequent retreat into extreme subjectivism, has surrendered its epiphanic capacities altogether. Rather, he suggests, modern art makes possible a new kind of 'interspatial' or 'framing' disclosure. In contrast to earlier 'epiphanies of being', where depth of meaning was taken to be *inherent* in the object, in modern art the subjectively refracted object can, in certain cases, set up 'a kind of frame or space or field within which there can be an epiphany'.[34] The disclosure is thus always indexed to a personal vision, but – according to Taylor – this does not mean that it simply dissolves into a private per-spective which can raise no broader claim to validity. He fully admits that 'We are now in an age in which a publicly accessible order of meanings is an impossibility.' Yet he does not in consequence deny the very existence of such an order; rather he suggests that 'The only way we can explore the order in which we are set with an aim to defining moral sources is through this part of personal resonance.'[35] In this domain, however, philosophy can play only a subsidiary role at best, paving the way for the profounder revelations of art.

In his 'Remarks on Discourse Ethics', Habermas has taken Taylor to task for this line of argument. He suggests that Taylor's division of labour between philosophical ethics, art and aesthetics is an 'evasion' which 'reveals the epistemological impasse in which a metaphysical ethics of the good finds itself'.[36] Modern art, Habermas contends, can no longer be tapped as a source of moral inspiration, as the Schlegel of the Athenaeum fragments had already clearly grasped. Furthermore: 'Even if we could accept an aesthetics that still believes in the ethical relevance of the world-disclosing power of modernism, its implications for philosophy would be of a *renunciatory* nature: it would either have to resign itself to the role of aesthetic criticism or itself become aesthetic. At any rate, it would have to abandon any pretension to convince on the basis of its *own* arguments.'[37]

Surprisingly, however, a few pages later Habermas adopts precisely this perspective himself. Stressing that his discourse ethics 'understands the operation of practical reason in purely epistemic terms', he admits that there remains the problem of how to explain 'what it means to *be* moral – the unique significance of morality in life as a whole – and thereby provide the will with a rational incentive to justice as such'.[38] Against his colleague Karl-Otto Apel, he suggests that this problem cannot be transformed into a task of philosophical justification: a good will, he contends, is awakened and fostered not through argumentation but through socialization into a form of life that complements the moral principle. Yet perhaps Habermas sensed while writing that this claim had given too much scope to contingency, for he immediately goes on to suggest that 'a comparable effect may also be produced by the world-disclosing power of prophetic speech and in general by those forms of innovative discourse that initiate better forms of life and more reflective ways of life – and also the kind of eloquent critique that enables us to discern these indirectly in works of literature and art'.[39]

Of course, Habermas might always argue that even the prophetic and aesthetic deliverances he invokes are only articulating a conception of the existential meaning of morality which is *relative* to a particular tradition, although this is certainly not the way such utterances would be understood by their authors. But there is reason to believe that he would not be entirely happy with restricting their relevance in this way. For in a number of recent essays Habermas has emphasized that religious discourse – and also, in a different way, the language of art – may continue to convey an existentially orientating and inspirational semantic charge, a sense of contact with the 'extraordinary' [*das Außeralltägliche*] or the 'unconditioned' [*das Unbedingte*], which cannot be entirely appropriated and discursively redeemed by philosophy. These claims are the sign of significant tensions which have emerged in his recent thought.

We can begin to trace these tensions in an essay on Max Horkheimer's late philosophy. Here Habermas argues that the collapse of metaphysics does not entail the disappearance from the world of all traces of the unconditional. Philosophical explication of the unavoidable normative presuppositions of communication allows us to 'recover the meaning of the unconditioned without recourse to metaphysics'[40] – namely, in the form of the force of claims to truth or rightness which, according to Habermas, 'burst every provinciality asunder'. At the same time, he warns that 'The meaning of the unconditional is not to be confused with an unconditional meaning that offers consolation.'[41] He again stresses that the philosophical demonstration of the *possibility* of the moral point of view, of its quasi-transcendental anchoring in the structure of communication, cannot in itself provide a motivating answer to the question: 'Why be moral?' And he continues: 'In *this* respect, it may perhaps be said that to seek to salvage an unconditional meaning without God is a futile undertaking, for it belongs to the peculiar dignity of philosophy to maintain adamantly that no validity-claim can have cognitive import unless it is vindicated before the tribunal of justificatory discourse.'[42]

But is this peculiar dignity of philosophy also its peculiar limitation? Or must we say, rather, that it is precisely the merit of the philosophical demand for grounding to expose the *cognitive* inadequacy of theological and religious discourse? Furthermore, is it so certain that the distinction between cognitive discourses and those which disclose meaning can be drawn in this rigorous way? In the context of these questions, the entire closing paragraph of Habermas's essay 'Themes in Postmetaphysical Thinking' deserves citation:

> In the wake of metaphysics, philosophy surrenders its extraordinary status. Explosive experiences of the extraordinary [*das Außeralltägliche*] have migrated into an art that has become autonomous. Of course, even after this deflation, ordinary life, now fully profane, by no means becomes immune to the shattering and subversive intrusion of extraordinary events. Viewed from without, religion, which has largely been deprived of its worldview functions, is still indispensable in ordinary life for normalizing intercourse with the extraordinary. For this reason, postmetaphysical thinking continues to coexist with religious practice – and not merely in the sense of the contemporaneity of the noncontemporaneous. This ongoing coexistence even throws light on a curious dependence of a philosophy that has forfeited its contact with the extraordinary. Philosophy, even in its postmetaphysical form, will be able neither to replace nor to repress religion as long as religious language is the bearer of a semantic content that is inspiring and even indispensable, for this content eludes (for the time being?) the explanatory force of philosophical language and continues to resist translation into reasoning discourses.[43]

In outlining this complex web of interrelations, Habermas acknowledges the continuing human need for contact with a transcendence which is more contentful and meaningful than the purely formal 'transcendence from within' to which we are exposed by the force of validity claims.[44] Indeed, elsewhere he has suggested that this contact is essential if public culture is not to decline into a stifling, demobilized complacency. He seems to concur with Taylor, despite their ostensible disagreements in other respects, that the life of even the most democratic polity will degenerate into oppressive and purposeless routine unless the transcendent sources of ethical energy and moral inspiration are periodically renewed:

> The inevitable banalization of everyday life in political communication also poses a danger for the semantic potentials on which such communication must draw. A culture without a thorn in its side [*eine Kultur ohne Stachel*] would be absorbed entirely by compensatory functions. . . . Even that moment of unconditionality which is stubbornly expressed by the transcending validity-claims of everyday communication is not sufficient. *Another* kind of transcendence is disclosed in the undefused force [*das Unabgegoltene*] which is disclosed by the critical appropriation of identity-forming religious traditions, and yet *another* in the negativity of modern art. The trivial must be allowed to shatter against the sheerly alien, abyssal, uncanny [*das schlechthin Fremde, Abgründige, Unheimliche*] which resists assimilation to what is already understood, although no privilege can now install itself behind it.[45]

Not only do these intuitions, which many will be surprised to find flowing from Habermas's pen, coincide with those of Taylor. There also seems to be a certain convergence with the recent thought of Derrida, in so far as this seeks to hold open the space of an 'experience of the impossible'. Derrida interprets this experience in various ways – as a messianic promise, which presupposes 'hospitality without reserve' towards the singularity of the event, or as a capacity to '*answer* [*répondre*] still for a gift which calls one beyond all responsibility', and which is in fact 'the good of the gift, of giving or donation itself'.[46] The exploration in Derrida's latest work of a basic pre-ontological structure of receptivity and donation which has *intrinsic* ethical significance is strongly reminiscent of Taylor's insistence on the indispensability and irreducibility of the human encounter with transcendent, empowering moral sources such as freedom, nature or – ultimately – God, although Derrida would, of course, be far more reluctant to provide such names. Habermas too, albeit with more circumspection, warns that in adapting philosophy to 'the conditions of a disenchanted and demythologized world' we must be careful to guard against 'losing the illumination of the semantic potential which was once preserved in myth'.[47] And he suggests that 'without a philosophical transformation of *one* of the great world religions this semantic potential could one day be lost; every generation must disclose this potential anew. . . .'[48]

This argument inevitably raises the question of why Habermas excludes philosophical discourse from that contact with the extraordinary, that resistance to disenchantment, which he considers entirely legimate in the religious and aesthetic spheres. How can he on the one hand command philosophy to stand sentinel at the gates of a disenchanted world, preventing the infiltration of regressive illusions, yet on the other expect it to absorb and rework the energies of art and – more especially – of religion, which derive from encounters with the transcendence of the 'sheerly alien, abyssal, uncanny'? And if philosophy, art and religion do find themselves radically at cross-purposes, as Habermas suggests, where should we look first in our need for existential orientation? In Habermas's view, no doubt, both Taylor and Derrida have strayed across what he ratifies as the 'Kantian' border into the mined terrain of metaphysics. But this objection simply raises the further issue of why philosophical discourse should be submitted to a *frontal* encounter with criteria of validity which are in fact apposite only for the specialized sciences, and which even Kant's philosophy could not possibly satisfy. For if, as Herbert Schnädelbach has argued, metaphysics is essentially an interpretative enterprise, which seeks to explicate 'the ultimate meaning of all contexts of meaning', then metaphysical questions are primarily concerned with *significance* rather than with *truth*.[49]

It seems safe to conclude, in the light of these difficulties, that the rivalry between the three forms of absolute Spirit, or self-disclosures of the unconditional, which Hegel sought to resolve by establishing the ascending sequence art–religion–philosophy, is likely to continue unabated as long as human beings are able to reflect on their experience and its relation to the world. But such an admission of permanent instability, of lack of fit between what we feel driven to say, the means of saying it, and the available procedures of justification, should not be used to legitimate the deflationary short circuit currently proposed by thinkers such as Rorty. Such a short circuit seeks to eliminate all traces of transcendence, of an imperative source of meaning, through what becomes – paradoxically – an objectivistic metaphysics of contingency. But a resistance to re-enchantment need not be equivalent to the endorsement of disenchantment, as many prominent twentieth-century thinkers, from Adorno to Wittgenstein to Merleau-Ponty, have known.

I would argue that Lacan should also be counted among this number. For Lacan, the modern world cannot be glibly placed under the sign of nihilism or the death of meaning. Rather, the symbolic meanings which have been drained from the desiccated public culture of our societies have found refuge in the phantasies, dreams and symptoms explored in psychoanalysis: 'It was by deciphering this speech [of the analysand] that Freud rediscovered the primary language of symbols, still living on in the suffering of civilized man.'[50] Furthermore, Lacan does not view such a symbolic language as merely the expression of an ultimately conventional system of cultural values without any deeper ontological resonance, as Habermas tends to do, despite his sense of the existential necessity of powerful symbolic resources. For Lacan affirms: 'that the question of his existence bathes the subject, supports him, invades him, tears him apart even, is shown in the tensions, the lapses, the phantasies that the analyst encounters'.[51] And this is a question which, 'beginning with himself, will extend to his in-the-world relation to objects, and to the existence of the world, in so far as it, too, may be questioned beyond its order'.[52] Thus, despite the 'profound alienation of the subject in our scientific civilization', it is still the case that 'creative subjectivity has not ceased in its struggle to renew the never-exhausted power of symbols in the human exchange that brings them to the light of day'.[53]

In the opening scene of *Götterdämmerung* the rope of fate which the Norns have been weaving breaks, confirming their mood of luminous melancholy and anxious yet resigned anticipation. The obscure compulsion of mythical knowledge, and of the world process in which it is embodied, has been shattered; Wotan's labyrinthine plan to bring about his own downfall and the end of divine power is nearing its conclusion; eternal knowledge is no more, and those endowed with the gift of prophecy have nothing further to reveal. ('Zu End' ewiges Wissen. / Der Welt melden / Weise nichts mehr.') Thus if Nietzsche caught much of the truth about Wagner in his brilliant protoype of aesthetic ideology-critique, he could do so only by simultaneously doing Wagner a profound injustice. For Wagner does not seek simply to hold his audience thrall to the mystification and compulsion of his mythic drama, but stages the very end of myth, the destruction of the gods and the emancipation of the human world from their domination, as part of this drama itself.

I would like to think that the essays in this volume could be read as pleas for a style of thinking which, in a similar way, would be bold enough to offer interpretations of the world expansive enough to frame all specific contexts of meaning, but would at the same time inscribe within itself the cautionary distance of a critical reflection on its own procedures. Just as the end of myth can itself only be recounted as myth, perhaps the story of the end of metaphysics will itself always open on to a metaphysical dimension. A style of philosophy which acknowledged this – in opposition to both the contextualism and formal universalism which today command wide allegiance – would view a commitment to metaphysical inquiry as an important aspect of the cognitive and imaginative transcendence of the given, and not one-sidedly as its ontological endorsement.

Far from being a discovery of recent – let alone postmodernist – thinking, the idea that metaphysics can no longer function foundationally, as 'first philosophy', has been central to the European tradition ever since the turmoil of post-Kantian idealism and its aftermath. By contrast, it is an unfortunate distinguishing feature of much contemporary theory to believe that metaphysics should also be suppressed in its role as 'last philosophy', to employ Michael Theunissen's attractive term.[54] In its residual yet irreducible guise as last philosophy, metaphysical exploration does not search for bedrock, but rather helps to hold open those fragile horizons of significance which lie *beyond* the dispersed and compartmentalized forms of modern inquiry. The closing of these horizons would surely signal the twilight of the human – and the destruction of hope for a more humane – world.

# Notes

1. Friedrich Nietzsche, *The Case of Wagner*, in *The Birth of Tragedy and The Case of Wagner*, trans. Walter Kaufmann, New York: Vintage Books 1967, p. 178.

2. Charles Taylor, *Sources of the Self: The Making of the Modern Identity*, Cambridge: Cambridge University Press 1989, p. 458.

3. *The Case of Wagner*, p. 176.

4. Richard Rorty, *Philosophical Papers Volume 1: Objectivity, Relativism and Truth*, Cambridge: Cambridge University Press 1991, p. 193.

5. Herbert Schnädelbach, 'The Face in the Sand: Foucault and the Anthropological Slumber', in Axel Honneth *et al.*, eds, *Philosophical Interventions in the Unfinished Project of Enlightenment*, Cambridge, MA: MIT Press 1992, p. 314.

6. Martin Heidegger, *Nietzsches Lehre vom Willen zur Macht als Erkenntnis*, *Gesamtausgabe*, vol. 47, Frankfurt am Main: Vittorio Klostermann 1989, p. 289/*Nietzsche: Volume 3: The Will to Power as Knowledge and as Metaphysics*, trans. Frank A. Capuzzi, Joan Stambaugh and David Krell, San Francisco: Harper & Row 1979, p. 177.

7. Jacques Derrida, *Of Grammatology*, trans. Gayatri Chakravorty Spivak, Baltimore: Johns Hopkins University Press 1976, p. 19.

8. Ibid.

9. Ibid., p. 20

10. Ibid., p. 23.

11. Jacques Derrida, 'Différance', in *Margins of Philosophy*, trans. Alan Bass, Sussex: Harvester Press 1982, p. 22.

12. Ibid.

13. See, for example, Jacques Derrida, 'Hors Livre', in *Dissémination*, Paris: Seuil 1972, p. 13/'Outwork' in *Dissemination*, trans. Barbara Johnson, London: Athlone Press 1981, p. 7.

14. Jacques Derrida, 'The Ends of Man', in *Margins of Philosophy*, p. 134.

15. Jacques Derrida, *Positions*, Paris: Éditions de Minuit 1972, p. 45/*Positions*, trans. Alan Bass, London: Athlone Press 1981, p. 33.

16. Ibid., p. 37/p. 26.

17. Manfred Frank, *Was ist Neo-Structuralismus?*, Frankfurt am Main: Suhrkamp 1984, p. 551/*What is Neo-Structuralism?* trans. Sabine Wilke and Richard Gray, Minneapolis: Minnesota University Press 1989, p. 433.

18. '. . . in my eyes, you remained in a semiology and never in a semantics, that is, you remained in a semiology concerned with the conditions of the sign. Since these conditions are not satisfied in the phonic order, you had to investigate another order, that of the trace, distanciation, spacing, etc. I say, however . . . precisely because there is a gigantic hole in your whole enterprise, because you have no theory of meaning.' (Paul Ricoeur, in 'Philosophy and Communication: Round-table Discussion between Ricoeur and Derrida', appendix to Leonard Lawlor, *Imagination and Chance: The Difference between the Thought of Ricoeur and Derrida*, Albany, NY: SUNY Press 1992, p. 136.)

19. 'Différance', pp. 22, 7.

20. See *Positions*, p. 61/*Positions*, p. 45.

21. Jacques Derrida, 'Force of Law: The "Mystical Foundation of Authority"', in Drucilla Cornell, Michel Rosenfeld and David Gray Carlson, eds, *Deconstruction and the Possibility of Justice*, London and New York: Routledge 1992, p. 21.

22. *Sources of the Self*, p. 489.
23. David Wood, 'Différance and the Problem of Strategy', in David Wood and Robert Bernasconi, eds, *Derrida and Différance*, Warwick University: Parousia Press 1985, p. 101.
24. *Positions*, p. 61/*Positions*, p. 44.
25. Jacques Derrida, *Spectres de Marx*, Paris: Galilée 1993, p. 102/*Specters of Marx*, trans. Peggy Kamuf, New York: Routledge 1994, p. 59.
26. 'Force of Law', p. 20.
27. *Of Grammatology*, p. 20 (emphasis added).
28. Jacques Derrida, 'Ousia et Grammē', in *Marges de la philosophie*, Paris: Éditions de Minuit 1972, p. 58 (emphasis added)/'Ousia and Grammē', in *Margins of Philosophy*, trans. Alan Bass, Sussex: Harvester Press 1982, p. 51.
29. *Spectres de Marx*, p. 126/*Specters of Marx*, p. 75.
30. Jacques Derrida, 'La structure, le signe et le jeu dans le discours des sciences humaines', in *L'écriture et la différence*, Paris: Seuil 1967, p. 411/'Structure, Sign and Play in the Discourse of the Human Sciences', in *Writing and Difference*, trans. Alan Bass, London: Routledge 1978, p. 280.
31. Jacques Derrida, 'Afterword', in *Limited Inc.*, Evanston, IL: Northwestern University Press 1988, p. 152.
32. Jürgen Habermas, 'Motive nachmetaphysischen Denkens', in *Nachmetaphysisches Denken*, Frankfurt am Main: Suhrkamp 1988, p. 43/'Themes in Postmetaphysical Thinking', in *Postmetaphysical Thinking*, trans. William Mark Hohengarten, Cambridge, MA: MIT Press 1992, p. 36.
33. *Sources of the Self*, p. 510.
34. Ibid., p. 477.
35. Ibid., p. 512.
36. Jürgen Habermas, 'Remarks on Discourse Ethics', in *Justification and Application: Remarks on Discourse Ethics*, trans. Ciaran Cronin, Cambridge: Polity Press 1993, p. 74.
37. Ibid.
38. Ibid., p. 79.
39. Ibid. Habermas's argument that our only recourse is to rely on socialization to provide the motivation to be moral sits uneasily with his claim that a 'basic anthropological trust' has been shattered by the moral horror of the twentieth century, and by the crimes of the Nazis in particular. On this, see the discussion in the interview 'The Limits of Neo-Historicism', in Peter Dews, ed., *Autonomy and Solidarity: Interviews with Jürgen Habermas*, London: Verso (revised edn) 1992, pp. 237–43, esp. p. 238.
40. Jürgen Habermas, 'To Seek to Salvage an Unconditional Meaning Without God is a Futile Undertaking: Reflections on a Remark of Max Horkheimer', in *Justification and Application*, p.141.
41. Ibid., p. 146.
42. Ibid.
43. 'Motive nachmetaphysischen Denkens', p. 60/'Themes in Postmetaphysical Thinking', p. 51.
44. See Jürgen Habermas, 'Exkurs: Transzendenz von innen, Transzendenz ins Diesseits', in *Texte und Kontexte*, Frankfurt am Main: Suhrkamp 1991.
45. Jürgen Habermas, 'Volkssouveränität als Verfahren', in *Faktizität und Geltung*, Frankfurt am Main: Suhrkamp 1992, pp. 630–31.
46. See *Spectres de Marx*, p. 111/*Specters of Marx*, p. 65; *Given Time I: Counterfeit Money*, trans. Peggy Kamuf, Chicago: University of Chicago Press 1992, pp. 31, 36.
47. Jürgen Habermas, 'Rückkehr zur Metaphysik – Eine Sammelrezension', in *Nachmetaphysisches Denken*, p. 275.
48. Jürgen Habermas, 'Metaphysik nach Kant', in *Nachmetaphysisches Denken*, p. 23/'Metaphysics after Kant', in *Postmetaphysical Thinking*, p. 15.
49. See Herbert Schnädelbach, 'Metaphysik und Region heute', in *Zur Rehabilitierung des animal rationale: Vorträge und Abhandlungen 2*, Frankfurt am Main: Suhrkamp 1992, p. 141.
50. Jacques Lacan, 'The Function and Field of Speech and Language in Psychoanalysis', in *Écrits: A Selection*, trans. A. Sheridan, London: Tavistock 1977, p. 63.

51. Jacques Lacan, 'On a Question Preliminary to Any Possible Treatment of Psychosis', in *Écrits: A Selection*, p. 194.

52. Ibid., pp. 194–5.

53. Ibid., pp. 70, 71.

54. See Michael Theunissen, 'Vorwort', in *Negative Theologie der Zeit*, Frankfurt am Main: Suhrkamp 1991, pp. 26–8.

# PART I

# Cross-Currents

# 1

# Adorno, Poststructuralism and the Critique of Identity

Over the past few years an awareness has begun to develop of the thematic affinities between the work of those recent French thinkers commonly grouped together under the label 'poststructuralism' and the thought of the first-generation Frankfurt School, particularly that of Adorno. Indeed, what is perhaps most surprising is that it should have taken so long for the interlocking of concerns between these two philosophical currents to be properly appreciated. Among the most prominent of such common preoccupations are: the illusory autonomy of the bourgeois subject, as exposed pre-eminently in the writings of Freud and Nietzsche; the oppressive functioning of scientific and technological reason, not least in its application to the social domain; the radicalizing potential of modernist aesthetic experience; and – in the case of Adorno, at least – the manner in which what are apparently the most marginal and fortuitous features of cultural artefacts reveal their most profound, and often unacknowledged, truths. Furthermore, these affinities have not merely been observed by outsiders, but are beginning to become part of the self-consciousness of participants in the two traditions themselves. Towards the end of his life, Michel Foucault admitted that he could have avoided many mistakes through an earlier reading of Critical Theory, and – in the last of several retrospective reconstructions of his intellectual itinerary – placed his own thought in a tradition concerned with the 'ontology of actuality', running from Kant and Hegel, via Nietzsche and Weber, to the Frankfurt School.[1] Similarly, Jean-François Lyotard has employed Adorno's account of the decline of metaphysics and the turn to 'micrology' in order to illuminate – partly by parallel and partly by contrast – his own interpretation of postmodernity;[2] while even Jacques Derrida, the least eclectic of recent French thinkers, has written appreciatively on Walter Benjamin, whose borderline position between the political and the mystical he clearly finds sympathetic.[3] On the other side, contemporary German inheritors of the Frankfurt School, including Habermas himself, have begun to explore the internal landscape of poststructuralism, and to assess the points of intersection and divergence with their own tradition.[4]

In the English-speaking world, it is the relation between the characteristic procedures of deconstruction developed by Derrida and the 'negative dialectics' of Adorno which has attracted the most attention: a common concern with the lability and historicity of language, a repudiation of foundationalism in philosophy, an awareness of the subterranean links between the metaphysics of identity and structures of domination, and a shared, tortuous love–hate relation to Hegel seem to mark out these two thinkers as unwitting philosophical comrades-in-arms. Up till now, however, the predominant tendency of such comparisons has been to present Adorno as a kind of deconstructionist *avant la lettre*.[5] The assumption has been that a more consistent pursuit of anti-metaphysical themes – and, by implication, a more politically radical approach – can be found in the work of the French Heideggerian than in that of the Frankfurt Marxist. It will be the fundamental contention of this essay that, for several interconnected reasons, this is a serious misunderstanding. First, although there are undoubtedly elements in Adorno's thought which anticipate Derridean themes, he has in many ways equally strong affinities with that mode of recent French thought which is usually known as the 'philosophy of desire'. It is only the exaggeration of the constitutive role of language in poststructuralism, it could be argued, and a corresponding antipathy – even on the intellectual Left – to the materialist emphases of Marxism, which have led to this aspect of Adorno's work being overlooked or underplayed. Second, from an Adornian perspective, it is precisely this lack of a materialist counterweight in Derrida's thought, the absence of any account of the interrelation of consciousness and nature, particularly 'inner nature', which can be seen to have brought forth the equally one-sided reaction of the philosophy of desire. From such a standpoint, different poststructuralist thinkers appear as dealing, in an inevitably distorting isolation, with what are in fact aspects of a single complex of problems. Finally, Adorno's concept of reconciliation, while far from immune to criticism, cannot be regarded as a simple 'failure of nerve' on his part, even less as an invitation to 'totalitarianism', to be contrasted with the harsher, less compromising vision of poststructuralism. It is, rather, the logical consequence of the attempt to think beyond a set of oppositions which – in their Nietzschean provenance – remain vulnerably brittle and abstract. In short, I hope to show, through an exploration of the central common theme of the critique of identity, that far from being merely a harbinger of poststructuralist and postmodernist styles of thought, Adorno offers us some of the conceptual tools with which to move beyond what is increasingly coming to appear, not least in France itself, as a self-destructively indiscriminate and politically ambiguous assault on the structures of rationality and modernity *in toto*.

## The Critique of Consciousness

In his 1973 essay on the painter Jacques Monory, Jean-François Lyotard makes significant use of the following tale from Borges's *Book of Imaginary Beings:*

> In one of the volumes of the *Lettres édifiantes et curieuses* that appeared in Paris during the first half of the eighteenth century, Father Fontecchio of the Society of Jesus planned a study of the superstitions and misinformation of the common people of Canton; in the preliminary outline he noted that the Fish was a shifting and shining creature that nobody had ever caught but that many said they had glimpsed in the depths of mirrors. Father Fontecchio died in 1736, and the work begun by his pen remained unfinished; some 150 years later Herbert Allen Giles took up the interrupted task. According to Giles, belief in the Fish is part of a larger myth that goes back to the legendary times of the Yellow Emperor. In those days the world of mirrors and the world of men were not, as they are now, cut off from each other. They were, besides, quite different; neither beings, nor colours nor shapes were the same. Both kingdoms, the specular and the human, lived in harmony; you could come and go through mirrors. One night the mirror people invaded the earth. Their power was great, but at the end of bloody warfare the magic arts of the Yellow Emperor prevailed. He repulsed the invaders, imprisoned them in their mirrors, and forced on them the task of repeating, as though in a kind of dream, all the actions of men. He stripped them of their power and of their forms and reduced them to mere slavish reflections. None the less, a day will come when the magic spell will be shaken off.
>
> The first to awaken will be the Fish. Deep in the mirror we will perceive a very faint line and the colour of this line will be like no other colour. Later on, other shapes will begin to stir. Little by little they will differ from us; little by little they will not imitate us. They will break through the barriers of glass or metal, and this time will not be defeated. Side by side with these mirror creatures, the creatures of water will join battle.
>
> In Yunnan, they do not speak of the Fish but of the Tiger of the Mirror. Others believe that in advance of the invasion we will hear from the depths of mirrors the clatter of weapons.[6]

For Lyotard this story condenses a critique of the modern subject which he shares with the majority of poststructuralist thinkers. Subjectivity presupposes reflection, a representation of experience as that of an experiencing self. But through such representation, which depends upon the synthesizing function of concepts, the original fluidity of intuition, the communication between the human and the specular worlds, is lost. Consciousness becomes a kind of self-contained theatre, divided between stage and auditorium: energy is transformed into the thought of energy, intensity into intentionality. Thus Lyotard writes:

Borges imagines these beings as forces, and this bar [the bar between representation and the represented] as a barrier; he imagines that the Emperor, the
Despot in general, can only maintain his position on condition that he represses
the monsters and keeps them on the other side of the transparent wall. The existence of the subject depends on this wall, on the enslavement of the fluid and
lethal powers repressed on the other side, on the function of representing them.[7]

This protest at the coercive unification implied by the notion of a self-conscious, self-identical subject is – of course – one of the central themes of
poststructuralism. It occurs in works such as the *Anti-Oedipus* of Deleuze
and Guattari, in which the schizophrenic fragmentation of experience and
loss of identity is celebrated as a liberation from the self forged by the
Oedipus complex. But it can also be found, in a more oblique form, in the
work of Michel Foucault. The models of enclosure and observation which
Foucault explored throughout his career are, in a sense, historically
specific, institutional embodiments of this conception of a consciousness
imposing its order upon the disorderly manifold of impulse. This is clearest in the case of the Panopticon which Foucault describes in *Discipline and
Punish*; but, in fact, as far back as *Madness and Civilization* he had
analysed what he terms 'the elaboration around and above madness of a
kind of absolute subject which is wholly gaze, and which confers upon it
the status of a pure object'.[8] Throughout his work the omnipresent look
reduces alterity to identity.

Traditionally, within the sphere of philosophy, it is perhaps the stream
of dialectical thought derived from Hegel which has most persistently
opposed this rigidity of the classifying gaze. Hegel's critique of the 'philosophy of reflection' is based on the view that any assumption abstracted
from experience and taken to be fundamental must necessarily enter into
contradiction with itself, including the assumption that subjectivity itself is
something self-contained, isolated from and standing over against the
object of knowledge. In Hegel's conception experience consists in the shifting reciprocal determinations of subject and object, and culminates in an
awareness that the very distinction between the two is valid only from a
restricted standpoint. As early as his essay on the difference between the
systems of Fichte and Schelling, Hegel had established this fundamental
principle of his philosophizing. 'The need of philosophy can satisfy itself',
he writes, 'by simply penetrating to the principle of nullifying all fixed
oppositions and connecting the limited to the Absolute. This satisfaction
found in the principle of absolute identity is characteristic of philosophy as
such.'[9] However, as this quotation makes clear, the dialectical mobilization
of the relation between subject and object in Hegel does not entail the
abandonment of the principle of identity. Hence, for poststructuralist
thought, the reliance on an Absolute which relativizes and reveals the
'reifying' character of conceptual dissection results in an even more

ineluctable form of coercion, since the movement from standpoint to standpoint is orientated towards a predetermined goal. The voyage of consciousness is undertaken only with a view to the treasure of experience which can be accumulated and brought home: the individual moments of the voyage are not enjoyed simply for themselves. This critique of Hegel is also, of course, implicitly or explicitly, a critique of Marxism, which is seen as attempting to coerce the plurality of social and political movements into a single unswerving dialectic of history.

One of the fundamental problems confronting poststructuralist thought, therefore – a problem which accounts for many of its distinctive features – is how to reject simultaneously both the repressive rigidities of self-consciousness and conceptual thought, *and* the available dialectical alternatives. In the quest for a solution to this difficulty, it is Nietzsche who plays the most important role. The central imaginative polarity in Nietzsche's work between the fluidity of the ultimate world of becoming, and the static systems of concepts laid over this fluidity, allows him to reveal the deceptiveness of all partial perspectives on reality, while also blocking the possibility of a historical totality of perspectives, which reveals what cannot be known through any one alone. Nietzsche's characteristic verbal compounds (*hineinlegen, hinzulügen* . . .) render unmistakable his view that all meaning, coherence and teleological movement is projected on to a world which, in itself, is blank, purposeless, indifferent, chaotic. This is a conception of the relation between thought and reality which is common to much of the Nietzsche-influenced philosophy of the 1960s and 1970s in France. Its most striking and systematically elaborated exemplification is perhaps to be found in Lyotard's *Économie libidinale,* which is centred on the notion of a 'grand ephemeral pellicule' constituted by the deployed surfaces of the body, which are swept by an incessantly mobile libidinal cathexis generating points of pure sensation or 'intensity'. This description of the libidinal band is perhaps best considered as a philosophical experiment, a paradoxical attempt to explore what experience would be like before the emergence of a self-conscious subject of experience. In Lyotard's view, this emergence can take place only through a cooling of intensity, a transformation of energy. Rendering more explicit the assumptions of his commentary on Borges, he writes:

> Theatricality and representation, far from being something one should take as a libidinal given, *a fortiori* as a metaphysical given, results from a certain kind of work on the labyrinthine and moebian band, an operation which imprints these special folds and creases whose effect is a box closed in on itself, and allowing to appear on the stage only those impulses which, coming from what will from now on be called the exterior, satisfy the conditions of interiority.[10]

Once the representational chamber of consciousness is constituted, then the libidinal band is inevitably occluded; *all* representation is misrepresentation. For Lyotard each segment of the band is 'absolutely singular', so that the attempt to divide it up into conceptual identities 'implies the denial of disparities, of heterogeneities, of transits and stases of energy, it implies the denial of polymorphy'.[11] This ontological affirmation of an irreducible plurality – in more or less sophisticated versions – has been one of the most influential themes of poststructuralism, and has had widespread political repercussions. It is, however, fraught with difficulties, which I would like to explore by looking a little more closely at the Nietzschean thought by which it is inspired.

## Knowledge and Becoming in Nietzsche

From the very beginning of his work, Nietzsche is concerned to combat the notion of knowledge as the mere reproduction of an objective reality, believing that forms of knowledge necessarily are and should be in the service of, and shaped by, human interests. This argument is already central to *The Birth of Tragedy,* where Nietzsche draws an unfavourable contrast between Greek tragedy at the height of its powers – a form of artistic creation which, through its blending of Dionysiac insight and Apollonian order, was able to confront the horror and chaos of existence, yet draw an affirmative conclusion from this confrontation – and the naively optimistic assumption of Socratic dialectic that reality can be exhaustively grasped in concepts. *The Birth of Tragedy* is directed against 'the illusion that thought, guided by the thread of causation, might plumb the furthest abysses of being, and even correct it'.[12] Throughout his work Nietzsche will stress the aversion of the human mind to chaos, its fear of unmediated intuition, and its resultant attempts to simplify the world by reducing diversity to identity. There is, however, an equally strong pragmatic tendency in Nietzsche, which suggests that this process of ordering and simplification takes place not simply because of an 'existential' need for security, but in the interests of sheer survival:

> In order for a particular species to maintain itself and increase its power, its conception of reality must comprehend enough of the calculable and constant for it to base a scheme of behaviour on it. The utility of preservation – not some abstract-theoretical need not to be deceived – stands as the motive behind the development of the organs of knowledge.[13]

It is on such considerations that Nietzsche bases his many paradoxical pronouncements on the nature of knowledge and truth – his statement, for example, that 'Truth is the kind of error without which a certain species of life cannot live.'[14]

A number of commentators have attempted to moderate the perplexing and scandalous effect of these formulations by suggesting that Nietzsche draws a distinction, implicitly at least, between two kinds of truth. His attack is directed against correspondence theories of truth, against the failure to consider the extent to which our language and our concepts shape the world, but does not exclude a deeper insight into the nature of reality which would merit the title 'truth'. Such attempts to render Nietzsche's position coherent are not entirely without textual support, but they also have a tendency to underplay the extent to which his paradoxical formulations betray a genuine dilemma. The Kantian element in Nietzsche's thought pushes him towards a thoroughgoing idealist epistemology, since – like Kant's immediate successors – he rejects the doctrine of the 'thing-in-itself' as incoherent. Thus, in *The Will to Power* he writes:

> The intellect cannot criticize itself, simply because it cannot be compared with other species of intellect and because its capacity to know would be revealed only in the presence of 'true reality'. . . . This presupposes that, distinct from every perspective kind of outlook or sensual-spiritual appropriation, something exists, an 'in-itself'. – But the psychological derivation of the belief in things forbids us to speak of 'things-in-themselves'.[15]

Yet despite his strictures, from *The Birth of Tragedy* onwards, where he contrasts the shallow optimism of science to an alternative Dionysiac insight into the nature of things, Nietzsche will repeatedly oppose a vision of ultimate reality to accepted truths. Indeed, in *The Birth of Tragedy* he employs the Kantian concept of the noumenal to illustrate precisely this opposition: 'The contrast of this authentic nature-truth and the lies of culture which present themselves as the sole reality is similar to that between the eternal core of things, the thing in itself, and the entire world of appearance.'[16] In general, Nietzsche's critique of metaphysics, and his denial of the ability of philosophy to establish epistemological criteria, drives him towards an idealism which argues that the structures of knowledge are constitutive of the object, while his insistence that all consciousness should comprehend itself as perspectival pushes him back towards a reinstatement of the distinction between appearance and reality.

I would argue that a similar dilemma, encapsulated in Nietzsche's dictum that 'Knowledge and Becoming exclude one another',[17] pervades the work of those poststructuralist thinkers who have been most directly influenced by Nietzschean schemas. We have already examined how Lyotard's motif of the libidinal band, which fuses a Freudian-inspired theory of cathexis with the doctrine of the Eternal Return, makes possible a denunciation of all theoretical discourses as 'apparatuses for the fixation and draining away of intensity'.[18] Lyotard, however, is too conscientious – and too restless – a figure to be satisfied for long with the monistic metaphysics of libido on which *Économie libidinale* relied. It can be no accident that shortly after the publication of this work he began to set off in a new direction, replacing the description of forms of discourse as '*dispositifs pulsionels*' (patterns of drive-investments) with the less ontologically loaded notion of 'language games', borrowed from Wittgenstein. In Lyotard's case, the attempt to develop a critique of objectifying theory from the standpoint of an ontology of flux represents an explicit, but only temporary, phase of his thought. With Foucault, however, the tension which this attempt implies is both a more covert, but also a more persistent, feature of his work. It is already apparent in *Madness and Civilization,* where Foucault wishes to develop a critique of the objectifying and alienating nature of modern psychiatric treatment and its theorizations, while also being conscious of the difficulty of appealing to the 'rudimentary movements of an experience' which would be 'madness itself'.[19] In *The Archaeology of Knowledge* Foucault renounces this approach: 'We are not trying to reconstitute what madness itself might be . . . in the form in which it was later organized (translated, deformed, travestied, perhaps even repressed) by discourses, and the oblique, often twisted play of their operations.'[20] He ostensibly adopts a position in which discourses are entirely constitutive of their objects. Yet the contradiction persists, since it is inherent in his attempt to develop a nondialectical form of critique. In the first volume of *The History of Sexuality*, for example, the oscillation between the epistemological and the ontological occurs in the form of an opposition between the apparatuses of sexuality and a tentatively – but persistently – evoked pre-discursive 'body and its pleasures'.[21] Foucault is able to avoid this dilemma in his final publications only by returning to a notion of self-constitution and self-reflection which he had hitherto denounced as illicitly Hegelian. One of the fundamental tenets of poststructuralist thought is tacitly abandoned when Foucault reinstates the relation between knowledge and its object as internal to consciousness; when he inquires:

> By means of what play of truth does man offer himself to be thought in his own being when he perceives himself as mad, when he considers himself as ill, when he reflects on himself as a living, speaking and labouring being, when he judges and punishes himself as a criminal?[22]

This is an unmistakably 'revisionist' retrospective.


## Adorno's Critique of Identity-Thinking

Having explored this fundamental difficulty of the poststructuralist position, I would now like to introduce the comparison with Adorno. One obvious point of entry would be the fact that both the poststructuralists and Adorno owe an enormous debt to Nietzsche, and in particular to his sense of the cost imposed by the forging of a self-identical, morally responsible subject, perhaps most vividly conveyed in the second essay of *On the Genealogy of Morals*. As I have already suggested, however, the full import of these parallels has been misunderstood, because of a failure to appreciate the gap between the general philosophical projects within which they occur. One of the most important distinctions in this respect is that Adorno is not content with a Nietzschean–Freudian, naturalist critique of consciousness, but takes up the discovery of the early German Romantics that the philosophy of pure consciousness is internally incoherent. In an illuminating article, Jochen Hörisch has shown that the original antecedents for Adorno's acute awareness of the loss of spontaneity imposed by the formation of the modern autonomous individual, his sense that the identity of the self must be coercively maintained against the centrifugal tendencies of impulse, can be traced back beyond Nietzsche to the critical engagement with Fichte's philosophy of Schlegel and Novalis. It is here, in thought partly inspired – like Adorno's own – by dismay at the failure of an attempted political realization of reason, that Adorno discovers a hidden history of subjectivity, an evocation of the pain of the process of individuation which is betrayed by logical incoherence. 'Early Romanticism', Hörisch argues, 'discovers suffering as the *principium individuationis* and as the "secret of individuality", which transcendental philosophy can conceal only at the cost of becoming entangled in unavowed contradictions. The pain of individuation derives from the inscription of a compulsory identity which passes itself off as an *a priori* structure of reason.'[23] Both aspects of this critique will be of crucial importance for Adorno: the demonstration of the structure of contradiction which *both* splits and constitutes the subject, and the sensitivity to the repression of inner nature which is demanded by the forging of such a subject. Adorno's critique of the modern subject, therefore, is as implacable as that of the poststructuralists, and is based on not dissimilar grounds; yet in contrast to that of Foucault, Deleuze or Lyotard it does not culminate in a call for the abolition of the subjective principle. Rather, Adorno always insists that our only option is to 'use the force of the subject to break through the deception of constitutive subjectivity'.[24] In order fully to understand the reasons for this difference of conclusion, we must turn to Adorno's account of the relation between concept and object, universality and particularity, and its opposition to that of Nietzsche.

From the very beginning, Nietzsche's work is haunted by a sense of the inherent fictionalizing and fetishizing tendencies of language and conceptual thought. In his early essay 'On Truth and Lies in an Nonmoral

Sense', Nietzsche remarks that every word immediately becomes a concept through the fact that

> it must not serve simply for the absolutely individualized original experience, to which it owes its birth, that is to say as a reminder, but must straight away serve for countless more or less similar cases, and that means must be matched to purely dissimilar cases. Every concept arises through the equating of what is not the same. [*Jeder Begriff entsteht durch Gleichsetzung des Nichtgleichen.*][25]

Throughout Nietzsche's work such remarks on the 'coarseness' of language, on the indifference to differences entailed by the use of concepts, are to be found. 'Just as it is certain', he continues,

> that one leaf is never quite like another, so it is certain that the concept leaf is constructed by an arbitrary dropping of individual differences, through a forgetting of what differentiates; and this awakens the idea that there is something in nature besides leaves which would be 'leaf', that is to say an original form, according to which all leaves are woven, drawn, circumscribed, coloured, curled, painted, but by clumsy hands, so that no example emerges correctly and reliably as a true copy of the original form. The overlooking of the individual gives us the form, whereas nature knows no forms and no concepts, and also no species, but only an X, which is unaccessible and indefinable to us.[26]

It is precisely such a view of the deceptive identity forged by concepts, as we have seen, which motivates Lyotard's evocation of the ineffably singular points of intensity which constitute the libidinal band, or Foucault's reluctant but repeated recourse to an uncapturable pre-discursive spontaneity – whether under the title of 'madness', 'resistance', or 'the body and its pleasures'.

Nietzsche's account of the manner in which real, particular leaves come to be seen as poor imitations of the concept 'leaf' captures precisely that process which Adorno refers to as 'identity-thinking'. 'The immanent claim of the concept', he writes, 'is its order creating invariance over against the variation of what is grasped under it. This is denied by the form of the concept, which is "false" in that respect.'[27] However, Adorno does not believe that this situation can be remedied simply by counterposing the contingent and particular to the universality of concepts. Rather, he argues, the assumption that what he terms the 'non-identical', what is left behind by the concept, is merely an inaccessible and undefinable X, the belief that 'nature knows no forms and no concepts', is itself the result of the primacy of the universal in identity-thinking. Adorno's philosophical effort is directed towards moving beyond the split between bare facticity and conceptual determination, through an experience of the contradiction which that split itself implies. Non-identity, Adorno suggests, 'is opaque only for identity's claim to be total'.[28] Thus, in the Introduction to *Against*

*Epistemology* [*Zur Metakritik der Erkenntnistheorie*], a series of critical essays on Husserlian phenomenology, he employs the following passage from *The Twilight of the Idols* to demonstrate that Nietzsche 'undervalued what he saw through':

> formerly, alteration, change, any becoming at all, were taken as proof of mere appearance, as an indication that there must be something which led us astray. Today, conversely, precisely in so far as the prejudice of reason forces us to posit unity, identity, permanence, substance, cause, thinghood, being, we see ourselves caught in error, compelled into error.[29]

Against the bent of this text, which is characteristic both of Nietzsche and of his poststructuralist followers, Adorno insists:

> The opposition of the stable to the chaotic, and the domination of nature, would never have succeeded without an element of stability in the dominated, which would otherwise incessantly give the lie to the subject. Completely casting away that element and localizing it solely in the subject is no less *hubris* than absolutizing the schemata of conceptual order . . . sheer chaos, to which reflective spirit downgrades the world for the sake of its own total power, is just as much the product of spirit as the cosmos it sets up as an object of reverence.[30]

Adorno's argument is that pure singularity is itself an abstraction, the waste product of identity-thinking.

Two major implications of this position are that the attempt by poststructuralist thought to isolate singularity will simply boomerang into another form of abstraction; and that what it mistakes for immediacy will in fact be highly mediated. These pitfalls are clearly exemplified by Lyotard's working through of the 'philosophy of desire' in *Économie libidinale.* The notion of a libidinal band composed of ephemeral intensities is an attempt to envisage a condition in which, as Nietzsche puts it, 'no moment would be for the sake of another'. But if every moment is prized purely for its uniqueness, without reference to a purpose or a meaning, to a before or an after, without reference to anything which goes beyond itself, then what is enjoyed in each moment becomes paradoxically and monotonously the same: in Lyotard's work of the mid 1970s any action, discourse, or aesthetic structure becomes an equally good – or equally bad – conveyor of intensity. Furthermore, Lyotard's own evocations betray his ostensible intention, since they make clear that such 'intensities' cannot be reduced to pure cathexis but are symbolically structured, coloured by remarkably determinate situations:

> the slow, light, intent gaze of an eye, then suddenly the head turns so that there is nothing left but a profile, Egypt. The silence which settles around her extends

to great expanses of the libidinal band which, it seems, belongs to her body. Those zones also are silent, which means that dense, inundating surges move noiselessly and continually towards 'her' regions, or come from these regions, down the length of slopes.[31]

It is important to note that Adorno does not avoid these difficulties by espousing a Hegelian position. He agrees with Hegel that, as a unity *imposed* on particulars, the abstract universal enters into contradiction with its own concept – becomes itself something arbitrary and particular. But he argues that even Hegel's solution – an immanent, self-realizing universal – fails to challenge the primacy of the universal as such. Identity-thinking, even in its Hegelian form, defeats its own purpose, since by reducing what is non-identical in the object to itself, it ultimately comes away empty-handed. For Adorno, the experience of this contradiction sparks off a further movement of reflection, to a position in which the non-identical is no longer viewed as the isolated particular which it is forced back into being by identity-thinking. The particular is now seen as standing in a pattern of relations to other particulars, a historically sedimented 'constellation' which defines its identity. 'What is internal to the non-identical', Adorno writes, 'is its relation to what it is not itself, and which its instituted, frozen identity withholds from it. . . . The object opens itself to a monadological insistence, which is a consciousness of the constellation in which it stands.'[32] This consciousness, in its turn, can be expressed only through a 'constellation' – as opposed to a hierarchical ordering – of concepts, which are able to generate out of the tension between them an openness to that non-identity of the thing itself, which would be 'the thing's own identity against its identifications'.[33] In other words, for Adorno there is no necessary antagonism between conceptual thought and reality, no inevitable mutual exclusion of Knowledge and Becoming. The problem is posed not by conceptual thought as such but by the assumption of the primacy of the concept, the delusion that mind lies beyond the total process in which it finds itself as a moment. The characteristics of reality which poststructuralist thought ontologizes are in fact merely the reflection of a historically obsolete imperiousness of consciousness, a lack of equilibrium between subject and object. 'What we differentiate', Adorno writes, 'will appear divergent, dissonant, negative for just as long as the structure of our consciousness obliges it to strive for unity: as long as its demand for totality will be its measure of whatever is not identical with it.'[34]

## Deconstruction and Negative Dialectics

One way of summarizing the argument so far would be to say that, for Adorno, the compulsive features of identity are inseparable from its internal contradictions: identity can become adequate to its concept only by acknowledging its own moment of non-identity. In the more naturalistic of the French thinkers influenced by Nietzsche, however, this logical dimension of the critique of consciousness is entirely absent. The ego is portrayed unproblematically as the internally consistent excluder of the spontaneity and particularity of impulse, with the consequence that opposition can take the form only of a self-defeating jump from the 'unity' of self-consciousness to a dispersal of intensities, or from the Oedipalized subject to a metaphysics of 'desiring machines'. In the work of Jacques Derrida, by contrast, a complementary one-sidedness occurs: the naturalistic dimension of Nietzsche's thought is almost entirely excluded in favour of an exploration of the contradictions implicit in the notion of pure self-identity. Derrida, in other words, shares a penchant for dialectics with Adorno, is sensitive to the unexpected ways in which philosophical opposites slide into one another, but is unable to link this concern with an account of the natural-historical genesis of the self.

The implications of this failure can perhaps best be highlighted by comparing Adorno's and Derrida's critiques of Husserlian phenomenology. Like Merleau-Ponty, whose account of the relation between consciousness and nature bears many affinities to his own, Adorno contests the very possibility of Husserl's transcendental reduction:

> the idealist may well call the conditions of possibility of the life of consciousness which have been abstracted out, transcendental – they refer back to a determinate, to some 'factual' conscious life. They are not valid 'in themselves'. . . . The strictest concept of the transcendental cannot release itself from its interdependence with the *factum*.[35]

It is important to note, however, that Adorno speaks of 'interdependence': he by no means wishes to effect an empiricist or naturalistic reduction of consciousness. Rather, his argument is simply that 'The mind's moment of non-being is so intertwined with existence that to pick it out neatly would be the same as to objectify and falsify it.'[36] Adorno, as a materialist, argues for the anchoring of consciousness in nature, while resisting any attempt to collapse the dialectic of subject and object into a metaphysical monism.

In Derrida's thought, however, the possibility of the transcendental reduction is never questioned as such. Rather, deconstruction incorporates the transcendental perspective, in an operation which Derrida terms 'erasure', but which – in its simultaneous cancellation and conservation – is close to a Hegelian *Aufhebung*. Thus, in *Of Grammatology* Derrida suggests that there is a 'short-of and a beyond of transcendental criticism', and that therefore 'the value of the transcendental arche must make its necessity felt before letting itself be erased'.[37] What this erasure consists in for Derrida is not the insistence on an irreducible break between facticity and the transcendental, which metaphysics has always dreamed of overcoming, but rather a 'reduction of the reduction', an appeal to what he explicitly terms an 'ultra-transcendental text'. For Derrida the incoherence of the concept of self-presence on which Husserl's theory of transcendental subjectivity is based reveals that the transcendental subject and its objects, along with the other characteristic oppositions of metaphysical thought, are in some sense – which he finds rather uncomfortable to expound – the 'effects' of a higher principle of non-identity for which his most common name is 'différance'. The result is a final philosophical position remarkably reminiscent of pre-Hegelian idealism. Since absolute difference, lacking all determinacy, is indistinguishable from absolute identity, Derrida's evocations of a trace which is 'origin of all repetition, origin of ideality . . . not more ideal than real, not more intelligible than sensible, not more a transparent signification than an opaque energy',[38] provide perhaps the closest twentieth-century parallel to the *Identitätsphilosophie* of the younger Schelling.

It appears, therefore, that Derrida's attempt to develop a critique of the self-identical subject which eschews any naturalistic moment results in a position no more plausible than Lyotard's monistic metaphysics of libido. Although Adorno did not live long enough to confront Derrida's position directly, his probable response to current comparisons and interassimilations of deconstruction and negative dialectics can be deduced from the critique of Heidegger's thought – undoubtedly the central influence on Derrida – which threads its way through his work. Heidegger is correct to suggest that there is 'more' to entities than simply their status as objects of consciousness, but – in Adorno's view – by treating this 'more' under the heading of 'Being' he transforms it into a self-defeating hypostatization:

> By making what philosophy cannot express an immediate theme, Heidegger dams philosophy up, to the point of a revocation of consciousness. By way of punishment, the spring which, according to his conception, is buried, and which he would like to uncover, dries up far more pitifully than the insight of philosophy, which was destroyed in vain, and which inclined towards the inexpressible through its mediations.[39]

For Adorno, whatever experience the word 'Being' may convey can be expressed only by a constellation of entities, whereas in Heidegger's philosophy the irreducibility of a relation is itself transformed into an ultimate. In the evocation of a Being which transcends the subject–object distinction, 'the moment of mediation becomes isolated and thereby immediate. However, mediation can be hypostatized just as little as the subject and object poles; it is only valid in their constellation. Mediation is mediated by what it mediates.'[40] *Mutatis mutandis,* one could also argue that Derridean *différance* is in fact differentiated by what it differentiates. While it is true that nature and culture, signified and signifier, object and subject would be nothing without the difference between them, this is not sufficient to ensure the *logical priority* of non-identity over identity which is crucial to Derrida's whole philosophical stance. The distinction between his position, according to which 'subjectivity – like objectivity – is an effect of *différance,* an effect inscribed in a system of *différance'*,[41] and that of Adorno, is clearly revealed by the following passage from *Negative Dialectics*:

> The polarity of subject and object can easily be taken, for its part, as an undia-lectical structure within which all dialectics take place. But both concepts are categories which originate in reflection, formulas for something which is not to be unified; nothing positive, not primary states of affairs, but negative through-out. Nonetheless, the difference of subject and object is not to be negated in its turn. They are neither an ultimate duality, nor is an ultimate unity hidden behind them. They constitute each other as much as – through such constitu-tion – they separate out from each other.[42]

## The Mirror and the Spell

By this point it will be clear that the frequent attempt of poststructuralist thinkers, and of literary and political commentators influenced by post-structuralism, to oppose the Nietzschean critique of identity to the coercive totalizations of dialectical thought is beset with intractable diffi-culties. Adorno, no less than recent French thought, criticizes Hegel's dialectic as being in many ways the most insidious, most ineluctable form of identity-thinking, yet at the same time his deeply dialectical sensibility perceives the self-defeating dynamic of a blunt prioritization of particu-larity, diversity, and non-identity. The dissolution of the reflective unity of the self in Deleuze or Lyotard leads only to the indifference of boundless flux, or to the monotonous repetition of intensity; while in Derrida's work the jettisoning of the materialist ballast of the Nietzschean and Freudian critique of consciousness results in the installation of difference as the principle of a new kind of 'first philosophy'. For Adorno, by contrast, non-identity cannot be respected by completely abandoning the principle of identity. 'To define identity as the correspondence of the thing-in-itself to its concept', he writes, is *hubris;* but the ideal of identity must not simply be discarded. Living in the rebuke that the thing is not identical with the concept is the concept's longing to become identical with the thing. This is how the sense of non-identity contains identity. The supposition of identity is indeed the ideological element of pure thought, all the way through to formal logic; but hidden in it is also the truth moment of ideology, the pledge that there should be no contradiction, no antagonism.[43]

Bearing this argument in mind, we are now perhaps in a position to return with more insight to the Borges story with which we began. It will already be apparent that the tale of the subduing of the mirror animals can be interpreted in terms not only of the libidinal critique of consciousness but also of the 'Dialectic of Enlightenment' which was first formulated by Horkheimer and Adorno during the early 1940s, and which continues to underpin *Negative Dialectics* and *Aesthetic Theory.* The humanization of the drives, represented by the transformation of the animals into reflections, does indeed result in a kind of mastery by the ego. But this mastery is bought at the price of a terrible isolation: in *Negative Dialectics* Adorno returns repeatedly to the pathos of a self helplessly confined within the circle of its own immanence, unable to make contact with anything external which does not turn out to be simply its own reflection. The need to break out of this isolation generates a tension at the heart of subjectivity itself, which poststructuralism, in general, is reluctant or unable to recognize. This inadequacy suggests that there might be substantive aspects of the story for which Lyotard has failed to account in his interpretation.

First, Lyotard describes the banishment and punishment of the animals as a simple act of force, of repression and containment, whereas Borges describes the Emperor as employing his 'magic arts', putting the animals under a spell. Significantly, the concept of a spell plays an important role in Adorno's philosophy; since enchantment can constitute a peculiarly intangible and non-apparent form of coercion, to speak of a spell suggests a state of compulsive selfhood in which actions are simultaneously autonomous and heteronomous, accompanied by an exaggerated subjective illusion of autonomy, but carried out by subjects nevertheless. The metaphor of the spell, in other words, captures both the repressive and enabling features of processes of socialization, which are portrayed as an aspect of the human conquest of nature in the interests of self-preservation. As Adorno writes in *Negative Dialectics*: 'The spell is the subjective form of the world spirit, the internal reinforcement of its primacy over the external processes of life.'[44] In the later critical theory of Habermas, this parallelism of the instrumental domination of outer nature and the repression of inner nature will be contested. Habermas will avoid Adorno's implication that emancipation from nature entails the closing down of all communicative sensitivity by attributing socialization and instrumental action to categorially distinct dimensions of historical development. Nevertheless, already, in its Adornian version, the Critical Theory position has a distinct advantage over that of the poststructuralists; for while figures such as Lyotard force themselves into a corner, where they can only denounce the dominance of the ego as an arbitrary coercion which should be abolished (whether it could is somewhat more problematic), Adorno perceives that compulsive identity, the sacrifice of the moment for the future, was necessary at a certain stage of history, in order for human beings to liberate themselves from blind subjugation to nature. To this extent such identity already contains a moment of freedom. Accordingly, the 'spell of selfhood' cannot be seen simply as an extension of natural coercion; rather, it is an illusion which could, in principle, be reflectively broken through by the subject which it generates – although the full realization of this process would be inseparable from a transformation of social relations. Furthermore, the result of such a breakthrough would not be the self-defeating inrush of the 'fluid and lethal powers' which Lyotard describes but, rather, a true identity – one which would be permeable to its own non-identical moment. One of the major differences between poststructuralism and Critical Theory is summarized in Adorno's contention that 'even when we merely limit the subject, we put an end to its power'.[45]

This brings us to a second point. Lyotard describes the mirror animals as 'monsters', but Borges specifies that the people of Canton believe the creature of the mirror to be a fish, 'a shifting and shining creature that nobody has ever caught'; while in Yunnan it is believed to be a tiger. In Adorno's thought it is under this double aspect that the non-identical appears to identity-thinking: on the one hand as something of tantalizing beauty which perpetually eludes our grasp; on the other as something menacing and uncontrollable – menacing precisely because of our inordinate need to control it. Yet we cannot enter into a relation with this creature either by smashing the mirror (the solution of the 'philosophers of desire') or by claiming – as Derrida claims – that both the true world and the reflected world are merely effects generated by its invisible surface. Rather, the only way to achieve this relation is to revoke the spell cast by the Emperor on the animals, which is also – as we have seen – a spell cast on himself.

It would not do to conclude, however, without stressing an important distinction between the lesson of Borges's tale and the philosophical position of Adorno. The story does contain an evocation of utopia, but Borges sets this in a distant, irrecoverable past. 'In those days [i.e., legendary times]', he tells us, 'the world of mirrors and the world of men were not . . . cut off from each other. They were, besides, quite different; neither beings, nor colours, nor shapes were the same. Both kingdoms, the specular and the human, lived in harmony; you could come and go through mirrors.' In Borges's version this initial accord is broken by an unexplained onslaught of nature, temporarily repulsed by humankind but destined to triumph in the end: 'a day will come when the magic spell will be shaken off', and this time the animals 'will not be defeated'. Adorno does not deny the possibility of such a calamitous conclusion to history: the 'clatter of weapons' from 'the depths of mirrors', which some believe will precede the final invasion, will undoubtedly sound, to our late-twentieth-century ears, like an announcement of ecological catastrophe or a three-minute nuclear warning. But Adorno does contest that such a terminus is inevitable. Our historical dilemma consists in the fact that the essential material preconditions for a reconciliation between human beings, and between humanity and nature, could have been installed only by a history of domination and self-coercion which has now built up an almost unstoppable momentum. As Adorno writes in *Negative Dialectics*: 'since self-preservation has been precarious and difficult for eons, the power of its instrument, the ego drives, remains all but irresistible even after technology has virtually made self-preservation easy'.[46] To suggest a prelapsarian harmony, in the face of this dilemma, is merely to fall resignedly into conservative illusion. Nevertheless, Borges's evocation of a state of peaceful interchange between the human and the mirror worlds provides a fitting image for that affinity without identity, and difference without domination – rather than coercive unity – which Adorno believes to be implied by the pledge that there should be 'no contradiction, no antagonism'.

## Notes

1. See 'Structuralism and Post-Structuralism: an Interview with Michel Foucault', *Telos* 55, Spring 1983, p. 200; and 'Un cours inédit', *Magazine littéraire*, no. 207, May 1984/'Kant on Enlightenment and Revolution', trans. Colin Gordon, *Economy and Society*, vol. 15, 1986.

2. See Jean-François Lyotard, 'Presentations', in Alan Montefiore, ed., *Philosophy in France Today*, Cambridge: Cambridge University Press 1983, pp. 201–4.

3. See Jacques Derrida, *La vérité en peinture*, Paris: Flammarion 1978, pp. 200–209/*The Truth in Painting*, trans. Geoff Bennington and Iain McLeod, Chicago: Chicago University Press 1987, pp. 175–89.

4. Axel Honneth, *Kritik der Macht*, Frankfurt am Main: Suhrkamp 1982/*The Critique of Power*, trans. Kenneth Baynes, Cambridge, MA: MIT Press 1991; Albrecht Wellmer, *Zur Dialektik von Moderne und Postmoderne*, Frankfurt am Main: Suhrkamp 1985/*The Persistence of Modernity*, trans. David Midgely, Cambridge: Polity Press 1991; Jürgen Habermas, *Der philosophische Diskurs der Moderne*, Frankfurt am Main: Suhrkamp 1985/*The Philosophical Discourse of Modernity*, trans. Frederick Lawrence, Cambridge MA: MIT Press 1988.

5. See, for example, Rainer Nägele, 'The Scene of the Other: Theodor W. Adorno's Negative Dialectic in the Context of Poststructuralism', *Boundary* 2, Fall – Winter 1982–3; Martin Jay, *Adorno*, London: Fontana 1984, pp. 21–2; and, above all, Michael Ryan, *Marxism and Deconstruction*, Baltimore, MD: Johns Hopkins University Press 1982, pp. 73–81.

6. Jorge Luis Borges, 'The Fauna of Mirrors', in *The Book of Imaginary Beings,* Harmondsworth: Penguin 1974, pp. 67–8.

7. Jean-François Lyotard, 'Contribution des tableaux de Jacques Monory', in Gérald Gassiot-Talabot *et al., Figurations 1960/1973,* Paris: Union Générale d'Editions 1973, pp. 155–6.

8. Michel Foucault, *Histoire de la folie à l'âge classique,* Paris: Gallimard (collection TEL edn) 1976, p. 479.

9. G.W.F. Hegel, *The Difference between Fichte's and Schelling's Systems of Philosophy,* Albany, NY: SUNY Press 1977, p. 112.

10. Jean-François Lyotard, *Économie libidinale,* Paris: Éditions de Minuit 1974, p. 11/ *Libidinal Economy,* trans. Iain Hamilton Grant, London: Athlone Press: 1993, p. 3.

11. Ibid., p. 294/ p. 247.

12. Friedrich Nietzsche, *Die Geburt der Tragödie aus dem Geiste der Musik,* in G. Colli and M. Montinari, eds, *Sämtliche Werke: Kritische Studienausgabe,* Berlin/New York 1980, vol. 1, p. 99 / *The Birth of Tragedy* in *The Birth of Tragedy/The Case of Wagner,* trans. Walter Kaufmann, New York: Vintage 1967, p. 95.

13. Friedrich Nietzsche, *The Will to Power,* ed. Walter Kaufmann, New York: Vintage 1967, pp. 266–7.

14. Ibid., p. 272.

15. Ibid., p. 263.

16. *Die Geburt der Tragödie,* pp. 58–9/*The Birth of Tragedy,* p. 61.

17. *The Will to Power,* p. 280.

18. *Économie libidinale,* p. 295/*Libidinal Economy,* p. 248.

19. Michel Foucault, 'Préface', in *Histoire de la folie à l'âge classique,* original edn, Paris: Gallimard 1961, p. vii.

20. Michel Foucault, *The Archaeology of Knowledge,* trans. A. Sheridan, London: Tavistock 1972, p. 47.

21. See, in particular, Michel Foucault, *The History of Sexuality,* Harmondsworth: Pelican 1981, pp. 150–59.

22. Michel Foucault, *L'usage des plaisirs,* Paris: Gallimard 1984, p. 13/*The Use of Pleasure,* trans. Robert Hurley, New York: Pantheon 1984, p. 7.

23. Jochen Hörisch, 'Herrscherwort, Gott und Geltende Sätze', in Burkhardt Lindner and W. Martin Lüdke, eds, *Materialien zur ästhetischen Theorie: Th. W. Adornos Konstruktion der Moderne,* Frankfurt am Main: Suhrkamp 1980, p. 406.

24. Theodor W. Adorno, *Negative Dialectics,* trans. E. B. Ashton, New York: Continuum 1973, p. xx.

25. Friedrich Nietzsche, 'Über Wahrheit und Lüge im äussermoralischen Sinne', in *Sämtliche Werke: Kritische Studienausgabe,* vol. 1, pp. 879–80/'On Truth and Lies in a Nonmoral Sense', in *Philosophy and Truth: Selections from Nietzsche's Notebooks of the Early 1870s,* trans. and ed. Daniel Breazeale, Sussex: Harvester Press 1979, p. 83.

26. Ibid., p. 880/p. 83.

27. *Negative Dialectics,* p. 153.

28. Ibid., p. 163.

29. Friedrich Nietzsche, *Götzendämmerung,* in *Sämtliche Werke: Kritische Studienausgabe,* vol. 6, p. 77/*The Twilight of the Idols,* trans. R.J. Hollingdale, Harmondsworth: Penguin 1968, p. 37; cited in Theodor W. Adorno, *Zur Metakritik der Erkenntnistheorie,* Frankfurt am Main: Suhrkamp 1970, p. 26/*Against Epistemology,* trans. Willis Domingo, Oxford: Blackwell 1982, p. 19.

30. Ibid., p. 27.

31. *Économie libidinale,* p. 40/*Libidinal Economy,* p. 29.

32. *Negative Dialectics,* p. 163.

33. Ibid., p. 161.

34. Ibid., pp. 5–6.

35. *Zur Metakritik der Erkenntnistheorie,* pp. 227–8/*Against Epistemology,* pp. 226–7.

36. *Negative Dialectics,* pp. 201–2.

37. Jacques Derrida, *Of Grammatology,* trans. Gayatri Chakravorty Spivak, Baltimore, MD and London: Johns Hopkins University Press 1976, p. 61.

38. Ibid., p. 65.

39. *Negative Dialectics,* p. 110.

40. Ibid., p. 99 (translation altered).

41. Jacques Derrida, *Positions,* Paris: Éditions de Minuit 1972, p. 40/*Positions*, trans. Alan Bass, London: Athlone Press 1981, p. 28.

42. *Negative Dialectics,* p. 176.

43. Ibid., p. 149.

44. Ibid., p. 344.

45. Ibid., p. 183. It is worth noting that the poststructuralist critique of consciousness, while exploiting Nietzsche's abstract opposition of particularity and conceptual identity, is in other respects extremely unfaithful to Nietzsche. Far from advocating a dissolution into impulse, Nietzsche is fully aware that the painfully acquired strength of self-discipline is a precondition for the liberation from discipline.

46. *Negative Dialectics,* p. 349.

# 2

# Foucault and the French Tradition of Historical Epistemology .

It has long been commonplace, in discussions of Foucault's work, to assume that the principal guidelines for his investigations into the history of the human sciences were directly derived from the French tradition of historical epistemology, whose most distinguished representatives are Gaston Bachelard and Georges Canguilhem. Mark Cousins and Athar Hussein express a common wisdom when they write, in their study of Foucault, that their subject 'adopted many of the methodological protocols of the French historians of science such as Bachelard, Canguilhem and Cavaillès. That history should not be written from the point of view of progress is the most important of them. Moreover, he has taken the displacement brought about by Canguilhem a great deal further by taking the methods of history of sciences outside the confines of histories of natural sciences'.[1]

This interpretation of Foucault's relation to his predecessors has been current ever since it was established at the beginning of the 1970s by Foucault's early, and sympathetic, Althusserian commentators. In 1971, for example, Dominique Lecourt suggested that Bachelard, Canguilhem and Foucault belonged to a common current of 'anti-positivism' (understood rather anomalously as the rejection of any general theory of scientific method) and 'anti-evolutionism' (understood as the denial of any unilinear growth of knowledge) in the philosophy of science.[2] Within this tradition, Foucault was portrayed as marking a shift of interest from the physical and biological to the human sciences. While Bachelard tends to define the matrix from which science emerges in terms of an atemporal psychology based on the conflict between reverie and rational reflection, image and concept, Canguilhem is far more interested in the social relativity and normative foundations of certain basic concepts, and even allows that the life sciences may be permanently dependent on certain figurative modes of expression, often of political or ideological origin. Placed in this lineage, Foucault can be seen as once more shifting the focus of attention, extending the consideration of ideological factors to include the social and institutional frameworks within which the human sciences have emerged.

It is certainly true that one keystone of the French epistemological tradition is the assumption that knowledge can be adequately understood only if it is studied in its historical development, as a situated dialectic of theory and experience, rather than being considered as the product of an encounter between a pre-given empirical reality and certain immutable faculties of the mind. Ultimately, the influence of this assumption in France can be traced back to Auguste Comte, who – in the first lesson of the *Cours de philosophie positive* – debunks the 'psychological method' ('the so-called study of the mind by the mind is a pure illusion') and argues that the task of positive philosophy is to trace 'the course actually followed by the human mind in action, through an examination of the methods really employed to obtain the exact knowledge that it has already acquired'.[3] Comte's determination to take history seriously also entails an appreciation of the fact that 'in order to devote itself to observation the mind needs some kind of theory',[4] an insight which was to remain central to the tradition as renewed by Bachelard and transmitted to the epistemology of the 1960s in France. In Foucault's writings, however, one rarely finds anything like an explicit philosophical argument for this approach. Rather, his position emerges from a skein of narrative whose ostensible concern may be more with political and social transformations than with the theory of the sciences. This is a technique which Foucault derives from Nietzsche, with whom he shares a profound suspicion of the traditional discourse of philosophy. Like Nietzsche, he is in search of a novel mode of expression which will evade absorption by 'the interiority of our philosophical reflection' without lapsing into 'the positivity of our knowledge'.[5]

*The Birth of the Clinic*, the first of Foucault's works to be written in the shadow of structuralism, offers a clear example of this oblique procedure. Apparently, Foucault is concerned to analyse certain transformations which took place in medical discourse at the end of the eighteenth century and beginning of the nineteenth, and their relation to the social and political upheavals of the French Revolution. But *The Birth of the Clinic* may also be read as a critique of phenomenological accounts of the status of scientific knowledge. In his later work, Maurice Merleau-Ponty had attempted to outline what he referred to as a 'genealogy of truth': he wished to show how discursive knowledge must, at some ultimate point, be anchored in a revelation of being which is prior even to the distinction of subject and object. Down to the very headings of its chapters ('Voir, Savoir'; 'L'invisible visible'), *The Birth of the Clinic* offers a subtly inverted echo of Merleau-Ponty's positions. In place of a 'genealogy of truth', Foucault proposes an 'archaeology of the gaze' which will show how supposedly immediate perception must be seen as a complex end-product, rather than as a point of departure. His historical analysis is directed towards a demonstration that the supposedly pristine look with which clinical medicine contemplates the body of the diseased patient is in fact the result of the crystallization of a complex set of procedures of observation and registration, institutional rules and forms of conceptualization. Similarly, his description of the faith of the initiators of clinical medicine – 'The gaze will be fulfilled in its own truth and will have access to the truth of things if it rests on them in silence, if everything keeps silent around what it sees'[6] – offers a sly allusion to the naïvety of phenomenology, its belief in the possibility of access to a purified, pre-linguistic level of experience. Far from providing an experiential foundation for a discourse of knowledge, for Foucault 'the original distribution of the visible and the invisible' is linked with 'the division between what is stated and what remains unsaid'.[7]

In Foucault, however, this argument goes far beyond anything to be found in Bachelard or Canguilhem. There can be no contesting that Bachelard's philosophy stresses the primacy of theory over experience: he often refers to his position as a rationalism – albeit an 'open rationalism' – in which the increasing conceptual coherence and mathematization of theory, rather than the increase of empirical range, is seen as the true mark of scientific advance, and he tirelessly criticizes philosophies which view scientific knowledge as the 'pleonasm of experience'.[8] Yet Bachelard never suggests that theories uniquely determine the facts to which they are applied, or that experience and experiment play no role in the construction of theory. And while he criticizes the abstract opposition between subject and object, which he sees as characteristic of traditional metaphysics, this is not a prelude to the reduction of both subject and object to the status of 'effects' of discursive systems, but in order to explore a more subtle dialectic between 'theory' and 'experiment', as it is manifested in the actual practice of the sciences. For Bachelard the task of an adequate philosophy of science is to steer a delicate course between realism and rationalism, rather than clinging unilaterally to one or other of these alternatives. Indeed, his conception of an 'open rationalism' consists precisely in the readiness of the scientist to revise his theories in the light of new evidence. 'When it is experimentation which brings the first message of a new phenomenon,' Bachelard states, 'the theoretician ceaselessly modifies the reigning theory, to enable it to assimilate the new fact'.[9] Nor is this adjustment limited to the superficial or *ad hoc* elements of theory, major transformations being attributed solely to conceptual innovation. In the concluding chapters of *La philosophie du non*, Bachelard suggests that no theoretical principle, not even fundamental logical principles such as the law of non-contradiction, can be assumed to be immune to revision in the light of novel experimental evidence.[10]

In Foucault's work, however, the relation between theory and experience is presented as one of unidirectional determination. Foucault – at least, the Foucault of the 1960s – adopts a view of the primacy of the discursive over the 'lived' which is clearly strongly influenced by structuralism. Thus, his denial of a 'heaven which glitters through the grid of all astronomies'[11] is an expression of his adherence less to Bachelardian epistemology than to the kind of viewpoint suggested by Lévi-Strauss's argument: 'there are no natural phenomena in the raw. These do not exist for man except as conceptualizations, seemingly filtered by logical and affective norms dependent on culture.'[12] Similarly, in *The Birth of the Clinic*, where Foucault argues that – at the level of his analysis – there is 'no distinction between theory and experience, methods and results; one had to read the deep structures of visibility in which field and gaze are bound together by *codes of knowledge*',[13] these codes tend to be seen merely as particular embodiments of the general codes of a culture. At the close of the book Foucault suggests that both the emergence of clinical medicine and the lyrical poetry of a Hölderlin can be seen as symptoms of a new consciousness of mortality, of an 'irruption of finitude', which characterizes one phase of nineteenth-century thought. In his next book, *The Order of Things*, Foucault greatly expands this conception, arguing that all the discourses of a particular epoch must be seen as determined by an underlying structure which he calls the *episteme*. This structure, which Foucault terms an 'historical *a priori*', constitutes the fundamental ordering principles of a culture, thereby providing an implicit ontology in which all its concrete modes of knowledge are rooted. As a result, there can be no possibility of any particular empirical discovery disturbing this ontology: change can come only with the global shift from one episteme to its successor. In Foucault's imaginative but implausible account, the history of Western culture since the Renaissance is divided into three immense and disconnected blocks.

In *The Archaeology of Knowledge*, the retrospective discourse on method which was the last of his books of the 1960s, Foucault greatly modifies this conception, under the guise of a correction of misinterpretations of his earlier work. He now denies that the episteme should be viewed as 'a form of knowledge or type of rationality which, crossing the boundaries of the most varied sciences, manifests the sovereign unity of a subject, a spirit or a period'.[14] If the term *episteme* is still to be used, it should be taken to denote a fluid system of disparate yet interlocking 'discursive practices'. However, this lessening of the rigidity of the episteme does not extend to the admission of a possible interaction between empirical discovery and the theoretical structure of science. Foucault insists that the object of a science 'does not await in limbo the order that will free it and enable it to become embodied in a visible and prolix objectivity'.[15] The task of the archaeology of knowledge is to account for the constitution of such objects 'without reference to the *ground*, the *foundation of things*, but by relating them to the body of rules that enable them to form as objects of discourse and thus constitute the conditions of their historical appearance'.[16] Its central assumption is that 'discourse is not a slender surface of contact or confrontation between a reality and a language, the intrication of a lexicon and an experience'.[17]

Thus, during the 1960s, Foucault attempts to produce a theory in which both subject and object are seen merely as effects of the field of discourse, rather than as its discursively situated but nevertheless interacting points of origin. Just as the objects of a science are a product of the discursive patterns of that science, so 'the subject (and its substitutes) must be stripped of their creative role and analysed as a complex and variable function of discourse'.[18] In order to explain the historical appearance of discourses, therefore, we need no recourse to existential or psychological considerations: this appearance is governed purely by 'codes of knowledge' or epistemes, or 'rules of formation'.[19] Yet in making this recommendation, Foucault, who appears to assume that the psychological subject and the transcendental subject of phenomenology exhaust the possibilities of theorization of the subject, entirely overlooks the importance of the moment of enunciation in discourse. His position rests on the characteristic structuralist confusion between the 'conditions of possibility' and the causes of an event. In isolating what – in reference to *The Order of Things* – he terms the 'formal laws' which govern a domain of statements, Foucault is not thereby enabled to explain why any particular statement should be produced on any particular occasion, just as Lévi-Strauss's isolation of a putative grammar of mythology does not explain specific instances of the production of myth, but only the rules in accordance with which such production must take place. Any structural analysis of this kind must be supplemented by a causal explanation of the individual event.

In *The Archaeology of Knowledge* Foucault attempts to overcome this problem by denying that he is seeking to achieve a formalization in the structuralist sense. His aim is, rather, to describe the immanent regularities of precisely those statements which have historically been produced. But this change, of course, fails to resolve the difficulty for a number of reasons. Firstly, Foucault himself admits that the description of regularities is an endless task, since there is a potentially infinite number of ways in which statements may be said to resemble and differ from each other: no definitive 'theory' can be achieved. Secondly, even if such a theory were possible, it would still have no explanatory force. Such a *post hoc* reconstruction would be of use only within a hermeneutical perspective; but since Foucault is relentlessly critical of projects of interpretation, and claims to be producing a neutral description of the domain of discourse, this possibility is excluded. Thirdly, the concentration on the immanent 'rules of formation' of discourse distracts attention from the fact that on many occasions (for example, the degeneration of a science in a climate of political terror) even the internal configuration of a discourse requires explanation in terms of external factors. One may conclude that what Foucault sees as the central question of 'archaeology' – 'for what reason did a certain statement appear and no other in its place?' – has been left unanswered.

Foucault's portrayal of the objects of scientific discourse as entirely constituted by that discourse contributes to the same impasse. Clearly, there is an important element of truth in his claim that 'one cannot speak of anything at any time; it is not easy to say anything new; it is not enough for us to open our eyes, to pay attention, or to be aware, for new objects suddenly to light up and emerge out of the ground'.[20] This insight into the priority of frameworks has become a commonplace in post-positivist philosophy of science. But in arguing for a total discursive determinism, Foucault takes a crucial step beyond both his contemporaries in the English-speaking world and even such an important influence on his thought as the work of Georges Canguilhem. It is true that in Canguilhem's *La connaissance de la vie*, one finds the assertion that 'theories never emerge from facts. Theories emerge only from previous theories, often of great antiquity.'[21] Yet Canguilhem immediately goes on to offer a crucial qualification of this statement, which reinstates the role of empirical evidence: 'Facts are merely the path, which is rarely direct, along which theories emerge from one another.'[22] In general, Canguilhem's Nietzsche-influenced philosophy of the aberrant and the exception forbids any determinism of the Foucaldian variety. He speaks of 'a certain anteriority of intellectual adventure over rationalization, a presumptuous overstepping [*dépassement*], resulting from the demands of life and action, of what it is already necessary to know and to have verified'.[23] For Foucault, by contrast, even 'discoveries' are rule-determined.

Part of Foucault's mistake consists in making the not uncommon leap from a discrediting of the belief in bare, pre-theoretical facts to the conclusion that there can be *no* discrepancy between the empirical implications of a theory and the observed course of events. But the fact that the description of events and processes is always *relative* to the vocabulary of a particular theory does not entail that such events must always be *consonant* with the implications of such a theory. Much recent philosophy of science in the English-speaking world has been concerned with precisely such discrepancies: with the fact that they continue to occur even in well-'tested' theories; with the *ad hoc* strategies which are devised to disarm their implications; with those moments of scientific crisis which are provoked by the accumulation of such discrepancies; and with the problem of the point at which it becomes 'rational' to abandon such a contradiction-burdened theory. In the work of Foucault, however, no such questions can be posed. Foucault's narratives of epistemic shifts communicate little sense of crisis. In *The Order of Things*, for example, the contemporary discoveries of palaeontology are attributed no role in the transition from the fixism of natural history to nineteenth-century evolutionary biology. And when Foucault does discuss a moment of scientific crisis, as in the tenth chapter of *The Birth of the Clinic*, he is careful to emphasize 'the difficulty of reaching an understanding when one was in agreement as to the facts'. He asserts that what was at stake was a pure clash of theoretical frameworks ('two incompatible types of medical experience'), not a situation in which one theory began to appear increasingly inadequate in the light of another.[24]

As the preceding discussion has indicated, theories of the coherence of systems of scientific concepts are closely linked with theories of continuity and discontinuity in the history of science. If each proposition of a science is seen as capable of facing the tribunal of experience independently, then science will be viewed as a gradual process of alteration and accumulation. If, on the other hand, the propositions of a science are seen as so closely interrelated that no one proposition can be changed without altering the sense of all the others, then each theory will determine its own set of 'facts', and there will be no common world of reference shared by different theories. Since Foucault emphasizes the solidarity of epistemes or 'regimes of discourse', discontinuity plays a central role in his account of the history of the sciences. This theme can indeed be traced back to Bachelard, who was concerned throughout his career to expose the notion of 'an abstract and invariable system of reason' which would underlie both 'common sense' and the successive stages of science. In contrast to this assumption, Bachelard affirms that 'thought is modified in its form if it is modified in its object'.[25] The history of science is characterized by 'epistemological discontinuities', after the occurrence of which a science is concerned with new objects, conducts its research according to new principles, and even adopts a new logic. There can be no simple linear accumulation of truths. Yet the status of discontinuity in Bachelard and Foucault is radically distinct.

## Bachelard's Epistemology

A number of commentators have pointed to the similarity between the innovations introduced into epistemology in France by Bachelard and his successors, and a similar transformation of philosophy of science in the English-speaking world initiated by the work of Kuhn, Hanson and others in the early 1960s.[26] In Kuhn's *The Structure of Scientific Revolutions* the history of science is seen as divided into a succession of paradigms – theoretical frameworks which are discontinuous in their background assumptions, the kinds of explanatory entities they posit, and their assessment of the phenomena which call for explanation. For Kuhn, the transformation between one paradigm and its successor is so comprehensive – his favoured analogy is the Gestalt-switch between two irreconcilable images – that he is led to argue: 'In so far as their only recourse to [the] world [of their research engagement] is through what they see and do, we may want to say that after a revolution scientists are responding to a different world.'[27] This formulation may be compared with Bachelard's affirmation: 'contemporary science, in inviting [the mind] to a new form of thought, conquers for it a new type of representation, and hence a new world'.[28] In both cases, theoretical frameworks appear to determine the very nature of reality.

This convergence, however, is far less close than it at first appears. In Kuhn's case, at least in his early statements of his position, the theory of paradigm changes leads towards relativism. Kuhn argues that since there can be no paradigm-independent access to reality, there can be no neutral standpoint from which to assess the comparative verisimilitude of different paradigms. Consequently, the history of science can no longer be viewed as an epic of cognitive progress: 'We may . . . have to relinquish the notion, explicit or implicit, that changes of paradigm carry scientists and those who learn from them closer and closer to the truth.'[29] None of these considerations applies to the work of Bachelard. Indeed, Bachelard's conception of the transition between scientific theories is a remarkably traditional one. It is true that he affirms an initial disjunction between everyday experience and the reality posited by science ('The world in which one thinks', Bachelard states, in *La philosophie du non*, 'is not the world in which one lives'[30]), but within the history of science itself, he refers far more frequently to a 'rectification' or 'recasting' of the organizing principles of a branch of science, rather than to a further process of rupture.

One of the comparatively rare occasions when Bachelard employs the term '*rupture épistémologique*' to refer to a break in scientific development, rather than to the initial break with the lived world, is to be found in *La philosophie du non*, in a passage concerned with the discovery of the atomic substructure of chemical elements. Yet even here Bachelard emphasizes that 'a non-Lavoisian chemistry . . . does not overlook the former and present usefulness of classical chemistry. It tends only to organize a more general chemistry, a panchemistry.'[31] In the final chapter of the book, he extends this observation: 'Generalization by the "no" should include what it denies. In fact, the whole rise of scientific thought over the last century derives from such dialectical reorganizations, which envelop what is negated.'[32] Behind its Hegelian phraseology, this account of scientific development differs little from the traditional realist conception of earlier scientific theories as 'limiting cases' of later theories, as approximately true or true given certain additional initial conditions. Such developments may involve a major reorganization of scientific knowledge – and in this sense there may be said to be 'discontinuity' – but there is no hint in Bachelard's work of 'incommensurability'. As a result, Bachelard has an extremely forthright view of science as a cognitively progressive enterprise. In a lecture delivered in 1951 he affirmed: 'The temporality of science is a growth in the number of truths, a deepening of the coherence of truths. The history of science is the story of this growth and of this deepening.'[33]

In Foucault's work, by contrast, a deep sensitivity to transformations in modes of discursive structuring, and even perceiving, between one period and another leads to a view of the history of science as composed of a succession – but not a progressive sequence – of regimes of discourse. A clear example may be found in *The Birth of the Clinic*, where Foucault discusses the emergence of anatomo-clinical medicine. He begins by criticizing, in a manner not markedly different from that of Bachelard, those theories which would present scientific change as the result of 'progress in observation, a wish to develop and extend experiment, an increasing fidelity to what can be revealed by sense-perceptible data, abandonment of theories and systems in favour of a more genuinely scientific empiricism'.[34] However, he goes on to suggest that:

> A more precise historical analysis reveals beyond these adjustments a quite different principle of transformation: it bears jointly on the type of objects to be known, on the grid that makes them appear, isolates them and carves up the elements relevant to a possible *savoir*, on the positions which the subject must occupy in order to map them, on the instrumental mediations which enable it to grasp them, on the modalities of registration and memory that it must put into operation, and on the forms of conceptualization that it must practice and that qualify it as a subject of legitimate knowledge.[35]

In short, what Foucault describes is a transformation so total as to leave no common denominator, reminiscent of a Kuhnian Gestalt-switch between paradigms. Significantly, he employs the two contrasting French terms for knowledge to draw a distinction which resembles Kuhn's distinction between changes at the level of the paradigm, and the puzzle-solving activity of 'normal science'. He suggests:

> that we are here concerned with an event which affects the arrangement of *savoir* is shown by the fact that *connaissance* in the order of anatomo-clinical medicine is not formed in the same way and according to the same rules as in the simple clinic. It is not a question of the same game, somewhat improved, but of a different game.[36]

The plausibility of this parallel is confirmed by a remark which Foucault makes at the very start of *The Birth of the Clinic*. He affirms that 'the old theory of sympathies spoke a vocabulary of correspondence, vicinities and homologies, terms for which the perceived space of anatomy hardly offers a coherent lexicon'.[37]

A second major difference between the work of Foucault and that of Bachelard concerns the relation between everyday experience (or what has come to be referred to, since Husserl, as the 'lifeworld') and science. In Bachelard it is possible to find a theory of the self-education of consciousness. This education begins with the observation of anomaly or incoherence in the spontaneous knowledge of the 'natural' mind, a discrepancy which eventually provokes a break with the comforting system of self-confirming assumptions: 'Objectivity appears on the level of detail, as a flaw in a picture.'[38] Once this break has taken place, the mind can be seen as divided between an ego which tends towards affectivity and illusion and a superego which is not simply the bearer of recrimination and the punitive aspects of culture, as in Freud, but which imposes an edifying shift towards the rational values of science. In Bachelard's view, this 'intellectual self-surveillance' leads to a doubling in which scientific method becomes conscious of itself. At this level, Bachelard suggests, the activity of self-surveillance 'declares itself absolutely free with respect to the entire historicity of culture'.[39] Accordingly, for Bachelard: 'In scientific thought, the concept functions all the better for the fact that it is severed from every afterimage. In its full exercise, the scientific concept is freed from all the slowness of its genetic evolution, an evolution which henceforward is a matter of mere psychology.'[40]

In Foucault's work, however, there is a firm rejection of this notion of a break between the realm of the image, or of ideology, and the realm of the concept. Thus in the preface to *The Birth of the Clinic*, in discussing the disjunction between the 'medicine of species' of the eighteenth century and the clinical medicine of the nineteenth, Foucault offers an allusive critique of Bachelard:

> What occurred was not a psychoanalysis of medical knowledge, nor any more or less spontaneous break with imaginary investments; 'positive' medicine is not a medicine that has made an 'objectal' choice in favour of objectivity itself. . . . Far from being broken, the fantasy link between knowledge and pain is reinforced by a more complex means than the mere permeability of the imagination.[40]

In *Madness and Civilization* and *The Birth of the Clinic* Foucault tends to speak of the world in which science is rooted in experiential or psychologistic terms. In later writings of the same decade, however, he more often portrays the supposed domain of experience and *connaissance* as being in fact a primary system of discursive *savoir*, out of which more formalized knowledges emerge as islands and archipelagos. In the preface to *The Order of Things*, for example, Foucault employs the Bachelardian term the 'unconscious of scientific knowledge', yet he does so not to refer to Bachelard's reservoir of archetypes but, rather, to denote a collective system of rules of the Lévi-Straussian kind. Even more significantly, he counters the assumption that 'The unconscious is always the negative side of science – that which resists it, deflects it, or disturbs it.'[42] Foucault would like to reveal a 'positive unconscious of knowledge: a level which eludes the consciousness of the scientist and yet is part of scientific discourse, instead of disrupting its validity and seeking to diminish its scientific stature'.[43] In *The Archaeology of Knowledge* he again takes up this argument, this time directing his fire more specifically against Althusserianism: 'Ideology is not exclusive of scientificity. . . . By correcting its errors, by clarifying its formulations, discourse does not necessarily undo its relations with ideology. The role of ideology does not diminish as rigour increases and error is dissipated.'[44]

## Canguilhem's History of Science

In stressing this indissoluble tie between image and concept, science and ideology, Foucault can indeed claim inspiration from his immediate mentor in the history and philosophy of science, Georges Canguilhem. Although he is in many respects a follower of Bachelard, Canguilhem does not uphold an absolute separation between the imagination and science. In *La connaissance de la vie*, he goes so far as to state: 'Perhaps it is true to say that, as far as the fundamental concepts which they apply in their principles of explanation are concerned, scientific theories are grafted on to ancient images, and we would even say on to myths.'[45] In passages such as this, Canguilhem appears to draw on a Bachelardian psychology of the imagination, even though he rejects Bachelard's exclusion of the imagination from science. In other places, however, he shows himself to be more sensitive to the social and political dimensions of image and metaphor – to the way in which, in a formulation of Michel Pêcheux's, 'practical ideological formations (conceptions of the world) intervene in biology in such a way that they are not purely and simply neutralized by the production of concepts'.[46] This view is more extensively developed in *Le normal et le pathologique*, where he argues that there can be no neutral and objective conception of normality in medicine and pathology. Normality and abnormality, health and sickness, are always ultimately dependent on the experience of the individual and – more generally – on judgements which are socially relative. It is the 'human experience of sickness which bears to the very heart of the problematic of the physiologist the concept of the nor-mal'.[47] More fundamentally: 'in questions of biology it is pathos which conditions the logos because it calls it forth'.[48]

Canguilhem has also influenced Foucault through his interest in the social and technical conditions which intervene in the history of the sci-ences. In *La connaissance de la vie*, for example, he argues that the Cartesian view of animals as mere machines should be seen not so much as a trans-position into ideology of a social phenomenon, capitalist production. Rather, it should be viewed as an exploitation of new forms of analogy made possible by the invention, during the Renaissance, of machines which could imitate human movements without requiring constant attention. Similarly, in an article in his *Études d'histoire et de philosophie des sciences*, Canguilhem traces the interrelation between advances in chemistry (the discovery of iodine), demographic surveys of the incidence of goitre and cretinism, the introduction of antiseptics and general anaesthetics into surgery, and the discovery of the function of the thyroid gland. He draws on this investigation to make the general point that the history of the sciences should not confuse 'an actual historical succession, with an all too easy log-ical reconstruction'. Its task should, rather, be 'to make us feel the opacity and the thickness of time'.[49] Such formulations are strongly reminiscent of Foucault. Indeed, Canguilhem's argument that 'the history of the sciences is related not only to a group of sciences without intrinsic cohesion but also to non-science, to ideology, to social and political practice',[50] appears to delineate precisely the Foucauldian field of research.

There remains, however, a crucial distinction between the approach of the two thinkers. Although Canguilhem fully considers the social and political factors which intervene in the history of the sciences, he does not consider these factors sufficient to explain the contours of this history. Their influence can be considered only as impinging on a process which possesses an immanent normativity, the normativity of 'an axiological activity, the quest for truth'.[51] This is not to say, however, that Canguilhem presupposes the existence of certain immutable principles of scientific rea-son. He follows Bachelard in affirming that there can be no *a priori* definition of rational procedure in the conduct of science, while at the same time refusing to suppose that the enterprise of science as a whole can be explained by irrational determinants. In this respect both Bachelard and Canguilhem appear close to the current in Anglo-Saxon philosophy of science represented by writers such as Polanyi and Toulmin, which argues that although the history of science must be seen as a rational process of inquiry, it is impossible to extract from this history a set of 'demarcation criteria' which would be applicable in all circumstances. In the history of science there is 'case law' but no 'canon law'. With reference to Bachelard, Canguilhem writes:

Reason is not founded in divine veracity, or in the requirement of the unity of the rules of the understanding. This rationalist demands of reason no other genealogical title, no other justification of its exercise, than science in its history.[52]

In a second respect, however, Canguilhem's position appears closer to that of Imre Lakatos, who considered the abandonment of the attempt to formulate general principles of scientific rationality as equivalent to a surrender to psychologism and sociologism. Like Lakatos, Canguilhem sees the history of science as constituted by the interplay of an 'internal' history, which deals with the filiation, displacement and transformation of concepts, and an 'external' history, which is concerned with psychological, social and political influences on the development of science. He further resembles Lakatos in affirming the primacy of internal history; for without some normative conception of what constitutes the rational growth of science, it becomes impossible to determine when an external, causal explanation is called for. For example, the need for an explanation of the decadence of a science in terms of social or political factors becomes apparent only if one has some independent conception of what scientific degeneration consists in. Similarly, the emergence of theories may need to be explained in terms of social or psychological contingencies, but the ultimate acceptance or rejection of these theories must be dependent upon their explanatory value. Canguilhem concludes that the historicity of science must be seen as representing the 'effectuation of a project which is internally normed, but traversed by accidents, delayed or sidetracked by obstacles, interrupted by crises, that is to say, moments of judgement and of truth'.[53]

In Foucault's work, however, this contrast between an immanent rationality of scientific knowledge and the contingencies of its historical development is entirely absent. Foucault tends, rather, to see scientific statements as locally necessary (in so far as they are determined by the underlying structure of a discursive formation) but globally contingent (in so far as this discursive formation itself is not susceptible to any ultimate rational justification). In this respect, Foucault must be classified as a representative of what Lakatos terms 'historiographical positivism', the view that the history of science can be entirely written as an 'external' history.[54] Indeed, at one point in *The Archaeology of Knowledge* Foucault claims this title for himself: 'If by substituting the analysis of rarity for the search for totalities, the description of relations of exteriority for the theme of the transcendental foundation, the analysis of accumulations for the quest for the origin, one is a positivist, then I am quite happy to be one.'[55] In *The Archaeology of Knowledge*, in other words, it is the facticity of discursive practices which determines what is to be counted as conceptual coherence, since according to Foucault 'one does not attach the constants of discourse to the ideal structures of the concept, but one describes the conceptual network on the basis of the intrinsic regularities of discourse'.[56]

It is evident that, according to such a view, the transition from one discursive formation to another cannot be seen as the result of a process of reasoned argument – both because for Foucault there is no theory-independent reality against which the forms of knowledge produced by different discursive formations could be compared, and because Foucault denies the possibility of a subject which could reflexively distance itself from a given field of discourse, and apply to this field independent criteria of rationality. Consequently, like other relativist accounts of the history of science, such as the earlier work of Kuhn, Foucault's work must have recourse to 'external', causal factors in order to explain scientific change itself. In the case of *The Structure of Scientific Revolutions* this external explanation appears to be provided by considerations of social psychology: the paradigm changes are ultimately seen as the results of collective preferences. In questions of paradigm choice, affirms Kuhn, 'there is no standard higher than the assent of the relevant community'.[57] For Foucault, of course, such a mode of explanation is ruled out, since he is firmly opposed to any form of psychologism. In its place he employs a combination of an immanent analysis of the discursive field and a consideration of the sociopolitical dependencies of this field. It is these dependencies, however, which are ultimately called on to explain the shift from one discursive formation to another.

Significantly, the attempt to erase the normative dimension of the history of science, as represented by the work of Kuhn, has been sharply attacked by Canguilhem. In the introduction to his anthology *Idéologie et rationalité dans l'histoire des sciences de la vie*, Canguilhem objects to the fact that Kuhn permits his normal, paradigm-guided science only

> an empirical mode of existence as a fact of culture. The paradigm is the result of a choice among its users. The normal is what is common, at a given period, to a collection of specialists in a university or academic institution. One believes one is dealing with concepts of philosophical criticism, whereas in fact one finds oneself at the level of social psychology.[58]

In general, Canguilhem is highly critical of any putatively 'objective' account of the history of science, which treats scientific statements simply as 'facts of discourse' like any others. Because it is centrally concerned with the vicissitudes of concepts, 'in no way can the history of science be the natural history of a cultural object'.[59] 'Natural history of a cultural object' would not, however, be an inappropriate designation for Foucault's approach to the human sciences.

By now it will be apparent that, in contrast to Foucault, the central emphasis of the French tradition of historical epistemology has been on the interdependence of the history and the philosophy of science as internally related components of a single project. In Canguilhem's phrase: 'without relation to the history of the sciences, an epistemology would be an entirely superfluous double of the science of which it claimed to speak';[60] while without a philosophically normative dimension, the history of science cannot even identify the contours of its object. This is the position of Bachelard, who argues at the beginning of *La formation de l'esprit scientifique* that 'the epistemologist must . . . sift the documents collected by the historian. He must judge them from the point of view of reason, indeed from the point of view of a reason which has evolved.'[61] It is also the position of Canguilhem, lucidly outlined in the lecture which serves as an introduction to his *Études d'histoire et de philosophie des sciences*, where he argues that the relation of the *history of science* to its object cannot be equated with the relation of a *science* to its object. The object of a science is determined by the ensemble of verified propositions which have been established about that object at a specific moment. There may well be changes in this ensemble of propositions, but these changes do not concern the science itself, whose object may be considered – in this sense – as non-temporal.[62] The history of the sciences, by contrast, is concerned precisely with the transformations of the concepts which define the objects of the sciences. Since the boundaries and transformations of a concept are always relative to a specific interpretation of that concept, the history of the sciences cannot itself be 'objective' in the scientific sense – it can be written only from a philosophical standpoint. For Canguilhem, the history of the sciences is not a description of discourses or practices, but a 'representation of meanings'.[63]

Yet even if these assumptions are granted, there still remains the problem of the epistemological standpoint from which the history of the sciences should be written. In Bachelard's work, this problem is approached through the introduction of the concept of 'recurrence'. Bachelard assumes that the only possible point from which to begin is the scientific values and attitudes of the present, since to deny these values would be to deny the rationality of the development of science itself, and it is difficult to see in what terms such a global denial could itself be rationally justified. Once this viewpoint has been adopted, the mass of documentation of the history of a science can be divided into what is 'lapsed' and what is 'ratified' – between those results which must be consigned to the prehistory of scientific knowledge, and those which can be integrated into the series of 'progressive formations of truth'.[64] This choice of standpoint, however, does not imply any form of dogmatism. The relation between what is 'lapsed' and what is 'ratified' is unstable, since such a recurrent history fully appreciates that the values and results on which it is based are themselves destined to be replaced by unforeseeable future discoveries and developments, and that the history of the sciences must therefore be continually rewritten. Canguilhem, who adopts the Bachelardian concept of recurrence, expresses the distinctiveness of this position in the following way:

> One sees the whole difference between recurrence, understood as a critical judgement of the past by the present of a science, assured, precisely because it is scientific, of being replaced and rectified, and the systematic and quasi-mechanical application of a standard model of scientific theory exercising a kind of epistemological policing function over the theories of the past.[65]

The scientific present does not embody an immutable truth, but offers the only non-arbitrary standpoint from which to view the scientific past.

In this respect, as in many others, Foucault's basic historiographical assumptions differ radically from those of the epistemological tradition from which his work is frequently assumed to have derived. But unfortunately, as we have seen, the majority of commentators read this tradition through Foucauldian spectacles, thereby producing a continuity which misrepresents Foucault's predecessors. One of the few authors who does not make this mistake is Gary Gutting. In *Michel Foucault's Archaeology of Scientific Reason* Gutting stresses the fact that both Bachelard and Canguilhem consider the history of science to be an inherently normative discipline, which would therefore undermine itself if it sought to achieve the status of neutral description.[66] Furthermore, Gutting explores in some detail Canguilhem's argument that the concept of a norm – whether biological, social, or, indeed, epistemological – 'cannot be reduced to an objective concept determinable by scientific methods'. This is because norms are ultimately the expression of a self-interpretation of life, which must itself be interpreted, and which cannot therefore be exhaustively defined by any empirical pattern of behaviour.[67] Yet when he moves on to discuss Foucault's archaeology, Gutting writes that its purpose is 'to describe in a neutral way the process whereby cognitive norms (whether genuinely scientific or not) are formed',[68] as if he had not already endorsed Bachelard's and Canguilhem's view that there can be no such normatively neutral access to norms.

Gutting is perhaps able to persuade himself that there is no fundamental philosophical divergence here because of his earlier argument that Bachelard's concept of an 'epistemological obstacle' and Canguilhem's concept of a 'scientific ideology' already challenge the distinction between 'internal' and 'external' history of science, in so far as they suggest that a scientific theory – as opposed to some extraneous factor – can itself both block and promote further scientific progress.[69] But here more discriminations are required. A scientific theory *as such* cannot be the cause of its own non-replacement by a superior theory, since otherwise such a replacement would never occur at all. At best one can say that a certain type of theory, while providing a *conceptual* springboard for later epistemic advances, also both expresses and invites certain psychological or ideological *investments*, which are the real causal – and thus, in retrospect, 'external' – factors which, for a while, hamper the achievement of such advances.

## Conclusion

Throughout the major part of his intellectual career, the deep political motivation of Foucault's thought results in a curious paradox. Foucault denies the epistemological privilege of the human sciences for the sake of those he portrays as the manipulated victims of their rise. Yet by reducing the history of the human sciences to an aleatory series of power–knowledge complexes, he places *himself* in a position of epistemological – indeed, metaphysical – privilege, no longer exposed to the challenge of an interpretative dialogue with those forms of knowledge whose 'dark side' of complicity with domination he so effectively exposes. Any such refusal of dialogue has itself inherent political dangers, in so far as it results in an autarkic vision, incapable of transformation and enrichment through exposure to alternative viewpoints. It is equally incapable of challenging power–knowledge complexes *philosophically*, by opening up the domains of experience which they conceal, since for Foucault such complexes are entirely constitutive of their objects.

The departure from the 'French epistemological tradition' which this approach involves can perhaps best be summarized by reference to the respective attitudes of Canguilhem and Foucault to the contrasting figures of Nietzsche and Husserl. Foucault suggested, on a number of occasions, that the key episode in his own intellectual development was the break, during the mid 1950s, with the optimistic rationalism of Husserlian phenomenology in favour of a Nietzschean perspectivism:

> I think that Nietzsche, who after all was almost a contemporary of Husserl, even though he stopped writing just when Husserl was about to begin, challenged and dissolved the Husserlian totalization. . . . Nietzsche discovered that the specific activity of philosophy is a diagnostic activity . . . what are we today? what is this 'today' in which we live? . . . ideologically, I remained an 'historicist' and Hegelian until I read Nietzsche.[70]

Canguilhem, however, despite his sympathy for vitalism's resistance to the objectification of the phenomenon of life, is critical of Nietzsche's account of scientific objectivity as the manifestation of a lowering of the tension of the will-to-power, and as therefore, in some sense, *contrary* to life.[71] Furthermore, during the mid 1950s, at precisely the time when Foucault was breaking with phenomenology, Canguilhem lectured on Husserl's *Crisis of the European Sciences* at the Sorbonne, and was clearly sympathetic to Husserl's account of the experiential impoverishment brought about by modern science, with its exclusive orientation towards technical achievement.[72] In other words, Canguilhem wishes both to preserve the enlightening power of science against Nietzsche's attacks ('Why cannot science, daughter of the fear of life, be accepted as a determination of the limits of life, and used courageously by life?')[73] and to endorse Husserl's dismay at the reduction of knowledge of the effectivity of its results, the effacement of subjectivity and the short-circuiting of the lifeworld – in short, his sense of the dangers of the modern separation of knowledge and wisdom. It is not a depreciation of science, he argues, to indicate the limits of its power.[74]

It is significant that Foucault, in his one major essay on Canguilhem, ignores this experience-centred dimension of his teacher's thought, and subtly assimilates his position to his own. For example, while apparently allowing the autonomy of 'the point of view of epistemology', as opposed to that of an empirical history of the sciences, in Canguilhem's thought, Foucault characterizes this as 'the investigation of the *internal normativity* of different scientific activities'.[75] He thereby transforms the normativity of knowledge back into an 'object' which varies in relation to different forms of knowledge, rather than viewing it – as Canguilhem does – as emerging in the space of dialogue between the history of science and its philosophically informed reconstruction. In general Foucault tries to simplify the complexities of Canguilhem's position in accordance with his own prejudices, arguing that his work belongs to a 'philosophy of *savoir*, rationality and the concept' as opposed to one of 'experience, meaning and the subject', and insisting that 'these two forms of thought constituted in France two frameworks which have remained profoundly heterogeneous'.[76] As we have seen, this dichotomy could not be less appropriate in Canguilhem's case. Indeed, a closer adherence to the perspective of his predecessor, in all its richness, might have enabled Foucault to develop a theoretical approach more consistent with his underlying critical purpose. It might have allowed him to trace a fragile thread of rationality, and thereby to discern a dialectic of oppressive application and emancipatory potential, in the history of the human sciences, without sacrificing any of the density of his account of their complicity with systems of administration and social control.

# Notes

1. Mark Cousins and Athar Hussein, *Michel Foucault*, London: Macmillan 1984, pp. 257–8.

2. See Dominique Lecourt, *Pour une critique de l'épistémologie*, Paris: Maspero 1972.

3. Stanislav Andreski, ed., *The Essential Comte*, London: Croom Helm 1974, p. 46.

4. Ibid., p. 22.

5. Michel Foucault, 'La Pensée du dehors', *Critique*, no. 229, 1966, p. 526/'Maurice Blanchot: The Thought from Outside', in *Foucault/Blanchot*, trans. Brian Massumi, New York: Zone Books 1987, p. 16.

6. Michel Foucault, *The Birth of the Clinic*, trans. A. Sheridan, London: Tavistock 1973, p. 108.

7. Ibid., p. xii.

8. Gaston Bachelard, *Le rationalisme appliqué*, Paris: PUF 1975, p. 38.

9. Ibid., p. 2.

10. See Gaston Bachelard, *La philosophie du non*, Paris: PUF 1975, chs 5–6/*The Philosophy of No*, trans. G.C. Waterston, New York: The Orion Press 1968, chs. 5–6.

11. Michel Foucault, *The Archaeology of Knowledge*, trans. A. Sheridan, London: Tavistock 1972, p. 191.

12. Claude Lévi-Strauss, *Structural Anthropology 2*, Harmondsworth: Penguin 1978, pp. 231–2.

13. *The Birth of the Clinic*, p. 98.

14. *The Archaeology of Knowledge*, p. 191.

15. Ibid., p. 45.

16. Ibid., p. 48.

17. Ibid.

18. Michel Foucault, 'What is an author?', in *Language, Counter-memory, Practice*, ed. Donald Bouchard, Oxford: Blackwell 1977, p. 138.

19. Michel Foucault, 'Réponse au cercle d'épistémologie', *Cahiers pour l'analyse*, no. 9, Summer 1968, p. 17.

20. *The Archaeology of Knowledge*, pp. 44–5.

21. Georges Canguilhem, *La connaissance de la vie*, Paris: Vrin 1965, p. 50.

22. Ibid.

23. Georges Canguilhem, *Idéologie et rationalité dans l'histoire des sciences de la vie*, Paris: Vrin 1977, p. 56.

24. *The Birth of the Clinic*, p. 174.

25. Gaston Bachelard, *Le nouvel esprit scientifique*, Paris: PUF 1978, p. 56/*The New Scientific Spirit*, trans. A. Goldhammer, Boston: Beacon Press 1984, pp. 53–4.

26. It should be noted that the French term '*épistémologie*' has a narrower connotation than the cognate English term, its meaning being closer to 'philosophy of science' than to 'theory of knowledge'.

27. Thomas Kuhn, *The Structure of Scientific Revolutions*, Chicago: University of Chicago Press 1974, p. 111.

28. *La philosophie du non*, p. 122/*The Philosophy of No*, p. 104.

29. *The Structure of Scientific Revolutions*, p. 170.

30. *La philosophie du non*, p. 110/*The Philosophy of No*, p. 95.

31. Ibid., p. 65/p. 55.

32. Ibid., p. 137/p. 117.

33. Gaston Bachelard, 'L'actualité de l'histoire des sciences', in *L'engagement rationaliste*, Paris: PUF 1972, p. 139.

34. *The Birth of the Clinic*, p. 136.

35. Ibid., p. 137.

36. Ibid.

37. Ibid., p. 3.

38. Gaston Bachelard, 'Discursive Idealism', *Graduate Faculty Philosophy Journal*, vol. 1, no. 2, Spring 1978, p. 5.

39. *Le rationalisme appliqué*, p. 80.

40. Gaston Bachelard, *La poétique de la rêverie*, Paris: PUF 1978, p. 46/*The Poetics of Reverie*, trans. Daniel Russell, Boston: Beacon Press 1971, p. 52.

41. *The Birth of the Clinic*, p. x.

42. Michel Foucault, *The Order of Things*, London: Tavistock 1974, p. xi.

43. Ibid.

44. *The Archaeology of Knowledge*, p. 186.

45. *La connaissance de la vie*, p. 79.

46. Michel Pêcheux, 'Idéologie et l'histoire des sciences', in Michel Pêcheux and Michel Fichant, *Sur l'histoire des sciences*, Paris: Maspero 1971, p. 38.

47. Georges Canguilhem, *Le normal et le pathologique*, Paris: PUF 1966, p. 172/*The Normal and the Pathological*, trans. Carolyn R. Fawcett and Robert S. Cohen, New York: Zone Books 1991, p. 234.

48. Ibid., p. 139/pp. 208–9.

49. Georges Canguilhem, *Études d'histoire et de philosophie des sciences*, Paris: Vrin 1968, p. 275.

50. Ibid., p. 18.

51. Ibid., p. 19.

52. Ibid., p. 200.

53. Ibid., p. 17.

54. See Imre Lakatos, *The Methodology of Scientific Research Programmes: Philosophical Papers: Volume I*, Cambridge: Cambridge University Press 1978, p. 135.

55. *The Archaeology of Knowledge*, p. 125.

56. Ibid., p. 62.

57. *The Structure of Scientific Revolutions*, p. 94.

58. *Idéologie et rationalité*, p. 23.

59. *Études d'histoire et de philosophie des sciences*, p. 18.

60. Ibid., p. 12.

61. Gaston Bachelard, *La formation de l'esprit scientifique*, Paris: Vrin 1977, p. 17.

62. See Georges Canguilhem, 'L'objet de l'histoire des sciences', in *Études d'histoire et de philosophie des sciences*.

63. Georges Canguilhem, *La formation du concept de réflexe aux XVII<sup>e</sup> et XVIII<sup>e</sup> siècles*, Paris: PUF 1955, p. 158.

64. See Gaston Bachelard, *L'activité rationaliste de la physique contemporaine*, Paris: PUF 1951, ch. 1.

65. *Idéologie et rationalité*, p. 21.

66. 'On such a model [i.e. that of Canguilhem], history of science is not a scientific discipline precisely because its explicitly normative intent excludes the value-free orientation characteristic of scientific analysis.' (Gary Gutting, *Michel Foucault's Archaeology of Scientific Reason*, Cambridge: Cambridge University Press 1989, p. 38.)

67. See *Michel Foucault's Archaeology*, pp. 46-52. The quotation is from Canguilhem, *On the Normal and the Pathological*, Dordrecht: Riedel 1978, p. 138.

68. *Michel Foucault's Archaeology*, p. 254.

69. See *Michel Foucault's Archaeology*, p. 17n, p. 45.

70. Paolo Caruso, *Conversazione con Lévi-Strauss, Foucault, Lacan*, Milan: V. Murcia and Co. 1969, pp. 116–17.

71. For Canguilhem's critique of Nietzsche, see 'De la science et de la contre-science', in Suzanne Bachelard *et al.*, *Hommage à Jean Hyppolite*, Paris: PUF 1971, pp. 177–80.

72. For a report of Canguilhem's lectures on Husserl, see Jean-Jacques Salomon, 'Georges Canguilhem ou la modernité', *Revue de Métaphysique et de Morale*, vol. 90, no. 1, January–March 1985.

73. 'De la science et de la contre-science', p. 180.

74. See 'Georges Canguilhem ou la modernité', pp. 58–9.

75. Michel Foucault, 'Georges Canguilhem: Philosopher of Error', *Ideology and Consciousness*, no. 7, Autumn 1980, p. 57.

76. Ibid., p. 52

# 3

# The Historicization of
# Analytical Philosophy

The reverse side of modernity is the permanent crisis of tradition. Perhaps one could even go so far as to define modernity as the uncompletable task of questioning what is handed down. Given this assumption, it seems reasonable to anticipate that on closer inspection the problem of tradition will turn out to have been one of the most important focuses of philosophical discussion over the last two hundred years. And indeed, from the young Hegel's critique of positivity, via Nietzsche's diagnosis of a 'consuming fever of history' which compensates precisely for the fragmentation of tradition provoked by the rise of an objectifying knowledge of the past, right up to the latest disputes surrounding the concept of postmodernity, European philosophy has repeatedly faced the question of tradition – of its repressive constraints or its indispensable power of orientation; of its anachronistic illusions or its sustaining continuity.[1]

Furthermore, the most significant 'continental' philosophers have never denied that an intrinsic relation to tradition also characterizes philosophical thinking, regardless of whether their own attitude to tradition was more positively or more negatively inflected. Husserl initially strove to achieve a new grounding for philosophy as a rigorous science, but in his later writings he was obliged to acknowledge the historicity of thought, and found himself confronted with the task of doing justice to this feature without exploding the framework of transcendental phenomenology. Derrida defends the need for a deconstruction of Western metaphysics, but nevertheless ruthlessly criticizes the view that one could escape the domination of the metaphysical tradition through recourse to a few contrived neologisms. Indeed, in the twentieth century only the analytical school constitutes a significant exception to this intellectual struggle – itself pervaded by tradition – with the question of the value of tradition.

It can scarcely be denied that analytical philosophy has been characterized from the very beginning by a deep hostility to tradition. This is why Hilary Putnam connects analytical philosophy with the world-view of cultural modernism in the third volume of his *Philosophical Papers*, entitled

*Realism and Reason*. According to Putnam, the desire to condemn and
overthrow tradition was definitive of this world-view, along with a fundamental expectation that the development of technology and the natural
sciences would permanently improve the condition of humanity. However,
not only did analytical philosophy turn its back on tradition – it allowed
its hostility towards tradition to become so powerful that it laid waste
the theoretical resources which might have made possible its own *self-
understanding* as a tradition. In the introduction to his study of the origins
of analytical philosophy, Peter Hylton points out that analytical philosophers have habitually treated all other analytically orientated philosophers
as contemporaries: 'analytical philosophy seems to think of itself as taking
place in a timeless moment'.[2] In such a perspective the interpretation of
Russell's logical atomism, for example, which was formulated shortly after
the turn of the last century, poses no specifically *hermeneutic* difficulties for
a contemporary philosopher. Since the validity or invalidity of arguments
is considered to be independent of context, one can defend or criticize
Russell's 'Theory of Definite Descriptions' just as one would defend or
criticize the theory of a colleague.

Currently, however, it is becoming ever clearer that the analytical movement is experiencing a certain exhaustion and crisis of orientation.
Nietzsche was convinced that 'when the historical sense reigns *without
constraint* and draws all its consequences . . . it uproots the future, because
it destroys illusions, and robs existing things of the atmosphere in which
alone they can live'.[3] But the example of contemporary analytical philosophy seems to suggest exactly the opposite. It is only because the
fundamental convictions of this tradition have become problematic, and
threaten to expose themselves as illusions, that questions concerning the
source of these convictions have begun to be posed. It is the immanent
development of analytical philosophy, and the theoretical difficulties this
development has encountered, which have brought about a newly reflective
openness and a novel awareness of history. Analytical philosophers have
begun to investigate the origins of their own tradition.

## From Hegel to Atomism

Peter Hylton's *Russell, Idealism, and the Origins of Analytical Philosophy* is
an interesting example of this shift of outlook. It was always known that
Russell passed through a Hegelian phase before he developed his logical
atomism, but only recently has it occurred to any analytical philosopher to
engage seriously with Russell's early writings, since it was considered obvious that Hegelianism was no more than a collage of metaphysical
absurdities. So Hylton's book is a testimony to the development of new

modes of thinking among more open-minded analytical philosophers, which have begun to take root despite long-standing prejudices. Furthermore, Hylton is well aware that a new interest in history cannot be incorporated into the stance of analytical philosophy without a wide-ranging revision of stubborn dogmas. In his methodological introduction, for example, he attacks the sharp distinction between philosophical activity and the history of philosophy, and makes a case for the importance of historical investigation for the understanding and evaluation of philosophical arguments. Because philosophy – in contrast to the sciences – always finds itself bringing its own methods and basic convictions into play, there is always the possibility that contemporary philosophizing will be able to learn from the past. Hylton concludes:

> Philosophy thus always has the hope of learning neglected lessons from its past. It is also, and perhaps more characteristically, always in a state of potential rivalry with its past, defining itself against its past, and threatened by it. . . . The deliberately ahistorical character of much history of philosophy seems to me not accidental, but a product of this insecure relation between philosophy and its past.[4]

Here Hylton is openly criticizing the predominant conception of the role of the history of philosophy in analytical philosophy. He is suggesting that a purely argumentative engagement with the classic texts of the history of philosophy can be seen as a kind of defence mechanism, which transforms the theories of the past into unsuccessful trial runs for later theories. Furthermore, such an engagement presupposes that there is nothing problematic about the task of identifying the content of earlier philosophical views. Against this, Hylton makes the objection that a philosophical theory has no determinate content and no unambiguously specifiable consequences, independently of how it is interconnected with other theories. Outside of formal logic, to which no philosophical argument is ever wholly reducible, there can be no decontextualized validity of arguments. Hylton's aim is to make these venerable hermeneutic insights fruitful for the self-understanding of analytical philosophy.

Hylton's book is primarily concerned with the influence of the British Hegelianism of the second half of the nineteenth century, particularly that of T.H. Green and F.H. Bradley. He tries to show how Russell's logical atomism arose out of a settling of accounts with the Hegelianism which he had defended at the beginning of his career. In fact, this enterprise closely follows the conception of the *philosophical* relevance of the history of philosophy which Charles Taylor has proposed in his essay 'Philosophy and its History'. Taylor argues that recourse to the most significant figures of the history of philosophy, in particular those who have introduced a 'change of paradigm', is indispensable if we are to break the spell of habitual figures of thought which have become almost instinctual. Only when we are clear about how unprecedented and precarious a certain philosophical picture originally was, are we in a position to take other possibilities seriously, and consider them without the blinkers of unreflective prejudice.[5]

Although this conception may seem relatively uncontentious from the standpoint of continental philosophy, Hylton is aware that he is attempting something iconoclastic within his own context:

> For one trained within the analytic tradition to study the history of that tradition might seem to be a small step. And so, in one sense, it is. . . . But in another sense it is a revolutionary move. Analytical philosophy has largely rejected historical modes of understanding. Attempts to apply that mode of understanding to analytic philosophy itself are so rare as to be non-existent.[6]

To justify the value of his new enterprise, Hylton suggests that his study 'may be useful not merely as a means of understanding the relevant works of Russell and Moore but as a way of gaining perspective on the tradition of twentieth-century analytical philosophy, and thus of learning something about our own philosophical situation.'[7] Hylton thus seems to assume that every philosopher finds herself in a 'philosophical situation', and that it can detract from her activity when she has no adequate conception of that situation. It is worth asking whether the classic authors of the analytical tradition could ever have regarded the expression 'philosophical situation' as meaningful, since it seems to imply that philosophical arguments do not possess timeless validity but derive their force, or lack of it, from the current state of discussion along with its presuppositions, which can never be entirely retrieved by reflection. Indeed, with regard to the question of objective philosophical truth and where it might lie, Hylton's position comes close to agnosticism. He is far from regarding the rise of analytical philosophy as an unambiguous step forward, a replacement of delusion and error by a reliable method. In the introduction to the second part of his study, he emphasizes:

> For every argument that Moore and Russell could mount against Idealism, there is an idealist reply which points out a distinction that is being neglected, or one that is drawn erroneously; an assumption smuggled in, or the sense of a term distorted.[8]

To illustrate Hylton's procedure, I will mention a couple of examples. In the early phases of their common reaction against Idealism, shortly before the turn of the century, Moore and Russell developed a metaphysics which Hylton describes as 'platonic atomism'. According to this metaphysics, the world consists of propositions and relations, which are absolutely independent both of each other and of the knowing mind. Relations and propositions are therefore both kinds of objects, but for platonic atomism distinctions between these different sorts of entities are of only secondary importance. Knowledge consists in the immediate contact between the mind and an isolatable object.

In addition, platonic atomism asserts that every proposition must be either true or false. However, as Hylton points out, this idea of the absoluteness of truth, a cornerstone of the analytical outlook, was taken over from the British Idealists. Russell agreed with his idealist predecessors that truth must be unconditional (in contrast to Kantianism, for example). The difference between them consists in the fact that the Idealists recognized stages of *relative* truth, through which one must ascend in order to attain absolute truth (though according to Bradley, this final truth can never be *discursively* attained[9]); whereas Moore and Russell share the view that each isolated proposition, taken on its own, can claim this absoluteness. Hylton calls this view 'Russell's assumption', and comments on it as follows:

> From the time of his rejection of Idealism onwards [Russell] takes it that truth is an absolute concept: either a thing is true or it is not, there can be no qualification and no degrees; and also that there are entities, independently identifiable, each of which has the property that it is absolutely and unqualifiedly true or equally unqualifiedly false. . . . This claim or assumption is largely hidden from the modern reader in the analytical tradition by the fact that such a reader has been educated to make the same assumption – to see it, indeed, as inevitable, and not as an assumption at all. The comparison with Idealism forces the assumption into the open. . . . Russell's assumption is required for ordinary truth-functional logic. For the modern reader this may simply contribute to the idea that there is no alternative to the assumption, but for Russell the assumption and modern logic were part of a single controversial view. He held that we have more reason to accept the assumption because it is required by logic. We can see that this shows that logic, in Russell's hands, was not a philosophically neutral tool, but a source of philosophical claims and of reasons for those claims.[10]

In this way Hylton's investigation throws new light on one of the fundamental assumptions of the analytical tradition. Other philosophers who have recently attempted to excavate the deep presuppositions of this tradition have also highlighted the central importance of the demand for absolute determinability. This demand is connected with the view of language as a representational medium which can in principle be characterized independently of the world which is represented. Only when language is viewed in this way, it is supposed, can it be adequate to the enterprise of the natural sciences. The natural sciences themselves, however, require no philosophical validation, since they provide their own legitimation through their instrumental success. They demonstrate that every meaningful question must have an unambiguous answer.[11]

A further achievement of Hylton's book consists in having cast doubt on a widespread assumption concerning Russell's place in the history of philosophy. It is still common on British university courses for Russell to be portrayed as the inheritor – via Mill – of the empiricism of the eighteenth century. But after his break with Idealism, Russell at first evinced no interest in epistemological issues: the assumption that the activity of the mind might play a role – however minimal – in the constitution of reality had to be unconditionally avoided. Only gradually, as a result of the emergence of difficulties in the project of 'platonic atomism' (how, for example, can the world consist of true and *false* propositions?), did Russell feel compelled to reintroduce epistemological considerations into his work. Thus empiricism was not a point of departure for Russell, but a terminus which he reached only after many detours. Hylton's investigations make it plausible to assume that many of the problems of the supposedly empiricist concept of 'acquaintance' in Russell arise from the fact that this concept already played a role in his earlier philosophy, where it was required to fulfil the role made vacant by the *lack* of an epistemology.[12]

## Rorty's 'Encapsulation' of Philosophy

Hylton's cautious treatment of the prehistory of analytical philosophy stands in sharp contrast to the unbuttoned rhetoric of Richard Rorty. Hylton's point of departure is evidently within the analytical tradition, and it is clear that he has reached his new evaluation of the philosophical significance of the history of philosophy only after considerable exertion. Hylton explicitly seeks to fend off the reproach that he has adopted a 'continental' perspective, insisting: 'The idea that we understand ourselves, and our intellectual activity, through understanding our history, does not . . . seem to depend on any questionable Hegelian metaphysics.'[13]

By contrast, among contemporary thinkers it is Richard Rorty who has – since the appearance of *Philosophy and the Mirror of Nature* – most successfully initiated a historicizing shift within analytical philosophy by appealing to the classic authors of the continental tradition, including Hegel. In his latest two-volume collection of essays, *Philosophical Papers: Volumes 1 and 2*, which consists of his principal writings from the 1980s, Rorty continues his attempt to mediate between the traditions, although the collection is divided up so that the first volume deals principally with analytical and the second with continental philosophers.

Rorty agrees with Hylton that one of the chief characteristics of analytical philosophy has been its lack of historical reflection. In the first essay of the second volume of these papers Rorty explicitly connects this lack with an isolation from continental philosophy:

Analytical philosophy has pretty well closed itself off from contact with non-analytical philosophy, and lives in its own world. The scientistic approach to philosophy which Husserl shared with Carnap lives on, forming a tacit presupposition of the work of analytical philosophers. Even though analytic philosophy now describes itself as 'post-positivistic', the idea that philosophy 'analyzes' or 'describes' some ahistorical formal structures – an idea common to Husserl, Russell, Carnap and Quine – persists. However, there is little metaphilosophical defense of this claim.[14]

But although Rorty repeatedly appeals to what Gadamer would term the 'Wirkungsgeschichtliches Bewußtsein' of continental philosophy (its awareness of the history of the reception of theories in which it stands as determining its own relation to its past), it is not difficult to show that his own attitude towards the philosophical tradition is in many respects closer to the typical attitude of analytical philosophy than to that of most continental traditions. There is a positive side to this, of course. In his essay 'Deconstruction and Circumvention', for example, Rorty develops an interesting criticism of those representatives of the Heidegger–Derrida school who implicitly or explicitly assume that the fate of the West can somehow be deciphered from the texts of metaphysics. Rorty protests: 'The claim, shared by Derrida and Heidegger, that the "ontotheological" tradition has permeated science, literature and politics – that it is central to the culture – is a self-deceptive attempt to magnify the importance of an academic speciality.'[14]

This critique is justified to the extent that the history of metaphysics consists fundamentally of theories and complexes of theories – not of a series of fateful terms which, as the knots in our conceptual net, supposedly hold our culture thrall to repressive illusions. But Rorty draws a false conclusion from this. He assumes that in undermining the view that the 'history of Being' must be regarded as a scarcely reversible process of decline, he has in fact succeeded in entirely dissolving the hold of the past over our current thinking. Furthermore, it does not follow from the insight that our culture is not *grounded* in the concepts of philosophy that philosophy is essentially just one more academic discipline among others, with no more intimate connection to the problems of everyday life than any other specialized area of research. Yet this assumption seems to lurk behind Rorty's blithe assertion that 'one of the less important side-shows of Western civilization – metaphysics – is closing down'.[16] Rorty describes this disempowering of the philosophical tradition, which he seeks to take further, as 'encapsulation', and he defends the view that this encapsulation is the real, unintended achievement of Heidegger's interpretation of the history of Western philosophy: 'Despite himself, what Heidegger did to the history of philosophy was not to deconstruct it but further to encapsulate and isolate it, thus enabling us to *circumvent* it.'[17]

These formulations recall Hylton's critical description of the efforts of analytical philosophy to evade what he calls 'the insecure relationship between philosophy and its past'. In the introduction to his book Hylton seeks to show that Rorty's conception of the history of philosophy in particular is better suited to the history of the natural sciences. Despite his renown as defender of a pluralist historicism, Rorty seems to harbour no doubts that his own version of pragmatism is superior to every previous philosophical position. The philosophical theories of the past are, in his view, merely unfortunate errors from which we have nothing to learn. Accordingly, he declares in his essay 'The Historiography of Philosophy: Four Genres':

> We should treat the history of philosophy as we treat the history of science. In the latter field, we have no reluctance in saying that we know better than our ancestors what they were talking about. We do not think it anachronistic to say that Aristotle had a false model of the heavens. . . . We should be equally willing to say that Aristotle was unfortunately ignorant that there are no such things as real essences, or Leibniz that God does not exist, or Descartes that the mind is just the nervous system under another description.[18]

In this statement one catches unmistakable echoes of the original programme of logical positivism. Indeed, Rorty admits that the pragmatist 'at first glance . . . looks like just another variety of positivist'.[19] But since he has read his Nietzsche, he also regards the belief in science as merely the last embodiment of 'metaphysical' belief in truth 'in itself'. He therefore asserts:

> If philosophy disappears, something will have been lost that was central to Western intellectual life – just as something central was lost when religious intuitions were weeded out from among the intellectually respectable candidates for philosophical articulation. But the Enlightenment thought, rightly, that what would succeed religion would be *better*. The pragmatist is betting that what succeeds the 'scientific' positivist culture which the Enlightenment produced will be *better*.[20]

This assertion might lead one to anticipate in Rorty's work a certain critical attitude towards the natural-scientific world-view which still plays a dominant role in our societies, one informed by the notion of a 'post-positivist' culture. But this is not how things stand. Rorty is unwilling to abandon either the naturalism of the scientific world-view or its physicalism (all processes are 'really' just segments of the network of causal relations between physical events). It is simply that he does not consider that such a world-view requires any *philosophical* underpinning: it is our modern common-sense ontology, to which we can legitimately have spontaneous recourse when it comes to dissolving illusory metaphysical problems. Rorty does indeed see himself as an opponent of the scientization of culture, yet the normativity of culture does not, in his view, pose any chronic problem which might seduce us towards thoughts of a neo-Kantian division between the natural sciences and the *Geisteswissenschaften*. Rorty wants to be 'naturalistic but not scientistic'.[21] His pragmatism 'wants to hold onto the materialistic world-view that typically forms the background of contemporary liberal selfconsciousness, while refraining from the claim that this view has been "established" by a method'.[22]

So Rorty's materialism and naturalism are ultimately a question of pure conviction, as he freely admits here. Accordingly, when, in the absence of persuasive grounds for adopting this philosophical orientation, one inquires into its deep cultural wellsprings, it becomes clear that Rorty is striving for the ideal of a *perfected* finitude of human life which has repeatedly exercised an almost irresistible force of attraction over modern consciousness. The internal tensions of Rorty's philosophy are strongly reminiscent, for example, of the theoretical problems of Left Hegelianism, and in particular of the problems of Feuerbach's 'Philosophy of the Future'. Rorty has gradually reached the conclusion, as did Feuerbach, that traditional philosophy is simply a continuation of theology by other means: both modes of thinking are characterized by the hypostatization of concepts which are artificially severed from their original rootedness in human life and practice. Rorty could surely subscribe without hesitation to the following quotation from Feuerbach's *Principles of the Philosophy of the Future*: 'Only when thought is separated from the human being, fixed in itself, do painful and unfruitful questions arise which are unsolvable from this standpoint.'[23] Furthermore, Rorty, just like Feuerbach, promises us a world-historical upturn, as soon as we have left behind the inflexible conceptual apparatus of philosophy. This is why he can welcome the Weberian 'disenchantment of the world' without reservation.[24] The problem is, however, that the naturalistic stance (of Rorty no less than of Feuerbach), which retains its own plausibility only as a weapon *against* philosophical hypostatizations, continually threatens to congeal into a new world-view – and, indeed, a positivistic one.

Thus although many regard Rorty as the outstanding representative of a new dialogue between the analytical and continental traditions, his own thinking reveals far stronger continuities with the basic assumptions of analytical philosophy. For Rorty, thought is not inextricably interwoven with the movement of tradition, for which one should therefore try to acquire as much sensitivity as possible. Rather, on his account we need to develop our awareness of the tradition only in order to come to the conclusion that we can consign it to the scrapheap without any major loss. Indeed, we *must* dispose of it in order to disclose the finitude of human beings as self-sufficient natural beings in a world without transcendence.

## Metaphor and Philosophy

In order to show why this project cannot succeed, I would like to investigate Rorty's treatment of the question of metaphor a little more closely. The choice of this theme is in no way arbitrary, since the phenomenon of metaphor, along with its differing interpretations, can be seen as a concentrated dramatization of the tension between behaviouristically orientated theories of language, on the one hand, and the conception of language as a world-disclosing power, on the other. Rorty himself makes it clear that an emphasis on the metaphorical foundations of philosophical language is one of the merits of continental philosophy, and that this emphasis is intimately connected with the sensitivity of continental philosophy to the historical transformation of world pictures:

> The analytical tradition regards metaphor as a distraction from [an ahistorical reality to which a given philosophical vocabulary may or may not be adequate] whereas the nonanalytical tradition regards metaphor as the way of escaping from the illusion that there is such a reality.[25]

At the same time, however, Rorty energetically defends Donald Davidson's theory of metaphor in both volumes of his *Philosophical Papers*. According to this theory, metaphorical expressions have no meaning other than their literal meaning, and in this sense they are for the most part literally false. Metaphors can be 'true' only when they are already 'dead' (incorporated into everyday language) – clearly a deeply ambivalent transfiguration. Davidson makes this proposal because he is convinced that only 'Literal meaning and literal truth conditions can be assigned to words and sentences apart from particular contexts of use. This is why adverting to them has genuine explanatory power.'[26] By contrast, a concept of 'metaphorical meaning' or 'metaphorical truth' gives us no help in explaining the functioning of metaphors: it is merely a redescription of what we understand when we grasp the point of a metaphor.[27]

According to Davidson, metaphors point towards previously unremarked aspects and similarities of things, and in this way they are able to spark off novel intellectual chain reactions. But this does not mean that we are entitled to consider a successful metaphor as a vehicle of truth. Metaphors have no 'specific cognitive content' which the listener or reader must grasp in order to understand them.[28] Rorty comments on this conception as follows: 'Davidson lets us see metaphors on the model of unfamiliar events in the natural world – *causes* of changing beliefs and desires – rather than on the model of *representations* of unfamiliar worlds which are "symbolic" rather than "natural".'[29]

But when one examines Rorty's appeal to Davidson more closely, it becomes clear that Rorty has brutally simplified the latter's conception.

Davidson asserts that metaphors have no cognitive content, but he does not contest the fact that metaphors open our eyes and sensitize us to new dimensions of a pre-predicative reality, which are not susceptible to exhaustive linguistic representation: 'If what metaphor makes us notice were finite in scope and propositional in nature, this would not in itself make trouble; we would simply project the content of the metaphor brought to mind onto the metaphor. But in fact there is no limit to what a metaphor calls to our attention, and much of what we are caused to notice is not propositional in character.'[30] By contrast, Rorty tries to make metaphor no different from any novel event in nature. He suggests that such a natural event also obliges us to rework our classificatory schemata, and to initiate a certain displacement in our conceptual grid of similarities and differences. But this equation is misleading. Considered in itself, no event in nature is characterized by an intrinsic capacity to point towards a specific range of new similarities, or by an internal – rather than contingent and associative – disclosure of a pre-predicative domain. Rorty is reluctant to acknowledge such a domain because the concept of the pre-predicative is straightforwardly incompatible with his 'materialist' ontology. However, the fact that metaphor in general imperils the habitual ontology of a scientized world has been highlighted by Paul Ricoeur in his book, *The Rule of Metaphor*. Ricoeur is of the view that we can do justice to the paradoxical 'it is' and 'it is not' of the metaphorical expression only if we undertake a revision of our objectifying world-view:

> It is precisely a question of establishing whether poetic language does not break through to a prescientific, pre-predicative level, where the very concepts of fact, object, reality, truth, as defined by epistemology, are *put in question* in favour of an oscillation of literal reference.[31]

It seems reasonable to assume that Rorty's rejection of this conception of metaphor is closely connected with his attitude to the history of philosophy. If one of the most important concerns of philosophy consists in the subtle, demanding task of an articulation of our implicit, deeply embedded conception of the world and of ourselves, then metaphor necessarily plays a key role in philosophical discourse. For Rorty, however, 'there is nothing deep down inside us that we have not put there ourselves, no criterion that we have not created in the course of creating a practice, no standard of rationality that is not an appeal to such a criterion, no rigorous argumentation that is not obedience to our own conventions'.[32]

This is why Rorty believes that philosophical theories of the past can pose no challenge to our contemporary modes of thought, even though he agrees that they are woven from metaphor. For either these metaphors are alive, and therefore as meaningless 'as birdsong' (in Rorty's phrase), or they are dead, already incorporated into our language, and therefore no longer capable of triggering new impulses of thought. Rorty describes 'the supersensory world, the Ideas, God, the moral law, the authority of reason' as 'dead metaphors which pragmatists can no longer find uses for'.[33] He evidently assumes that we can reach a firm and final understanding of these expressions – and that philosophical metaphors, therefore, conceal no inexhaustible power of articulation, since there is simply no pre-linguistic dimension of our experience of the world to be disclosed.

Thus, in the final reckoning, Rorty's compromise between analytical and continental philosophy cannot be sustained. His naturalistic background ontology, which presupposes a fully determinable reality, inhibits his understanding of our relation to traditions, including those of philosophy. It is true that Rorty was one of the first to draw attention to the status of analytical philosophy as a tradition, but in his view the development of traditions is dependent purely on causal contingencies, and this means that tradition can raise no claim to rational interpretability.[34] To make clear the gulf between Rorty's approach and the main currents of twentieth-century continental philosophy, one need only recall the following passage from Gadamer's *Wahrheit und Methode*: 'The same thing is as true of understanding as of language. Neither is to be grasped simply as a fact that can be empirically investigated. Neither is ever simply an object, but rather encompasses everything which can ever become an object.'[35]

## Putnam's Anti-Reductionism

A happier example of the new flexibility and openness of analytical philosophy is provided by the work which Hilary Putnam has published over the last fifteen years or so. What is perhaps most interesting about Putnam's collection of articles *Realism and Reason: Philosophical Papers Volume 3* is that here, for the first time, he ventures beyond his earlier discussions, which remained, despite their pathbreaking features, within the inherited framework of analytical philosophy, and risks some generalizations concerning the historical development and cultural significance of the analytical movement as a whole. In the introduction to this volume, Putnam confesses:

> I have come to see that one cannot come to grips with the real problems of philosophy without being more sensitive to the epistemological position of the philosopher. . . . Becoming more sensitive to that position had consequences I did not expect. It led me to think about questions which are thought to be more the province of 'continental philosophy' than of 'analytical philosophy', for instance, to think about the fact that our notions of rationality evolve in history, and about the fact that one's own philosophical tradition has both a past and a future.[36]

Thus the immanent development of Putnam's thinking has thrown up questions which threaten to disrupt the self-understanding of analytical philosophy. For this reason, it is important to note that Putnam's path of development has taken precisely the opposite direction to that of Rorty. Since the publication of *Philosophy and the Mirror of Nature* Rorty has become ever more intolerant of the 'transcendental' features of continental philosophy. In several essays in the second volume of his *Philosophical Papers* he polemicizes against those interpreters of Derrida who fondly imagine that Derrida has discovered new, non-empirical 'conditions of possibility' of such phenomena as metaphor, self-reflection, and perhaps even metaphysical discourse in general. Rorty argues that there can only be conditions of actuality, not of possibility.[37] This is why he assures his readers that Derrida's approach is based on an identification of language and social practice, even though this interpretation can scarcely be reconciled with Derrida's own self-understanding. In fact, Derrida's radicalized and expanded conception of language as the 'general text' embraces 'everything which can ever become an object', to employ the formula of Gadamer's cited above. But Rorty will only allow that Derrida occasionally falls into the temptation of treating language as if it were a trans-human power.[38] Putnam, by contrast, has put ever more distance between himself and the persistent naturalism and realism of the analytical tradition, and it is precisely this shift in his views which has brought him into the vicinity of continental philosophy. An example from one of the essays in *Realism and Reason* may make this development clearer.

In 'Vagueness and Alternative Logic', Putnam investigates the fundamental assumption which Hylton identifies behind the innovations of the early Russell. Like the majority of later analytical philosophers, Russell started from the presupposition that every sentence must be either unqualifiedly true or unqualifiedly false, since either it mirrors the corresponding objects or it does not. Russell rejects the British Idealists' assumption that there can be grades or stages of truth, even though this assumption is apparently more compatible with everyday speech, in which we habitually describe various sorts of assertions as being 'partly' true or false, even when they cannot be broken down into components which are in turn unequivocally true or false.

Thus the analytical principles of bivalence and complete semantic determinability cannot be smoothly harmonized with everyday usage. In the analytical tradition there are two major and distinct approaches to the problem of resolving the 'indeterminacy' of everyday language. Either one assumes that the imprecision of everyday language is unavoidable, in which case it makes sense to put the nuances of linguistic usage under the microscope in order to bring unnoticed and potentially misleading distinctions of meaning to light; or, if one regards everyday language as dangerously but curably imprecise, then the assumption must be that it could, in principle, be translated into a precise, unambiguous language – that of the natural sciences, for example. Putnam addresses the problems of this second approach with reference to one of its outstanding representatives, Quine. The fundamental problem of this approach in Putnam's view lies in the fact that the criteria of 'rationality' which we must apply in order to evaluate the viability of a translation schema cannot themselves be part of the idealized language. Putnam draws from this the following anti-reductionist lesson:

> If ordinary language lacks significant truth, then why is the language of science, or any theory stated in that language, better off? Such terms as 'electron', 'charge' and 'mass' have themselves a certain vagueness. And even if they did not, why should we *accept* any theory which contains these terms? Because the theory is a good *explanation* of certain *phenomena*? But . . . there are no 'explanations' and no 'phenomena'! (Explanation and phenomenon are vague words too.) If ordinary language cannot be used to say anything significant, then it cannot be used to invent or to justify a *better* language.[39]

Once a philosopher has taken on board this moral of the irreducibility of everyday language, there is always the danger that she will immediately react by plunging into a pluralism of language games which abandons any criteria beyond the rules of habitual cultural practices. But in Putnam's view this approach is no less reductionist than its scientistic counterpart, since a definition of truth in terms of agreement with the norms of a culture cannot itself be based on these norms. This is why he asserts:

> It is true that we speak a public language, that we inherit versions, that talk of truth and falsity only makes sense against the background of an 'inherited tradition', as Wittgenstein says. But it is also true that we constantly remake our language, and that we make new versions out of old ones, and that we have to use reason to do all this, and, for that matter, even to understand and apply the norms we do not alter or criticize. Consensus definitions of reason do not work, because consensus among grown-ups *presupposes* reason, rather than defining it.[40]

Regarded from this angle, Rorty's reasons for contesting the idea that metaphors have a distinctive meaning or specific cognitive content become clearer. For if the *appropriate* understanding of metaphors, which are a form of linguistic innovation, is a rational activity in the sense that one must in principle be in a position to give reasons for the preferred interpretation, then rationality cannot be exclusively defined with reference to existing norms. Here a further distinction between Davidson's theory of metaphor and Rorty's simplifying transcription of it becomes apparent.

For if a metaphor is comparable to an unprecedented event in nature which sets new trains of thought in motion, then there can be no question of the *appropriateness* of its intepretation. Davidson, in contrast to Rorty, disputes that metaphor functions as the bearer of a specific 'message', but not that 'Many of us need help if we are to see what the author of a metaphor wanted us to see and what a more sensitive or educated reader grasps.'[41]

Thus Davidson does not entirely exclude the question of communicative intention, and this difference of opinion between Davidson and Rorty points once more to the fact that Rorty's philosophy rests on the two incompatible pillars of realism and conventionalism. Rorty's analytical training has left its traces in the form of his natural-scientific background ontology, and has also had the consequence that his encounter with the hermeneutic insights of the continental tradition has merely encouraged him to effect a crude reduction of normativity to dominant cultural norms. In contrast, Putnam, by the beginning of the 1980s, had already reached the conclusion that a naturalistic or conventionalistic evasion of the normative dimension of truth and rationality could almost be considered as defining the untranscendable limits of analytical philosophy:

> I shall call any conception according to which there are institutionalized norms which define what is and what is not rationally acceptable a *criterial* conception of rationality. In sum, what the logical positivists and Wittgenstein (and perhaps Quine as well) did was to *produce philosophies which leave no room for the rational activity of philosophy*. This is why these views are self-refuting . . . arguing about the nature of rationality is an activity that *presupposes* a notion of rational justification wider than the positivist notion, indeed wider than institutionalized criterial rationality.[42]

## Putnam's Diagnosis of Philosophical Modernism

But if, like Putnam, one reaches the conclusion that there is a fundamental contradiction at the basis of a significant – indeed, epoch-making – philosophical movement, then it will seem plausible to seek a historical and cultural dimension to the success of this movement. In a few of the more 'experimental' essays in *Realism and Reason* Putnam attempts to characterize this dimension. In 'Convention in Philosophy', for example, he investigates three decisive features of the self-understanding of analytical philosophy:

(1) Analytical philosophy is non-ideological: which means above all that it is non-political and non-moralizing.
(2) Analytical philosophy consists of piecemeal problem solving. Analytical

philosophers need not have integrated positions; they write articles proposing and discussing arguments on specific philosophical problems and topics.
(3) . . . analytical philosophy for a long time regarded value theory as second-class philosophy, and a concern with literature, the arts, culture and the history of culture as at best optional for an analytical philosopher.[43]

According to Putnam, this self-understanding was always a blend of truth and self-deception. The motor of analytical philosophy was a strong, albeit implicit, ideological programme, which he now connects, as we have already seen, with the internal tensions of cultural modernism. This programme, most clearly embodied in the work of the Vienna Circle, inevitably provoked a counter-movement within analytical philosophy. But this counter-movement (of which Wittgenstein's late philosophy is the most celebrated example) was no less hostile to tradition than were the positivists, and thus was also an expression of cultural modernism. Putnam is now of the view that it was only this debate between an optimistic and a pessimistic response to modernity which kept the dynamic of analytical philosophy alive. At the end of the last essay in *Realism and Reason*, he asserts:

> The 'motor' of analytical philosophy was logical positivism . . . not because all analytical philosophers were positivists, but because the arguments pro-and-con positivism were what kept analytical philosophy in motion. Analytical philosophy has already begun to lose shape as a tendency with a strong ideological current at its centre.[44]

It would seem that the developments of the last decade or so have justified Putnam's diagnosis. However, the confirmation has taken the form not only of an accelerating *rapprochement* between analytical and continental modes of thought in some areas, but also of an ever-widening gulf within the analytical tradition between those philosophers (Cavell, MacIntyre, Taylor, to name only the most influential) who possess a certain sensitivity to the social context and implicit moral and political assumptions of philosophical positions, and those who have bunkered down behind the barricades of a supposedly purely technical discipline, and treat any contact with other currents of thought as a potential source of infection. Yet even this defensive reaction is a kind of negative response to the higher level of historical self-reflection which analytical philosophy has attained over the last ten years. There are, therefore, good grounds for suspecting that the attainment of this level of reflection will prove irreversible – for as we know, even repressed possibilities of insight have their unavoidable consequences. Thus a tradition whose identity paradoxically consisted in its inability to grasp itself as a tradition appears to have entered a phase of dissolution – a phase which, fortunately, also promises the release of new energies.

# Notes
1. Reviewing Peter Hylton, *Russell, Idealism, and the Origins of Analytical Philosophy*, Oxford: Clarendon Press 1990; Richard Rorty, *Philosophical Papers Volume 1: Objectivity, Relativism and Truth*, Cambridge: Cambridge University Press 1991, and *Volume 2: Essays on Heidegger and Others*, Cambridge: Cambridge University Press 1991; Hilary Putnam, *Realism and Reason: Philosophical Papers Volume 3* (Cambridge Paperback Library edn), Cambridge: Cambridge University Press 1989.

2. *Russell, Idealism, and the Origins of Analytical Philosophy*, p. vii.

3. Friedrich Nietzsche, 'On the Uses and Disadvantages of History for Life', in *Untimely Meditations*, trans. R.J. Hollingdale, Cambridge: Cambridge University Press, p. 95.

4. *Russell, Idealism, and the Origins of Analytical Philosophy*, pp. 6 ff.

5. See Charles Taylor, 'Philosophy and its History' in Richard Rorty, J. B. Schneewind and Quentin Skinner, eds, *Philosophy in History*, Cambridge: Cambridge University Press 1984.

6. *Russell, Idealism, and the Origins of Analytical Philosophy*, p. vii.

7. Ibid., p. 1.

8. Ibid., p. 105

9. See Robert Stern, 'British Hegelianism: A Non-Metaphysical View?', *European Journal of Philosophy*, vol. 2, no. 3, December 1994.

10. *Russell, Idealism, and the Origins of Analytical Philosophy*, p. 10.

11. See Mark Sacks, 'Through a Glass Darkly: Vagueness in the Metaphysics of the Analytical Tradition', in David Bell and Neil Cooper, eds, *The Analytic Tradition*, Oxford: Blackwell 1990. The appearance of this book is itself an indication of the emergence of a new historical sensibility amongst analytical philosophers. See also Michael Dummett, *The Origins of Analytic Philosophy*, London: Duckworth 1993.

12. *Russell, Idealism, and the Origins of Analytical Philosophy*, pp. 328 ff.

13. Ibid., p. 16.

14. *Philosophical Papers Volume 2*, p. 21.

15. Ibid., p. 87.

16. *Philosophical Papers Volume 1*, p. 218.

17. *Philosophical Papers Volume 2*, p. 105.

18. Richard Rorty, 'The Historiography of Philosophy: Four Genres', in *Philosophy in History*, p. 49.

19. Richard Rorty, 'Introduction: Pragmatism and Philosophy', in *Consequences of Pragmatism*, Minneapolis: Minnesota University Press 1982, p. xvii.

20. 'The Historiography of Philosophy: Four Genres', p. 49.

21. *Philosophical Papers Volume 1*, p. 35.

22. Ibid., p. 65.

23. Ludwig Feuerbach, *Grundsätze der Philosophie der Zukunft*, in *Theorie Werkausgabe*, Frankfurt am Main: Suhrkamp 1975, vol. 3, p. 316/*Principles of the Philosophy of the Future*, trans. Manfred H. Vogel, Indianapolis: Hackett 1986, p. 67.

24. See *Philosophical Papers Volume 1*, where Rorty advocates a 'philosophical superficiality and light-mindedness' which 'helps along the disenchantment of the world' (p. 193).

25. *Philosophical Papers Volume 2*, p. 23.

26. Donald Davidson, 'What Metaphors Mean', in *Enquiries into Truth and Interpretation*, Oxford: Clarendon Press 1984, p. 247.

27. Ibid.

28. Ibid., p. 262.

29. *Philosophical Papers Volume 1*, p. 163.

30. 'What Metaphors Mean', p. 263.

31. Paul Ricoeur, *La métaphore vive*, Paris: Seuil 1975, p. 319/*The Rule of Metaphor*, trans. Robert Czerny with Kathleen McLaughlin and John Costello, London: Routledge & Kegan Paul 1986, p. 254.

32. 'Introduction: Pragmatism and Philosophy', p. xiii.

33. *Philosophical Papers Volume 2*, p. 210.

34. In *Contingency, Irony and Solidarity* (Cambridge: Cambridge University Press 1989), Rorty writes of 'the random factors which have made some things subjects of conversation for us and others not, have made some projects and not others possible and important' (p. 17).

35. Hans-Georg Gadamer, *Wahrheit und Methode*, Tübingen: J.C.B. Mohr 1960, p. 382/*Truth and Method*, trans. William Glen-Doepel, London: Sheed & Ward 1979, p. 365.

36. *Realism and Reason: Philosophical Papers Volume 3*, p. vii.

37. *Philosophical Papers Volume 2*, p. 55.

38. Ibid., p. 3.

39. Hilary Putnam, 'Vagueness and Alternative Logic', in *Realism and Reason*, p. 277.

40. Ibid., p. 240.

41. 'What Metaphors Mean', p. 264.

42. *Realism and Reason*, p. 191 (emphasis added).

43. Ibid., p. 180.

44. Ibid., p. 303.

# —PART II—

# Deconstruction

# 4

# Nietzsche and the Critique of
## *Ursprungsphilosophie*

In a celebrated section in *Twilight of the Idols,* Nietzsche describes what he takes to have been the role of 'reason' in philosophy. Reaffirming an advocacy of 'historical philosophizing' [*historisches Philosophieren*] which has been central to his work ever since the opening paragraphs of *Human, All-too Human,* he suggests that one of the most dangerous idiosyncrasies of philosophers has been 'to confuse the first and the last':

> They place that which comes at the end – unfortunately! for it ought not to come at all! – namely, the 'highest concepts', which means the most general, the emptiest concepts, the last smoke of an evaporating reality, in the beginning, as the beginning. This again is nothing but their way of showing reverence: the higher may not grow out of the lower, may not have grown at all. . . . That which is last, thinnest and emptiest is put first as cause in itself, as *ens realissimum.*[1]

For Nietzsche, the role allotted to the I or ego [*das Ich*] in modern thought is the most obvious embodiment of this inversion. The ego recommends itself for such a role, because of our apparently immediate awareness of the contents of consciousness: 'To derive something unknown from something known alleviates, calms, gratifies and furthermore gives a feeling of power.'[2] Yet this immediacy of self-knowledge is, for Nietzsche, an illusion; consequently, so are the unity and identity which the ego projects into things:

> Formerly, alteration, change, any becoming at all, were taken as proof of mere appearance, as an indication that there must be something which led us astray. Today, conversely, precisely in so far as the prejudice of reason forces us to posit unity, identity, permanence, substance, cause, thinghood, being, we see ourselves caught in error, compelled into error.[3]

Nietzsche's arguments against the 'philosophy of origins', and his connection of such philosophy with the coercive imposition of an identity whose model is that of the self-conscious subject, have had an important impact on contemporary intellectual life, particularly through the mediation of recent French thought. Yet Nietzsche's position is clearly not unproblematic, for the undermining of original identity, and consequently of any comprehensive conceptualization of reality, seems to depend – either surreptitiously or explicitly – on an ontology of flux which is incompatible with the critical motifs in his own thought. Thus, in the section of *Twilight of the Idols* which we have been considering, Nietzsche suggests that even Heraclitus did injustice to the senses in so far as he considered them to be the purveyors of an illusion of stability and identity.[4] Yet it can scarcely be denied that our experience of the empirical world is characterized by both (relative) change *and* (relative) identity. It is not clear in what sense Nietzsche can appeal to an absolute priority of becoming, or insist upon the *inherently* falsifying and fetishizing function of concepts.

These difficulties are no less prominent in the work of those recent French thinkers who have been influenced by Nietzsche, as can be seen from Foucault's famous essay on 'Nietzsche, Genealogy, History'.[5] Here Foucault seeks to give a condensed exposition of Nietzsche's critique of *Ursprungsphilosophie*, and to delineate his genealogical alternative. According to Foucault, Nietzsche frequently employs the concept of 'origin' [*Ursprung*] in a stressed opposition to those of 'descent' [*Herkunft*] and 'emergence' [*Entstehung*]. The origin is the traditional goal of philosophers; the pursuit of the origin consists in 'an attempt to capture the exact essence of things, their purest possibilities, and their carefully protected identities . . .; this search assumes the existence of immobile forms that precede the external world of accident and succession'.[6] *Entstehung* and *Herkunft*, by contrast, form the object not of a philosophical quest, but of a new kind of history. The question of 'descent' is the question of the transmission and intermingling of racial and social characteristics, and of the body as the 'inscribed surface of events';[7] while 'emergence' must be understood in terms of the 'non-place' of opposition between forces which deprives the phenomenon of any single source.[8] Thus Nietzschean genealogy, in its concern for *Herkunft* and *Entstehung*, shatters the identity of the subject and erases the uniqueness of the source. Genealogy, he suggests, is opposed to 'the search for "origins"' and to 'the meta-historical deployment of ideal significations'.[9] Throughout this text, Foucault opposes the conflictuality, singularity and dispersion of the real events of history described by genealogy to the 'profound intentions and immutable necessities' of *Ursprungsphilosophie*. Yet in describing the standpoint of genealogy he finds himself entangled in a contradiction that is similar to the one we have already encountered in Nietzsche. For on the one hand he argues that the aim of genealogy is to 'leave things undisturbed in their own dimension and intensity',[10] to respect the actual complexity and diversity of events; while on the other he argues that genealogy is directed against the ideal of 'apocalyptic objectivity'. Nietzsche's version of historical sense, he claims is explicit in its perspective and acknowledges its system of injustice. . . . It is not given to a discreet effacement before the objects it observes and does not submit itself to their processes; nor does it seek laws, since it gives equal weight to its own sight and to its objects.[11]

Foucault does not attempt to reconcile these two accounts: genealogy is presented as being both 'gray, meticulous and patiently documentary',[12] and marked – like all interpretations – by an element of the coercive and the arbitrary.

The extent to which 'Nietzsche, Genealogy, History' can be read as a methodological manifesto for Foucault's work of the 1970s, rather than simply as an exposition of Nietzsche, is open to debate. Even if we set this question aside, however, it is clear that difficulties similar to those which emerge in that essay have characterized Foucault's thought ever since the beginning. Thus in his most explicit phase of methodological reflection, around the time of *The Archaeology of Knowledge*, Foucault describes himself as being committed to a 'pure description of the facts of discourse', despite the fact that his own theory of discursive formations is directed precisely against any phenomenological conception of pure description.[13] The conclusion of *The Archaeology of Knowledge* is one of the few places in Foucault's work where this tension between objectivism and relativism is explicitly reflected upon. Here Foucault admits that the attempt to bypass any inquiry into the conditions of possibility of knowledge runs the risk of accusations of naivety; he therefore tries – without notable success – to define a status for his historical description of discursive formations which would be neither that of science nor that of philosophy.[14] Ultimately, however, Foucault's sympathies lie with the scientific challenge to philosophical perspectives: 'if you recognize the right of empirical research, some fragment of history, to challenge the transcendental dimension, then you have ceded the main point'.[15]

In similar forms, the difficulties which I have outlined in Foucault's work also occur in that of the other French thinkers of the 1960s and 1970s most directly influenced by Nietzsche. In Jean-François Lyotard's *Économie libidinale*, the autonomy and priority of the concept and of consciousness are challenged from the standpoint of an ontology of force. However, the impossibility of justifying this ontology theoretically then leads to an aestheticization of philosophical discourse. But this aestheticization in turn requires some form of justification, and when the political consequences in terms of which the suspension of truth-claims was legitimated turn out not to be those which were anticipated, then the entire structure begins to collapse. By the time of *Just Gaming* (1979), Lyotard has renounced his metaphysics of libido and admitted that 'it is not true that the quest for intensities or things of that kind can provide the substance of a politics, because there is the problem of injustice'.[16]

## Derrida and Schelling

There is one thinker within the field of poststructuralism, however, whose work does not fall victim to these difficulties. Although Jacques Derrida has been deeply influenced by Nietzsche, his primary training as a philosopher was within the tradition of Husserlian phenomenology, and as a consequence he has always retained a sense of the integrity of the transcendental perspective, and of its invulnerability to direct historicist or naturalistic inversions. One obvious testimony to this difference of outlook is Derrida's review of Foucault's *Madness and Civilization*, which challenges the coherence of Foucault's conception of an empirical history of reason. For Derrida, 'the internal and autonomous analysis of the philosophical content of philosophical discourse' must take priority over any historical insertion of it.[17] We cannot write the history of reason until we know what reason is – and history alone can never tell us this, since in any historical investigation reason is presupposed. In consequence, Derrida concludes – with deliberate provocation – that the reduction of the hyperbolic *cogito* to 'intraworldliness' is itself potentially a form of totalitarian enclosure no less dangerous than those which Foucault attacks.[18]

It should be noted that Derrida's objections are not aimed simply against direct attempts to invert the relation of priority between the essential and the factual. More generally, Derrida is opposed to any philosophical strategy intended to blur or weaken the line between the empirical and the transcendental realms. This opposition is clearly exemplified in his earliest major essay, his 'Introduction' to Husserl's posthumously published text on 'The Origin of Geometry', an exploration of the problem of origins which had also intrigued Merleau-Ponty. Interestingly, Merleau-Ponty reads this late meditation by Husserl as one symptom of a shift away from *Ursprungsphilosophie*, as Nietzsche understands it: genetic phenomenology can be seen as an attempt not to place the ideal and immutable at the origin but, rather, precisely to see how idealities – such as those of geometry – emerge out of the flux and instability of the lifeworld.[19] More generally, Merleau-Ponty perceives in Husserl's later work a renunciation of the view that transcendental reflection can function independently of all empirical investigation. He suggests that the later Husserl

> seems to admit that the philosopher could not possibly have immediate access to the universal by reflection alone – that he is in no position to do without anthropological experience or to construct what constitutes the meaning of other experiences and civilizations by a purely imaginative variation of his own experiences.[20]

Merleau-Ponty is not, of course, advocating the elimination of the transcendental perspective. But he is challenging its self-sufficiency, and suggesting that such a challenge emerges by virtue of the internal dynamic of Husserl's phenomenology itself.

Derrida, however, in his 'Introduction' to 'The Origin of Geometry', is explicitly hostile to this softening of the distinction between transcendental and empirical inquiry. For Derrida, to admit that empirical facts could have any status other than that of examples for the procedure of imaginative variation 'contradicts the very premiss of phenomenology', which is that 'essential insight *de jure* precedes every material historical investigation, and has no need of facts as such to reveal to the historian the *a priori* sense of his activity and objects'.[21] In general, Derrida opposes Merleau-Ponty's thesis of an *historicization* of phenomenology, which implies that, to the very extent to which Husserl in his later work makes history an explicit object of inquiry, his phenomenology is able to liberate itself from history, rather than being unwittingly subject to it. Derrida writes: 'We could then be tempted by an interpretation diametrically opposed to that of Merleau-Ponty, and maintain that Husserl, far from opening the phenomenological parentheses to historical factuality under all its forms, leaves history more than ever *outside* them.'[22]

Derrida's resistance to the dilution of the transcendental perspective cannot help but raise questions about his own attitude to the philosophy of origins. For if Derrida defends the primacy of transcendental inquiry, he must surely also be committed to the derivative status of the empirical. Yet one of the most prominent and influential of Derrida's themes has been the criticism of all philosophical conceptions of origin. It is precisely the absence of origin – or of a *telos*, its mirror-image or counterpart – which blocks the possibility of interpretative closure and opens up the dissemination of the text. Thus Derrida's strategy must take the form of an internal dismantling of the transcendental perspective, which prevents it from performing its founding or originating role, without lapsing into what he would consider to be the incoherence of a prioritization, or even an equal enfranchisement, of empirical inquiry.

In order to clarify what is at stake here, it may be useful to refer to an earlier episode in the history of philosophy, in which the status of transcendental philosophy was similarly at issue: the clash between Fichte and Schelling, which was perhaps the crucial episode in the development of German Idealism. The parallel suggests itself, because the difficulties which Schelling confronted in his attempt to move beyond what he considered to be Fichte's subjective idealism are close to those which Derrida encounters in his effort to transcend the phenomenology of Husserl. In both cases, what is confronted is a conception of philosophy as 'systematic self-investigation',[23] as the reflexive explication of the structure of consciousness. In Husserl, it is true, this explication is eidetic and descriptive, whereas in Fichte it is dialectical-deductive. Yet what is common to both is the conviction that a standpoint has been attained which cannot be gone beyond: there can be no knowledge more fundamental than self-knowledge, since in all other knowledge the knowing subject is presupposed. Thus, in the 1794 *Wissenschaftslehre*, Fichte opposes 'the concept of an existent that is supposed, from a certain viewpoint, to subsist independently of presentation', on the grounds that 'whatever we may think, we are that which thinks therein, and hence . . . nothing could ever come to exist independently of us, for everything is necessarily related to our thinking'.[24] Similarly, in the *Cartesian Meditations*, Husserl argues:

> Every imaginable sense, every imaginable being, whether the latter is called immanent or transcendent, falls within the domain of transcendental subjectivity, as the subjectivity which constitutes sense and being. The attempt to conceive the universe of true being as something lying outside the universe of possible consciousness, possible knowledge, possible evidence, the two being related to one another merely externally by a rigid law, is nonsensical.[25]

Such positions appear, at first sight, to be impregnable. Yet Schelling, in his divergence from Fichte, focuses on one crucial weakness. Transcendental idealism claims to have found an absolute starting point, yet any self-consciousness contains a duality of subject and object, even though the object here is merely the subject reflected upon by itself. Yet every object is conditioned by its relation to a subject, just as every subject is conditioned by its relation to an object, so that neither taken alone, nor the two in their relation, can constitute the absolute standpoint that is claimed. Schelling had already developed this argument clearly in his exuberant early essay of 1795, 'Vom Ich als Prinzip der Philosophie Überhaupt':

> Since the subject is thinkable only in regard to an object, and the object only in regard to a subject, neither of them can contain the unconditional because both are conditioned reciprocally, both are equally unserviceable. Furthermore, in order to determine the relationship of the two, an ulterior reason for the determination must be presupposed, owing to which both are determined. For one cannot say that the subject alone determines the object, because the subject is only conceivable in relation to the object, and vice versa, and it would amount to the same if I were to treat as unconditional a subject determined by an object or an object determined by a subject.[26]

In this essay, Schelling resolves the difficulty by distinguishing between the subject and what he terms the 'absolute I', which is beyond the subject–object relation. Eventually, however, he comes to appreciate that what is beyond this relation can be characterized neither in objective nor in subjective terms but, rather, takes the form of an 'absolute indifference' [*absolute Indifferenz*] with regard to all determinations. From the new standpoint of Schelling's *Identitätsphilosophie*, Fichte's insistence on the primacy of the evidence of reflection, his assertion that 'one cannot begin from a being . . . but must begin from a seeing',[27] simply confirms the limitations of his philosophy, since the metaphor of vision implies the duality of viewer and viewed. In his reply to Fichte, Schelling argues that 'The necessity of beginning from seeing keeps you and your philosophy locked within a thoroughly conditioned sequence.'[28] He points out:

> Either you must never move outside seeing, as you express it, and this means outside subjectivity, and *every I*, as you say at one point in the *Wissenschaftslehre*, must be and remain the absolute substance, or, if you go out to an unconceptualizable real ground, then the whole reference back to subjectivity is valid only in a preliminary sense.[29]

It is difficult to overlook the parallels between Schelling's argument and Derrida's critique of Husserl. Derrida, as we have seen, resists any externalist reduction – or even qualification – of transcendental consciousness. Rather, he focuses on the discrepancy between the claim of the immediacy of the relation of phenomenological self-presence, and the necessarily conditioned nature of any such relation. Like Schelling, Derrida insists on the derivative status of the classical oppositions of philosophy, and attempts to climb beyond them: 'Subjectivity – like objectivity – is an effect of différance, an effect inscribed in a system of différance.'[30] It could be said in reply, of course, that such a comparison is superficial. Schelling transcends the subject–object relation towards absolute identity, a point of ultimate closure and security, whereas Derrida's *différance* implies perpetual deferral of any such point. Yet even this objection is not as convincing as may at first appear – firstly, because a *différance* which is prior to all determinate differences collapses into absolute identity: as François Wahl noted long ago, 'a bare concept of *différance* is a contradiction, since difference has to be specified'.[31] Secondly, because it follows from Schelling's argument that the absolute cannot become an object of consciousness, cannot be made present any more than *différance*. It is not surprising, therefore, that Schelling's thought – like that of Derrida – is accompanied by an incessant reflection on its own conditions of meaningfulness. The restless character of the work of both Derrida and Schelling can be seen not as a manifestation of inconsistency but, rather, as a logical consequence of their point of departure: it is only through the repeated development, and repeated collapse, of philosophical terminologies and strategies that something of the nature of philosophy's 'impossible' object can be obliquely indicated.[32]

If there is any plausibility in this parallel between Derrida and Schelling, the status of Derrida's attack on the concept of origin clearly needs to be reassessed. Derrida shows the impossibility of an origin, in the sense of an epistemological ground which could be made present. But he cannot be said to have abandoned the concept of origin, if by 'origin' we understand the unconditioned source of the conditioned structures of experience. This distinction is drawn by Derrida himself in many of his statements concerning *différance* and the trace. Thus, in *Of Grammatology* he writes: 'There cannot be a science of *différance* itself in its operation, as it is impossible to have a science of the origin of presence itself, that is to say of a certain non-origin.'[33] And a little later in the same chapter he remarks:

> The trace is in fact the absolute origin of sense in general. Which amounts to saying once again that there is no absolute origin of sense in general. The trace is the *différance* which opens appearance and signification. Articulating the living upon the non-living in general, origin of all repetition, origin of ideality, the trace is not more ideal than real, not more intelligible than sensible, not more a transparent signification than an opaque energy, and no concept of metaphysics can describe it.[34]

Elsewhere Derrida himself has stressed that 'neither/nor' is simultaneously 'either/or',[35] so that in the light of such passages it is difficult to deny the proximity of his *différance* to Schelling's *absolute Indifferenz*.

It seems that Derrida has avoided the contradictions of a reductive critique of *Ursprungsphilosophie* at the cost of reinstating the position against which the critique was directed. Nothing could be 'thinner' and 'emptier' – to employ Nietzsche's terms – than the *différance* which Derrida makes responsible not simply for the semantic instability of the text, but for the movement of the world and of history in general. The defence which is frequently made of Derrida at this point – that he is engaged in some form of parody of the philosophy of origins – is scarcely adequate; for if Derrida did not become involved in a dubious argumentative strategy against transcendental philosophy, he would have no need of concepts of parody and of the '*sous rature*' in order to ward off the implications of his own position. The inherent difficulties of this strategy were perceptively pinpointed at an early date by Christopher Macann, in an article whose phenomenological standpoint produces an intriguing convergence with Nietzsche: 'Does Derrida's concept of "trace" or "*différance*" represent a transcendental critique of Husserl's transcendental analysis?' It may seem so at first:

> And yet this return to an original principle, unlike Husserl's descriptions of the *Umwelt* or the *Lebenswelt*, seems to take us away from concrete structures of experience and to involve us in abstractions more abstruse than those of Husserl's transcendental analysis. Is the concept of the trace arrived at by a kind of reduction of the transcendental reduction to one single constitutive principle? But then, how can a principle attained exclusively through philosophical reflection be ascribed to consciousness as the condition of its realization?[36]

In fact, this is precisely the response which Fichte makes to Schelling when he suggests that the latter's absolute identity is purely negative and formal.[37]

## Adorno on the Philosophy of Origins

Now that we have reached this point, it seems legitimate to ask whether there is any sense in which Nietzsche's critique of *Ursprungsphilosophie* can be retained as a resource of contemporary thought, given the difficulties both of an externalist reduction of the standpoint of consciousness and of Derrida's attempts to transcend that standpoint. I would argue that a positive answer to this question can be found in the work of Adorno, a thinker who plays off Nietzsche's insights against those of the dialectical tradition, in particular in his critique of Husserl's phenomenology: *Against Epistemology*.[38]

The significance of Adorno's position can perhaps best be brought out through a contrast with Derrida's assumption that the oppositions of metaphysics have always been thought within the horizon of their own overcoming; the duality of signifier and signified, for example, within the horizon of an ultimate unmediated presence of meaning. Derrida draws the following conclusion: 'The *paradox* is that the metaphysical reduction of the sign needed the opposition it was reducing. The opposition is systematic with the reduction.'[39] Yet the second statement by no means follows from the first, unless one confuses a *historical* with an *essential* relation. For it could equally well be argued that duality has posed the most persistent problem and the most persistent block to projects of 'metaphysical reduction'. It is in this sense that Adorno appropriates the Nietzschean emphasis on the non-originality of conceptuality and consciousness:

> The qualification of the absolutely first in subjective immanence founders because immanence can never completely disentangle the moment of nonidentity within itself, and because subjectivity, the organ of reflection, clashes with the idea of an absolutely first as pure immediacy.[40]

Adorno should not, of course, be taken to mean that subjectivity as currently lived and philosophically construed provides a barrier against the delusion of origins. Rather, his argument is that the suppression of nonidentity, the collapsing of subjectivity into pure self-presence – against which Derrida protests – and the compulsive features of this suppression – which other poststructuralist thinkers have highlighted – are the expression of a historically and socially determined drive for control. This is why it is insufficient to oppose to identitarian principles an 'abstract asservation of polarity'.[41] Against the reductiveness even of duality, Adorno takes up the lesson of Nietzsche's thought that the philosophy of origins can be dissolved, and the non-self-sufficiency of the subject acknowledged, only in the open-ended dialectic of concrete experience. Yet he moves beyond both Nietzsche and his more recent French followers in suggesting that the general possibility of such experience is a political question: the question of the practical overcoming of a redundant domination.

## Notes

1. Friedrich Nietzsche, *The Twilight of the Idols*, trans. R.J. Hollingdale, Harmondsworth: Penguin 1968, p. 37.
2. Ibid., p. 51.
3. Ibid., p. 36.
4. Ibid., p. 37.
5. Michel Foucault, 'Nietzsche, Genealogy, History', in Donald F. Bouchard, ed., *Language, Counter-memory, Practice*, Oxford: Blackwell 1977.
6. Ibid., p.142.
7. Ibid., p.148.
8. Ibid., p.150.
9. Ibid., p.140.
10. Ibid., p.154.
11. Ibid., p.157.
12. Ibid., p.139.
13. See Michel Foucault, 'Réponse au cercle d'épistémologie', *Cahiers pour l'analyse*, no. 9, Summer 1968, pp. 9–40.
14. See Michel Foucault, *The Archaeology of Knowledge*, trans. A. Sheridan, London: Tavistock 1972, pp. 205–8.
15. Ibid., p. 203.
16. Jean-François Lyotard and Jean-Loup Thébaud, *Au Juste*, Paris: Christian Bourgois 1979, pp. 170–71/*Just Gaming*, trans. Wlad Godzich, Manchester: Manchester University Press 1985, p. 90.
17. Jacques Derrida, 'Cogito and the History of Madness', in *Writing and Difference*, trans. Alan Bass, London: Routledge 1978, p. 44.
18. Ibid., p. 57.
19. For Merleau-Ponty's interpretation of the later Husserl, see 'Le philosophe et son ombre', in *Éloge de la philosophie*, Paris: Gallimard 1960/'The Philosopher and His Shadow', in *Signs*, trans. Richard C. McCleary, Evanston: Northwestern University Press 1964.
20. Maurice Merleau-Ponty, 'The Philosopher and Sociology', in John O'Neill, ed., *Phenomenology, Language and Sociology*, London: Heineman Educational 1974, p. 104.
21. Jacques Derrida, *Edmund Husserl's Origin of Geometry: An Introduction*, Stony Brook, NY: N. Hays 1978, p. 112.
22. Ibid., p. 116.
23. Edmund Husserl, *Cartesian Meditations*, trans. Dorion Cairns, The Hague: Martinus Nijhoff 1973, p. 83.
24. J.G. Fichte, 'Second Introduction to the Science of Knowledge', in Peter Heath and John Lachs, eds, *The Science of Knowledge*, Cambridge: Cambridge University Press 1982, p. 71.
25. *Cartesian Meditations*, p. 84.
26. F.W.J. Schelling, 'Of the I as Principle of Philosophy', in Fritz Marti trans. and ed., *The Unconditional in Human Knowledge*, Lewisburg, PA: Bucknell University Press 1980, p. 74.
27. J.G. Fichte, 'Letter to Schelling', 31 May–7 August 1801, in Walter Schulz, ed., *Fichte–Schelling: Briefwechsel*, Frankfurt am Main: Suhrkamp 1968, p. 126.
28. F.W.J. Schelling, Letter to Fichte, 3 October 1801, in *Briefwechsel*, p. 135.

29. Ibid., p. 134.

30. Jacques Derrida, *Positions*, trans. Alan Bass, London: Athlone Press 1981, p. 28.

31. 'Un concept nu de différance est contradiction, car la différence ne peut manquer d'être spécifiée', (François Wahl, *Qu'est-ce que le structuralisme: Philosophie*, Paris: Seuil [Collection Points edn] 1973, p. 186).

32. On this aspect of Schelling's thought, see Wolfgang Wieland, 'Die Anfänge der Philosophie Schellings und die Frage nach der Natur', in Manfred Frank and Gerhard Kurz, eds, *Materialien zu Schellings philosophischen Anfängen*, Frankfurt am Main: Suhrkamp 1975, pp. 250–54.

33. Jacques Derrida, *Of Grammatology*, trans. Gayatri Chakravorty Spivak, Baltimore, MD and London: Johns Hopkins University Press 1976, p. 63.

34. Ibid.

35. *Positions*, p. 43.

36. Christopher Macann, 'Jacques Derrida's Theory of Writing and the Concept of the Trace', *Journal of the British Society for Phenomenology*, vol. 3, no. 2, May 1972, p. 199.

37. J.G. Fichte, 'Letter to Schelling', 15 January 1802, in *Briefwechsel*, p. 152.

38. Theodor Adorno, *Against Epistemology*, trans. Willis Domingo, Oxford: Blackwell 1982.

39. Jacques Derrida, 'Structure, Sign and Play in the Discourse of the Human Sciences', in *Writing and Difference*, p. 281.

40. *Against Epistemology*, p. 23.

41. Ibid., p.183.

# 5

# Writing in the Lifeworld:
# Speech-Acts, Metaphor
# and Deconstruction

At one point in the unpublished notes which were written between 1872 and 1874, in the wake of *The Birth of Tragedy,* and were intended to form the *Philosophenbuch*, a work on the nature of philosophy and the role of the philosopher, Nietzsche comments: 'Without untruth there is neither society nor culture. The tragic conflict. Everything good and beautiful depends upon illusion: Truth kills; indeed kills itself (insofar as it recognises that it is grounded in illusion).'[1]

The dialectics of this suicide of truth are tortuous. Truth is not what it takes itself to be, since it is grounded not in reason or evidence, but in illusion. Nevertheless, according to Nietzsche, such truth possesses the power to lay bare its own grounding in illusion. But if truth reveals the illusion which is its own foundation, it can do so only by recognizing this illusion *as* illusion – that is, by taking itself as the fundamental, non-illusory truth. Yet in so doing it would cancel its own insight into the necessary foundation of truth in illusion, in the very same movement in which this truth is affirmed. Is the truth that truth is grounded in illusion itself grounded in illusion, or not?

In diverse embodiments this dizzying spiral is common to all the major strands of postmodernist thinking. What distinguishes such thinking from more traditional forms of scepticism and relativism, however, is the claim that there is more than a structure of argument at issue. Theoretical postmodernism's connection to an epochal notion of postmodernity is established by the assumption that the process of the self-undermining or implosion of truth is not simply a philosophical manoeuvre, but a historical development which has taken – or is currently taking – place in the contemporary world.[2] In Nietzsche's later thought, of course, the positive and negative dimensions of this process, which he comes to term 'nihilism', are held in a difficult tension. This tension is abandoned in postmodernism, which – notoriously – provides both 'pessimistic' and 'optimistic' varieties of its central thesis: Baudrillard's displacement of the true/false distinction by the 'gigantic simulacrum' of the hyperreal on the one hand;[3] Lyotard's 'networks of uncertain and ephemeral narratives' which 'can undermine the great institutionalized narrative apparatuses' on the other.[4]

Against the obvious objection that the kind of relativism they espouse is self-refuting, postmodernist thinkers – often appealing to Nietzsche – point to the intractable difficulties which have always been encountered by attempts to establish an objective and definitive grounding of truth-claims. If such a grounding cannot be provided, it is assumed, then relativism is the *only* possible option, and the contradictory consequences will simply have to be braved – just as Nietzsche speaks defiantly of '*my* truths'. But what if there were a middle path, a third option? In this case, the assumption that the historically proven failure of ultimate grounding legitimates a relativist position would no longer be compelling.

This is one context in which Derrida's work acquires a special interest. Derrida does not, of course, endorse the category of the 'postmodern'. If anything, he has recently been moving towards a conception of himself as a modern thinker. Nevertheless, the fundamental spiral of his thought often appears to enact – on a more rarefied philosophical level – the Nietzschean pattern of implosion which we have just considered. Furthermore, Derrida – particularly in his earlier work – regards deconstruction not as a subjective option, or even as a method, but rather as a characterization of the contemporary historical process, which is in some sense *determined* by the whole history which precedes it. 'By a slow movement whose necessity is hardly perceptible,' he asserts in *Of Grammatology*, 'everything that for at least some twenty centuries tended towards and finally succeeded in being gathered under the name of language is beginning to let itself be transferred to, or at least summarized under, the name of writing.'[5] And according to the earlier Derrida, it is writing – understood *with* Nietzsche and *against* Heidegger – which 'is not originarily submitted to the logos and to truth'.[6]

At the same time, Derrida is almost alone among his French contemporaries in being fully alert to the pitfalls of a simplistic anti-foundationalism and relativistic pluralism. Because he is steeped in the phenomenology of Husserl and Heidegger, he cannot permit himself any false naivety about transcendental and foundational issues. He once confessed, in the course of a discussion which will occupy us further: 'I don't believe in an overcoming of the transcendental. On the contrary, I think the transcendental questions are indispensable, and that it's necessary to repeat them endlessly, even up to the point where we examine the questions themselves in the history of their forms.'[7] If the first part of this statement is sincere, then what Derrida means by an examination of the history of transcendental questions cannot amount to a simple historicization of them, and his thought, therefore, has the interest of presenting the process of destructive self-implication which we have just examined, while striving to avoid the incoherence of its dominant theorizations. While many forms of postmodernism are content to re-enact – whether self-consciously or not – the familiar patterns of contextualism and cultural relativism, Derrida's project has always been to move beyond the transcendental position of Husserlian phenomenology, not to lapse beneath its level of rigour.[8]

Thus, whereas Baudrillard describes a 'nihilist system' which has 'the power to invert everything, even that which negates it, into indifference',[9] and Lyotard describes a pluralism of incommensurable language games, Derrida is careful to avoid any determinate delineation of what might emerge from the process of the self-destruction of truth, of some new (anti-)principle 'beyond' truth and falsehood. He repeatedly invokes such a 'beyond', but he usually does so indirectly, through an open-ended series of negations, as at the conclusion of his essay 'Ousia and Grammē': 'Such a *différance* would lead us to think, already and again, a writing without presence and without absence, without history, without cause, without arche, without telos, disrupting absolutely every dialectic, every theology, every ontology.'[10] More recently, Derrida has explicitly reflected on this method of delineation and its proximity to the procedures of 'negative theology', in an essay called 'Comment ne pas parler'.[11] Even though this essay is over-defensive, and cannot be regarded as entirely vindicating Derrida's approach, it certainly suggests that only an intense and hyper-cautious reflexivity could provide the basis for a viable philosophical model of the self-undermining movement invoked by theories of a transition from modernity to postmodernity – one which would not collapse into a naive relativism.

Thus the following discussion is motivated by the assumption that if even Derrida's account of this movement proves incoherent, then the epochal claims of postmodernist thought, which are usually presented in a far less sophisticated manner, will have been shown to be unsustainable. My strategy will be to concentrate on two examples of Derrida's approach to cases of destructive self-implication: firstly, his account of Austin's speech-act theory in 'Signature, Event, Context';[12] secondly, the account of metaphor in 'White Mythology' and his subsequent dispute with Paul Ricoeur over the philosophy of metaphor. I shall seek to show that these two cases reveal a similar flaw in Derrida's philosophical assumptions – a flaw whose consequence is that his thought ultimately lapses back into an incoherence indistinguishable from that of a naive 'postmodern' logic of implosion, despite his best effort to distance himself from this position.

## Derrida and Austin

Derrida begins 'Signature, Event, Context' with an exposition of his now familiar account of writing. Writing has the potential to function in the radical absence of its author, and of any empirically determined readership – in other words, its effectivity is not bound to any context. The notion of context, however, plays a crucial role in J. L. Austin's book *How to Do Things with Words*, the fountainhead of the tradition of speech-act theory. Here Austin initiates the exploration of 'performative' uses of language, such as promising or naming, in which the words 'I promise to . . .' or 'I name this ship . . .' are not the *description* of something the speaker does, but are themselves the very *act* in question. In Austin's account, in order for such a performative speech-act to be, not 'true', but 'happy', a complex set of circumstantial conditions must be met. To give a trivial example: in a marriage ceremony the person conducting the proceedings must be authorized to do so, the partners must normally not be of the same sex, and so forth, in order for the words 'I do' to have their performative effect.[13] But if we understand all language to be inhabited by writing in Derrida's sense, and apply this understanding to the dimension of language explored by Austin, the conclusion forced upon us is that it is impossible to specify necessary and sufficient conditions for the success of performative speech acts. We can never 'saturate the context', as Derrida puts it, and thereby guarantee the success of the speech-act in question. Austin's 'failure' itself consists in trying to specify the conditions of success and failure, in particular by attempting to make the notion of conscious intention 'a determining focus of the context'.[14] In giving this primacy to intention, Austin – for all his adventurousness – simply repeats the classic logocentric attempt to suppress the 'dissemination' of writing.

On closer inspection of Austin's original argument, however, it quickly becomes apparent that Derrida's assimilation of Austin to the tradition of logocentrism requires a bizarre level of hermeneutic violence. At the core of Derrida's reading lies the following claim:

> Austin's approach is quite remarkable, and typical of the philosophical tradition from which he wishes to disassociate himself. It consists in acknowledging that the possibility of the negative (here, of *infelicities*) is certainly a structural possibility, that failure is an essential risk of the operations under consideration, and then, in an almost simultaneous gesture, in the name of a kind of ideal regulation, in excluding this risk as accidental, external, having nothing to teach us about the linguistic phenomenon being examined.[15]

Notoriously, Derrida then goes on to accuse Austin of excluding 'non-serious' uses of language as 'etiolated' and 'parasitical', of seeking to marginalize the fictive and assuming its subordination to literal truth.

Austin does indeed exclude overtly fictional and aesthetic uses of language, in the sense of situations in which the usual pragmatic expectations of participants are *explicitly* suspended. He states: '[There] are parasitic uses of language, which are "not serious", not the "full normal use". The normal conditions of reference may be suspended, or no attempt made at a standard perlocutionary act, no attempt to make you do anything, as Walt Whitman does not seriously incite the eagle of liberty to soar."[16] However, Austin is far from insensitive to the kinds of inexplicit, semi-conscious, and even unconscious 'play-acting' which are essential to everyday speech in the form of insincerities, disguises or simple ambivalences of feeling, and so on. In these cases, he is perfectly willing to admit that there are no sharp borderlines to be drawn between the serious and the non-serious, as we shall see in more detail in a moment. Thus, Austin's exclusion of overtly fictional, jocular or ironic speech-acts amounts to no more than the claim that, for the purpose of analysing pragmatic features of language, cases in which some of those features are *self-consciously suspended* are of little use: actors who threaten violence to each other on stage do not expect to be assaulted later in the dressing-room. Furthermore, Derrida's claim that Austin does not consider that pragmatic failures or 'infelicities' offer any illumination of the phenomenon of language under consideration,[17] seems extraordinary in view of the fact that much of *How to Do Things with Words* is taken up with the classification and discussion of different kinds of 'infelicities', precisely for the sake of what they tell us about the pragmatics of language.

The continuation of Derrida's argument is equally puzzling:

> the value of risk or exposure to failure, even though it can affect *a priori* the totality of conventional acts, as Austin acknowledges, is not investigated as an essential predicate, or as a law. Austin does not wonder what consequences flow from the fact that a certain possibility – that a possible risk – is always possible, is in a certain sense a necessary possibility. And if such a necessary possibility is recognized, does it still constitute an accident? What is a success when the possibility of failure continues to constitute its structure? The opposition success/failure of the illocution or perlocution thus seems here to be very insufficient and highly derivative.[18]

The crucial glide here, in Derrida's formulations, is from the notion of a necessary possibility of failure to the notion that the possibility of failure – in a new and more fundamental sense – *constitutes the structure of success.* Austin himself is far from underestimating the 'necessary possibility of failure'. He does not think that the *possibility* of failure is accidental, as Derrida's question implies, but, rather, any specific *empirical* failure. Austin states, for example:

It is *inherent in the nature* of any procedure that the limits of its applicability, and therewith, of course, the 'precise' definition of the procedure, will remain vague. There will *always* occur difficult or marginal cases where nothing in the previous history of a conventional procedure will decide conclusively whether such a procedure is or is not correctly applied to such a case.[19]

Derrida, however, seems to want to go beyond this insight – to suggest what could be termed the *possibility of necessary failure* (as opposed to the necessity of possible failure), and thus to propose a notion of failure as preceding and constituting the opposition of success and failure in the usual sense. The clearest indication of this comes at the end of the section on Austin in 'Signature, Event, Context', where Derrida states that the fact that there are 'effects' of consciousness, speech, performativity, ordinary language, 'does not exclude what is in general opposed to them term by term, indeed rather presupposes it, *in a dissymmetrical fashion*, as the general space of their possibility'.[20] It is this emphasis on dissymmetry which highlights Derrida's commitment to a version of the destructive self-implication of postmodernist thought.

But why should failure be such a condition of possibility – thus entailing the constitutive *impossibility* – of success? Derrida's argument, if one reads partly between the lines, seems to run as follows: because of the distinctive reflexivity of language, the recognition of a speech-act *as* successful is an essential component of its success. In order for a speech-act to be recognized as successful, however, the context would have to be saturated – all the necessary and sufficient conditions would have to be *known* to be satisfied. Thus Derrida states: 'In order for a context to be exhaustively determined in the sense required by Austin, it would at least be necessary for the conscious intention to be totally present and actually transparent to itself and to the others, since it is a determining focus of the context.'[21] But because of what Derrida in this essay describes as 'iterability', or the dependence of the apparent identity of linguistic terms on an open-ended structure of referral, no context can be determined by conscious intention in this way. Hence no speech-act can ever be successful.

At first sight this seems an absurd conclusion, yet there is clear evidence that it is the conclusion towards which Derrida – *nolens, volens* – is driven. I am referring here to a passage later in 'Signature, Event, Context', where Derrida adopts the position of an imaginary interlocutor to voice the most obvious objection to his own position:

Someone might indeed say to me: you cannot claim to give an account of the so-called graphematic structure of the speech act on the basis merely of the occurrence of performative failures, however real these failures may be, and however effective or general their possibility. You cannot deny that there are also performatives which succeed, and you need to be able to give an explanation of them: people open meetings – Paul Ricoeur did it yesterday. People say

'I am asking a question', people make bets, people challenge, people launch boats, and people even get married sometimes. Such events, it appears, have taken place. And if a single one of them took place on a single occasion, you would need to be able to account for it.[22]

Derrida's self-induced embarrassment at this point is betrayed by the fact that, in ostensibly replying to his own question, he in fact sidesteps to a *different* question – that of the supposed singularity of the event in relation to its citational or iterative structure: 'I would say perhaps. First we would have to agree on the question of what it means for something to "happen" . . .'[23]

Derrida, I would suggest, finds himself in this difficulty because of his assumption that unless the context – *per impossibile* – can be saturated, no speech-act can proceed successfully. However, one needs to be cautiously aware of what could be *meant* by saturation of a context here. Derrida makes the following statement: 'This conscious presence of the speakers or hearers participating in the carrying out of a performative, their conscious and intentional presence to the totality of the operation, implies teleologically that no remainder escapes the present totalization.'[24] But when saturation is described in this way, a requirement is established which is indeed impossible to fulfil, even ideally or 'teleologically'. But is this the appropriate way to describe saturation? Derrida does not consider the possibility that the ensemble of conditions might be in force in some sense *other* than being present to a totalizing consciousness. Perhaps because of his early training in the rigorously reflective exigencies of Husserlian phenomenology, it does not seem to occur to him to mobilize a notion of the *pre-reflective* as a means of addressing the problem of context.

What I mean by this can be illustrated by a passage from the work of Hilary Putnam, where, as part of a critique of empiricist philosophies of social science, he develops an argument concerning direct language learning:

If I go to a gas station and say *bedok et hashemen*, and the attendant punches me in the nose (and the same thing happens at other gas stations) my faith in my translation of *bedok et hashemen* as 'check the oil' will be shaken. But notice what is going on! I am assuming (1) the attendant wants to sell gas and oil; (2) it is not *obligatory* in Israel to say 'bevakasha' *(please)* when making a request; (3) if someone wants to sell oil, and a customer asks 'check the oil' in the language of the seller (and no obligatory politeness-rules have been violated) the seller will check the oil . . .; (4) someone driving up to a gas station will be treated as a customer. Each time I check my 'analytical hypothesis' (i.e. my translation skills) in a new context, a *new* list of psychological/sociological hypotheses of the order of (1)–(4) will be imported from 'general background knowledge', or whatever. The whole list of such things that I use and believe cannot, obviously, be *written down* in advance.[25]

The situation described by Putnam is a familiar one. It is impossible *in principle* to spell out or make explicitly present to consciousness the totality of background conditions for the success of a translation, or – by strict analogy – of a performative utterance. But this does not mean that these background conditions cannot be assumed to be operative as a totality, in the form of what phenomenology has taught us to call the 'lifeworld'; nor that – in the event of breakdown or failure – the relevant condition cannot be reflectively identified. Totality, we could say, *excludes* presence, and presence *excludes* totality. Against this it might be argued that Derrida's 'general text' cannot be equated with writing in the empirical sense. If anything, its non-objectifiable and all-embracing status would seem to identify it as a radicalized successor to the notion of the lifeworld. But, as Charles Spinosa has argued, the incessant mobility which the displacement of the concept of the lifeworld – the 'totality of involvements' or 'context of assignments' of *Being and Time* – by that of *différance* would introduce can itself be seen as a *hypostatization* of those privileged moments when a shift in the background presuppositions of interpretation occurs. In this sense, the thought of a primordial *différance* simply repeats the abstractive fallacy of objectifying metaphysics. Such thinking projects those features of the world which emerge only at the point of *breakdown* of a practical totality of involvements back into this totality itself, where they are employed as the basis of a theoretical 'explanation' of everyday practices.[26]

To put the point in another way: because of his fixation with the 'metaphysics of presence', Derrida assumes that to be saturated, a context must be *present* to consciousness. He suggests, for example, that Austin's ideal is 'self-presence of a total context, transparency of intentions, presence of meaning to the absolutely singular unicity of a speech-act, etc.'.[27] He cannot, it seems, accommodate the notion of a context which is *neither* present *nor* absent (to consciousness), but is *pre-reflectively* saturated. To take up the terms employed by Putnam, if the 'general background knowledge' cannot be 'written down', this is because the lifeworld is precisely that which writing cannot inscribe. This resistance to inscription is something which Derrida himself almost stumbles across at the beginning of 'Signature, Event, Context', when he suggests that the ways of proceeding at a conference are governed by 'a kind of implicit but structurally vague consensus' which prescribes that communication should take place 'within the horizon of an intelligibility and a truth of meaning'.[28] Such a consensus constitutes a 'semantic horizon' of the kind which Derrida, by the end of the essay, too easily assumes can be 'ruptured' by the 'intervention of writing'.[29] But how can something be 'ruptured' which does not have sufficient structure to be broken, which is too elusive even to be brought to consciousness, except in fragments? We can see, in this way, how Derrida's notion of writing is literally utopian, heir to the transcendental consciousness of Husserl in its effort to suppress its own context.[30]

Accordingly, Derrida's repeated discovery of transcendental motifs in Austin's text can perhaps best be read as a form of 'projective identification', which occludes the real radicality of Austin's position. Derrida suggests, for example, that when Austin defines six types of infelicities:

> By means of the values of 'conventionality', 'correctness' and 'wholeness' which contribute to this definition, we discover those of a context which is exhaustively definable, of a consciousness which is free and present to the totality of the operation, of a meaning [*vouloir-dire*] absolutely full and master of itself: the teleological jurisdiction of a total field of which *intention* remains the organizing centre.[31]

The least one can say about these remarks is that Austin's position is unrecognizable in them. Austin does *not* suggest the need for a consciousness present to the totality of the operation; and he does *not* give intention the centrality which Derrida assumes.

With regard to the first point, Austin stresses – as we have already seen – that there is always an unpredictably various range of things which can go wrong with any conventional act: 'There will always occur difficult or marginal cases where nothing in the previous history of a conventional procedure will decide conclusively whether such a procedure is or is not correctly applied to such a case.'[32] One important implication of this, which Austin does not emphasize, is that it is always logically possible for a flaw to be discovered *retrospectively* in what was taken to be correct procedure: there is never any punctual guarantee of success. With regard to the second point, Austin is far from giving intention the sovereign role which Derrida suggests, again reading through his Husserlian spectacles. Certainly, Austin sees intention as a component of the speech-act, but he has serious doubts about the extent to which it is *necessary*: 'For example, if I say "I congratulate you" must we really have a feeling, or rather a thought, that you have done or deserved well?'[33] Furthermore, Austin is fully aware of the difficulties involved in the *independent* identification of intentions. Such identification can scarcely be direct, since it often depends on the subsequent performance of certain actions: does the failure to surrender possession after saying 'I give' indicate the breakdown of the *original* intention or of a *corollary* intention?[34]

In fact, as Derrida nowhere mentions, Austin – with the help of some lines from Euripides – devotes a substantial passage in the first chapter of his book to debunking the notion of intentions as internal happenings in principle independent of language – as what he calls 'fictitious inner acts':

> we are apt to have a feeling that [words'] being serious consists in their being uttered as (merely) the outward and visible sign, for convenience or other record or for information, of an inward and spiritual act: from which it is but a short

step to go on to believe or assume without realizing that for many purposes the outward utterance is a description, *true* or *false*, of the occurrence of the inward performance. The classic expression of this idea is to be found in the *Hippolytus* (1. 612), where Hippolytus says . . . 'my tongue swore to, but my heart (or mind or other backstage artiste) did not'.[35]

Thus it appears that Austin's view of intention is remarkably close to the view expressed by Derrida himself: 'It is less a matter of opposing citation or iteration to the non-iteration of an event than of constructing a differential typology of forms of iteration. . . . In this typology the category of intention will not disappear, it will have its place, but from this place it will no longer be able to command the whole stage and the whole system of utterances.'[36]

## Derrida and Ricoeur on Metaphor

I now want to show that a structure of argument similar to that of the essay on Austin, and generating similar problems, can also be found in Derrida's discussions of philosophy and metaphor. Although any one of a range of themes in Derrida's work could have been chosen for this parallel demonstration, his treatment of metaphor, and his exchange on the issue with his eminent contemporary, Paul Ricoeur, has a particular interest in the present context. As we shall see, the discussion can again be seen as gravitating around the crucial question of the status of the lifeworld.

Derrida's central argument in his major essay on metaphor, 'White Mythology', is that theories of metaphor have always been articulated within the conceptual field of Western metaphysics, which is itself structured by certain fundamental 'metaphors'. Derrida affirms that 'metaphor, in all its essential traits, is a classic philosopheme, a metaphysical concept. It is therefore caught in the field which a general metaphorology of philosophy would like to dominate. It emerged from a network of philosophemes which themselves correspond to tropes or to figures which are contemporary or in systematic solidarity with it.'[37] Examples of such metaphors would be notions such as 'theory', 'foundation' or 'concept', all of which depend upon the sublimation – in Derrida's view, never fully achieved – of an original 'sensuous' meaning into an 'intellectual' meaning. For example: 'The fundamental corresponds to the desire for a firm and ultimate ground, for a terrain on which to construct, for the earth as the support of an artificial structure';[38] and such connotations cannot be completely 'erased' by philosophical abstraction. The conclusion Derrida draws from this 'paradox of auto-implication', as Ricoeur terms it, is a radical one: 'Metaphor is less in the philosophical text (and in the rhetorical text co-ordinated with it), than the latter is in metaphor. And metaphor can no longer receive its name from metaphysics, other than by a catachresis, so to speak, which tracks it via the philosophical phantom of metaphor: as "untrue metaphor".'[39]

Thus Derrida's position depends, firstly, upon the assumption that fundamental 'metaphors' – which can therefore no longer be termed metaphors – remain operative at the basis of philosophical definitions of metaphor. Secondly, Derrida assumes that such definitions necessarily rely on a distinction between 'literal' truth and a (putatively temporary) figurative deviation from that truth, with the consequence that if the distinction between 'literal' and 'metaphorical' truth is itself 'metaphorical', then the entire structure of philosophical thinking about metaphor – indeed, of 'metaphysics' in general – will begin to totter.

In his critical response to this account, Ricoeur contends that the distinction between 'living' and 'dead' metaphors remains defensible – concepts such as 'concept' or 'theory', for example, have long since lost any figurative charge which they might originally have possessed, just as the French word 'tête' no longer evokes the Latin word for a pot ['testa']. Consequently, although philosophical discourse makes frequent – and inevitable – use of metaphors, it cannot be said to be 'in' metaphor in quite the manner which Derrida maintains. Ricoeur does not deny that such concepts can have their 'figurative' content reawakened – both Hegel and Heidegger were virtuosi in this domain – but this reawakening does not demonstrate that the term functions primarily as a metaphor. As Ricoeur states: 'The reanimation of a dead metaphor is a positive operation of delexicalization which is equivalent to the production of a new metaphor.'[40]

The obvious Derridean riposte at this juncture would be to suggest that the very distinction between living and dead metaphor involves a claim to distinguish between literal and figurative meaning which must be grounded in the 'metaphysics of presence'. Ricoeur's reply to this objection is to claim that the contrast of literal and figurative meaning does not require the belief in 'the illusion that words might have in themselves a proper meaning, that is to say, primitive, natural, original'.[41] And his argument continues as follows: 'We have certainly admitted that the metaphorical use of a word can always be opposed to its literal use; but literal does not mean proper in the sense of original, but simply current, usual: the literal meaning is that which is lexicalized.'[42]

Here Ricoeur is relying on the results of his earlier discussions of 'interactionist' theories of metaphor, the impetus for which was first provided by I. A. Richards. In *The Philosophy of Rhetoric* Richards introduced the distinction between 'tenor' and 'vehicle' which, he claimed, were usually described by 'clumsy descriptive phrases' such as 'the original idea' and 'the borrowed one', or 'the underlying idea' and 'the imagined nature'.[43] As Ricoeur points out, the advantage of this distinction is that it entirely bypasses the traditional distinction between literal and metaphorical meaning, since it is in the *tension* between tenor and vehicle that the metaphor consists. This tension can be described as that between an 'is' and an 'is not', as a 'play of semantic pertinence and impertinence'.[44] Ricoeur's argument does not, however, entail that the distinction between literal and metaphorical utterance cannot now be reformulated in a new way:

> The only criterion of metaphor, in fact, is that the word gives two ideas at once, that it contains both 'tenor' and 'vehicle' in interaction. By contrast, this criterion can serve to define literal meaning: if one cannot distinguish tenor and vehicle, then the word can be provisionally regarded as literal. . . . But, in this case, literal meaning has nothing to do with proper meaning. Furthermore, literal language becomes extremely rare, outside of the technical language of the sciences.[45]

It will be evident that Ricoeur's reply is directed to the same hitch in Derrida's strategy which has already been identified in the attempted deconstruction of Austin. Just as Derrida assumes that in order for a speech act to be successful the context must be 'consciously' saturated, surveyed from an exhaustively objectifying vantage point, so he assumes that – for philosophy to 'master' metaphor – an absolute, 'non-metaphorical' distinction between literal and figurative meaning must be established, outside of any horizon of a shared language. But just as, for Austin, there can be no 'guaranteed' success of speech acts, only an ongoing process of adjudication in which new rules and discriminations are continually introduced to address unforeseen (and unforeseeable) eventualities, so – for Ricoeur – the acknowledgement of the inescapability of metaphor does not radically undermine the philosophical project of conceptual articulation in the manner which Derrida suggests. If the concept of metaphor is not considered to be *essentially* tied to a battery of 'metaphysical' distinctions, then there is no reason why metaphor should not be employed in a reflective process of self-exploration and self-clarification. This process can never be definitively concluded, but at the same time it is certainly not self-defeating, as Derrida's account implies.[46] Philosophy and poetry, according to Ricoeur, have different, albeit intersecting, dynamics; and the philosophical effort to approach the non-objective can be accepted as inescapably dependent on metaphor, without being reducible to it. As Ricoeur once stated, in the course of a discussion with Derrida: 'There is a sort of incommunicability behind us and, secondly, before us there is the task of communication. And I think that this idea of incommunicability behind and a task of communication in front cannot be overcome philosophically.'[47]

## Derrida's Response to Ricoeur

In the first part of his essay 'The *retrait* of metaphor', Derrida develops a reply to Ricoeur which focuses on two principal issues. First, he denies that he endorses the understanding of metaphor as a deviation from the proper to the figurative, or as a transfer from the sensible to the intelligible. Second, he denies that he accepts a conception of the evolution of metaphor into concept as involving a process of 'wearing away' [*usure*] in which an 'original' figurative meaning would be slowly eroded into a literal one. Thus Derrida writes: '"White Mythology" constantly questions the current and currently philosophical interpretation of metaphor (including in Heidegger) as a transfer from the sensible to the intelligible.'[48] Similarly, he claims that his intention was to 'deconstruct a philosophical concept, a concept based on the schema of the worn out metaphor [*la metaphore usée*], or privileging for significant reasons the trope called metaphor.'[49] Fundamentally, Derrida's defence is to suggest that the conceptions of metaphor which Ricoeur criticizes are precisely those which he, too, is concerned to deconstruct.

This defence, however, raises a crucial issue about the philosophical functioning of deconstruction. For although Derrida can reply that he is not *endorsing* the 'metaphysical' conception of metaphor, he does not advocate any *alternative* conception, since his claim is that the concept of metaphor belongs *inherently* within 'metaphysical' schemas, and thus that phenomena can be described *as metaphor* only in the manner which Ricoeur contests. Thus, in 'White Mythology' Derrida suggests that the 'condition of impossibility' of describing metaphor in the philosophical text is constituted by the fact that 'metaphor remains, *in all its essential characteristics,* a classical philosopheme, a metaphysical concept . . .'[50] It is this claim, of course, which generates the dynamic of implosion, or destructive self-implication, which is also characteristic of postmodernist thinking. But if metaphor can be thought in ways which do not require a 'metaphysical' conception of proper or original nomination or meaning, but merely – as Ricoeur suggests – a distinction between lexicalized and innovative usage, then this potential for self-undermining is defused.

Derrida thus seems vulnerable to Ricoeur's accusation that he assumes an implausible unity and coherence of Western philosophical thinking, under the rubric of the 'metaphysics of presence', in order to provide the target of deconstruction – a target which includes the concept of metaphor, considered to be essentially tied to the 'vocation of pure nomination'. For example, when Derrida writes: 'the whole of this aforesaid history of Western metaphysics would be a vast structural process, where the *epoche* of Being withholding itself in withdrawal would take, or rather would present, an (interlaced) series of guises', he remains dependent on a figure of thought, that of the 'history of Being' [*Seinsgeschichte*], ultimately derived from Heidegger.[51] But in a discussion of Heidegger's account of metaphysics, Ricoeur confesses: 'I cannot see in this enclosing of the previous history of Western thought in the unity of "metaphysics" [*la métaphysique*] anything other than the spirit of vengeance which . . . [Heidegger's] thought invites us to renounce, as well as the will-to-power which – for this thought – appears inseparable from it.'[52] And he continues: 'Why should this philosophy refuse to all its predecessors the benefit of the rupture and the power of innovation which it grants to itself? The moment has come, it seems to me, to deny oneself the convenience, now become a lazy habit of thought, of gathering the whole of Western thinking under a single term – metaphysics.'[53] Ricoeur's parallel critique of Derrida focuses on the latter's identification of a handful of tropes – such as those of the 'home' and of the 'sun' – which are purported to dominate and organize Western philosophy as a whole. He contests this circular complicity in which metaphor, understood 'metaphysically' as a deviation from proper nomination, in turn marks philosophy indelibly as metaphysics. On the contrary, he argues: 'The metaphors of the sun and the home reign only to the extent that they are selected by philosophical discourse. The metaphorical field in its entirety is open to all the figures that play on the relations of the similar and the dissimilar in any region of the thinkable whatsoever.'[54]

## Metaphor and Metaphysics

Derrida also has a reply to this criticism of course: he has never hypostatized the unity of metaphysical thinking in this way; he has always emphasized that such thinking is always internally traversed and disrupted by its apparent limit or border.[55] Later in the 'The *retrait* of metaphor', Derrida seeks to demonstrate this specifically in terms of the dynamics of metaphor. He first suggests, extrapolating from Heidegger: 'One might be tempted to say: metaphysics, which corresponds in its discourse to the withdrawal [*le retrait*] of metaphor, tends to assemble, in their resemblance, all the metonymic lags [*écarts*] in a grand metaphor of Being and of the truth of Being. The assemblage would be *the* language of metaphysics [*le langage de la* métaphysique].'[56] Derrida then goes on to argue, however, that this putative unity is destroyed by the fact that the notion of the 'withdrawal of Being' which makes this metaphorical process possible cannot itself be a metaphorical notion: '"Withdrawal of Being" cannot have a literal or proper meaning to the extent that Being is not "something" [*quelque chose*], a determinate entity which one can designate. For the same reason, since the withdrawal of Being gives rise to the metaphysical concept of metaphor and to its withdrawal, the expression "withdrawal of Being" is not *strictu sensu* metaphorical.'[57] In Derrida's account, this spiralling movement has the following consequence:

> Far from proceeding from a word or a known or determinate meaning (withdrawal) in order to think what is the case with Being and with metaphor, I would only succeed in comprehending, understanding, reading, thinking withdrawal, allowing it to be announced in general, on the basis of the withdrawal of Being as the withdrawal of metaphor in all the polysemic *and* disseminal potential of withdrawal.[58]

Derrida has an important point here concerning any attempt to make statements about 'Being', which has significant implications for Ricoeur's position. As we have seen, Ricoeur argues that the concept of literal language is not foundational but privative – the literal is merely whatever lacks metaphorical tension, and such tension is revealed in a relation between tenor and vehicle characterized by a simultaneity of truth and falsehood. But since nothing can be truly *or* falsely predicated of Being itself, the distinction between literal and metaphorical language collapses in this case. Thus the implication of Ricoeur's position that all language can be located in a force-field defined by the poles of the literal and the metaphorical must be mistaken. But Derrida's position is not thereby at the same time vindicated. For Derrida is still relying, in 'The *retrait* of metaphor', on a basic conception of metaphor as *deviation* from an original denomination (he refers to 'a determinate entity which one can designate'), in order to show that the condition of possibility of metaphysics itself – the withdrawal of Being – deviates from this model of deviation, and thus must be understood 'quasi-metaphorically', or as a 'supplementary fold of metaphor'.[59] He still has to assume the unity of metaphysics, grounded in this view, in order to generate the subsequent dissemination, or what he also terms the 'generalizing catastrophe'.[60] Furthermore, what Derrida describes in these melodramatic terms (the fact that there is no meaning which can be fixed prior to metaphorical entanglements, since all such entanglements presuppose the doubly metaphorical displacement of Being) is a commonplace of interactionist accounts of metaphors, which fully acknowledge that the 'vehicle' impacts back on the 'tenor'.[61]

Similarly, in Ricoeur's account, the emergence of metaphor disrupts not an impossible but an imperative literality, since it is indicated not by a deviation or substitution but, rather, by a triple tension: between 'tenor' and 'vehicle', between a literal interpretation which 'perishes at the hands of semantic impertinence' and a new interpretation 'whose sense emerges through nonsense', and between 'identity and difference in the play of resemblance'.[62] The consequence of this view may be that the language of

Being can be neither literal nor metaphorical – but Ricoeur has in a sense already acknowledged this in his account of the essential tension between philosophy and poetry as disclosures of the world. Thus, there is no need to follow Derrida in assuming that the 'ontological' event of the withdrawal of Being implies a 'withdrawal' (or the 'double trait' – *re-trait*) of an 'ontic' or 'metaphysical' understanding of metaphor, with its supposedly disseminative consequences. Rather, it could be argued, it is metaphor itself, in its unresolvable tension, which reveals the strain between the ontological and the ontic, between existential and relational meaning, implicit in our experience as a whole.

Because he adopts this view of metaphor, Ricoeur repudiates the Heideggerian assumption that the 'language of metaphysics' pervades even our everyday experience. In this he agrees with Hans-Georg Gadamer, who, in an essay on Hegel and Heidegger, inquires: 'But can a language or a family of languages ever legitimately be called the language of metaphysical thinking, merely because metaphysics was thought in it, or not even that – was anticipated in it? Is not language always the language of the homeland, and of the enactment of becoming-at-home in the world?'[63] For Ricoeur, to take the metaphoricity of language seriously is to challenge our habitual modern objectivist ontology, but it is not to step beyond the everyday into a rareified and privileged domain of poetry, thinking, or even deconstruction. Thus Ricoeur writes: 'what poetic discourse brings into language is a pre-objective world where we find ourselves from birth, but also into which we project our ownmost possibilities. Thus we must shatter the reign of the object, in order to allow to be, and to be spoken, our primordial belonging to a world which we inhabit, that is to say which, simultaneously, precedes us and receives the imprint of our activity.'[64]

## Proximity and Presence

By this time the parallels will have emerged between the dynamic of Derrida's response to Austin and that of his debate with Ricoeur. In the case of Austin, it became clear that the possibility of drawing a distinction between success and failure does not depend upon a pre-given, exhaustive set of criteria. Rather, the more precise articulation of what we mean by the 'success' of a speech act takes place through reflection on what appears as failure: it involves a further articulation of the lifeworld, and of the interpretative potentialities which are conveyed within it. Similarly, metaphorical usage is not identified by contrast with an absolute canon of proper usage but, rather, itself makes possible a distinction between literal and metaphorical usage, in terms of the absence or presence of a tension between 'tenor' and 'vehicle', or between 'focus' and 'frame', to employ

Max Black's more sophisticated extension of Richards's terminology.[65] Reflection on metaphor is thus part of a process of articulation which *precedes* the distinction between figurative and literal on which traditional philosophical theories of metaphor are based. As Ricoeur says: 'poetic language . . . makes . . . a breakthrough at a prescientific, ante-predicative level, where the very notions of fact, of object, of reality, of truth, as these are limited by epistemology, are put into question'.[66] But if Derrida, in general, is unreceptive to this line of argument, this is not because he has overlooked its possibility. Rather, it is because, for Derrida, notions of the ante-predicative and the pre-reflexive, not to mention that of 'our primordial belonging to the world', are still contaminated with the metaphysics of presence. It is this conviction of Derrida's which must now be examined.

A fruitful place to begin is his well-known essay on 'The Ends of Man'. In this text Derrida begins by suggesting that the predominant interpretation of the thought of Hegel, Husserl and Heidegger in postwar France was marked by an erroneous anthropologizing tendency. Against this approach Derrida seeks to show that these thinkers should, rather, be understood as both *within* and *beyond* anthropocentric thought; that the concept of consciousness in Hegel and Husserl, for example, cannot simply be reduced to the concept of *human* consciousness. Heidegger represents a more complex case, because of his explicit interrogation of the links between metaphysics and humanism. But even here Derrida detects the recurrence of a dubious anthropocentrism. On his account, this tendency is already apparent in the opening paragraphs of *Being and Time,* where Heidegger explains the privileged position of *Dasein* in the posing of the 'question of Being'.

Heidegger's explanation of this privilege is that the process of questioning is nothing other than the mode of being of *Dasein.* Accordingly, this mode of being must first be clarified, before the general question of Being can be posed.[67] *Dasein* is the entity which is 'ontically' distinguished by the fact that, in its very being, it is concerned about its being.[68] Derrida, however, comments on this privilege as follows:

> It is governed by phenomenology's principle of principles, the principle of presence and of presence in self-presence, such as it is manifested to the being and in the being that *we* are. It is this self-presence, this absolute proximity of the (questioning) being to itself, this familiarity with itself of the being ready to understand Being, that intervenes in the determination of the *factum*, and that motivates the choice of the exemplary being, of the text, the good text for the hermeneutic of the meaning of Being.[69]

In fact, in Heidegger's account, what is decisive is not 'proximity' as such but, rather, what he terms the 'being related back or prior relatedness [*Rück-oder Vorbezogenheit*] of that which is asked about to questioning as a mode of being of a being', although this – of course – *entails* a certain proximity of questioner and questioned.[70] But even setting this issue aside, what is remarkable about Derrida's formulations is the persistent equation of *proximity* and *(self)-presence*. It is striking that the German terms '*Vorhandenheit*', '*Anwesenheit*', '*Gegenwärtigkeit*'and '*Präsenz*' do not appear at any point in the passages of Heidegger to which Derrida is referring. Certainly, Heidegger describes the Being of Dasein as 'disclosed' [*erschlossen*] to itself. But why should disclosure be equated with 'presence', especially when Heidegger himself emphasizes that this disclosure is a matter not of direct apprehension but of understanding [*Verstehen*]? Indeed, Derrida goes on to admit that 'this proximity, this identity or self-presence [the appositions should be noted] of the "entity that we are" – of the inquirer and of the interrogated – does not have the form of subjective consciousness, as in transcendental phenomenology.' He nevertheless objects to the fact that Heidegger practises 'a style of reading which "makes explicit", practises a continual bringing to light, something which resembles, at least, a coming into consciousness, without break, displacement or change of terrain'.[71] However, such a process of reading would be complicit with the metaphysics of *presence* only if it could be brought to completion; if the paradoxical – and metaphorical – tension between 'is' and 'is not' could be resolved.

In fact, the undermining of the equation of presence and proximity can be seen as standing at the very beginning of post-Hegelian philosophizing, and in Left Hegelian thought it is central to the kind of complex attempt to outflank Hegel which also typifies deconstruction. One of the main targets of Feuerbach's attack on Hegelian thought, for example, and – by implication – on the metaphysical tradition as a whole, is the presupposition of (the need for) presuppositionlessness. In his 1841 essay 'Über den "Anfang der Philosophie"' ('On the "Beginning in Philosophy"'), Feuerbach argues that 'The task of science in general is not to cancel the object [*den Gegenstand aufzuheben*] – i.e. to be without presuppositions, God forbid! but, rather, to make what is not objective objective. But what is not an object is not given in a conceptualizable way [*begreiflicher Weise*] – thus all science begins without a datum, begins without ground [*bodenlos*].'[72] At this point the question arises: 'what is the non-objective?' [*das Nichtgegenständliche*]. And Feuerbach answers: 'Everything which is – even the most sensuous, even the most common everyday thing, as long as it is only an object of life-enjoyment or common perception [*nur ein Gegenstand des Lebensgenusses oder der gemeinen Anschauung*] and not of science'.[73] Feuerbach goes on to suggest that it is not the 'beyond' or the 'realm of spirits' which should be seen as non-objective and unapproachable – rather, this beyond has been thoroughly objectified, and 'human beings . . . have lived rather in the light of another than in the light of this world'. Indeed, what is truly hidden is what is closest to us: 'The nearest is what is furthest for the human being; precisely because it does not count for him as a mystery, it is a mystery; because it is always – it is never – an object.'[74] In contrast with this metaphorical tension – in the sense of Ricoeur's simultaneous 'is and is not' – implied by Feuerbach's view of the world in which we are immersed ('because it is always – it is never – an object'), in contrast with this invocation of groundlessness which is nevertheless not an 'anti-foundationalism', Derrida can be seen as seeking a resolution, a change of terrain through a step beyond the horizon – a writing of the lifeworld.[75]

## Conclusion

Perhaps the previous sentence should be couched in the past tense, for some of the recent developments in Derrida's thinking suggest that the equation of presence and proximity has become problematic for him too. In *Of Grammatology* Derrida had suggested:

> There is not a single signified that escapes, even if recaptured, the play of signi-
> fying references that constitute language. The advent of writing is the advent of
> this play; today such a play is coming into its own, effacing the limit starting
> from which one had thought to regulate the circulation of signs, drawing along
> with it all the reassuring signifieds, reducing all the strongholds, all the out-of-
> bounds shelters which watched over the field of language.[76]

Now, however, he stresses that even the most elementary allocution depends upon a primordial co-appurtenance: 'We would not be together in a sort of minimal community – but one which is also incommensurable with any other – speaking the same language, or praying for translation within the horizon of the same language . . . if a sort of friendship had not been sealed before any other contract. . . .'[77] Furthermore, Derrida states: 'this *anterior* affirmation of being-together in the allocution . . . can no longer be simply integrated, above all it cannot be *presented* as a being-present . . . within the space of ontology, precisely because it opens this space'.[78] In other words, an affirmation of being-together here plays the role of precondition of the space of ontology which was formerly allotted to *différance*, but it is clear that such an affirmation is something radically other than *différance*. For what is at issue is not the quasi-sceptical reduction of every mode of being to a trace or 're-mark' but, rather, the acknowledgement of a *mode of being* (and, indeed, of a 'together' of proximity and belonging – and thus of the *proper*) which is prior to all presence – to all objectification of entities. Such co-belonging surely constitutes an 'out-of-bounds shelter which watches over the field of language'. Since it can neither be brought to presence nor shattered by *différance*, it is fundamentally comparable in its structure to what I have here been calling the 'lifeworld'.

Derrida's conception of such a pre-reflective domain, at least in these passages, is resolutely anti-monological. It is based on the relation between speakers, and in this it differs from phenomenological articulations of the lifeworld, including that of Heidegger. Still, it does not consist in mere acknowledgements of the formal interplay of responsibility and otherness. For that *'sorte de consensus structurellement vague'* which Derrida had fleetingly evoked at the beginning of 'Signature, Event, Context', and which was there seen as constituting a 'limit' or a 'regulation' of the 'circulation of signs', has been redisovered as the implicit assumption of semantic agreement which provides the initial purchase necessary even for operations which radically question such agreement. Derrida now acknowledges that there must be a *relatively* stable core of shared meanings for deconstructive operations to have something to work upon: 'what I sought to designate under the title of "doubling commentary" is the "minimal deciphering" of the "first" pertinent or competent access to structures that are relatively stable (and hence destabilizable!), and from which the most venturesome questions and interpretations have to start'.[79] Indeed, he now emphasizes that 'no research is possible in a community (for example, academic) without the prior search for this minimal consensus and without discussion around this minimal consensus'.[80] These statements seem to represent an acceptance of a polarization within language between a stability (which cannot be captured and employed as a ground) and a process of destabilization, which is comparable to Ricoeur's account of the polarization between the literal and the metaphorical – and, indeed, to Austin's account of the relation between performatives and their 'infelicities'. The question that remains is whether the acknowledgement of this polarity or dualism (which *cannot* be deconstructed, since deconstruction begins from it) represents no more than a minor adjustment of Derrida's philosophical strategy. For it may well be that it not only undermines the foundations of postmodern anti-foundationalism but also represents the beginning of an unravelling of the strategy of deconstruction, viewed as an operation which could be strictly opposed to hermeneutics and critique.

This limitation of the thought of delimitation, marked by that fact that 'speech' is no longer put under suspicion as a metaphysical category in Derrida's work, represents a crucial turning point, for it means that what I have here called the 'lifeworld' can be neither definitively shattered nor entirely objectified.[81] At the same time, Derrida could hardly deny that this affirmation, this 'friendship prior to all friendships', touches us with the utmost proximity. We may thus conclude that his earlier thinking was not able to provide that third way between foundationalism and relativism which might have rescued postmodern claims concerning an epochal crisis of foundations from a naive pluralism. Rather, it simply reproduced the self-destructive dynamic of postmodern thinking in an even more comprehensive form. It is to Derrida's credit that he has come to appreciate this complicity, and to seek remedies for it. But at the same time his most recent work, in its exploration of forms of proximity beyond presence, leaves us with the puzzling question of what difference still remains between critical hermeneutics and deconstruction.

## Notes

1. Friedrich Nietzsche, *Sämtliche Werke: Kritische Studienausgabe,* ed. Giorgio Colli and Mazzino Montinari, Berlin and New York: de Gruyter 1967–77, vol. 7, p. 623/*Philosophy and Truth: Selections from Nietzsche's Notebooks of the Early 1870s,* trans. and ed. Daniel Breazeale, Sussex: Harvester Press 1979, p. 92.

2. A classic statement of this view, which also locates the crucial epochal break in Nietzsche's assault on truth in the 1870s, may be found in Gianni Vattimo, 'Nihilisme et postmoderne en philosophie', in Vattimo, *La fin de la modernité,* Paris: Seuil 1987, pp. 169–85/'Nihilism and Postmodern in Philosophy', in *The End of Modernity,* trans. John R. Snyder, Cambridge: Polity Press 1988, pp. 164–81.

3. See Jean Baudrillard, *Simulacres et Simulation,* Paris: Galilée 1981, pp. 16 ff/*Simulacra and Simulation,* trans. Sheila Faria Glaser, Ann Arbor, MI: University of Michigan Press 1994, pp. 12 ff.

4. See Jean-François Lyotard, *Instructions païennes,* Paris: Galilée 1977, p. 34.

5. Jacques Derrida, *De la grammatologie,* Paris: Éditions de Minuit 1967, pp. 15–16/*Of Grammatology,* trans. Gayatri Chakravorty Spivak, Baltimore: Johns Hopkins University Press 1976, p. 6.

6. Ibid., p. 33/p. 19.

7. Jacques Derrida, in 'Philosophy and Communication: Round-table Discussion Between Ricoeur and Derrida', appendix to Leonard Lawlor, *Imagination and Chance: The Difference between the Thought of Ricoeur and Derrida,* Albany, NY: SUNY Press 1992, p. 158.

8. 'A thought of the trace can no more break with a transcendental phenomenlogy than be reduced to it.' (*De la grammatologie,* p. 91/*Of Grammatology,* p. 62.) For a discussion of the anti-relativism of Derrida's thought see my *Logics of Disintegration,* London: Verso 1987, pp. 4–11.

9. *Simulacres et Simulation,* p. 236/*Simulacra and Simulation,* p. 163.

10. Jacques Derrida, *Marges de la philosophie,* Paris: Éditions de Minuit 1972, p. 78/*Margins of Philosophy,* trans. Alan Bass, Sussex: Harvester Press 1982, p. 67.

11. Jacques Derrida, 'Comment ne pas parler', in *Psyché: inventions de l'autre,* Paris: Galilée 1987.

12. In *Marges de la philosophie,* pp. 367–93/*Margins of Philosophy,* pp. 309–30.

13. See J. L. Austin, *How to Do Things with Words,* Oxford: Oxford University Press 1962, esp. chs 1–4.

14. *Marges de la philosophie,* p. 389/*Margins of Philosophy,* p. 327.

15. Ibid., p. 385/p. 323.

16. *How to Do Things with Words,* p. 104.

17. *Marges de la philosophie,* pp. 384–5/*Margins of Philosophy,* p. 323.

18. Ibid., p. 385/p. 324.

19. *How to Do Things with Words,* p. 31 (emphasis added).

20. *Marges de la philosophie,* p. 390/*Margins of Philosophy,* p. 327 (emphasis added).

21. Ibid., p. 389/p. 327.

22. Ibid., p. 388/p. 326.

23. Ibid.

24. Ibid., p. 384/p. 322.

25. Hilary Putnam, *Meaning and the Moral Sciences*, London: Routledge 1978, p. 69.

26. See Charles Spinosa, 'Derrida and Heidegger: Iterability and *Ereignis*', in Hubert L. Dreyfus and Harrison Hall, eds, *Heidegger: A Critical Reader*, Oxford and Cambridge, MA: Blackwell 1992, esp. note 65, pp. 296–7.

27. *Marges de la philosophie*, p. 387/*Margins of Philosophy*, p. 325.

28. Ibid., p. 368/p. 310.

29. Ibid., p. 392/p. 329.

30. Stanley Cavell makes a similar point, in a rich discussion of the Austin–Derrida encounter which I read only after completing this essay, when he suggests that what 'Derrida is objecting to here is something he was already in flight from, the specter of the ordinary'. In Cavell's view, Derrida's gesture of demoting our everyday acts to perpetually uncertain 'effects' unhappily 'further[s] the air of implication that there is something more to do – a further reality to assess, a fullness of certainty to apply – than human beings can compass.' (See 'Seminar on "What Did Derrida Want of Austin?"', in Stanley Cavell, *Philosophical Passages: Wittgenstein, Emerson, Austin, Derrida* [The Bucknell Lectures in Literary Theory, vol. 12], Oxford: Blackwell 1994, p. 74; and the text under discussion, 'What Did Derrida Want of Austin,' in ibid. pp. 42–65.)

31. *Marges de la philosophie*, p. 384/*Margins of Philosophy*, p. 323.

32. *How to Do Things with Words*, p. 31.

33. Ibid., p. 41.

34. Ibid., p. 43.

35. Ibid., pp. 9–10.

36. 'Signature, évènement, contexte', in *Marges de la philosophie*, p. 389/'Signature, event, context', in *Margins of Philosophy*, p. 326. In his essay 'With the compliments of the author: reflections on Austin and Derrida' (*Critical Enquiry*, no. 8, Summer 1982), Stanley Fish presents an account of the relation between Austin and Derrida which accords with my own, in so far as Austin is not considered to be vulnerable to Derrida's deconstruction. However, Fish's reasons for arguing this are that Austin's theory is already 'Derridean' in its subordination of 'truth' to performative context, and in its constant undermining of its own categories and aims. In my view, this account is too charitable both to Austin and to Derrida. First, as Geoffrey Warnock has pointed out, the fact that – in Austin's words – 'The truth or falsity of a statement depends not merely on the meanings of words but on what act you were performing in what circumstances' (*How to Do Things with Words*, p. 144), does not entail that the assessment of truth or falsity falls away as an autonomous dimension in the determination of the 'happiness – or otherwise – of performatives' (see Warnock, *J.L. Austin*, London: Routledge 1989, pp. 133–45). Secondly, Fish's claim that Derrida 'thinks of a context as a structure of assumptions' (p. 708) presents us with a domesticated, 'pragmatized' Derrida, for whom semantic indeterminacy is merely a matter of degree, depending on the density of the assumptions governing any specific context of communication. It defuses the radical consequences of Derrida's 'dissymmetrical' inversion of success and failure, which would undermine even the (relative) stability of such 'assumptions'.

37. 'La mythologie blanche', in *Marges de la philosophie*, p. 261/'White Mythology', in *Margins of Philosophy*, p. 219.

38. Ibid., p. 267/p. 224.

39. Ibid., p. 308/p. 258.

40. Paul Ricoeur, *La métaphore vive*, Paris: Seuil 1975, p. 370/*The Rule of Metaphor*, trans. R. Czerny *et al.*, London: Routledge & Kegan Paul 1986, p. 291.

41. Ibid., p. 369/p. 290.

42. Ibid., p. 369/pp. 290–91.

43. I. A. Richards, *The Philosophy of Rhetoric*, New York: Oxford University Press 1965, p. 97.

44. See *La métaphore vive*, pp. 310–11, 368–9/*The Rule of Metaphor*, pp. 247–56, 290.

45. Ibid., p. 107/p. 81.

46. Ibid., pp. 374–84/pp. 259–303.

47. Paul Ricoeur, in 'Philosophy and Communication: Round-table Discussion between Ricoeur and Derrida', pp. 135–6.

48. Jacques Derrida, 'Le retrait de la métaphore', in *Psyché: inventions de l'autre*, p. 70/'The *retrait* of Metaphor', *Enclitic*, vol. 2, no. 2, Fall 1978, p. 13.

49. Ibid., p. 71/p. 14.

50. *Marges de la philosophie*, p. 261/Margins of Philosophy, p. 219 (emphasis added).

51. 'Le retrait de la métaphore', p. 79/'The *retrait* of Metaphor', p. 20.

52. *La métaphore vive*, p. 395/*The Rule of Metaphor*, p. 311.

53. Ibid., p. 396/p. 311.

54. Ibid., p. 374/p. 295.

55. 'Le retrait de la métaphore', p. 72/'The *retrait* of Metaphor', p. 14.

56. Ibid., p. 79/p. 21.

57. Ibid., p. 89/pp. 22–3.

58. Ibid., pp. 81–2/p. 23.

59. Ibid., p. 80/p. 21.

60. It may be objected that Derrida has increasingly challenged the unity of Heidegger's 'history of Being' in his later writings, further developing the argument of 'Le *retrait* de la métaphore'. For example, in *La carte postale*, he states: 'If the post (technology, position, "metaphysics") is announced at the "first" sending, then there is no longer *metaphysics*, etc. . . . nor even the *envoi*, but *envois* without destination.' (*La carte postale*, Paris: Flammarion 1980, pp. 73–4/*The Post Card: from Socrates to Freud and Beyond*, trans. Alan Bass, Chicago: University of Chicago Press 1987, pp. 65–6.) Similarly, in an interview from 1983 he asked: 'Does one have the right to speak of a – of *the* – Western metaphysics, of *its* language, of a single destiny or "sending forth of being", etc.?' ('An Interview with Jacques Derrida', in David Wood and Robert Bernasconi, eds, *Derrida and Différance*, Warwick University: Parousia Press 1985, p. 125.) However, Ricoeur's point is that whether one thinks of metaphysics as a unitary history or as an uncontainable dispersion triggered by an original 'withdrawal', a historically implausible disjunction between previous philosophy and this supposedly unprecedented thinking of metaphysics is still presupposed.

61. See, for example, Max Black's famous paper on 'Metaphor', where he writes: 'It was a simplification, again, to speak as if the implication-system of the metaphorical expression remains unaltered by the metaphorical statement. . . . If to call a man a wolf is to put him in a special light, we must not forget that the metaphor makes the wolf seem more human than he otherwise would.' (In *Models and Metaphors*, Ithaca, NY: Cornell University Press 1962, pp. 44–5). It is thus clear that Heidegger's claim that 'The metaphorical exists only within metaphysics', where it is viewed as a semantic transfer from the sensible to the intelligible (*The Principle of Reason*, trans. Reginald Lilly, Bloomington and Indianapolis: Indiana University Press 1991, p. 48) presupposes the substitution theory of metaphor. For Heidegger's counter-examples – which have deeply influenced Derrida, and which Heidegger uses to show that his own discourse is not metaphorical – rely simply on the suggestion that the tenor impacts on the vehicle. This is a suggestion which the interaction theory, but not the substitution theory, can readily accept. For example, in the 'Letter on Humanism' Heidegger states: 'The talk about the house of Being is no transfer of the image "house" to Being. But one day, we will, by thinking the essence of Being in an appropriate(ing) way . . . more readily be able to think what "house" and "to dwell" are.' ('Letter on Humanism', in David Krell, trans. and ed., *Basic Writings*, New York: Harper & Row 1977, pp. 236–7). It is surprising that David Wood, who knows both the analytical and continental literature on metaphor, should still not see that Heidegger's position depends on the equation of the *phenomenon* of metaphor with a particular *theory* of metaphor, as indeed does that of Derrida (see David Wood, 'Metaphor and Metaphysics', in *Philosophy at the Limit*, London: Hutchinson 1990, esp. pp. 36–7). As we have seen, there are independent reasons for assuming that talk of Being is neither literal nor metaphorical, but not all Heidegger's counter-examples are of such talk. He also suggests, for example, that Hölderlin's description of language as the 'flower of the mouth' should not be seen as metaphor (see 'On the Way to Language', in *On the Way to Language*, New York: Harper & Row 1971, p. 100).

62. *La métaphore vive*, p. 311/*The Rule of Metaphor*, p. 247.

63. Hans-Georg Gadamer, 'Anmerkungen zu dem Thema "Hegel und Heidegger"', in Hermann Braun and Manfred Riedel, eds, *Natur und Geschichte: Karl Löwith zum 70 Geburtstag*, Stuttgart, Berlin, Cologne, Mainz: W. Kohlhammer 1967, p. 130.

64. *La métaphore vive*, p. 387/*The Rule of Metaphor*, p. 306.

65. See Black, 'Metaphor', pp. 25–47. In his well-known essay 'What metaphors mean', Donald Davidson develops a series of objections to the interactionist account of metaphor associated with Richards and Black. Davidson's central contention is that metaphor cannot be understood in terms of the interplay between a 'literal' and a 'figurative' meaning: metaphor 'is something brought off by the imaginative employment of words and sentences and depends entirely on the ordinary meanings of those words and hence on the ordinary meanings of the sentences they comprise.' Davidson's reason for arguing thus is that 'No theory of metaphorical meaning or metaphorical truth can help to explain how metaphor works', whereas 'literal meaning and literal truth conditions can be assigned to words and sentences apart from particular contexts of use', and therefore have 'genuine explanatory power' (Davidson, 'What Metaphors Mean', in *Enquiries into Truth and Interpretation*, Oxford: Clarendon Press 1984, pp. 259, 247). However, I do not think these objections are damaging to Ricoeur's project, which is *not* one of using a notion of metaphorical meaning or truth to 'explain' metaphor. Rather, Ricoeur wants to draw ontological consequences from the fact that metaphors can be true, and Davidson does not want to deny that there may be 'such a thing as metaphorical truth' (p. 257). Indeed, Davidson's theory, in which metaphorical statements are 'false' in so far as truth conditions can be assigned to them, yet can reveal a truth (albeit psychologistically interpreted in terms of 'visions, thoughts, and feelings inspired by metaphor') for which such conditions cannot be assigned, seems fundamentally congruent with Ricoeur's account, in which metaphor is characterized by 'an "is not", itself implied in the impossible literal interpretation, but present in filigree in the metaphorical "is"' (*La métaphore vive*, p. 312/*The Rule of Metaphor*, p. 248).

66. *La métaphore vive*, p. 319/*The Rule of Metaphor*, p. 254.

67. Martin Heidegger, *Sein und Zeit*, Tübingen: Niemeyer 1927, p. 7/*Being and Time*, trans. John Macquarrie and Edward Robinson, Oxford: Blackwell 1978, pp. 26–7.

68. Ibid., p. 12/p. 33.

69. Derrida, 'Les fins de l'homme', in *Marges de la philosophie*, p. 150/'The Ends of Man', in *Margins of Philosophy*, pp. 125–6.

70. *Sein und Zeit*, p. 8 (section 2). The Macquarrie and Robinson translation has 'relatedness backward or forward', which misses the sense of temporal anticipation in '*Vor*bezogenheit'.

71. *Marges de la philosophie*, pp. 150–51/*Margins of Philosophy*, p. 126.

72. Ludwig Feuerbach, 'Über den "Anfang der Philosophie"', in Wilhelm Bolin and Friedrich Jodl, eds, *Sämtliche Werke*, 2nd edn, Stuttgart: Frommann-Holzboog 1956, vol. 2, p. 205.

73. Ibid., p. 206.

74. Ibid.

75. The main drawback of Lawrence Lawlor's otherwise informative book on the Derrida–Ricoeur debate is that it fails to see this ultimately self-defeating consequence of Derrida's position. Lawlor summarizes the opposing positions as follows: 'for Ricoeur mediation derives from immediacy, while for Derrida mediation precedes immediacy (presence)' (*Imagination and Chance*, p. 50). Apart from confirming the currency of the false equation of immediacy and presence which is one of the central concerns of this essay, there are a number of problems with this formulation. Firstly, Ricoeur does not *derive* mediation from immediacy, or think they can be collapsed together, as his account of language as suspended between incommunicability and the task of communication makes clear (see p. 101 above). Secondly, Lawlor does not see that to assert: 'for Derrida mediation itself is prior to presence or immediacy' (p. 124) not only reduces the immediate to an illusion but renders the concept of mediation incoherent, since there is nothing to *mediate*. The result is the self-defeating installation of a kind of Hegelianism, a reading of 'the logical structure of *différance* (of supplementarity, of mimicry, of the hymen, of the same) as relation not unity, a relation that, being none of the relata, establishes the relata out of itself' (ibid.). Even Hegel, however, never subordinates the immediate to mediation in such an unqualified way.

76. *De la grammatologie*, p. 16/*Of Grammatology*, p. 7.

77. Jacques Derrida, 'The Politics of Friendship', *The Journal of Philosophy*, vol. 45, 1988, pp. 632–44.

78. Ibid., p. 637.

79. Jacques Derrida, 'Afterword: Toward an Ethic of Discussion', in *Limited Inc.*, trans. S. Weber, Evanston, IL: Northwestern University Press 1988, p. 145.

80. Ibid., p. 146.

81. 'The Politics of Friendship', p. 637.

# Deconstruction and German Idealism: A Response to Rodolphe Gasché's *The Tain of the Mirror*

Proponents of deconstruction have often been faced with the problem of defining the originality of Derrida's work, by contrast with earlier episodes in the history of European philosophy. Particularly in the earlier years of Derrida's reception there were many enthusiasts ready to proclaim that deconstruction represented a radical break in the history of thought, echoing Derrida's own willingness at the time to suggest that 'all Western methods of analysis, explication, reading, or interpretation' have been produced within the 'greatest totality', that of 'logocentric metaphysics'.[1] Thus in 1973 Sarah Kofman asserted: 'Derrida does not address himself to the understanding, to ears accustomed to the paternal logos. He bursts the eardrums of such ears. Philosophizing with a hammer, like Nietzsche, he traduces logocentric philosophy which wishes to hear the voice of truth as close to itself as possible, in the sphere of intimacy.'[2] More recently Christopher Norris has made the typical claim: 'to think of deconstruction as a "method" is to pull it back into the orbit of those traditional concepts and categories which (as Derrida argues) have organised the discourse of Western reason from the time of its Greek inception', thereby implying that deconstruction properly lies outside this orbit.[3]

Yet even such a connoisseur of Derrida as David Wood has difficulty, when the chips are down, in defining deconstruction as anything other than the *continuation* of a well-established tradition in Western philosophy, perhaps even of *the* central post-Kantian tradition. At the end of his *Philosophy at the Limit*, Wood writes: 'The transformation of the philosophical project is arguably a perennial task, and the curling back of critique onto itself is something philosophy can neither prevent, nor finally come to terms with. This essential restlessness is a necessary limit to a historically dominant conception of the philosophical project.'[4] With this argument as backdrop, Wood tries to show that deconstruction is 'no arbitrary move, but one in which philosophy turns to consider, in the most serious way we know today, its own conditions of possibility'.[5] But he is also aware that the 'historically dominant' conception of philosophy which this self-scrutiny challenges has been on the defensive for at least two hundred years. Indeed: 'Derrida has been influenced by a tradition of thinkers, which would include Kant, Hegel, Marx, Nietzsche, Husserl and Heidegger . . . for whom the theme of the end of metaphysics has been a central concern.'[6] Furthermore, as Wood stresses, 'the uncovering of relations, principles, concepts, etc., that we ordinarily take for granted is a classic philosophical activity',[7] so that his defence of deconstruction seems ultimately to amount to no more than the claim that deconstruction represents the most intensely self-reflexive form of contemporary philosophical activity. At the end of one essay on Derrida, he remarks that 'Philosophy on the move is the only possible transgression of metaphysics. There is no other place to go.'[8]

These issues have acquired increasing political importance in recent years, because of the way in which deconstruction has been enlisted by certain versions of postmodernist theory to mount a full-scale assault on the dualistic and hierarchical structures which are assumed to be essential to philosophical reason. If Derrida's work is in some sense, however tenuous, qualitatively distinct from the corpus of Western philosophy, then it can legitimately be mobilized for such a purpose. However, if Wood is right, then a deconstruction which abandoned its claims to continuity with the philosophical tradition would also lose the capacities which distinguish critique from sheer denunciation. But unfortunately, Wood's more sober account of the philosophical lineage of deconstruction fails for the most part to highlight the historical intertwining of power and reason as a significant issue for deconstruction at all. Wood often seems to treat reflexivity as a form of *l'art pour l'art*, and thus teeters on the brink of political complacency.

It is in this context that the work of Rodolphe Gasché acquires a distinctive importance. For Gasché's writings, and in particular his book *The Tain of the Mirror*, are widely respected as the most compelling defence of the specifically philosophical credentials of Derrida's thought, albeit a defence which tends to repress the textually playful and disruptive elements of deconstruction.[9] Gasché argues forcefully that the claim that locating deconstruction in the history of philosophical thought would defuse its 'alterity and explosive potential' ends up 'idealizing its operations', and thereby 'flattens it and renders it indifferent'.[10] In particular, Derrida's work does not legitimate a privileging of 'literature', and of a certain 'deconstructive' discourse of literary criticism over philosophy, on the pretext that the self-referentiality of 'literature', its sensitivity towards its own textuality, exposes the naive orientation of philosophy towards presence and truth. On the contrary, for Gasché this very characterization of literariness relies on 'the model of a conscious subjectivity, that is, of a self-reflexive presence',[11] and in fact represents no more than an intensified prolongation of New Critical aestheticism. Seeking to stem this tide, Gasché argues that 'deconstruction in the first place represents a critique of reflexivity and specularity.

It is the lack of awareness of this essential feature of deconstruction that has caused the easy accommodation of deconstruction by contemporary American criticism.'[12] Accordingly, he suggests, the full significance of deconstruction can be grasped only when the role of the concept of reflection in modern European philosophy is appreciated in its historical complexity. Yet at the same time Gasché also insists: 'strictly speaking, deconstruction can no longer be situated within a history of ideas and the continuum of philosophical thought on which such a history rests'.[13] Indeed, Derrida's work makes possible a radical dismantling of philosophy which goes beyond the mere intensification of reflexivity.

## The Problem of Reflection

One of the central aims of Gasché's major work on deconstruction, *The Tain of the Mirror*, is thus to correct defects in Derrida's reception by thoroughly exploring the relation between Derrida's work and the moment in European thought when the problems of specularity and reflection were explored with the greatest inventiveness and intensity, namely that of German Idealism. In Gasché's account, reflection is the central category of the modern philosophy of subjectivity, which first emerges with Descartes: 'from the moment it became the chief methodological concept for Cartesian thought, it has signified the turning away from any straightforward consideration of objects and the immediacy of such an experience towards a consideration of the very experience in which objects are given'.[14] Subsequently, in Kant's philosophy, this activity was given an even more ambitious role. In the form of 'transcendental reflection' its task was now to explore the subjective dimension in which the conditions of possibility of all knowledge are located. The basic problem to which this enterprise gives rise, however, is that – through the act of reflection – the subject radically separates itself from, and opposes itself to, the very domain of objects which its transcendental activity is supposed to constitute. Thus, for Kant's successors, the methodology of reflection was seen as contradicting its own aim – that of turning back on experience, and comprehending the fundamental polarity of subject and object which structures and subtends it.

In more metaphorical terms, the main difficulty for the reflective standpoint is posed by the task of establishing the fundamental identity of the two poles of the reflective relationship, of knower and known. If what is mirrored in the other is to be recognized as ultimately identical with the knowing subject, then some criterion of identification must be available *prior* to the process of reflection: no amount of gazing into a mirror will – *per se* – inform the viewer that what is perceived is an image of herself. As

Gasché puts the issue, the mirror must mirror its own process of reflecting in order for the identity of reflector and reflected to be established.[15] In his account, the thought of Fichte, Schelling and the Jena Romantics attempts in various ways to deal with this problem, but ultimately remains entangled in the dualisms of reflection. It is only with the work of Hegel that a viable resolution is found.

As Gasché explains, by introducing the notion of 'absolute reflection' or 'speculation' Hegel is able to escape the difficulties which emerge when reflection is seen as arising from one pole of the reflective relation, whether subjective or objective, or indeed from both taken together. Thus:

> Hegel's criticism of the metaphysics of reflection is guided by the notion of totality. If reflection is an operation produced *between* a figure and its image in the mirror, *between* a subject and an object, then the poles or extremes of the process of reflection are no longer the essential part of that process but its mean, or the whole of all the relations and of the process between them. The medium in which reflection takes place, this middle which splits into opposed poles and from which they borrow their meaning, becomes the real subject of reflection.[16]

Of course, Gasché does not mean to imply that there can be no further advance of thought beyond Hegel, only that any 'post-Hegelian' thought must avoid lapsing back into a naive one-sidedness which Hegel definitively overcame:

> if one is to address the principal deficiencies of the theories of subjectivity, of consciousness and self-consciousness – that is, of reflection – recourse to Hegel's speculative and dialectical solution is unavoidable . . . yet it would be erroneous to believe that the inevitable pathway through Hegel means that one has no choice but to accept the Hegelian solution. It is to affirm, for the moment only, and foremost, that all criticism of reflection . . . must take its standards from the Hegelian project.[17]

Thus the presentation of Hegel's achievement is intended to function only as a prelude to the discussion of Derrida, where 'the very successfulness of successful philosophical solutions to the aporias of reflection'[18] will be challenged.

But how can success be unsuccessful? In other words, what could possibly function as the limit or blind spot of Hegelian absolute reflection, whose very aim is to overcome all oppositions between inside and outside, between a 'before' and beyond' of the limit, between opacity and transparency? This is the central problem with which Gasché wrestles in the second half of his book.

## Derrida beyond Hegel?

For Gasché, the limit of philosophical thought in general, including that of Hegel, is determined by the fact that philosophy cannot account for its own 'space of inscription', and that the process of inscription gives rise to inconsistencies which the essentially idealizing movement of philosophical thought suppresses:

> All the gestures of philosophy – reflection and transcendentalization, all the themes of philosophy, but primarily those of subjectivity, transcendentality, freedom, origin, truth, presence – are impossible without the differences and discrepancies that permeate philosophical texts. Yet these same disparities also limit the scope of these gestures and of the purity and coherence of the philosophical concepts or themes. Deconstruction is an attempt to account for these various and essentially heterogeneous aporias and discursive inequalities with what I have called infrastructures.[19]

As examples of 'infrastructures' Gasché cites '*différance*', 'supplementarity', 'iterability', and other key Derridean terms, which together 'represent the systematic exploration of . . . the space of inscription'.[20]

Gasché is careful to emphasize, however, that the elusive working of the infrastructures does not simply generate the discrepancies which permeate philosophical texts, thereby undermining the project of idealization, the search for a pure coherence of truth and meaning. At the same time, they render this project *possible*. To put the argument at its simplest: without supplementarity and iterability there could be no self-returning movement of reflection, since reflection can be nothing other than a repetition of experience which seeks to make good what is lacking in the apparent plenitude of its immediacy. Yet at the same time supplementarity and iterability undermine the self-coincidence for which reflection strives, marking the supposedly original identity which is recovered as always already a repetition. Accordingly, Gasché argues, if reflexivity is understood as the central principle of any supposedly self-grounding philosophical system, then deconstruction 'is a meditation on the *general system*, or on what makes systematicity as such both necessary and impossible'.[21] Against more 'literary' versions of deconstruction – which, in his view, overemphasize the moment of disruption – Gasché repeatedly stresses that Derrida's work seeks to straddle both the impossibility *and* the necessity of systematizing thought.

Yet Gasché's own approach immediately poses the following problem: how can the chain of 'infrastructures' play its ambivalent role without occupying a 'transcendental' position in relation to the structure of the philosophical text, thereby reinstating a dualism of condition and conditioned which would be vulnerable from the standpoint of Hegelian speculation? It should be noted that the fact that the infrastructures function simultaneously as conditions of possibility *and* conditions of impossibility does not in itself put their transcendental status into question, for even Kant's categories can be said to function in this way. The Kantian categories specify transcendental conditions of the experience of objects, if by this we mean knowledge of 'appearances'. But they can also be seen as embodying conditions of the 'impossibility' of experience, if we insist that experience in the emphatic sense must involve an encounter with the world as it ultimately is, not with one aspect of a reality of which the other aspect is constitutively inaccessible. Thus Hegel asserts against Kant, in the shorter *Logic*: 'It argues an utter want of consistency to say, on the one hand, that the understanding only knows phenomena, and, on the other, assert the absolute character of this knowledge, by such statements as "Cognition can go no further".'[22] However, the fact that it is precisely Hegel who identifies all transcendental structures as conditions of possibility *and* impossibility in this way points to a central philosophical problem which Gasché will be forced to confront in his book.

In the second and third parts of *The Tain of the Mirror* Gasché sometimes characterizes the infrastructures as 'quasi-transcendentals' because of their dual enabling/disabling role.[23] But often he is less guarded, referring to '*structure* in Derrida', for example, as 'the transcendental opening that represents the condition of possibility of the minor structures and the accidents that they suffer'.[24] Indeed, Gasché has a tendency simply to reverse the ferocious demolition of the transcendental standpoint undertaken in the first part of the book, and to play the transcendental card *against* Hegelian speculation. Thus he writes at one point, without qualification:

> The mark's *transcendental* opening withdraws in its representation, making manifest the limits of *speculative Aufhebung*, which is incapable of accounting for the re-mark *as such*, not only because this infrastructure cannot be phenomenologized and experienced, but also because at least one representation of it – that is, at least one figure in which it disappears – is left unaccounted for. This last figure is ultimately the figure of *Aufhebung* itself.[25]

The problem with this manoeuvre, of course, is that every infrastructure which is shifted into the position of a 'condition of possibility' of speculation opens up a duality of condition and conditioned which is in its turn ripe for the speculative overcoming endorsed in the first part of *The Tain of the Mirror*. For example, Gasché suggests that the infrastructures 'to some extent continue Husserl's (and Heidegger's) research into the *a prioris* of meaning (including that of Being)'.[26] Yet he then goes on to claim that 'the infrastructures question the very *differences* between the *a priori* and the world they open'.[27] What Gasché is aiming for is suggested by his claim that the infrastructures are neither 'empirical *nor* transcendental' but, rather, 'instances of an intermediary discourse, concerned with a middle in which the differends are suspended and preserved, but which is not simply a dialectical middle'.[28] Yet he is unable adequately to explain why this middle is *not* dialectical, and how it escapes the Hegelian sublation. Indeed, as this and many other passages demonstrate, Gasché is ultimately driven to the expedient of asseveration: infrastructures suspend and preserve, but they are not 'dialectical'; they have 'a structure and function similar to transcendentals without actually being one'.[29] In consequence, his repeated reference to the '*quasi*-transcendental' status of the infrastructures seems to be more an index of philosophical embarrassment than a genuine solution. For, as an exponent of deconstruction must be the first to be aware, it is simply not possible to prevent the kind of semantic 'contamination' which would suck the infrastructures back into an unequivocally transcendental function – or at least into a role as equivocal as that of any other transcendental item.

Conversely, however, if Gasché were to insist that his exposition has defined an 'other' resistant to speculative appropriation, then he would have to explain why this does not detract from Hegel's success in the original context of German Idealism. For on Gasché's own account, it looks as though Hegel is relying on the possibility of a reflexive self-return to support his speculative solution. For example, Gasché concludes his chapter on Hegel by announcing: 'Absolute reflection is the full exposition of all the logically possible moments of the *logos*, a process which is completed as soon as the *logos* is folded back into itself.'[30] However, he does not ask what this 'folding back into itself' could consist in, if not precisely in an achieved self-coincidence. This self-coincidence must, in addition, *know itself* as such, for if it were known only from an *external* standpoint, the 'full exposition' of the moments would not have been completed. But how can this conception be defended – even temporarily – against Gasché's later claim that the 'arche-trace' is that which 'prevents a self from being self'?[31] And why does not the notion of the 'medium in which reflection takes place' as the 'real subject of reflection' simply displace the original problem, without doing anything to resolve it?

## The Limits of Reflection in German Idealism

In general, it seems that Gasché's historically indexed defence of Hegel relies on the assumption that Hegel's predecessors were deluded by a naive methodology of reflection, which conflicted with their totalizing ambitions. But there now exists a mass of scholarship which suggests the contrary – namely, that thinkers such as Fichte, Novalis and Schelling were concerned precisely with what they saw as an intrinsic, irresoluble conflict between reflection and totalization. To put it at its simplest: these thinkers became aware that the return-into-self of reflection requires that the self be *identified* as that which is to be returned to. But since – proto-deconstructively – they were also aware that there can be no identity without difference, a detour via the other (the Fichtean 'not-I') proved necessary to the supposedly absolute identity of the 'I'. This contradiction had already become the basic motor of Fichte's philosophy by the time he came to give the lectures known as the *Wissenschaftslehre nova methodo* in 1798–9.[32] It seems barely to differ from Gasché's claim that 'the arche-trace must be understood as the fold of an irreducible "bending-back", as a minimal (self-)difference within (self-)identity, which secures selfhood as self-presence through the detour of oneself (as Other) to oneself'.[33]

It may well have been a discomfiting sense of the proximity of Idealist concerns which led Gasché to treat Walter Schulz's classic essay on these issues so peremptorily and dismissively. In 'Das Problem der absoluten Reflexion' Schulz argues that a deep dilemma confronts the project of German Idealism with respect to its conception of the absolute, a conception which emerges from consideration of the unique structure of self-consciousness. Far from functioning as a stable ground, Schulz suggests, 'Absolute subjectivity can in no way be conceptually grasped, because it eludes every attempt to pin it down. Being underivable from anything else, it is in itself its own self-transcending, in other words it is the self-presupposing capacity to posit itself endlessly ever anew.'[34] Absolute subjectivity, on this account, bears a striking resemblance to those conditions of simultaneous possibility and impossibility which are central to *The Tain of the Mirror*'s account of deconstruction. For it generates an antinomy which Schulz describes in the following way:

> The *thesis* of this antinomy maintains: there is nothing in the domain of entities on the basis of which absolute subjectivity could be comprehended and derived; thus it must be the principle from which all worldly being is constructible and comprehensible. – The *antithesis* maintains, on the contrary: absolute subjectivity cannot be determined in itself; so that it is impossible to bring it into play as the principle of an intelligible construction of what is.[35]

The problem highlighted here could be summarized in the contention that in so far as the absolute is *absolute*, it cannot even function as an ultimate principle, for in order for it to do so it would have to be determined in some way, even if only *as* such a principle.

In Schulz's account, the typical response of the later Fichte and Schelling to this problem consists in an internal 'doubling' of the absolute, which places the 'pure' absolute, understood as the divine, beyond conceptual determination. Thus, in the later versions of his *Wissenschaftslehre*

Fichte describes the absolute knowledge on which he had formerly grounded his system as merely a translucent image [*Bild*] of the infinite divine life;[36] while Schelling argues from 1809 onwards that 'God contains himself in an inner basis of his existence, which, to this extent, precedes him as to his existence, but similarly God is prior to the basis as this basis, as such, could not be if God did not exist in actuality.'[37] Significantly, Gasché also finds himself struggling with the theory of an 'originary doubling' in the second part of *The Tain of the Mirror*: 'Such a theory must conceive of an *a priori*, and from the start irreducible, double, a "double rootedness", of a duplication that constitutes the simple, and only within which it can emerge as a simplicity.'[38] The difference would be that whereas Gasché writes incoherently of a *constitution* of the simple – incoherently, because the idea of constitution contradicts the very concept of the simple – the later Fichte and Schelling will try to think the simultaneity of primordial simplicity *and* primordial duality.

It is also important to note that, as Schulz emphasizes, Hegel was unable to escape this problem, despite his efforts to identify fully the external contingency of nature and history and the inner necessity of spirit. Hegel:

> declares on the one hand that absolute spirit is already complete in itself, and on the other hand also maintains that this absoluteness must constantly demonstrate itself to be in-and-for-itself through the process of its circular positing. In sum, the paradoxical dialectic of the circular movement consists in the fact that the circle, which is never completed and yet always already at its end, is the movement which posits the dissolution of everything fixed as the only constant.[39]

Taking a cue from Schulz, one can detect Hegel's unease with his own position at the end of the *Science of Logic*, where he writes:

> hence it may indeed be said that every beginning must be made with the absolute, just as all advance is merely the exposition of it, in so far as its in-itself is the notion. But because the absolute is at first only in-itself it equally is *not* the absolute, nor the posited notion, and also not the idea; for what characterizes these is precisely the fact that in them the *in-itself* is only an abstract, one-sided moment. Hence the advance is not a kind of superfluity; this it would be if that with which the beginning is made were in truth already the absolute. . . . Only in its consummation is it the absolute.[40]

The obvious query which can be raised at this point (and this is the later Schelling's question to Hegel) is: how can the absolute *become*? Is not submission to a condition of development or emergence inconsistent with the very concept of the absolute?[41] We could also ask in the present context: in what sense is this *not* the problem which the theory of infrastructures is meant to address? In other words, in what sense is Derrida's deconstruction of the philosophy of reflection, as Gasché presents it, qualitatively distinct from the explorations of the antinomies of reflection to be found in German Idealism itself?

This philosophical question highlights the fact that Gasché operates with an extremely trite historical account of Hegel's relation to his predecessors, one whose outline was first made canonical by Hegel himself in his lectures on the history of philosophy.[42] Gasché recounts an all too familiar story in which 'the transcendental science (of Kant and Fichte) and the science of Nature (of Schelling)' are readily synthesized by Hegel in his concept of an 'absolute totality'.[43] But as Gasché, with his extensive knowledge of recent German philosophy, must surely know, this construal of events has been washed away by a vast wave of scholarship over the last forty years. In an essay on Hegel and Hölderlin dating from 1970, for example, Dieter Henrich could already assume that 'it has long been clear that the path from Kant to Hegel cannot be represented as an ascent which leads, step by step, to higher insight'.[44] And more recently, Rolf-Peter Horstmann has written:

> The efforts of the more recent research on Idealism, at least, point unambiguously toward the destruction of the picture, first proposed to the world by Hegel himself, of a homogeneous process of development leading from Fichte to Hegel. This destruction has gone so far that . . . [one colleague] could declare without fear of contradiction, in a report on Fichte research which appeared some time ago, that to accept the thesis derived from Hegel would be 'today . . . a confession of professional incompetence'.[45]

In light of these comments, Gasché's historical account of the problem of 'reflection' must be considered tendentious, to say the least. Perhaps it is time to look more closely at the dynamics of German Idealism.


## Jacobi and the History of German Idealism

In our latest images of the history of German Idealism, the figure of Friedrich Jacobi has come to play an increasingly central role, as Horstmann's recent book *Die Grenzen der Vernunft*, which presents a *vue d'ensemble* of Idealism from the standpoint of current German scholarship, testifies.[46] Jacobi is now seen as so significant because in the course of the 'Pantheism Dispute', which pitted him against the leading thinkers of the German Enlightenment, including Kant, Mendelssohn and Herder, he raised in a pathbreaking form the question of the *intrinsic* limits of philosophical system and philosophical explanation.[47] Indeed, it would be no exaggeration to claim that Jacobi develops a strategy, a 'double game' with the history of philosophy, which already anticipates later disman-tlings of metaphysics, from Nietzsche to Heidegger and Derrida. For on the one hand Jacobi maintains that, to the extent that one pursues the philosophical project of exhaustive explanation, which he sees as reaching its first culmination in Spinoza's system, one will end with a denial of those fundamental, undemonstrable truths, such as the truth of our own free agency, which are constitutive of the human world. On the other hand he can see no *rationally compelling* grounds for resisting the deter-ministic dynamic of the philosophical project, once one has accepted that comprehensive explanation is its central intellectual imperative (and how could one conclude otherwise?). Jacobi's strategy must, therefore, be to show that philosophical explanation, taken to its limit, leads to results which are *existentially* incoherent, and thus puts itself in question. As he writes: 'The heart of the matter is that, out of fatalism, I draw a conclusion immediately opposed to fatalism, and to everything which is connected with it.'[48]

Of course, such a position can be reached only by 'going through' meta-physics, not by circumventing it in a naive appeal to common sense, and this clearly puts Jacobi in a profoundly ambivalent relation to his target. In his *Letters on the Doctrine of Spinoza* (1785) he emphasizes that he has never been able to gain the advantage over Spinoza as far as philosophical argument is concerned, or 'with pure metaphysics'.[49] As he puts it: 'I love Spinoza because, more than any other philosopher, he has brought me to the complete conviction that certain things cannot be deduced: one must not close one's eyes before them, but simply accept them as one finds them.'[50] Thus what gives Jacobi's position its sophistication is his view that the transition to '*Glaube*' (belief or faith) can occur only as a dialec-tical reversal – or what he famously describes as a 'salto mortale' – at the outer limit of the project of explanation.[51]

Furthermore, since, by means of this leap, we enter a domain which is not susceptible to explanatory conceptualization, the dimension of *Glaube* cannot be in direct *competition* with philosophy: the leap in some sense requires the continued existence of metaphysics as its springboard. This is why Jacobi appeared to his contemporaries as the exponent of a unique 'double theory', as Dieter Henrich has termed it, which both expounds a compelling version of Spinozism and invokes dimensions of experience which seem to dissolve under the pressure of Spinozist explanatory rigour, yet also threaten to undermine it.[52] For Jacobi, 'Every path of demon-stration leads to fatalism.'[53] He therefore declares: 'the greatest achievement of the seeker is to disclose and reveal being [*Dasein*]. . . . Explanation is only his means, a path to the goal, the immediate and never the ultimate aim.'[54] Conversely, there must be something sheerly given to provide the leverage for explanation even to begin, and the dimension of

*Glaube* therefore haunts the philosophical enterprise as it seeks to establish a rationally self-supporting, comprehensive system.

This basic pattern of Jacobi's thinking informs his most famous text, *On the Doctrine of Spinoza*, but it also appears in perhaps even more dramatic guise in the long open letter he wrote to Fichte in 1799. Here Jacobi maintains that 'All human beings, in so far as they strive for knowledge, set up . . . pure philosophy as their ultimate goal, even without knowing it; for human beings know only in so far as they conceptualize [*begreifen*], and they conceptualize only in so far as – transforming subject matter into mere form – they make the form their subject matter, and their subject matter into nothing.'[55] Furthermore – and here Jacobi agrees with Fichte – the principle of such a pure philosophy can only be the 'I':

> A science which has itself alone as object and no content besides, is a science in itself [*eine Wissenschaft an sich*]. The I is a science in itself, and indeed the only one. It knows itself, and it would be contrary to its concept to know or perceive something outside itself. . . .[56]

However, the collusion between what Jacobi calls his '*Unphilosophie*' and Fichte's '*Alleinphilosophie*' lasts only up to the point when Fichte drives philosophy up against its immanent limit. As Jacobi states: 'Both of us want, with equal seriousness and zeal, that the science of knowing . . . should become complete; only with the difference that *you* want it so that the ground of all truth can show itself in the science of knowing; whereas I want the completion, so that this ground can be revealed: the *true itself* [*das Wahre selbst*] is necessarily outside it.'[57]

This conception of the true as breaking through at the point where the thinker runs up against the limit produced by the subjectivized, self-reflexive enclosure of philosophical knowledge already suggests anticipatory affinities with deconstruction. One might, of course, object that Derrida would not refer to what glimmers through the fractures of metaphysical thinking as 'the true' – for him, this concept is itself too metaphysically freighted. However, Jacobi makes clear that what he means by the true cannot be reduced to something *known*: 'All philosophers were trying to get behind the form of the thing, to the thing itself, behind truth, to the true: they wanted to *know* the true – not *knowing* that, if the true could be *known* by human beings, it would necessarily cease being the true, and become . . . a mere creature of human invention.'[58] Thus, for Jacobi, what is 'beyond' metaphysics is conceptually inaccessible, and therefore constantly liable to be dismissed as a delusion: 'Truly, my dear Fichte, it would not put me out . . . if you wished to describe as chimericalism [*Chimärismus*] what I oppose to the idealism which I attack as *Nihilism* – I have displayed my *un*-knowing [*Nicht*-Wissen] in all my writings.'[59] One is again reminded of Derrida's constant exposure of the fragility of his own position, and his warnings against the belief that we can simply step 'beyond' metaphysics into a new form of theory.

In his neglect of the problematic opened up by Jacobi, Gasché simply follows Hegel, who tries to demolish Jacobi's position in *Faith and Knowledge*, and in Chapter 5 of the *Encyclopaedia Logic* ('Third Attitude of Thought to Objectivity: Immediate or Intuitive Knowledge'). In the latter text Hegel bluntly denies the duality of belief and knowledge, arguing that 'it is unquestionably a fact of experience, firstly, that what we believe is in our consciousness – which implies that we *know about it*; and secondly, that this belief is a certainty in our consciousness – which implies that we *know* it'.[60] In the earlier *Faith and Knowledge*, however, Hegel attacks this dualism from another angle, arguing against the fracture between finite and infinite which is implied by Jacobi's reading of Spinoza. In one extraordinary passage he writes: 'Attached to the ring, which it offers as a symbol of Reason, there is a piece of skin from the hand that offers it; and if Reason is scientific connection, and has to do with concepts, we can very well do without that piece of skin.'[61] Despite Hegel's claim, it now seems clear, with two hundred years of hindsight, that the ring of reason cannot be brought so cleanly off the human finger, and that this piece of skin – whether as memento, wound, offering or castration – has been a catalyst and irritant at the core of European philosophy ever since. An important spur to the rewriting of the history of German Idealism has been the appreciation that it was Schelling, rather than Hegel, who first struggled to come to terms with the implications of this essential contamination of reason, without abandoning reason's legitimate claims.[62]

Not surprisingly, therefore, Schelling has a more complex relation to Jacobi than does Hegel. In his lecture series *On the History of Modern Philosophy* he stresses that 'Jacobi had the clearest insight into the fact that rational systems do not really explain anything in the last analysis.'[63] Schelling's criticisms thus concern only the fact that Jacobi 'saw no other possibility of knowledge outside that of negative knowledge. . . . The only knowledge left to him in relation to his substantial knowledge was to close his eyes in the face of it, to want to know nothing about it.'[64] Accordingly, Schelling's aim is to find a more intricate account of the belief/knowledge relation, which can do justice to both sides without overcoming the distinction speculatively in favour of knowledge, as Hegel tends to do. Some inkling of the difficulty of this task, which defines Schelling's philosophy from the *Philosophical Inquiries into the Nature of Human Freedom* onwards, can perhaps be conveyed by the following quotation:

But if, in relation to such an opposition, both belief and knowledge are supposed to be *in* philosophy, are supposed to be philosophical (and Jacobi certainly made a determined claim, despite his doctrine of non-knowledge, that he had *also* established a philosophical doctrine), then both belief and knowledge had to be explained philosophically. But a system that asserted a philosophical knowledge and a belief that was *totally opposed to philosophical knowledge*, yet was likewise philosophical, would have, in order even only *formally* to exist, to be the system of a philosophical, i.e. philosophically grasped, dualism.[65]


## *Différance* and Idealization

'A belief that was *totally opposed to philosophical knowledge*, yet . . . likewise philosophical' – again the anticipation of the liminal games of deconstruction is remarkable. Indeed, in the remainder of this essay I wish to show that Schelling – in the most intense and imaginative phases of his work – was grappling with issues which are often nowadays located on the terrain of deconstruction. Furthermore, he also struggled with the dilemmas which deconstruction itself confronts in seeking to articulate itself as a quasi-theoretical position – dilemmas which are particularly apparent in *The Tain of the Mirror*.

The central problem here concerns how Gasché, given his conception of the infrastructures, can provide any account of the emergence of relatively *stable* differences which do not immediately differ from themselves and therefore collapse, proving unable to function as the condition of the identities and relations which constitute a *world*. In other words, given that the infrastructures are 'the conditions of possibility (and impossibility) of the conceptual differences as well as discursive inequalities',[66] why do not these contradictory conditions immediately cancel each other, and thus implode? This question is rendered all the more urgent by Gasché's argument that the 'purification and idealization' of the infrastructures is impossible, because 'the function represented by each infrastructure also applies to itself, so that it remains essentially dislocated from itself'.[67] For if an infrastructure such as '*différance*' is internally dislocated, non-self-identical, how can it function as the 'productive and primordial constituting causality, as one would say in traditional philosophy, of differends and differences',[68] which suggests that in some sense it is *beyond* such differences? Conversely, if *différance* possesses the minimal identity of a 'causality', it must be an 'effect' of itself (since all identity is an 'effect' of *différance*), and therefore exemplify precisely the type of reflexively self-constituting process which Gasché wishes to undermine. It seems that if Gasché is to avoid this outcome, any infrastructure which he nominates for a transcendental role will itself be instantly sucked back down into the vortex of the infrastructures. Of course, Gasché acknowledges this – but he does not fully take on board its consequences for what he terms the 'explicatory power of inscription'.[69]

A number of contemporary philosophers who have written on transcendental arguments have suggested that such arguments typically begin from some indubitable fact about experience, then try to show that this feature would not be possible without a richer complex of features which function as its non-empirical preconditions. In the example given by Charles Taylor, commenting on Merleau-Ponty, the intrinsically orientated character of our perceptual experience points to that fact that such experience *must* be that of an embodied agent.[70] In Gasché's case the fundamental given feature seems to be the internal limit encountered by processes of idealization. As Gasché puts it: 'deconstruction is . . . the attempt to account for the heterogeneity constitutive of the philosophical discourse'.[71] Yet the infrastructures do not so much enrich our picture of the preconditions of such heterogeneity, and thus enhance our comprehension of its necessity, as offer weak redescriptions of it – weak, because the operation of the infrastructures is less complex than the process it is meant to account for. Furthermore, by feeding the infrastructures back into this process, Gasché himself seems to deny that they can be anything other than such redescriptions. And it is not clear why this feeding back does not threaten to destroy the 'indubitable fact' which even Gasché's version of transcendental argumentation must rely on – namely, heterogeneity itself.[72]

A similar issue recurs throughout Derrida's own work. For an attentive reader must surely wonder why the notion of pure 'presence', supposedly pursued by metaphysics, must be considered as illusory or factitious, whereas the notion of a pure iterability or *différance* is not – indeed, it must in some sense be considered as 'foundational'. In *Of Grammatology* Derrida writes: 'The literal [*propre*] meaning does not exist, its "appearance" is a necessary function – one which must be analyzed as such – in the system of differences and metaphors.'[73] But since, as Derrida stresses, our interpretative activities necessarily presuppose a notion of literal meaning, and since this notion *can* be acknowledged within philosophy as an orientating though *unattainable* ideal, why should not the notion of what Derrida terms the '*pure* movement which produces difference'[74] be considered merely as the contrary pole of idealization, as the adjective 'pure' implies? Does not the assumption that there is a 'system' of some kind which gives rise to the illusion of literalness or presence itself involve a curious literalism? This question can be put in another way. Given that presence – as well as absence – are everyday features of our world, just as the grasping of meaning – as well as opacity and incomprehension – are features of our linguistic encounters, why should we not regard the play of *différance*, or the logic of supplementarity, as itself a hypostatization of *one aspect* of our experience which is no less deceptive than the ideal of absolute presence? Derrida states aphoristically that 'signification is formed only within the hollow of *différance*'.[75] One could equally claim that *différance* is the shadow of signification.

If it were taken as definitive, this inversion of Derrida would encapsulate the views of a thinker such as Jürgen Habermas, who suggests that difference and dissension can occur only against an implicit background of agreement, which in turn relies on processes of idealization which are always-already in train. Yet the implication of this view for agreement concerning truth, which Habermas considers as also *securing* truth under the ideal communicative conditions which figure as a telos internal to language, is that dissension and misunderstanding could in principle be eliminated – and this implication itself has paradoxical consequences. For, as Albrecht Wellmer has recently inquired, how could an 'ideal speech situation' be realized without undermining the very conditions of communication which it is intended to bring to transparency? Wellmer appeals specifically to Derrida in formulating his claim that 'Insofar as the idea of the ideal communication community includes the negation of the conditions of finite human communication . . . it implies the negation of the natural and historical conditions of human life, of finite human existence . . . ideal communication would be the death of communication.'[76] Thus a decisive philosophical issue is undoubtedly being highlighted in Gasché's account of the infrastructures as blocks to idealization, but Gasché's way of developing this account simply falls into an incoherence complementary to that of the 'ideal speech situation'. This is where Schelling's thinking in the 'Ages of the World' acquires its relevance.

## Schelling's 'Ages of the World'

Schelling's three drafts for the project he termed the 'Ages of the World' [*Die Weltalter*], written between 1811 and 1814, begin by describing an unresolvable conflict within a basic polarity which embraces many of the oppositions discussed so far: difference and identity, singularity and universality, materiality and ideality, textuality and meaning. In deconstructive terms, Schelling's fundamental suggestion is that any attempt to pin down the ideality of a truth or meaning will quickly fall prey to the material play of the signifying medium from which it seeks to abstract. In Schelling's more mythopoetically vivid language, this 'logic of supplementarity' is described as a struggle between two primordial 'wills' – in other words, pure potentialities for beginning, for bringing into being. The first of these, which he calls the 'will which wills nothing', is captured by the gravitational pull of a second will, which crystallizes within the absolute featurelessness of the first, and which Schelling terms the 'determinate will which wills something'.[77] This second will can be understood as the longing of the first will simply to *be*, since – for Schelling – 'existence is ownness, is separation [*Existenz ist Eigenheit, ist Absonderung*]'.[78] However, the transparent pure will and the opaque determinate will – or what Schelling frequently terms '*das Seyende*' and '*das Seyn*' – are also envisioned as the two poles of a fundamental proto-ontological tension, or – in language which Schelling borrows from Boehme – as an expansive, communicative 'love' and an involuted, self-consuming 'anger'.

In Schellings's first draft of the *Weltalter*, the contractive will 'captures' the pure will and transforms it from something outflowing into something 'suffering, enclosed, latent'.[79] In the more prosaic terms of the theory of predication which Schelling develops most clearly in the third *Weltalter* draft, there exists a basic tension between the singularity of the subject and the universality of the predicate, each of which wishes to be the 'whole of being'. Again, Schelling portrays the conflict which emerges between the 'expansive, self-communicating essence'[80] of 'predicative being', and the 'dynamic darkness . . . positive inclination to obscurity'[81] of 'pronominal being', to employ the helpful epithets proposed by Wolfram Hogrebe.[82] In this version, however, Schelling makes clear why the conflict cannot be quelled through the conjunction of 'A' and 'B' – his notations for these principles of being – within a propositional structure (just as for Derrida the tension between the materiality of the text and the ideality of meaning cannot be resolved hermeneutically in an 'interpretation'). The reason is that if the antithesis between singularity and universality is a genuine one, then a new antithesis will arise between the *unity* of A and B in the propositional structure (Hogrebe terms this 'propositional being') and their irreducible opposition *as* A and B: 'To say there should be both antithesis and unity therefore means: the negating principle, the affirming principle, and again the unity of the two – each of these three should be a particular principle separated from the others.'[83] The problem here is the ensuing proto-ontological rivalry: 'Each of these powers is able to be for itself, as unity is unity for itself, and each of the opposites is the whole, complete essence. . . . Thus each has also precisely the same claims to be the essence, that which is ["das Seiende"].'[84] Again, in deconstructive terms, the coherence and stability of the meaning of the text turns out to be merely another supplement, a further mark in the chain of 're-marks'.

The result is an incessant 'rotary movement' [*rotatorische Bewegung*] which is unable to attain a stable state of 'being', and which Schelling evokes with great poetic intensity: 'Since there is thus an incessant urge [*Drang*] to be, and that primal essence nevertheless cannot be, it remains in a state of perpetual desire [*Begierde*], as an incessant seeking, an eternal, never quieted passion [*Sucht*] to be.'[85] In the distinctive sonorities of the earlier *Weltalter* drafts, Schelling describes how the emergence of a third will, the effective will [*wirkender Wille*] or the propositional bond between 'A' and 'B' fails to put a brake on the cyclical dynamic.[86] This is described as

> an involuntary movement, which – once begun – repeats itself over and over again; for through each contraction the effective will becomes sensitive to love as the first will, so that it decides once more to expand: however, through this separation the other will, in the form of a craving for existence, is aroused again within it, and since it cannot break loose from this will, since its own existence consists in the fact that it is both wills, contraction immediately arises out of the expansion, and there is no escape.[87]

Indeed, not only is there no escape, but in Schelling's account this vortex or merry-go-round of ontological potentialities [*Umtrieb, wirbelnde Bewegung*] becomes ever more frantic, culminating in what he terms a 'wild, self-dismembering madness, which is still the innermost trait of all things'.[88]

At this point, however, it is important to highlight the distinction between Schelling's *Weltalterphilosophie* and the dynamic of deconstruction. For Derrida the play of *différance* is directly at work in the 'staging' of the present, just as for Gasché the infrastructures both limit and delimit the space of reflexivity. Of course, this involves the relegation of *différance* to the status of an absolute past, a 'past which was never present' – but it is by no means clear how this displacement can occur. For if 'presence is always belated with regard to itself and comes *ex post*, as an effect, to the absolute past to which it must relate in order to be constituted',[89] how can this phenomenon which is *derivative* of *différance* summon the force to drive *différance* from the stage? Schelling's answer to this conundrum is that it is not just *différance*, but the 'rotary movement' driven by the conflict of *différance and* its idealizing occlusion, or more generally by the compulsive struggle of metaphysical opposites, which must *itself* be repressed [*verdrängt* – as in Freud] in order for time and space to unfold and frame a world. He reaches this conclusion via reflection on the kind of situation described by Derrida, when he asserts: 'It is because of *différance* that the movement of signification is possible only if each so-called "present" element, each element appearing on the scene [or stage – *scène*] of presence, is related to something else than itself, thereby keeping within in itself the mark of the past element, and already being hollowed out by the mark of its relation to the future element.'[90] For if all differentially constituted elements must appear on a 'scene of presence', then the 'scene of presence' itself cannot be simply an 'effect' of *différance*. Indeed, this scene must force the play of *différance* into the wings. For if the scene of presence, as opposed to *particular* 'present' entities, were *itself* differentially constituted, then even the 'illusion' of presence would be immediately demolished by *différance*. There would thus be no possibility even of the apparent processes of delay and detour which Derrida considers essential to temporalization and spatialization,[91] since if something is *delayed*, then something *else* must be occurring on the scene of presence in its stead. Without this fundamental occupancy or resistance, *différance* – as temporalization and spatialization – would never be able to 'constitute' time and space at all. So how does this stabilization occur? In other words – how can there be a world?

## Schelling's Theory of Time

Schelling discerns an affinity between 'propositional being' and what he terms the 'pure godhead' (as opposed to the 'primal being' [*Urwesen*], beleaguered successor to the creator God, who is trapped in the frenzy of the rotary movement). The godhead is that which is 'in itself neither what is nor what is not, but only the eternal freedom to be'.[92] Because it is 'sublimely above being and non-being', and is therefore also called by Schelling '*das Überseyende*', the pure freedom to be (or not be) serves as a pole of attraction for the dimensions of being caught in the *Umtrieb* – it functions *as* being in relation to their radical instability: 'For although in itself it neither is what is nor what is not, it can stand towards everything else only as that which is – not that it is annulled as what in itself neither is nor is not, but that it is just as what neither is nor is not.'[93] In particular *das Überseyende*, which can be understood as the pure *space* of propositionality, and thus of world-disclosure, attracts and polarizes the propositional mode of being, which, as the balancing bond between subject and predicate, has the closest affinity to it. It thereby disrupts the equipolarity of the rotary movement, arousing the longing for an escape from the vortex through a disintrication of the modes of being. The escape itself, however, can be grasped only as a 'self-doubling' [*Selbstverdoppelung*] in which the primordial being finally manages to distance itself from the torment which it itself is. Schelling views this process metaphorically as a human moment of decision, which brings the relief of externalization in a crystallizing word: 'All confusion, the whole chaotic state in which we find ourselves inwardly at the beginning of each new process of development, derives from that searching for and not being able to find the beginning. The discovered beginning is the discovered word, through which all conflict is resolved.'[94]

More specifically, Schelling's proposal is that time and space are the forms in which the madness of the rotary movement is repressed. The conflict between the modes of being is rendered containable, though by no

means extinguished, by being dispersed across the three emergent dimensions of time (past, present and future), since in this way the three modes
can evade the 'necessity of mutual inexistence'[95] by each simultaneously
being and not being:

> Past time is not annulled time. What has past can, to be sure, not be as present,
> but must be as something past at the same time with the present. What is future
> is, to be sure, not as something that now is, but is simultaneously with the pre-
> sent, as something that is in the future. And it is equally absurd to consider
> being past as well as being future as a complete non-being. . . . Thus it is only
> the contradiction at its climax ['in der höchsten Steigerung'] which breaks eter-
> nity, and, instead of one eternity, posits a succession of eternities (aeons) or
> times. But just this succession of eternities is what we commonly call time.
> Therefore eternity opens out into time in this decision.[96]

Schelling summarizes this process in the words: 'Now for the first time
there arises a before and after, a real articulation, and therefore compo-
sure.'[97]

In the current context, perhaps the most important feature of this narrative is the idea that the rotary movement must be consigned to an
absolute past, a past 'prior' to time, if the world is to begin. Schelling
argues that since the very notion of a beginning of the time of the world
presupposes – in apparent self-contradiction – a time which has already
been, 'the beginning which is truly a beginning cannot first have to await
the elapse of this [time], but rather it must be past from the very beginning.
A beginning of time is thus unthinkable unless a whole mass [*eine ganze
Masse*] is simultaneously posited as past and another as future; for only
through this polarized holding-apart [*polarisches Auseinandersetzen*] does
time arise at every moment.'[98] The past *of* time itself can only be the rotary
movement, since it is precisely this immediately self-destructive conflict of
principles which must be overcome for the dimensionality of time to
become actual. Thus timeless logical torment is transformed into the
opaque singularity, the stubborn 'iterability' divided against itself, which
lies at the heart of nature, and upon which strata of intentionality and
meaning have always-already been superimposed. As Schelling writes:

> The primordial state of contradiction, that wild fire, that life of passion and
> desire, is posited as past by the godhead which is, by that supernatural essence
> of freedom. But because the godhead, which is from eternity, can never come to
> be, that primordial state is posited as an eternal past, a past which did not first
> become past, but was the past primordially and from all eternity.[99]

It could thus be said that Schelling shares with Derrida a sense that the
world is riven by a fundamental proto-ontological inconsistency ('*différance*'). But in Schelling this awareness is articulated in the view that the

oscillation between *différance and* its idealizing negation, which is driven by the 'necessity of mutual inexistence', lies entombed in the 'abyss of what is past'.[100] It is unable to break though into the present, where it would entail the destruction of those *actual* differences which weave the fabric of reality. In the first version of the *Weltalter* Schelling remarks that when the 'one unfathomable being' in which everything was originally enclosed is correctly viewed by the mind, then:

> new abysses disclose themselves in it, and man discovers, not without a kind of horror similar to that which he experiences when he finds that his dwelling has been built over the seat of a primordial fire, that even in the primal being itself something had to be posited as past before the present time became possible, that what is past still remains concealed in the ground, and that the same principle which – in its quiescence – sustains us and holds us, would consume and annihilate us if it became effective.[101]

More succinctly, towards the end of the third draft of the *Weltalter*, Schelling affirms that 'without continual solicitation to madness there would be no consciousness'.[102]

This claim should not be understood as representing the triumph of the self-identity of consciousness over *différance*. Rather, Schelling's point is that the emergence of *genuine* differences, in the form of the opening up of a world stretched between the incommensurable dimensions of past, present and future, involves a constant struggle against what might be termed the 'pseudo-difference' of the rotary movement. In this sense Schelling's account of the rotary movement implies a critique of those who would view iterability, supplementarity, or even dissemination as representing some kind of emancipatory open-endedness, rather than a dismally repetitive closure. But despite the audacity of this conception, a deconstructive critic would no doubt be inclined to argue that since *das Überseyende* remains the encompassing space of disclosure which orientates the world towards the overcoming of conflict, it is still the case that Schelling's conception is grounded in a suspect teleology of reconciliation and unity.

It should be noted, however, that Schelling's theory of time as the diremption and interlacing of the modes of being implies that the unity towards which the world is moving is neither an illusory projection (however transcendentally necessary) nor a state which could in principle be realized in the present. As we have seen, in Schelling's conception, the present is the point of separation from – and repression of – the past. But this separation occurs only for the sake of resolving the conflict between the two 'principles of being' – pronominal and predicative – which past and present respectively embody. It is thus driven by an anticipation of the future as the domain of the third, propositional principle, where the conflict between past and present will be quelled. For this reason Schelling claims that 'time is in every moment the whole of time, in other words past, present and future, and this whole begins not from the past, not from the limit, but from the middle point, and is equivalent to eternity in every moment'.[103]

This conception of time as the intertwining of three coexistent eternities allows Schelling to portray unity or reconciliation not merely as *constitutive* of the present, but as 'present' in the present, though never fully realizable in it. In other words, on Schelling's view, 'the future is actually the time in time [*die Zukunft sei eigentlich die Zeit in der Zeit*]'.[104] He writes of a unity that 'can only be one which is always becoming, always generating itself, and, in a word, one which is from the present standpoint always futural [*zukünftig*]'.[105] In theological terms, for Schelling God is 'non-*existent*' [nicht*existierend*], but this is not equivalent to his being 'non-existent' [nichtexistierend]. Rather, it means that God, understood as ultimate reconciliation, 'also *is*, precisely in that he is not [*qua*] being [*seiend*]. He is only as not being, [that is, he is] in a state of envelopment (*implicite, in statu involutionis*), which is a transition (means) to real revelation.'[106]

## Schelling's World-Formula

Of course, it might be still objected that there remains a 'regulative idea' of unity, of reunification and reconciliation, in the *Weltalter*, even if it can never be achieved in present time, and this would be sufficient to support the deconstructive riposte to Schelling. But here Schelling makes one of his most astonishing moves. Throughout the *Weltalter* he stresses the power of negation as the driving force of development:

> For beginning in any case lies only in negation. . . . In order that a movement may now begin or come to be, it is not sufficient for it merely not to be; it must explicitly be posited as not being. Thus a ground is given for it to be. The starting-point (*terminus a quo*) of a movement is not an empty, inactive one, but a negation of movement; the movement actually arising is an overcoming of this negation.[107]

Towards the end of the third draft of the *Weltalter*, however, Schelling reflects that the ultimate point of polarization, that which is 'above being' [*das Überseyende*], must itself flip over into an ultimate power of negation in relation to the actual world of the potencies [*Potenzen*], or the temporalized versions of the principles of being. It must become the 'one' over against the 'all'. Thus the ineffable, contractive force of singularity is not only the driving force of the beginning, a 'never to be cancelled beginning, a never attainable root of reality',[108] but also the terminal pole of attraction.

Yet the pure freedom of the *Überseyende*, the pure potentiality to be or not be, does not take the form of a fully self-conscious identity returning to itself out of the world, but, rather, of an *a priori* blackout, a lapse into unconsciousness which has always-already occurred. Schelling writes:

> the one, or the potency drawing into itself is, with respect to nature, a highly spiritual power, indeed pure spirit, although not acting with freedom and deliberation . . . this negating power does not know itself, therefore also not its own state, does not know the freedom of decision, by virtue of which it is what alone is active. It had to be thus. The higher life had to sink again into unconsciousness of itself, in order that there might be a true beginning.[109]

In *Prädikation und Genesis*, his brilliant commentary on the *Weltalter*, Wolfram Hogrebe emphasizes how the singularity of 'B' (the contractive will) makes possible both idealizing, communicative progress and opaque, self-destructive regress. Schelling's deepest intuition, Hogrebe suggests, is that:

> the singular *unum* is first and last. The first: it preceded the elementary predication, the last: it remains autonomous over against all predication, 'something which no-one can fully fathom' [*Ein Ding, das keiner voll aussinnt*]. Pronominal being cannot be cancelled predicatively or propositionally, and this means: *semantic idealism shatters against pronominal being*. Something or other [*Irgendeins*] is the pre-rational spur of the rational. There is meaning only because there is madness, affirmation because negation, consistency because inconsistency, consciousness because an unconscious.[110]

Thus that which orientates is also that which disorientates. This, it could be said, is Schelling's account of the 'identity of identity and non-identity'. Yet his version of this fundamental – indeed unavoidable – structure does not involve an *Aufhebung* of conflictual opposition of the kind which Derrida finds so suspect. This resistance to *Aufhebung* is strikingly encrypted in the 'world-formula' [*Weltformel*] which Schelling gives in the third version of the *Weltalter*:

$$\left( \frac{A^3}{A^2 = (A = B)} \right) B$$

This formula can be understood in many ways. We could say that $A^2$ is the ideality of a signified emerging from its identity with the materiality of the signifier ($A = B$), and that $A^3$ is the interpretation which brings about and stabilizes this emergence. In more traditional German Idealist terms we could say that $A^2$ is self-consciousness standing opposed to its own unconscious identity with nature, and that $A^3$ is *Geist*, the overarching identity of subjectivity's identity and non-identity with nature. We could also speak, as Hogrebe does, of the constellation of pronominal, predicative and propositional being.[111] But however we approach the formula, the important point is that it suggests that any hermeneutic posture, articulation of spirit, or propositional disclosure is itself only an expression of a singular, materially embedded perspective on the world. This is why Schelling adds the 'B' outside the bracket, which he describes as 'the fire which consumes being within itself, which thus makes that which is attracted one with itself . . . that which is attracted and drawn in is eternal nature, the all; that which attracts or draws in is one'.[112] It is 'B' which both supports and undermines the world: 'B' – to return to Gasché's terms – is the condition of possibility *and* impossibility of system.

As I have already suggested, with this daring construction Schelling almost seems to be trying to break the deadlock between two of the major contending positions in European philosophy today: Habermasian critical theory, with its suspect reliance on a telos of ideal communication, on the one hand; and the implicitly autodestructive vortex of deconstruction on the other. Like Derrida, and against Habermas, Schelling sets an unsublatable, pre-logical inconsistency at the heart of being. But unlike Derrida, he realizes that this very inconsistency must also function as the *motor* of an idealizing and reconciling tendency which is not *imposed* on a recalcitrant reality by 'phallogocentrism', or by 'ethico-theoretical decisions' which 'privilege the idea of presence', as Gasché suggests, but is, rather, internal to its very structure.[113]

I say 'unlike Derrida'. But it is perhaps worth pointing out that some of the more recent innovations in Derrida's thought read like a belated recognition of Schelling's insight that pure '*différance*' would destroy itself, since 'eternal destruction [*Zerrüttung*], eternal chaos, eternal torment and anguish is impossible'.[114] In now defining deconstruction itself – at least in one of its dimensions – as 'the undeconstructible', and thus exempting it from its own reflexive movement, Derrida has acknowledged that the *space* of the play of *différance* (or what he had earlier referred to as the 'scene of presence') must itself lie beyond the play of *différance*, as does *das Überseyende* in Schelling.[115] Furthermore, by defining deconstruction in this sense as 'justice', Derrida has also recognized that the undeconstructible functions as 'the chance of the future, of the promise or the appeal' – in other words, induces a constitutive ethical polarization of temporality towards emancipation or messianic reconcilation.[116] Like the Schelling of the *Weltalter*, Derrida has become intensely concerned with the absolute singularity of the promissory 'here-now' [*ici-maintenant*], which brings both peace and disruption, discord and concord, and without which there would be no future, and thus no time.[117] Indeed, in a radical reversal of his earlier views, where nothing could 'exceed' *différance*, the 'here-now' (which is not, of course, to be equated with presence) appears to have become its 'condition of possibility': 'No *différance* without alterity, no alterity without singularity, no singularity without here-now.'[118]

## Conclusion

Doubtless more than enough has now been said to indicate the problems of Gasché's account of the relation between deconstruction and German Idealism. Whatever the divergences in cultural context and philosophical vocabulary – and they are indeed deep – it is hard to overlook the fact that Schelling is wrestling with a problem closely allied to Gasché's central preoccupation: how is it possible to overcome the dualistic structure of reflection without endorsing a speculative *Aufhebung* of this dualism? Or: how is it possible to think the 'identity of identity and non-identity' in a non-Hegelian way? This proximity is even reflected in some of Gasché's terminological innovations. For example, Gasché is forced to assert that deconstruction represents, in a certain sense, 'a methodical principle of philosophical foundation and grounding',[119] despite the fact that the very notion of foundation reinstates a dualism of 'ground' and 'grounded'. To tackle this problem he then has recourse to the argument that 'Deconstruction repeats or mimes grounding in order to account for the difference between a ground and that which is grounded, with what can no longer be called a ground . . . an infrastructure is not what is called a ground in traditional philosophical language. It is, on the contrary, a non-fundamental structure, or an abyssal structure, to the extent that it is without a bottom.'[120] These formulations echo uncannily the closing pages of the *Philosophical Inquiries*, Schelling's prelude to the *Weltalter*, where his sense of the abyss [*Abgrund*] of the 'primal ground' [*Urgrund*] leads him to characterize it as the 'un-ground' [*Ungrund*] – a term which later Gasché 'reinvents' to describe the infrastructures.[121]

Given the virtuosity of Schelling's explorations in this area, it is surprising to find Gasché so summarily dismissing him for his supposedly 'romantic and abstract tendencies',[122] while thinkers distinguished merely by their post-Hegelian chronology are treated as having advanced beyond the problematic of absolute reflection. Indeed, it seems as though almost any philosophical position can be read as a challenge to the project of metaphysics, as long as it is located historically after Hegel. Thus Gasché cites 'Nietzsche, Dilthey, the later Husserl and the early Heidegger' as exemplifying 'a type of philosophy that cannot comfortably be placed within the usual philosophical classifications', and hence as waystones on the path towards Derrida. He writes, for example: 'What Nietzsche and Heidegger thematize as life is something that escapes, at least up to a certain point, the classical opposition of the rational and the irrational', and that 'spirit, life, in Dilthey, is essentially the non-reflexive source of reflection and self-reflection. As the source of all reflexivity, it forever escapes reflection.'[123] What is surprising here is Gasché's confidence that Nietzsche's mockery of the injunction 'know thyself', or Dilthey's cumbrous ruminations on the unfathomability of *das Leben*, represent a powerful challenge to Hegelian totalization, since these thinkers can scarcely be said to rival the dizzying intricacy of the treatments of the transreflexive ground of reflexivity *within* German Idealism itself.

But despite the affinities explored so far, there is one final objection which will no doubt be raised against the juxtaposition of Schelling and Derrida – an objection focused on the question of language. David Wood has proposed the elegant definition: 'deconstruction reflexively applies to philosophy itself the defamiliarizing operation philosophy usually reserves for outer application'.[124] But since the corpus of philosophy consists of texts, deconstruction is a form of attention to philosophical writings, in particular to their 'unconscious textuality'.[125] It might therefore be argued that Derrida is separated by the gulf of the 'linguistic turn', by an irreversible heightening of philosophical sensitivity towards language which has occurred in the twentieth century, from any Idealist or post-Idealist metaphysics, no matter how wayward. But is the situation so clear?

In the 'Introduction' to *Philosophy at the Limit*, for example, Wood states:

> If there is one thing Nietzsche, Wittgenstein, Heidegger, Foucault and Derrida have each taught us it is that the traditional epistemologically centred demarcation of the subject's relation to the world, in which knowledge (especially perceptual) provides the guiding thread, is fatally undercut by the linguistic character of our being. And *language* understood in this way cannot be assigned a place within the traditional topological scheme of regions and linear limits. It is not merely a thickening of the boundary, or the darkening of a mediating lens. It is the irreversible displacement of all insight drawn from the visual field, even when this is reflected through an active subject.[126]

But the force of this argument depends on what is meant by the 'linguistic character of our being'. If this character is supposed to be exclusive or definitive, then such a claim can be made plausible only by an optical parody of all accounts of the subject. It would perhaps be less misleading to speak of the linguistic *dimension* of our being . And in this case the difference between pre- and post-Nietzschean philosophy (even if one makes the questionable concession that Nietzsche's thought does place such a dominant stress on language in its exploration of the human) would be one of emphasis, not a radical break. Indeed, Schelling could be said to begin not from the linguistic character of *our* being but from the linguistic character of being *as such*, in so far as the internal tensions of propositional structure are seen as mapping – and, in fact, as ultimately identical with – the fissures and diremptions of reality as a whole. But he insists on what deconstruction often prefers to forget: that the linguistic character of being also implies the ontological character of language.

Furthermore, this focus on language is a matter not just of theory, but of philosophical practice. Schelling's *Weltalter* fragments famously begin, in all three versions, with an aphoristic reflection on the dimensions of time, our differing forms of awareness of them, and the distinct discursive modalities of this awareness.[127] Consistent with this motto, the *Weltalter* texts are not a 'theory' of the absolute past but a 'retelling' of it, presented in a unique mytho-metaphysical style which deliberately oscillates between narrative and dialectical modes. Given Schelling's emphasis on resistant singularity, on the 'incomprehensible basis of reality in things, the irreducible remainder which cannot be resolved into reason',[128] can it really be supposed that he expects his project to 'escape from its status as writing, to transcend the particularity of its physical form, the actual language it employs', or that he considers language as 'a transparent vehicle of meaning and truth', as David Wood suggests philosophy typically does?[129] Indeed, does not Wood's definition of the text (presumably the 'general text') as 'a struggle between order and chaos, a desperate attempt to exchange its own materiality for transparency', summarize rather neatly the central 'proto-ontological' insight of the *Weltalter*, which sends its shock-waves through Schelling's writing? As Hogrebe suggests, do not the drafts of the *Weltalter*, in seeking to convey a sense of this struggle, of the seething inconsistency which underpins the world, frequently 'explode philosophical discourse in an orgy of imagery [*orgiastische Bildlichkeit*]'?[130]

One might also ask: Can defenders of deconstruction both have their cake and eat it? Can they both appeal to the irreversibility of the lingustic turn *and* expand the concept of the text so far that it includes 'consciousness, subjectivity, the real world . . .?'[131] If the 'general text' really is this inclusive, then surely the deconstructive engagement with it will sooner or later find itself confronted with the metaphysical issues which such foci of philosophical attention have traditionally raised. If it is not, then claims for the epochal significance of deconstruction will be that much harder to sustain. Certainly, there does not seem to be anything specifically 'linguistic' about the problems of reflexivity with which Gasché deals; and in fact, in much deconstructive writing questions of language seem to be the idiom rather than the substance of the discussion.

I began with the vexation which commentators have long felt in seeking to define the 'break' represented by Derrida's work in relation to the philosophical tradition – with the problem of being both inside and outside without triggering a Hegelian sublation. Similar difficulties are generated by the fact that deconstruction seems to lose the scope of its social and political implications when it is construed as no more than a highly reflexive approach to the reading of texts (in the restricted sense), whereas the more these implications are emphasized, the more deconstruction appears as a recognizably philosophical position, confronted with familiar dilemmas which cannot be rhetorically outmanoeuvred. Given the fundamental character of these tensions, it is hardly surprising that one kind of attempt to evade them uses deconstruction to mount a *political* critique of the Western intellectual tradition which considers itself exempt from the necessity of giving any consistent *philosophical* account of itself. And to the extent that Gasché, despite his stress on philosophical accounting, considers the infrastructures to constitute something which can be clearly labelled and quarantined as 'metaphysical conceptuality',[132] he can be seen as ultimately giving succour to this tendency. For it will be clear by now that many of Gasché's generalizations about the character of 'metaphysics' or 'philosophical discourse' are either tautological or misleading. He claims, for example, that 'logical contradictions' are the 'only discrepancies for which the philosophical discourse can account'.[133] Yet what do Schelling's *Weltalter* speculations explore, if not precisely forms of inconsistency and difference which are prior to the emergence of meaning, rationality and logic? Are they metaphysical or not? And, ultimately, what is the politics of this question?

It should be stressed that the assumption of the preceding argument has not been that a critique of *The Tain of the Mirror*, or of any other significant work in a deconstructive vein, is tantamount to a comprehensive critique of Derrida himself, whose writings always contain twists and complexities which escape the earnestness or frivolity of his followers. The assumption, rather, is that, as with the splintering of the Hegelian school after Hegel's death, significant deconstructive positions – and Gasché's work certainly counts as such – will reveal certain of the tensions and fractures *internal* to their philosophical source, as if under a magnifying glass. Robert Bernasconi admitted as much, in one of the best reviews of *The Tain of the Mirror*, when he suggested that 'by presenting the systematic reading of Derrida so whole-heartedly, Gasché has redrawn and polarized the debate about the meaning of Derrida's contribution to philosophy'.[134]

There is thus good reason to believe that our traversal of German Idealism on a path which cuts across Gasché's deconstructive reading – and his reading of deconstruction – has challenged those assumptions of deconstruction with which we began, concerning its own relation to the history of philosophy. For perhaps the very construction of the metaphysical tradition on which even Derrida himself relies is an implausible idealization – not just in the familiar deconstructive sense that the fracture between metaphysics and its 'exterior' runs through the heart of every metaphysical text but, rather, in the sense that this fracture itself has been an explicit focus of concern in the modern period – since as early as the interventions of Jacobi, at least. In short, we need not adopt the solution by which even some of Derrida's admirers are tempted: namely, an acceptance that deconstruction is ultimately the continuation of philosophy – and perhaps not even by other means. We need not deny, therefore, that deconstructive procedures have a significant role to play in disentangling the tensions and collusions between reason and domination. But at the same time, both political denouncers of – and reluctant collaborators with – the 'metaphysics of presence' should be confronted with the fact that counter-discourses on the 'margins of philosophy' constitute a complex, stratified heritage which cannot be neatly separated from the mainstream philosophical tradition. A greater awareness of this heritage would not only help to puncture the illusions of radical novelty which are such a damaging feature of contemporary intellectual life; it would also disrupt any homogenizing conception of the Western intellectual tradition, and thus of its supposedly *global* complicity in the exclusion of whatever currently figures as its 'Other'.

## Notes

1. Jacques Derrida, *Of Grammatology*, trans. Gayatri Chakravorty Spivak, Baltimore, MD and London: Johns Hopkins University Press 1976, p. 46.
2. Sarah Kofman, 'Un philosophe "unheimlich"', in Lucette Finas *et al.*, *Écarts: quatre essais à propos de Jacques Derrida*, Paris: Fayard 1973, p. 125.
3. Christopher Norris, *Jacques Derrida*, London: Fontana 1987, p. 20. It is symptomatic of the difficulties I wish to discuss that Norris immediately goes on to contradict himself: 'Derrida's stress on textuality and writing is *not* in any sense a break with philosophy, or a declaration of intepretative freedoms hitherto undreamt under the grim repressive law of conceptual clarity and truth' (ibid., p. 21).
4. David Wood, *Philosophy at the Limit*, London: Hutchinson 1990, p. 153.
5. David Wood, 'Beyond Deconstruction?', in A. Phillips Griffiths, ed., *Contemporary French Philosophy*, Cambridge: Cambridge University Press 1987, p. 193.
6. Ibid., pp. 192–3.
7. Ibid., p. 193.
8. David Wood, 'Difference and the Problem of Strategy', in David Wood and Robert Bernasconi, eds, *Derrida and Différance*, Warwick University: Parousia Press 1992, p. 103.
9. See, for example, Bernard Flynn's review in *Review of Metaphysics*, vol. 41, no. 1, September 1987; or Robert Bernasconi's review, entitled 'Deconstruction and Scholarship', in *Man and World*, vol. 21, 1988, pp. 223–30. Although Bernasconi is more sceptical than Flynn, he still concludes with the assertion: 'By presenting the systematic reading of Derrida so wholeheartedly, Gasché has redrawn and polarised the debate about the meaning of Derrida's contribution to philosophy, and issued a challenge to everyone concerned with this question.' More recently, Fredric Jameson has echoed the general admiration for Gasché's 'transformation of "deconstruction" into a full-fledged philosophical system' (Fredric Jameson, 'Marx's Purloined Letter', *New Left Review*, 209, January–February 1995, p. 83).
10. Rodolphe Gasché, 'The Law of Tradition', in *Inventions of Difference: On Jacques Derrida*, Cambridge, MA: Harvard University Press 1994, p. 58.

11. See Rodolphe Gasché, 'Deconstruction as Criticism', in *Inventions of Difference*, esp. pp. 53–7.

12. Ibid., p. 23.

13. Ibid., p. 62.

14. Rodolphe Gasché, *The Tain of the Mirror*, Cambridge, MA: Harvard University Press 1986, p. 13.

15. See ibid., ch. 3.

16. Ibid., p. 62.

17. Ibid., p. 74.

18. Ibid., p. 79.

19. Ibid., p. 174.

20. Ibid., p. 224.

21. Ibid., p, 185.

22. *The Logic of Hegel*, trans. William Wallace, Oxford: Clarendon Press 1975, p. 91.

23. See *The Tain of the Mirror*, pp. 316–17.

24. Ibid., p. 147.

25. Ibid., p. 223 (emphasis on 'transcendental' and 'speculative' added).

26. Ibid., p. 245.

27. Ibid., p. 249.

28. Ibid., p. 151.

29. Ibid., p. 316

30. Ibid., p. 54.

31. Ibid., p. 192.

32. 'But the determinate activity cannot be posited without the opposed activity, from which the determinate is derived, being posited also. A self-positing cannot be comprehended unless a non-positing of self is posited along with it'. (J.G. Fichte, *Wissenschaftslehre nova methodo* [lecture transcript of K. Chr. Fr. Krause 1798/9], Hamburg: Felix Meiner Verlag 1982, p. 36/*Foundations of Transcendental Philosophy* [*Wissenschaftslehre*] *nova methodo*, trans. D. Breazeale, Ithaca, NY: Cornell University Press 1992, p. 123.)

33. *The Tain of the Mirror*, p. 192. The classic account of (non-Hegelian) Idealism as a critical engagement with the model of reflection is, of course, Dieter Henrich, 'Fichte's Original Insight', in Darrel Christensen *et al.*, eds, *Contemporary German Philosophy*, vol. 1, 1982, pp. 15–54. In Henrich's view – the direct opposite of Gasché's – Hegel, far from resolving the antinomies of reflection theories of self-consciousness, never even fully grasped them. In contrast to his major rivals, his account of self-consciousness continued to presuppose a reflection structure, albeit an intersubjectively expanded one.

34. Walter Schulz, 'Das Problem der absoluten Reflexion', in *Vernunft und Freiheit: Aufsätze und Vorträge*, Stuttgart: Reclam 1981, p. 14.

35. Ibid., p. 15.

36. See J.G. Fichte, 'Die Wissenschaftslehre in ihrem allgemeinen Umrisse (1810)', in I.H. Fichte, ed., *Fichtes Werke*, Berlin and New York: de Gruyter 1971, vol. 2/'The Science of Knowledge in its General Outline', trans. Walter E. Wright, *Idealistic Studies*, vol. 6, 1976.

37. F.W.J. Schelling, *Philosophical Inquiries into the Nature of Human Freedom*, trans. James Gutman, La Salle, IL: Open Court Classics 1936, p. 33.

38. *The Tain of the Mirror*, p. 226.

39. 'Das Problem der absoluten Reflexion', p. 19.

40. Hegel, *The Science of Logic*, trans. A.V. Miller, Atlantic Highlands, NJ: Humanities Press 1969, p. 829.

41. For a discussion of Schelling's critique of Hegel from this angle, see Jürgen Habermas, 'Dialektischer Idealismus im Übergang zum Materialismus – Geschichtsphilosophische Folgerungen aus Schellings Idee einer Contraction Gottes', in *Theorie und Praxis: Sozialphilosophische Studien*, Frankfurt am Main: Suhrkamp 1978.

42. 'Fichte created a great sensation in his time; his philosophy is the Kantian philosophy in its completion'. . . . 'It was Schelling, finally, who made the most important, or, from a philosophical point of view, the only important advance upon the philosophy of Fichte'. . . . '[Schelling's] defect is that this Idea in general, its distinction into the ideal and the natural world . . . [is] not shown forth and developed or necessitated by the Notion'. . . . 'The present

standpoint of philosophy is that the Idea is known in its necessity.' (*Hegel's Lectures on the History of Philosophy*, trans. E.S. Haldane and Frances H. Simpson, Atlantic Highlands, NJ: Humanities Press 1975, vol. 3, pp. 479, 512, 542, 545.)

43. See *The Tain of the Mirror*, p. 56.

44. Dieter Henrich, 'Hegel und Hölderlin', in *Hegel im Kontext*, Frankfurt am Main: Suhrkamp 1975, p. 10.

45. Rolf-Peter Horstmann, *Die Grenzen der Vernunft: Eine Untersuchung zu Zielen und Motiven des Deutschen Idealismus*, Frankfurt am Main: Anton Hain 1991, pp. 27–8.

46. See ibid., esp. ch. 2.

47. See, for example, Frederick Beiser, *The Fate of Reason: German Philosophy from Kant to Fichte*, Cambridge, MA: Harvard University Press 1987, chs 2–3; Kurt Christ, *Jacobi und Mendelssohn: Eine Analyse des Spinozastreits*, Würzburg: Königshausen & Neuman 1988; Wilhelm Schmidt-Biggemann, 'Sprung in die Metaphysik oder Fall ins Nichts: Eine Alternative im Pantheismusstreit', in *Theodizee und Tatsachen: Das Profil der Deutschen Aufkärung*, Frankfurt am Main: Suhrkamp 1988, pp. 150–64.

48. *Über die Lehre des Spinoza, in Briefen an Herrn Moses Mendelssohn*, in F.H. Jacobi, *Werke* (reprographic reprint, Darmstadt: WBG 1980), vol. 4/1 and 2, p. 59.

49. Ibid., p. 161.

50. Ibid., p. 29.

51. On this, see Gilbert Kirschner, 'La conception de l'histoire de la philosophie de F.H. Jacobi', in Klaus Hammacher, ed., *Friedrich Heinrich Jacobi: Philosoph und Literat der Goethezeit*, Frankfurt am Main: Vittorio Klostermann 1971.

52. See Dieter Henrich, *Der Grund im Bewußtsein: Untersuchungen zu Hölderlins Denken*, Stuttgart: Klett-Cotta 1992, ch 5.

53. *Über die Lehre des Spinoza in Briefen an Herrn Moses Mendelssohn*, p. 223.

54. Ibid., p. 72.

55. Letter from Jacobi to Fichte, Eutin, 3–21 March 1799, in Werner Röhr, ed., *Appellation an das Publikum: Dokumente zum Atheismusstreit Jena 1798/99*, Leipzig: Reclam 1991, p. 158/'Open Letter to Fichte', in Ernst Behler, ed., *Philosophy of German Idealism*, New York: Continuum 1992, p. 126.

56. Ibid., p. 158/p. 127.

57. Ibid., p. 156–7/p. 125.

58. Ibid., p. 161/p. 130.

59. Ibid., p. 164/p. 136.

60. *The Logic of Hegel*, p. 97.

61. G.W.F. Hegel, *Faith and Knowledge*, trans. Walter Cerf and H.S. Harris, Albany, NY: SUNY Press 1977, p. 117.

62. The pathbreaking text here, of course, is Walter Schulz, *Die Vollendung des Deutschen Idealismus in der Spätphilosophie Schellings*, Pfullingen: Neske 1955.

63. F.W.J. Schelling, *On the History of Modern Philosophy*, trans. Andrew Bowie, Cambridge: Cambridge University Press 1994, p. 172.

64. Ibid.

65. Ibid., p. 175.

66. *The Tain of the Mirror*, p. 184.

67. Ibid., p. 200.

68. Ibid., p. 198.

69. Ibid., p. 163.

70. See Charles Taylor, 'The Validity of Transcendental Arguments', *Proceedings of the Aristotelian Society* 1979, pp. 151–65.

71. *The Tain of the Mirror*, p. 135.

72. These problems with Gasché's procedure have been tellingly mocked by Richard Rorty: 'In particular, I object to the idea that one can be "rigorous" if one's procedure consists in inventing new words for what one is pleased to call "conditions of possibility" rather than playing sentences using old words off against each other.' ('Is Derrida a transcendental philosopher?', in *Essays on Heidegger and Others: Philosophical Papers Volume 2*, Cambridge: Cambridge University Press 1991, p. 124.) Rorty takes himself to be demolishing transcendental arguments, and the transcendental dimension of Derrida's work, altogether, but this is

clearly not the case. Transcendental arguments can be said to render the necessity of certain structures rationally intelligible through an exploration of the unimaginability of alternatives. To this extent their conclusions are always provisional, since what is unimaginable may always turn out to be historically determined – but this does not make them *intrinsically* deceptive. (See Eckhart Förster, 'How are Transcendental Arguments Possible?', in Eva Schaper and Wilhelm Vossenkuhl, eds, *Reading Kant*, Oxford: Blackwell 1989; Rüdiger Bubner, 'Kant, Transcendental Arguments and the Problem of Deduction', *Review of Metaphysics*, vol. 28, no. 3, March 1975; and Hermann Krings, 'Knowing and Thinking: On the Structure and History of the Transcendental Method in Philosophy', in Darrell E. Christensen *et al.*, eds, *Contemporary German Philosophy*, vol. 4, 1984.) It is precisely in the ingenuity with which he carries out such explorations, I would contend, that the interest of Derrida's work lies.

73. *Of Grammatology*, p. 89.

74. Ibid., p. 62.

75. Ibid., p. 69.

76. Albrecht Wellmer, 'Wahrheit, Kontingenz, Moderne' in Harry Kunneman and Hent de Vries, eds, *Enlightenments: Encounters between Critical Theory and Contemporary French Thought*, Kampen (the Netherlands): Kok Pharos 1993, p. 30. Derrida, of course, would suspect this direct appeal to finitude, since it threatens to set up a new dualism.

77. F.W.J. Schelling, 'Die Weltalter. Erstes Buch. Die Vergangenheit. Druck I' (1811), in Manfred Frank, ed., *Ausgewählte Schriften*, Frankfurt am Main: Suhrkamp 1985, vol. 4, pp. 229–30/pp. 17–18. The second page number refers to the pagination of the original published edition of the first two drafts of 'The Ages of the World', Manfred Schroter, ed., *Die Weltalter. Fragmente in den Urfassungen von 1811 und 1813*, Munich: Biederstein & Leibniz 1946. This pagination is also given in Frank's edition.

78. Ibid., p. 230/p. 18.

79. Ibid., p. 234/p. 22.

80. F.W.J. Schelling, *The Ages of The World*, trans. Frederick de Wolfe Bolman Jr, New York: Columbia University Press 1942, p. 101. This is a translation of the third version of the *Weltalter*, the only one to appear in Schelling's *Sämmtliche Werke*, Stuttgart: Cotta 1856–61, edited by his son (part 1, vol. 8, pp. 195–344).

81. Ibid., p. 98.

82. See Wolfram Hogrebe, *Prädikation und Genesis. Metaphysik als Fundamentalheuristik im Ausgang von Schellings "Die Weltalter"*, Frankfurt am Main: Suhrkamp 1989, pp. 80 ff.

83. *The Ages of the World*, p. 103.

84. Ibid. This, of course, is the point, at the core of his thinking, where Schelling resists the Hegelian notion of *Aufhebung*.

85. Ibid., p. 119.

86. Schelling, following Kant, understands a will to be an unconditioned *capacity* to begin or initiate – to bring into being. Hence the terminology of 'wills' reflects the 'proto-ontological' status of the processes he describes: these involve drives towards being which collapse back on themselves, failing fully to come into being.

87. 'Die Weltalter. Druck I', p. 247/p. 35.

88. Ibid., p. 255/p. 43.

89. *The Tain of the Mirror*, p. 198.

90. Jacques Derrida, 'Différance', in *Margins of Philosophy*, trans. Alan Bass, Sussex: Harvester Press 1982, p. 13 (trans. altered).

91. See ibid., p. 8.

92. *The Ages of the World*, p. 121.

93. Ibid., pp. 127–8.

94. Ibid., pp. 227–8. See *Prädikation und Genesis*, pp. 99–105, for a helpful commentary on this process. I owe the characterization of *das Überseyende* as 'Propositionsraum' or 'Propositionsdimension' to Hogrebe's pioneering work. See also Andrew Bowie, *Schelling and Modern European Philosophy: An Introduction*, London: Routledge 1993, ch. 5.

95. *The Ages of the World*, p. 120.

96. Ibid., p. 191.

97. Ibid., p. 135.

98. 'Die Weltalter. Druck I', p. 287/p. 75.

99. *The Ages of the World*, p. 142.

100. Ibid., p. 132.

101. 'Die Weltalter. Druck I', p. 225/p. 13.

102. *The Ages of the World*, p. 229.

103. 'Die Weltalter. Druck I', p. 292/p. 80. On Schelling's theory of time in the *Weltalter*, see Wolfgang Wieland, *Schellings Lehre von der Zeit*, Heidelberg: Carl Winter – Universitätsverlag 1956; Manfred Frank, *Zeitbewußtsein*, Pfullingen: Neske 1990, esp. pp. 110–35. Wieland's Heideggerian reading downplays the reconciliatory core of futurity in the *Weltalter*, viewing the future as no more than the endless holding open of the 'separation' [*Scheidung*] of the present (see esp. pp. 42–4).

104. 'System der gesammten Philosophie und der Naturphilosophie insbesondere', in *Ausgewählte Schriften*, vol. 3, p. 284.

105. 'Die Weltalter. Druck I', p. 272/p. 60.

106. *The Ages of the World*, p. 205.

107. Ibid., p. 111.

108. Ibid., p. 204.

109. Ibid., pp. 201–2.

110. *Prädikation und Genesis*, p. 114.

111. See ibid., pp. 112–13.

112. *The Ages of the World*, p. 201.

113. See 'Deconstruction as Criticism', p. 36; *The Tain of the Mirror*, p. 136. Gasché's suggestion is inconsistent because the term 'decision' seems intended to imply an (ultimately) arbitrary imposition. But any such decision could only be an 'effect' of the play of infrastructures, and therefore just as essential/non-essential as that which it supposedly suppresses. Talk of the 'privileging' of speech over writing, etc., entails similar problems.

114. 'Die Weltalter. Druck I', p. 266/p. 54.

115. See Jacques Derrida, 'Force of Law: The "Mystical Foundation of Authority"', in Drucilla Cornell, Michel Rosenfeld and David Gray Carlson, eds, *Deconstruction and the Possibility of Justice*, London and New York: Routledge 1992, pp. 14–15. In describing the infrastructures as the 'systematic exploration' of the 'space of inscription', Gasché also implicitly allows this space to *encompass* the play of the infrastructures, but he fails to perceive the consequences of this for his general position.

116. See Jacques Derrida, *Spectres de Marx*, Paris: Galilée 1993, p. 60/*Specters of Marx*, trans. Peggy Kamuf, New York: Routledge 1994, p. 31.

117. See ibid., p. 68/p. 37.

118. Ibid., p. 60/p. 31.

119. *The Tain of the Mirror*, p. 121.

120. Ibid., pp. 154–5.

121. See *Philosophical Inquiries into the Nature of Human Freedom*, pp. 87 ff. Gutman's translation ('the groundless') captures the vertigo of Schelling's term, though not its philosophically significant morphology. Gasché describes the infrastructures as 'ungrounds' on p. 175 of *The Tain of the Mirror*. For an interesting preliminary comparison of Derrida's work and Schelling's treatise on freedom as investigations into the preconditions of metaphysics, see Fiona Steinkamp, 'Différance and Indifference', *Journal of the British Society for Phenomenology*, vol. 22, no. 3, October 1991.

122. *The Tain of the Mirror*, p. 73.

123. Ibid., p. 81.

124. David Wood, 'Deconstruction and Criticism', in *Philosophy at the Limit*, p. 44.

125. Ibid., p. 48.

126. *Philosophy at the Limit*, pp. xviii–xix. These paragraphs continue a lively discussion with David Wood which followed my presentation of an early draft of this essay at the University of Warwick in May 1992. I hope he will forgive me for returning so obsessively to these issues, and take this as a tribute to a long-standing partner in debate.

127. 'What is past is known, what is present is discerned, what is future is divined./The known is retold, the discerned is represented, the divined is foretold [or prophesied].' (Das Vergangene wird gewußt, das Gegenwärtige wird erkannt, das Zukünftige wird geahndet./Das

Gewußte wird erzählt, das Erkannte wird dargestellt, das Geahndete wird geweissagt.) (*The Ages of The World*, p. 83.)

128. *Philosophical Inquiries into the Nature of Human Freedom*, p. 34.

129. 'Deconstruction and Criticism', p. 48.

130. *Prädikation und Genesis*, p. 116. Hogrebe's account of the *Weltalter* is framed by the argument that the project represents Schelling's attempt to realize the 'mythology of reason' anticipated by the 'Oldest System-Programme of German Idealism'. For a new English translation see 'The "Oldest System-Programme of German Idealism"', trans. Taylor Carman, *European Journal of Philosophy*, vol. 3, no. 2, August 1995.

131. 'Deconstruction and Criticism', p. 63.

132. *The Tain of the Mirror*, p. 166.

133. Ibid., p. 135.

134. 'Deconstruction and Scholarship', p. 230.

# PART III

# Critical Theory

# Lifeworld, Metaphysics and the Ethics of Nature in Habermas

It would scarcely be contentious to claim that the question of the ethical relation between human beings and nature poses considerable difficulties for Habermas's version of critical theory. Indeed, Habermas himself seems to consider these difficulties as a price worth paying for the advances he has made on other fronts. In his view, it is an advantage of his philosophy that it detaches an analysis of intersubjective structures, which provides the normative basis for critique, from unanswerable and outmoded 'metaphysical' questions concerning the place of human subjectivity in the world as a whole.[1] In the work of the earlier Frankfurt School, by contrast, one often finds an extremely close – although admittedly obscure – relation between the oppression and exploitation which characterize class society, and the reckless domination and exploitation of external nature, which is seen as reaching its culmination in modern technological society. Indeed, in one of his last publications, *Counterrevolution and Revolt*, Marcuse attempted once again to present the idea of a 'liberation of nature' as an essential precondition for the liberation of society. According to Marcuse, human beings have lost touch with what he calls 'the true *Forms* of things, distorted and denied in the established reality'.[2] A qualitative break with the repression of modern society would be possible only if the 'life-enhancing, sensuous, aesthetic qualities inherent in nature' could be made manifest through an abolition of the instrumental violation of nature.[3]

The metaphysical presuppositions of Marcuse's argument remain unclarified, and are perhaps even incoherent, since he equivocates on the question of whether the potentialities of nature are 'bearers of *objective values*' which are independent in principle from human interests, or whether they merely embody 'objective *qualities* . . . which are essential to the enhancement and fulfillment of life'.[4] But despite this, Marcuse's position acquires a striking contemporary relevance when one observes how emphatically he foregrounds the gender-specific character of the instrumental domination of nature, in a way which anticipates feminist debates of the last two decades. '*Destructive* productivity . . .', he declares, is 'the ever more conspicuous feature of male domination; inasmuch as the "male principle" has been the ruling mental and physical force, a free society would be the "definite negation" of this principle – it would be a *feminine* society'.[5]

On the other hand, it cannot be doubted that, as Habermas claims, the displacement of the centre of gravity of critical theory from the relation between society and nature to the intersubjective web of social relations has represented a theoretical and political advance in many respects. For it is only a theory of communication and its distortions, of the kind to which Habermas first gave a key role within critical theory, which makes possible a balanced assessment of the tensions between regression and progress in the development of contemporary societies, an assessment which does not underplay, or even ignore, the democratic potential of the modern constitutional state. The normative basis of the critique of existing social relations becomes far clearer in Habermas's work, since here the predominance of instrumental or functional reason results from an inadequate realization of the fundamental democratic principles of modernity, whose content, he contends, can be formalized on the basis of a universal pragmatics. At the same time, however, Habermas has no specifically *philosophical* resources which would allow him to appraise the current state of the relation between humanity and nature. Theoretically, Habermas operates with the assumption that dialectical interactions can occur only in the relations between human subjects, not within the relation between human beings and nature. Nature can be thematized only as a phenomenon which is disclosed *within* the linguistic intersubjectivity of the lifeworld. The metaphysical aspiration to penetrate into the depths of nature, and to characterize the essential features of nature '*an sich*' in conceptual terms, have entirely lost their former plausibility, according to Habermas. Indeed, he regards *any* attempt to elaborate a knowledge of nature other than that framed by the cognitive interest in instrumental control of nature, which structures our access to nature in a quasi-transcendental manner, with deep suspicion.[6]

Furthermore, Habermas's basic outlook, in both its cognitive and its moral dimensions, stresses the unique linguisticality of human interactions, and thus separates human beings from all other natural beings in a radical way. He considers that only beings who use language, and thereby acquire capacities for self-reflection and responsibility towards others, can properly be considered as subjects of morality. Furthermore, he believes it is impossible to demonstrate philosophically the existence of an intrinsic, non-anthropocentric value or telos of nature, since any such supposed demonstration would stray beyond those limits of human knowledge which Kant established once and for all.[7] At the same time, however,

Habermas does not contest the fact that human beings are capable of moral experiences of non-human nature. On the contrary, since the beginning of the 1980s he has made two distinct attempts to explain this possibility, without entirely exploding the framework of his discourse ethics.

In his 'Reply to My Critics' (1982), Habermas expressed the view that the anthropocentric orientation of discourse ethics needed to be supplemented by an ethics of sympathy [*Mitleid*]. In this context, he appealed to the notion of anamnetic solidarity as it functions in the thought of Walter Benjamin. Such solidarity, he suggested, represents an attempt to address the problem of past injustice which is perhaps made most vivid by the thought that even a future 'just' society could not avoid being plagued by 'bad conscience'. It could not simply 'forget' its own status as the end result of a history full of horror. For not even an achieved state of justice could eradicate the suffering of past generations, or answer their unheard cries for help. Anamnetic solidarity, Habermas suggests, signifies an attempt to sustain at least a 'compassionate solidarity with the despair of the tormented who have suffered what cannot be made good again',[8] without which even justice would become something unjust.

Habermas then makes the suggestion that our deeply ingrained feelings of moral obligation in relation to nature can be interpreted in the light of the concept of anamnetic solidarity. We can extend to non-human creatures a 'compassion for the violation of moral or bodily integrity' which is 'a limit concept [*Grenzbegriff*] of discourse ethics, just as nature-in-itself is a limit concept of the transcendental–pragmatic theory of knowledge'.[9] But ingenious though it is, this comparison seems inapposite. For one thing, the concept of 'nature-in-itself' indicates a total epistemic inaccessibility, whereas in the case of anamnetic solidarity what is suggested is a *different kind* of moral accessibility. The role of the concept of 'nature-in-itself' is merely to hold open a gap, to prevent any determinate state of natural science from being taken as an account of nature as such, while also reassuring us that the effort to know nature is not the vain pursuit of a *merely* constructed object. Anamnetic solidarity, by contrast, does not point towards the goal of moral striving but, rather, provides a moral *supplement* which discourse ethics requires for internal reasons, but cannot itself provide.

To put this in another way: the appeal to the notion of anamnetic solidarity can be seen as a necessary consequence of the strict universalism of discourse ethics. For if violations of morality can be identified across contemporary cultures, then they can also be identified in that 'other country' which is the past. It is important to remember, however, that what is at issue here is not simply human suffering as such but, rather, specifically *unjust* suffering, as identified by the criteria of discourse ethics.

Accordingly, simply to suggest the extension of anamnetic solidarity – by analogy – to non-human nature is to beg the question of what would *constitute* injustice in this domain. Furthermore, unless one explicitly adopts a theological perspective – and Habermas is extremely reticent on this issue – the *redemptive power* of anamnetic solidarity in relation to the victims of the past remains entirely obscure, whereas we could, given the necessary moral and political will, take effective action to improve the lot of those fellow creatures who populate the natural world.[10]

It is perhaps as a result of these inadequacies that Habermas has made a second, very different attempt, a decade after the first, to theorize the moral relation between human beings and nature. At the end of his 'Remarks on Discourse Ethics' (1991) Habermas expresses the view that we can have duties towards animals to the extent that we stand in *quasi-communicative relations* with them. Morality, he suggests in this context, is a kind of 'protective institution', which arises from our awareness that no human being can preserve his or her integrity alone, because 'the integrity of individuals requires the stabilization of a network of symmetrical relations of recognition, within which the nonreplaceable individuals can secure their fragile identities in a *reciprocal* fashion only as members of a community'.[11] The relations in which we stand to certain animals, Habermas now argues, give rise to analogous obligations:

> Like moral obligations generally, our quasi-moral responsibility toward animals is related to and grounded in the potential for harm inherent in all social interactions. To the extent that creatures participate in our social interactions, we encounter them in the role of an alter ego, as an other in need of protection; this grounds the expectation that we will assume a fiduciary responsibility for their claims.[12]

Habermas makes use of this argument because he is convinced that the prohibition of arbitrary acts of cruelty against animals cannot be relativized to specific forms of life. Since, in Habermas's semi-technical definition, 'ethical issues' of the good life – as opposed to 'moral' issues of justice – depend on the identity-forming values and ideals of specific traditions, and can therefore raise no claims to universal validity, they fail to capture the 'categorical' character of the prohibition on the unnecessary infliction of pain on living creatures.

This argument, however, is scarcely more convincing than Habermas's earlier proposal. This is firstly because, in Habermas's theory, the moral respect due to human beings derives from their status as potential participants in moral discourse, not merely from their communicative capacities as such. On Habermas's account, it cannot be moral to do something to other human beings which they would not agree, after free and fair discussion, to be in their interest, so that the constraint derives from the hypothetical outcome of an ideal consensus. In the case of animals, however, there can be no such restriction. The mere fact of standing in a communicative relation of some kind to another being is not sufficient to generate a normative limit on purely self-interested behaviour towards that being – the sceptic can always reply to Habermas that the feelings that arise by *analogy* with the situation of human communication are simply misleading, that they encourage us to overlook the essential moral differences.

Secondly – and just as problematically – we have a strong sense that it is morally wrong to inflict unnecessary suffering on non-human creatures even when we stand in no communicative relations to them, and Habermas needs to be able to account for this. Indeed, Habermas himself stresses the strength of this prohibition by calling it 'moral' or 'quasi-moral', in the sense of categorical rather than culturally relative. Yet since this prohibition cannot be moral in the Habermasian technical sense of being grounded in the concepts of the theory of communicative action, it suggests that there may be an awareness of the 'good' which is not merely relative to the implicit presuppositions of a specific sociocultural form of life, in the way that Habermas's account of the ethical domain implies. Indeed we find ourselves confronted by the question of whether there might not be certain ethical issues, and specifically problems connected with our relations to nature, which call for a universally valid response.

## Seel's Aesthetics of Nature

Martin Seel, a representative of what might be termed the 'third generation' of Critical Theory, makes an attempt to identify such *ethical* universals in his book *Eine Ästhetik der Natur* (*An Aesthetics of Nature*). Seel begins from the assumption that it is possible to distinguish three fundamental forms of the aesthetic encounter with nature, which he classifies as 'contemplation', 'correlation' and 'imagination'. Contemplation implies absorption in the aimless, self-sufficient consideration of an object, particularly of a natural object whose form is uncontaminated by human purposiveness. According to Seel, this contemplative relation to nature discovers no hidden meaning of things. On the contrary, the advantage of contemplation consists precisely in the fact that this attitude makes possible a temporary escape from the meaning-saturated network of social relations, which can – on occasion – threaten to become stifling. In this context Seel raises the objection against Habermas that 'Total communication . . . would be a kind of suffocation within the communality of a shared cultural horizon. Communicative life has ethical value only as a partial value.'[13]

By contrast, 'correlation' refers to the experience of nature – for example, of a landscape – as a successful realization of favourable conditions for human life. To react to a landscape corresponsively means: 'I *experience* the landscape as the presence of modes of existence which promise fulfilment, which transcend the disadvantages which would otherwise also be present.'[14] Indeed, at a second level correlation ultimately embraces the interlacing of all the modes of our aesthetic relation to nature, since this relation is itself part of a fulfilled way of life.[15] Lastly, Seel defines imagination as an encounter in which nature is experienced as if it were the work of an artist. From this perspective nature can even be said to be superior to every work of art, precisely because it brings forth its artwork-like images without any conscious intention. Here Seel picks up the thread of a thought of Adorno's, arguing: 'it [is] the insignificance of natural beauty, grasped as if it were an aesthetic image, the fleeting, elusive quality of its mode of expression which makes it into a permanent corrective both of artistic production and of the experience of art'.[16] Nature perceived imaginatively allows us a glimpse of new, unprecedented possibilities of life and meaning, and in this way liberates us from too narrow an existential enclosure within existing social relations.

According to Seel, contemplation, correlation and imagination are not merely three qualitatively different attitudes to free nature. They also function as models for three possibilities of experience which are internal to the general *form* of the good life. For: 'under modern conditions only those forms of life can be successful, which offer possibilities for the conscious intensification, the conscious variation, and the conscious suspension of their primary orientation'.[17] In order to lead a good life, we need the opportunity to distance ourselves from the current meaning of our activities and relations to others, just as we need the freedom to imagine for ourselves an alternative, non-realized way of life, and also the possibility of experiencing our existing way of life as harmonious and life-enhancing. For this reason Seel maintains that 'In the successful realization of an aesthetic relation to the world . . . we find a form of successful relation to the world *in general*.'[18]

Although Seel gives only incidental treatment to the question of our ethical relation to nature, he vigorously defends the view that only a philosophical explication of the aesthetic dimension of nature can provide the guidelines for a viable environmental ethics. An ethics of nature must take the form of an ethics of *aesthetic* nature, because – as he puts it – 'only the aesthetics of nature can account for the full meaning of a non-instrumental interaction with nature, and in this way ground the duty to preserve nature, which makes this interaction possible'.[19] Seel does not contest the fact that an ethics of nature must take into account, for example, the economic and ecological dimensions of our relation to nature. In these cases, however, he insists that it is a matter of the preservation or destruction of necessary *conditions* of a favourable life for all, whereas the aesthetic dimension concerns a dimension of the fulfilled life as such. Thus under no circumstances will Seel admit that an ethics of nature could be concerned with a value or purposiveness of nature *'an sich'*. Accordingly, Seel's approach, despite its considerable expansion of the scope of an ethical consideration of nature beyond what is allowed by Habermas, remains strictly anthropocentric:

> The economic, ecological and aesthetic preservation of nature is in the reflective interest of every human being. . . . It is part of the right to autonomy of every human being. His or her right to self-development is – among other things – a right to free nature. Nature has no rights over against human beings, rather human beings have a right to nature, against other human beings.[20]

## Limits of a Lifeworld-Centred View of Nature

It seems legitimate to doubt, however, whether the idea of a universal right to the aesthetic enjoyment of nature is sufficient to bring about the reorientation of our environmental consciousness which is necessary today. It is interesting that even Habermas expresses doubts about the sufficiency of a purely anthropocentric environmental ethics, which he supports with the following remarks of Joel Whitebook:

> Even if it could be shown *theoretically* that it is not necessary to move from the standpoint of anthropocentrism to formulate solutions to the environmental crisis, a question would still remain at the level of *social psychology*. For it is difficult to imagine how the conflict between society and nature is going to be solved without a major transformation in our social consciousness – e.g. a renewed reverence for life.[21]

Yet despite this concession, Habermas agrees with Seel that a metaphysical support for this psychological reorientation is neither necessary, nor to be provided by means of philosophical reflection. Both thinkers share the view that a philosophical characterization of nature as a whole would transgress the bounds which Kant definitively established for human knowledge, and lapse back into the arbitrariness of pre-critical thinking. Seel emphasizes that,

> since the emergence of modern science . . . there is no longer a unitary nature, which could function as the support of a closed theory of our being in and with nature. The object of mathematical physics, of the life-sciences or geo-sciences, of medical physiology or psychological therapy, the nature of my kitchen garden, the appearance of an aesthetic landscape – even if these concepts of nature cannot simply be lined up alongside one another, no more comprehensive concept is in prospect from the standpoint of which the question of the definitive, favourable relation to nature could be answered in general.[22]

He goes on to draw the conclusion that 'the question of the appropriate relation to nature . . . becomes transformed into the question of the right relation between our relations to nature'.[23]

But it is easy to see the *reductio ad absurdum* towards which this line of argument tends. Is nature viewed from my kitchen window qualitatively distinct from what I can see through my living-room window? Is the nature I drive through different from the one I take a walk through? Hence we are faced with the question: is this anthropocentric – even sceptical – reticence sustainable? Is it possible to abandon every philosophical notion of how nature must be, beyond our various modes of access to it? We may get closer to an answer to this question if we pursue a little further the tacit implications of Seel's conception of the relation between human beings and nature.

Seel concludes his book by affirming, as he has done several times in the course of his discussions, that nature is 'neither a subject, nor like a subject' [*weder Subjekt noch subjekthaft*], just as he asserts that 'an aesthetics of nature needs no metaphysics'.[24] However, one could raise the objection that a basic metaphysical conviction is already implicit in the attempt to deny external nature every trace of subjectivity. Seel's conception is, fundamentally, dualistic. On the one hand, he repeatedly emphasizes that human beings are 'living natural beings' [*lebende Naturwesen*]. On the other, he also makes it clear that human beings must be regarded as 'subjects' who are capable of reflectively choosing and pursuing their own life projects. But if nature is not at all subject-like [*subjekthaft*], and yet human beings are simultaneously both natural beings and subjects, then the two dimensions of human existence which Seel identifies appear to enter into contradiction. One might ask: where does the subjective freedom of human beings emerge from, if pre-human nature reveals no self-related structures and no capacity – even an unreflective one – for self-determination in accordance with an immanent norm? Presumably Seel would not deny that the animal world seems characterized by the pervasiveness of purposive action, and since he remains agnostic about the character of nature '*an sich*', he has no reason to insist that any such apparent purposiveness, any such 'proto-subjectivity' (as it might be called), must ultimately be explicable in non-intentional terms. These genetic considerations would not, of course, be a decisive objection to Seel's position if he were strictly Kantian in the sense of considering phenomenal nature purely as the correlate of a transcendental process of constitution, although he would still be faced with the conundrum of the relation between nature and freedom. However, Seel evidently wishes to embed the 'transcendental' dimension of the human relation to the world (the fact that this is not simply a relation *between* inner-worldly entities) *within* natural history; hence the genetic question cannot be avoided.

Seel, no doubt aware of this, does make the concession that the modern natural sciences are 'one-sided': 'No matter to what extent physics is able to write the history of nature, the historical reality of human beings and their difficult relation to external nature, out of which even the history of physics as a form of knowledge has emerged, cannot itself figure in this history.'[25] Yet he also appears to believe that the philosophical investigation of the domain of nature can be undertaken only in the form of a hermeneutics or a phenomenological description of the plural modes of experience and knowledge within which we encounter nature. All the paths of access to nature, however – including that of the modern natural sciences – presuppose the background structure of the lifeworld, 'the historical reality of human beings', which frames our human perspectives on the world in general. It is the fact not only that this world falls outside the purview of the natural sciences, but also that the terms which are essential to its description cannot be *reduced* to natural-scientific terms, which sets a *cognitive* limit to the natural sciences.[26] As we have just noted, this sense of a limit could be avoided only if Seel were to consider nature as the correlate of a purely transcendental process of constitution, which would itself have no naturalistic dimension. But, as Seel's inclusion of the history of the natural sciences within human history suggests, he does not in fact endorse the correspondence of natural-scientific objectivity and extra-mundane subjectivity, which alone would enable him to avoid the requirement that the natural sciences be supplemented by a further philosophical form of inquiry into nature. This form can be appropriately characterized as 'metaphysical', since it would strive to give us at least some intuition of how nature must be constituted '*an sich*', given that it has brought forth the subjectivity of human beings and the history of their experiences of nature.

Seel – influenced, like Habermas, by the Weberian thesis of the disenchantment of the world – refuses this type of philosophical reflection, since he equates the concept of metaphysics with the attempt to develop a philosophical interpretation of the objective meaning of the totality of being, and of the purpose of human life within such a totality. According to Seel, 'the thread of a global mediation between human praxis and natural being has been broken'.[27] Similarly, Habermas maintains that:

> The perspective from which metaphysics distinguished essence from appearance vanishes together with the anticipation of the totality of beings. In science phenomena are traced back to more and more fundamental structures whose depth matches the range of explanatory theories; but these structures no longer stand within the referential network of a totality. They no longer throw light on the individual's position in the cosmos, upon one's place in the architectonic of reason or within the system.[28]

Against this view one could object that a philosophical reflection on the constitution of nature *'an sich'* becomes indispensable when – like Habermas – one both acknowledges the transcendental dimension of the lifeworld and rejects 'the assumption of a transcendental consciousness, without origins as it were'.[29]

Talk of nature *'an sich'* in this context should not be misinterpreted as advocacy of a revival of objectivistic metaphysics. Philosophical inquiry into the 'nature of nature' need not raise a suspect claim to have deciphered the 'objective meaning in being', as Habermas puts it.[30] Many of the influential philosophers of the twentieth century – Maurice Merleau-Ponty, Theodor Adorno and Charles Taylor, for example – have felt compelled to contest the cognitive exclusivity of the natural sciences in the domain of nature, without believing that it is possible to establish a metaphysical theory of nature. Since for all these thinkers subjectivity emerges from nature, yet also remains a part of – intrinsic to – nature, we cannot, as thinking subjects, make nature the target of a theory of any kind without distorting an essential co-belonging. But this fact does not preclude philosophical elucidations of a reality which merits the title 'Natur *an sich*' in so far as it cannot be *reduced* to the forms of its interpretation. Furthermore, such elucidations need not fall victim to the illusion, which both Seel and Habermas so fear, that one could derive detailed prescriptions for the conduct of human life from a totalizing speculation on the meaning and purpose of nature. They can freely advertise their own provisional status.

## The Return of *natura naturans*

It is interesting to observe that Habermas seems to be far more aware than Seel that at least a residue of a 'metaphysical' conception of nature must be retained in contemporary philosophy, as the recent dispute with his leading contemporary Dieter Henrich has revealed. In his polemic 'What is Metaphysics? – What is Modernity? Twelve Theses against Jürgen Habermas', Henrich argued that Habermas's philosophy finds itself torn between the contradictory tendencies of naturalism and transcendentalism. Habermas's position, he claimed, is philosophically inconsistent, because – on the one hand – it presupposes a pragmatic and socio-scientific conception of language and communication, and – on the other hand – also draws on the tradition of transcendental phenomenology in its elaboration of the concept of the lifeworld.[31] In replying to this criticism, Habermas insisted that his naturalism was not to be confused with the physicalism of the modern natural-scientific world-view: 'It seems to me that it has been clear since Marx that the normative content of modernity can be taken up and preserved even and especially under materialist premisses.' And he continued: '"Nature in itself" does not coincide with objectivated nature. What Marx had in mind is the emergence in natural history of the sociocultural form of life of *homo sapiens*, which goes beyond physically objectified nature to conceptually include, as it were, a piece of *natura naturans*.'[32]

Habermas's gesture towards the double terminology of *natura naturata* and *natura naturans* is as surprising as it is illuminating. For this conceptual distinction, which ultimately derives from Neo-Platonism, was first systematically elaborated by the Scholastics, and reappears once more with Spinoza. It was eventually taken up and elaborated by German Idealism, in particular by Schelling, in the wake of the Spinoza-renaissance of the German Enlightenment.[33] In another passage where Habermas makes use of this terminology, he refers explicitly to Schelling, and one is reminded that Habermas began his intellectual career with a dissertation on this philosopher. Indeed, there is reason to suspect that Schelling has continued to play a significant – albeit muted – role in Habermas's thinking ever since.[34] It seems important for our purposes, therefore, to cast a brief glance at the kind of role which the distinction between *natura naturata* and *natura naturans* plays in Schelling's own thought.

In the fullest statement of his identity philosophy, the unpublished 'Würzburg System' of 1804, Schelling equates *natura naturans* with the infinite self-affirmation of a pantheistically interpreted God, while *natura naturata* is understood as the world of dependent – and thus transient – things.[35] The characterization of *natura naturans* as the spontaneous creative principle of the natural world has the consequence that even the most elementary forms of the material world conceal a core of self-relatedness, without which the emergence of organic life, and ultimately the conscious life of humanity, would remain inexplicable. Schelling asserts: 'Everything is a primal germ, or it is nothing. [*Alles ist Urkeim oder nichts.*] Every part of the material world is not only alive, but is also a universe of different kinds of life, even when a rigid selfhood represses this infinite life. . . . The inorganic is only the negation of the organic, death only repressed life.'[36] Habermas would presumably reject such assertions as extravagant speculation, yet – as we have seen – even he must admit that, in the final analysis, we cannot rest content with understanding nature in terms of a physicalistic world-view inspired by the natural sciences. If this is indeed the case, then the question is raised of whether it might not be legitimate at least to speculate about an alternative image of nature to that which predominates in our technological society, and about what its ethical consequences might be.

Here we are beginning to reach the heart of the matter. Habermas strives, although not entirely consistently, to abandon every 'metaphysical' conception of nature, because he fears that normative insights which are presumed to have metaphysical backing could be used to override the democratic consensus of the members of a society. For this reason he maintains that philosophy as 'interpreter' – that is, in one of the two key roles he attributes to philosophy – can concern itself only with the meaning-complexes of a *specific* lifeworld, not with the totality of the world as such. The norms of linguistic praxis which specify the priority of the principle of an unlimited communication community over all substantive convictions can claim universal validity, whereas *ethical* arguments concerning the meaning and purpose of life are only ever valid relative to a specific form of life.[37] But here Habermas finds himself entangled in contradiction. For since, according to his own conception, philosophy – apart from its 'reconstructive' use – functions as the reflective articulation of the intuitions of a specific lifeworld, there can be no 'neutral' viewpoint from which Habermas can describe a plurality of lifeworlds, each with its own value orientation, embedded in a natural context understood in materialist terms. This 'sophisticated naturalism', as Charles Taylor has called it,[38] is itself a metaphysical view which claims an objectivity which transcends the confines of any specific lifeworld, despite Habermas's attempts to present it as a scientific hypothesis.[39]

But if the logic of Habermas's position forces him to make transcultural philosophical claims in this way, the force of his argument that ethical convictions can never raise a claim to validity which goes beyond the bounds of a specific form of life is considerably weakened. It should be noted that on this point Habermas finds himself faced not merely with a theoretical but also with a practical dilemma. This is because he insists on the fact that philosophical reflection can only explain the possibility and structure of the moral point of view, but can provide no generally valid grounds to justify *why* we should be moral. In this case, Habermas suggests, we have to rely on 'socialisation into a form of life that complements the moral principle', or even on 'the world-disclosing power of prophetic speech and in general . . . every innovative discourse that initiates better forms of life, and more reflective ways of life'.[40] However, Habermas goes on to contest the idea that 'world-disclosing arguments' can be regarded as philosophical arguments. This conclusion is disturbing, because it seems to deprive Habermas of any philosophical means to foster *concretely* the moral mode of being with whose *formal* possibility he is so intensely concerned. Perhaps it would be wiser of him to recognize as legitimate the world-disclosing function of philosophy, which has played such a central role in the history of thought, while at the same time emphasizing the essential condition of a post-Kantian fallibilism: that the world cannot be *exhausted* as an object of thought.

That such a fallibilism need not be equated with ethical relativism is shown by the writings of Hans Jonas, and in particular by his major work on the environmental crisis, *Das Prinzip Verantwortung* (*The Imperative of Responsibility*). In the course of his discussions, Jonas frequently stresses: 'it is a commonplace that it follows from the nature of philosophical knowledge and its concerns that it must strive for the ultimate, and yet always remain exposed to the conflict of opinions'.[41] Nevertheless, he seeks to demonstrate the incoherence of a reductionistic physicalism, and to make plausible a conception of nature which reveals many similarities with Schelling's *Naturphilosophie*. Indeed, Jonas shares not only with Schelling, but also with contemporary thinkers such as Thomas Nagel, the conviction that mind is an objective feature of reality, or that – as he puts it – 'subjectivity or inwardness is an ontologically essential datum within being'.[42] As a result, he rejects not only scientific reductionism but any form of idealism which would consider material nature merely as a constituted correlate of consciousness. But since, for familiar reasons, he also rejects Cartesian dualism, Jonas is led to propose that there must be a tendency towards the realization of a dimension of inwardness or subjectivity internal to the original stuff of the world:

> Since finality – striving towards a goal – appears in a subjectively manifest form in certain natural beings, namely living beings, and can hence become effective in an objectively causal way, it cannot be entirely alien to nature, which brought it forth; it must itself be 'natural', and indeed in conformity with nature, conditioned by nature and autonomously generated by nature. It follows that final causes – and thus also values and differences of value – must be included in the concept of the world's causality, which cannot be entirely neutral.[43]

Building on this conception of the essential purposiveness of nature, Jonas asserts, in *Das Prinzip Verantwortung*: 'we can discern in the capacity to have purposes something which is "good in itself", concerning which we intuitively know that it is infinitely superior to all purposeless being'.[44] In having purposes, Jonas suggests, being affirms itself, and 'the mere fact that being is not indifferent towards itself turns its difference from nonbeing into the fundamental value of all values, the primary "Yes"'.[45] This self-affirmation becomes explicit at the level of organic life, where the organism maintains itself against the constant threat of dissolution and death. Furthermore, in human existence it attains the level of self-consciousness, becomes aware both of itself and of all other purposive self-affirmation. The fact that only human beings can thus actively foster purposiveness is, for Jonas, sufficient to make the responsibility of human beings for other human beings, and in particular for the sheer continuation of human life as such, into 'the primordial image of all responsibility'.[46] The central argument of *Das Prinzip Verantwortung* is that in an age of global ecological crisis, the fundamental task of the preservation of human life must displace utopian projects of social transformation which have, in any case, traditionally implied an exploitative attitude to nature.

It is clearly important to consider how discourse ethics might respond to the challenge posed by Jonas's elaboration of what he presents as a metaphysically warranted ethical insight. Although Habermas has not discussed Jonas directly, Karl-Otto Apel has responded respectfully to his work, and the weaknesses in Apel's reply usefully highlight some of the vulnerable points of a discourse-ethical approach to ecological issues, and to the ethics of nature. Apel claims that discourse ethics, because of its founding principle of consensus guided by the ideal of an unlimited community of communication, must take into account the hypothetical interests of future generations. This seems plausible enough since, given the universal scope of discourse, there is no reason to exclude the hypothetically attributed views of individuals who will exist, but happen not to exist at present, from the discussion of moral issues pertinent to them. But Apel then goes on to claim that Jonas's basic postulate – that 'there should also be a humanity in the future' – can also be derived from the grounding principle of discourse ethics, presumably since the criteria of coherence and consensus employed by discourse ethics require the maximum possible scrutiny, and thus an indefinite continuation of the human speech community.[47]

This further claim, however, seems highly implausible. For first, as Habermas has argued against Apel, although the refusal to seek (moral or cognitive) truth through consensus can be seen as a violation of the normative import of the counterfactual pragmatic presuppositions of communication, this does not mean that commitment to such a search is itself a moral obligation grounded in or derived from this normativity. Habermas insists that 'Communicative reason, unlike practical reason, is not itself a source of norms of right action . . . Normativity and rationality *overlap* in the field of justification of moral insights . . . and at any rate cannot sustain an existential understanding of self and world.'[48] And this objection seems justified. For there is indeed something bizarre about Apel's suggestion that we are under an obligation, by virtue of the mere fact of communicating with others, to ensure the generational continuity of a speech community which could amplify consensus towards an infinite ideal – in other words, to procreate! However, even if we shift the focus – following Habermas – to the issue of the *justification* of moral norms, as opposed to the supposed ethical implications of communication as such, the prospects do not look much better. Habermas's principle of universalization states that a norm is valid when the consequences of its being generally followed could be accepted by all concerned as consonant with their interests. But what sense could it make to consult human beings – even in a hypothetical, 'advocatory' manner – about a norm of action which, if followed, would result in their never coming into existence? Human beings who do not yet exist *will* have interests when they do exist, but the idea of a non-existent being having an interest in existing or not seems downright incoherent.[49]

Given these difficulties of the discourse-ethical approach, and given that Habermas already discerns a kernel of truth in the concept of *natura naturans*, it would seem to be open to him – and perhaps even advisable for him – to accept the universality of the basic ethical insight proposed by Jonas, at least until its cultural relativity can be demonstrated. Significantly, Habermas does not try to avoid appealing to what he calls the 'unmistakeable language' of our 'moral intuitions' when it is a matter of evaluating the permissibility of cruelty to animals. Furthermore he has, on occasion, described our human reaction to the destruction of the environment in a manner which suggests a deep-rooted – and perhaps even ontologically grounded – sympathy between human beings and the natural world:

> It is true that the timebombs of a ruthlessly exploited nature are quietly yet stubbornly ticking away. But while outer nature broods in its way on revenge for the mutilations we have inflicted on it, nature within *us* also raises its voice. . . . We cannot be deceived, for example, by the crippling sadness which overcomes us amidst a landscape destroyed and poisoned, stifled in its expression, by the hands of human beings and the detritus of civilization.[50]

Such passages in Habermas seem to indicate that he cannot avoid at least the tendency to reach beyond the limits of his quasi-Kantian conception of nature, in order to give an appropriate description of our unease when we are confronted with the condition of nature in our technological civilization. For according to Habermas here, it is not – as Seel suggests – our *aesthetic* sense for natural beauty and sublimity which turns the protection of the environment into a *moral* duty. Rather, it is 'nature in us', which functions as a sounding board for the silent lament of a violated outer nature, and thus potentially awakens an ethical sensitivity to the need for a less instrumental relation to nature.

Of course, no *specific* duties towards nature can be derived from these obscure anticipations of an 'ontological' sympathy; rather, the possibility in principle of a reorientation, which would be more than a matter of 'social psychology' – to use Whitebook's term – and would tincture all social and personal goals and decisions to a greater or lesser extent. It thus appears that Habermas has posed what he terms the 'basic philosophical question' falsely. For what is fundamentally at issue is not 'how an ethics of nature should be grounded today, without recourse to the substantial reason of religious or metaphysical world-views, and thus on the level of learning attained by our modern understanding of the world', as he puts it,[51] since this presupposes that a modern understanding of the world can be exclusively scientific. It is true that the speculatively inclined will no doubt continue to engage indefinitely in dispute about the constitution of nature 'in-itself', and in this sense the restoration of a dominant, exclusive world-view would be unthinkable without the use of horrendous violence. But in order to foster a new awareness of the claims of nature, philosophy need only make clear the insuperable limits of a *scientized* understanding of the world, and to show at least the plausibility of the assumption of an inwardness of nature, which we might still refer to as *natura naturans*, by means of arguments which are both rational and world-disclosive. For ultimately the belief that a post-technological ethics of the fragile world we inhabit could do without any speculative dimension whatsoever is surely no less an illusion than the antiquated conviction of possessing the one uniquely true metaphysical picture of nature.

## Notes

1. In an essay on Horkheimer, Habermas claims that 'Unified metaphysical thought – however negatively accented – transposes solidarity, which has its proper place in linguistic intersubjectivity, communication, and individuating socialization, into the identity of an underlying essence, the undifferentiated negativity of the world-will.' See 'To Seek to Salvage an Unconditional Meaning without God is a Futile Undertaking: Reflections on a Remark of Max Horkheimer', in Jürgen Habermas, *Justification and Application. Remarks on Discourse Ethics*, trans. Ciaran Cronin, Cambridge: Polity Press 1993, p. 143.

2. Herbert Marcuse, *Counterrevolution and Revolt*, Boston, MA: Beacon Press 1972, pp. 69–70.

3. Ibid., pp. 63–74.

4. Both phrases occur on p. 69.

5. Ibid., pp. 74–5.

6. In 1982 Habermas observed: 'it is important to note that the approaches to an interpretative account of natural history – phenomenological, morphological, anthropological-evolutionary – have not overcome the stage of natural *philosophy*; that they have not been able to develop into alternative *within* science.' ('A Reply to My Critics', in John B. Thompson and David Held, eds, *Habermas: Critical Debates*, London: Macmillan 1982, p. 243.)

7. See Jürgen Habermas, 'Rückkehr zur Metaphysik? – Eine Sammelrezension', in *Nachmetaphysisches Denken*, Frankfurt am Main: Suhrkamp 1988.

8. 'A Reply to My Critics', p. 247.

9. Ibid.

10. For a general critique of Habermas's use of the concept of anamnetic solidarity, see Dieter Teichert, 'Anamnetische Solidarität? Zum Begriff historischer Erinnerung bei Benjamin, Habermas und Ricoeur', *Konstanzer Berichte*, 1993/1, Zentrum für Philosophie und Wissenschaftstheorie, University of Konstanz. Teichert makes it clear that, without redemptive theological premises which Habermas cannot employ, anamnetic solidarity tends to become instrumentalized – a remembrance of the past for the sake of the present.

11. Jürgen Habermas, 'Remarks on Discourse Ethics', in *Justification and Application*, p. 109.

12. Ibid.

13. Martin Seel, *Eine Ästhetik der Natur*, Frankfurt am Main: Suhrkamp 1991, p. 325.

14. Ibid., p. 90.

15. See ibid., pp. 293–8.
16. Ibid., p. 165.
17. Ibid., p. 288.
18. Ibid., p. 298.
19. Ibid., p. 342.
20. Ibid., p. 346.
21. Cited in 'A Reply to My Critics', p. 247.
22. *Eine Ästhetik der Natur*, p. 13.
23. Ibid., p. 15.
24. Ibid., p. 366.
25. Ibid., p. 25.
26. As Hilary Putnam has argued in many recent papers, any attempt to translate our everyday epistemic notions into physicalistic terms will presuppose precisely those concepts of appropriateness, explanatory adequacy, and so forth, which it is intended to reduce. See, for example, 'Vagueness and Alternative Logic', in *Realism and Reason: Philosophical Papers Volume 3*, Cambridge: Cambridge University Press (paperback edn) 1989.
27. *Eine Ästhetik der Natur*, p. 13.
28. Jürgen Habermas, 'Themes in Postmetaphysical Thinking', in *Postmetaphysical Thinking: Philosophical Essays*, trans. William Hohengarten, Cambridge: Polity Press 1992, p. 35.
29. 'A Reply to My Critics', p. 242.
30. 'Rückkehr zur Metaphysik? – Eine Sammelrezension', p. 271.
31. See Dieter Henrich, 'Was ist Metaphysik – was Moderne? Zwölf Thesen gegen Jürgen Habermas', in *Konzepte*, Frankfurt am Main: Suhrkamp 1987, pp. 22 ff.
32. 'Metaphysics after Kant', in *Postmetaphysical Thinking*, p. 20.
33. See the article '*Natura naturans/naturata*', in Joachim Ritter and Karlfried Gründer, eds, *Historisches Wörterbuch der Philosophie*, Basel/Stuttgart: Schwabe 1984, vol. 6.
34. In an interview, Habermas refers to Schelling's *Weltalter* ('Ages of the World') as an inspiration for the ideas of 'felicitous interaction, of reciprocity and distance, of separation and of successful, unspoiled nearness' which underpin his theory of communicative action. See 'The Dialectics of Rationalization' in Jürgen Habermas, *Autonomy and Solidarity: Interviews*, ed. Peter Dews, London: Verso (revised edn) 1992, p. 125.
35. F.W.J. Schelling, *System der gesammten Philosophie und der Naturphilosophie insbesondere*, in Manfred Frank, ed., *Ausgewählte Schriften*, Frankfurt am Main: Suhrkamp 1985, vol. 3, pp. 209 ff. The first part of this text has been translated as 'System of Philosophy in General and of the Philosophy of Nature in Particular', in Thomas Pfau, trans. and ed., *Idealism and the Endgame of Theory: Three Essays by F.W.J. Schelling*, Albany, NY: SUNY Press 1994. Schelling's explication of the distinction between *naturans* and *naturata* is on pp. 183–5 of this translation.
36. Ibid., p. 398.
37. See Jürgen Habermas, 'On the Pragmatic, the Ethical and the Moral Employments of Practical Reason', in *Justification and Application*.
38. See Charles Taylor, *Sources of the Self*, Cambridge: Cambridge University Press 1989, p. 67.
39. '. . . whatever form materialism appears in, within the horizon of a scientific and fallibilistic mode of thought it is a hypothesis which can only claim plausibility for the time being.' (Jürgen Habermas, 'Transzendenz von innen, Transzendenz ins Diesseits', in *Texte und Kontexte*, Frankfurt am Main: Suhrkamp 1991, p. 129.)
40. 'Remarks on Discourse Ethics', p. 79.
41. Hans Jonas, *Das Prinzip Verantwortung*, Frankfurt am Main: Suhrkamp 1989, p. 326/*The Imperative of Responsibility*, trans. Hans Jonas with the collaboration of David Herr, Chicago: University of Chicago Press 1984, p. 186.
42. Hans Jonas, *Materie, Geist und Schöpfung*, Frankfurt am Main: Suhrkamp 1988, p. 17.
43. Ibid., p. 23.
44. *Das Prinzip Verantwortung*, p. 154/*The Imperative of Responsibility*, p. 80.
45. Ibid., p. 155/p. 81.
46. Ibid., p. 184/p. 98.

47. See Karl-Otto Apel, 'Verantwortung heute – nur noch Prinzip der Bewahrung und Selbstbeschränkung oder immer noch der Befreiung und Verwirklichung von Humanität?', in *Diskurs und Verantwortung*, Frankfurt am Main: Suhrkamp 1992, pp. 198–216, esp. p. 203.

48. 'Remarks on Discourse Ethics', p. 81.

49. For an exploration of the paradoxes which arise for discourse ethics from the need to include *potential* human beings within an *actual* consensus, see Micha Brumlik, 'Über die Ansprüche Ungeborener und Unmündiger. Wie advokatorisch ist die Diskursethik?', in Wolfgang Kuhlmann, ed., *Moralität und Sittlichkeit*, Frankfurt am Main: Suhrkamp 1986.

50. Jürgen Habermas, *Vergangenheit als Zukunft*, Zurich: Pendo Verlag 1991, p. 125/*The Past as Future*, trans. and ed. Max Pensky, Lincoln, NB: University of Nebraska Press 1994, p. 94.

51. 'A Reply to my Critics', p. 248 (translation altered).

# Modernity, Self-Consciousness and the Scope of Philosophy: Jürgen Habermas and Dieter Henrich in Debate

One of the least noted features of the strife between Habermas and his postmodernist opponents over the 'philosophical discourse of modernity' is the number of assumptions which both sides share in common, despite the energy of the arguments between them. Habermas and his critics coincide in the view – ultimately derived from Heidegger – that the history of philosophy is susceptible to an epochal analysis, and that the era of the philosophy of the subject, which is also the culminating era of metaphysical thinking, is currently drawing to a close. Indeed, it is remarkable that *The Philosophical Discourse of Modernity* gives the celebrated account of the 'death of man' in Foucault's *The Order of Things*, viewed as a postmortem on the monological subject, almost unqualified endorsement. Habermas is convinced that Foucault's account of the unstable oscillation between transcendental and empirical dimensions characteristic of 'anthropological' thinking, in which the figure of man functions ambiguously as both subject and object, as both ground and goal of knowledge, accurately transcribes the symptoms which inform us that 'the paradigm of the philosophy of consciousness is exhausted'.[1] His disagreement is only with Foucault's solution, which relies on a concept of power which oscillates just as much between transcendental and empirical status as the concept of 'man' it supplants: 'Foucault did not think through the aporias of his own approach well enough to see how his theory of power was overtaken by a fate similar to that of the human sciences rooted in the philosophy of the subject . . . To the objectivism of self-mastery on the part of the human sciences there corresponds a subjectivism of self-forgetfulness on Foucault's part.'[2] By contrast, Habermas's own answer to the insoluble dilemmas of *Subjektphilosophie* involves the advocacy of a shift in basic philosophical models: 'the paradigm of the knowledge of objects has to be replaced by the paradigm of mutual understanding between subjects capable of speech and action'.[3] Only a communicative paradigm, Habermas contends, is able to overcome the dynamic of self-objectification and reification which is built into any philosophy centred on the self-reflecting subject, and against which postmodernist thinking is also centrally – if ineptly – directed.

From the standpoint of his critics, of course, Habermas does not go nearly far enough. The shift to an intersubjective paradigm, as the very term suggests, does not provide a sufficiently radical escape from the dominance of subjectivity. As Fred Dallmayr has written:

> Despite the claimed exit from subjectivity, the same spheres or dimensions [as those of Kantian rationalism] clearly resurface in Habermas's model with its various divisions or tripartitions. . . . In the light of this intrinsic continuity, one can reasonably doubt the asserted 'paradigm shift' – away from subject- or ego-centred reason – given that the various dimensions of the model all pay homage to the same centring (being classifiable respectively into subject-object, subject-subject, and subject-to-itself relationships).[4]

Here, as in other responses to Habermas, the essentially metaphysical aspect of modern philosophy is taken to consist in its establishment of categorial distinctions between rationality dimensions. The retention of these distinctions is viewed as already implying a form of reification, regardless of whether they are seen as anchored in the capacities of the subject or, rather, as the result of the historical unfolding of the intrinsic structure of a *communicative* reason. Furthermore, the elaboration and defence of this communicative rationality are not seen as an adequate counter to, but rather as complicit with, the continued social and political dynamic of subjectivism and individualism. As Jay Bernstein has argued:

> the revelation that the very lifeworld which is the ground and repository of our collective life has been as lifeworld systematically "de-worlded", suggests that rationalization has distorted and deformed reason *intrinsically* by trisecting it, by categorically disallowing where needed an unmetaphorical intermeshing of validity claims. More precisely, the structures of the lifeworld have been distorted such that they appear, almost always and nearly everywhere, to accord with the claims of subject-centred reason.[5]

Habermas's reply to this disquiet is that an 'abstract negation' of the principle of subjectivity will simply result in a submission of human individuals to an anonymous pre-subjective principle or power. The only way in which the aspirations to freedom and self-determination awkwardly conveyed by the philosophy of the subject can be preserved is by providing an account of the subject as essentially constituted through its relations with others, so that even its basic capacities for self-consciousness and reflection are seen as an internalization of dialogue, not as a form of potentially all-embracing objectification. In Habermas's account, the subject is not deconstructed or exploded; rather, 'the self-relation emerges out of an *interactive* context'.[6]

## Henrich on Subjectivity and Self-Preservation

But what if the Heideggerian assumption of both Habermas and the post-modernists were incorrect? What if the subject of modern philosophy cannot be simply reduced to a principle of domination? This is the possibility which is opened by the work of Dieter Henrich, outstanding scholar of German Idealism and leading contemporary of Habermas, who has written extensively on the theory of subjectivity, and with whom Habermas has been engaged in debate over the past decade or so. At the most general level, Henrich has criticized an over-easy recourse to the language of epochal transformations and paradigm shifts, which can readily become a historicist evasion of philosophical issues. There is a depressing pertinence to Henrich's claim that:

> promises of enlightenment accompanied by declarations of a paradigm shift fade especially quickly if they depend not only on a methodically new beginning but also on curtailing the problem. They actually invite proclamations of further paradigm shifts, shifts that today once again dilute and even inundate efforts at diagnosing the modern world.[7]

However, Henrich's reservations are not limited merely to the use made of the concept of a paradigm shift. He has developed a complex historical and philosophical argument which contests the Heideggerian account of the status of the subject upon which both Habermas and the postmodernists largely rely.

The fullest statement of Henrich's position is to be found in his article 'Die Grundstruktur der modernen Philosophie' ('The Basic Structure of Modern Philosophy'), which was published in 1976. Here Henrich gives Heidegger the accolade of having elaborated the 'interpretation of modernity' which 'penetrates deepest'. This is because 'It brings the Cartesian element of modern consciousness pre-eminently into view and interprets it as the expression of a tendency to understand every entity as primarily an object of methodical knowledge – as possible theme of a confirmation [*Feststellen*] of the knowing subject which has attained certainty.'[8] However, Henrich contends, this diagnosis, despite its undeniable power, does not do justice to the relation between self-consciousness [*Selbstbewußtsein*] and self-preservation [*Selbsterhaltung*] in modern philosophy, since it necessarily reduces the former to the latter. In order to sustain his position, Heidegger must show that self-consciousness is nothing other than the 'unconditional domination over something transparently present', thus collapsing the connection between self-consciousness and self-assertion into an identity.[9] But against this Henrich argues that even if it is true that I cannot put myself at my own disposition without some activity on my part, this does not entail that the disposability as such is the result of my own activity: 'I cannot ground the continuity of that interpretative relation to myself, on the basis of which I preserve my being, without activity. But this does not mean that I could – and would need to – open up for myself the very possibility of a relation to myself.'[10]

Henrich's essay emphasizes the intimate connection between the concepts of self-consciousness and self-preservation in modernity, while insisting that the distinction between them cannot be simply collapsed. The historical corollary of this standpoint is his argument that the relation between these concepts long predates Hobbes and Descartes, since it emerged first in Stoic thinking, and was transmitted thence to the modern West. Breaking with the Aristotelian thought that self-preservation is orientated towards the realization of the *eidos* of a particular being, and thus ultimately guided by the teleological world order which determines this *eidos*, the Stoics identified a self-acquaintance, an awareness of one's own essence, which was prior to the awareness of one's relation to the world order. Only on the basis of this awareness of oneself was it possible to desire to preserve oneself.[11] Explicating this thought in contemporary philosophical terms, Henrich argues that self-preservation would not be necessary, if self-consciousness did not include an awareness of being dependent on conditions which are not under its own control. The experience of dependence on an unfathomable ground of selfhood, rather than the striving for total self-domination, gives rise to the various constellations of modern thought and experience. Even the experience of modern technology, Henrich suggests, forces an awareness that the self cannot be *causa sui*; that – as the possibility of standing in a relation to itself – it has an origin other than whatever it brings under its control. In Henrich's words: 'Self-consciousness hopes for a reason for its own being and activity, with regard to which it already knows that it would be meaningless to represent it as a further context of controllable objectivity.'[12]

From this perspective Henrich explains that the dynamism of modern consciousness is not simply a matter of will-to-power, but arises from the situation of a self which knows that there are conditions of its being which cannot be captured by an objective knowledge of the cosmos [*Kosmoswissen*]. The restless urge to explore and break boundaries can be understood in terms of the attempt by such a self to comprehend itself in the only way possible, through ceaseless experimentation: 'It strives to put itself in ever new situations, and to test new possibilities of being. And yet in this it is not concerned with the expansion of its power, but first and foremost simply with confirming its being, which is incomprehensible to it, anew.'[13] Consequently, Henrich argues that what he calls 'Baconianism' (which Heidegger equates with modernity as such) should be seen as only one of a range of philosophical responses to the paradoxical position of the modern self. The three most significant alternatives are: an attempt to show the newly autonomous self to be at home in a totality which is fundamentally homogeneous with it, which Henrich attributes to thinkers such as Leibniz and Hegel; scepticism, which reacts to the unknowability of the ground of consciousness, and is thus an essential strand in the modern experience of the world; and theories such as those of Marx, Nietzsche and Freud, in which reason and subjectivity have only the status of means or functions in the service of a more fundamental self-sustaining process.[14]

Significantly, in the little-read closing pages of the first volume of *The Theory of Communicative Action*, Habermas feels obliged to address Henrich's account of self-consciousness and self-preservation in detail. In terms of the general structure of Habermas's philosophical position, this need arises because he must definitively establish the 'exhaustion' of the paradigm of *Subjektphilosophie*, suggested by the dead-end of Adorno's *Negative Dialectics*, before moving on to expound his communicative grounding of a critical social theory. Habermas begins by rehearsing the well-known aporia of the 'reflection theory' of self-consciousness, of which Henrich himself has given a classic account in his pathbreaking essay on 'Fichte's Original Insight', and later in a major text on '*Selbstbewußtsein*'.[15] If self-consciousness, understood as an identity of knower and known, is taken as the defining feature of the subject, and if it is also considered to be constituted by the reflexive relation of a subject turning back to view itself as an object, then the problem arises that the subject must *pre-exist* the relation in which it is supposed to consist, in order to effect this turning back.[16] A second major difficulty is posed by the fact that in order to turn back and grasp its identity with itself, the subject must be able to *recognize* the target of reflection as itself – but this *presupposes* an awareness of self, which is precisely what the relation of reflection is intended to explain.[17]

In his article on self-consciousness, Henrich seeks to resolve these problems by dropping the assumption that consciousness must belong to an 'I' or a self. He suggests that consciousness can be understood as an 'event' [*Ereignis*] or dimension in which awareness and awareness of awareness are fused, even prior to the emergence of the self. As an 'active principle of organization of the field of consciousness', the self – when it emerges – is part of what consciousness is aware of. But this structure is to be understood as an '(implicit) self-less consciousness of the self', not as an explicit reflection of the self upon itself. Such reflection may occur, of course, but this activity of the self cannot be taken as the primordial phenomenon of consciousness:

> Only by virtue of the fact that [consciousness] makes possible activities which can be attributed to the self is it appropriated in a derivative sense by the self, becomes freely available as explicit knowledge in reflection, and thus apparently resembles a productive self-generation which causes its own presuppositions to be forgotten.[18]

For Habermas, the notion of this primordial consciousness is not only philosophically incoherent, but ideologically suspect. In its radical depersonalization it evokes echoes of Eastern mysticism, on the one hand, but is also readily assimilable by the objectifying approaches of neurology (to which Henrich himself alludes in 'Self-Consciousness') or Luhmannian systems theory, on the other. This paradoxical diremption of Henrich's position into mysticism and objectivism suggests to Habermas the *correctness* of the earlier Frankfurt School's 'primal history of subjectivity':

> If one tries to keep the model of a subject relating itself to objects and yet would like to get behind the reflective structure of consciousness, then the only solution which is consistent is the one Henrich wants to avoid: the subsumption of consciousness under categories of self-preservation. That is what Adorno and Horkheimer maintain: there are no 'intrinsic criteria of correctness' to be derived from the reflexivity of an objectifying relation apart from those of a cognitive-instrumental confirmation of states of affairs.[19]

In line with this argument, Habermas suggests that the self-contradictory concepts with which both Adorno and Henrich attempt to break out of the cage of *Subjektphilosophie* – a selfless self-consciousness, the identification of the non-identical – indicate that the only viable solution must involve a shift of paradigm.

## Habermas's Communicative Paradigm

As is well known, the philosophical core of Habermas's alternative, intersubjective paradigm is derived from the work of George Herbert Mead, to whom he had referred approvingly as early as his essay on 'Labour and Interaction'.[20] According to Mead, self-consciousness arises through the process whereby the organism internalizes the attitudes of others to itself, a process which has adaptational value, since it enables an individual to anticipate the responses of others. Thus for Mead, the solution to the 'essential psychological problem of selfhood or of self-consciousness' is to be found by referring to the process of social conduct or activity in which the given person or individual is implicated: the context of interaction precedes the emergence of individual perspectives on that interaction. The individual

> enters his own experience as a self or individual not directly or immediately, not by becoming a subject to himself, but only in so far as he first becomes an object to himself just as other individuals are objects to him or in his experience; and he becomes an object to himself only by taking the attitudes of other individuals toward himself within a social environment or context of experience and behaviour in which both he and they are involved.[21]

Summarizing his account, Mead affirms that 'The self, as that which can be an object to itself, is essentially a social structure, and it arises in social experience.'[22]

Habermas has long relied on Mead's interactionism for his basic account of the genesis of the self. But in *The Theory of Communicative Action* he also draws heavily on the work of Ernst Tugendhat, in particular *Self-Consciousness and Self-Determination*, in order to give his convictions a theoretical articulation powerful enough to counter the assumptions of Henrich's approach. In Habermas's view, Tugendhat provides a *reductio ad absurdum* of traditional theories of self-consciousness, including those of Henrich and his pupils in the 'Heidelberg School', thus reinforcing his claims that the paradigm of the 'philosophy of consciousness' is exhausted. Tugendhat, of course, draws heavily on Mead, as well as on Heidegger and Wittgenstein.

*Self-Consciousness and Self-Determination* makes a determined attack on two presuppositions of the traditional theory of self-consciousness from which Henrich begins. The first is that in the case of self-consciousness we find a unique relation which involves a subject becoming an object of cognition for itself; the second is that this relation is characterized by an identity of subject and object, or of knower and known, which is itself simultaneously known. In Tugendhat's view, Henrich himself has given a powerful demonstration of the irreducible difficulties to which these assumptions give rise. But his preferred solution, a 'non-egological' theory of consciousness, threatens to dissolve the very phenomenon which was to be explained. Henrich finds himself in the absurd position of preferring to abandon the very concept of self-knowledge, rather than give up the traditional model of what such knowledge consists in.[23]

Tugendhat's alternative model of self-consciousness is based on the fundamental conviction, expounded at length in his introductory lectures on analytical philosophy, that knowledge essentially takes the form not of the representation of an object but, rather, of the understanding of a proposition. Critically exposing the metaphorics of vision which has permeated the history of European epistemology, Tugendhat argues that knowing is always knowing *that*, and hence susceptible to articulation in language. There are no ineffable encounters between the mind and reality: 'the intending of an object is not only a dependent part of a propositional consciousness, but it is based in turn on a propositional consciousness, on the holding true of an existential proposition'.[24] On this basis, Tugendhat argues that self-knowledge cannot consist in the reflexive relation of a subject to itself as object – the erroneous model which causes Henrich so much travail – but, rather, in the cognitive relation between a person and a proposition, where the proposition describes a state of consciousness of this person ('I am in love'). By characterizing self-consciousness in terms of the understanding of such "'I $\phi$'" sentences' (as he calls them), Tugendhat is apparently able to undermine the assumption that self-consciousness involves an identity of knower and known, since on one side we have the person who knows, and on the other a proposition about this same person. But of course, this structure alone is not sufficient to give an account of self-consciousness, unless Tugendhat is able to explain how the speaker of such an "'I $\phi$'" sentence' knows who the pronoun 'I' refers to, namely him- or herself. And this he must do without recourse to notions of a peculiar object, the 'I', which is identified by the subject as itself. For otherwise, the problem raised by Henrich – how can I identify this object as myself without already being familiar with myself? – would simply recur.

Tugendhat's answer to this problem is to claim that an identification *does* take place in self-consciousness – but not from the standpoint of the speaker. Linguistic mastery of the use of the term 'I' involves the – at least implicit – knowledge that conscious states which I attribute to myself in the first person can be attributed to me, as an entity identifiable by others through my physically observable features, in the third. The meaning of the term 'I' is determined by its interchangeability, according to viewpoint, within a *system* of deictic terms. Thus Tugendhat writes:

> The essential difference between 'I' and 'this human being' (or more generally this such-and-such) is that, with 'this', one refers to an object on the basis of an observation, but with 'I' one does not. However, this does not, of course, mean that an observable, but immaterial, object is referred to. Rather, just as we earlier had to say that the entity is indeed not identified [by a deictic term], but is meant as identifiable, so we must also say: it is indeed not observed, not perceived – when I refer to it by saying 'I' – but is meant as observable, as perceivable.[25]

In this way Tugendhat claims to have dissolved what he views as the untenable consequence of Henrich's amalgamation of a relation of identity and a cognitive relation – namely, the notion that the Fichtean formula 'I = I' captures the cognitive core of self-consciousness, and is not simply a nonsensical tautology. In Tugendhat's theory, one might say, cognition and identification are separated and distributed between the first- and third-person standpoints. In the self-attributions of psychological states which may be taken as paradigm cases of self-consciousness, the epistemic component is a proposition, whereas what is identified as the subject of this proposition is myself as a person, a psychophysical entity distinguished in terms of its unique track through time and space. In this way Tugendhat seeks to achieve his own version of a shift to an intersubjective paradigm which will finally dissolve transcendental illusions concerning the status of the 'I'.

## Henrich's Reply to Tugendhat

Tugendhat's argument, however, has not gone uncontested. The Tübingen philosophers Manfred Frank and Gianfranco Soldati have subjected his views to detailed criticisms, which centre on the vulnerability of the claim that *all* knowledge must be propositionally structured.[26] What is more, in an article published in 1989 Henrich himself developed a powerful – even devastating – reply to Tugendhat, which inevitably also ricochets against Habermas's arguments for the achievements of the communicative paradigm shift. Fundamentally, Henrich contests that a division of labour between first-person and third-person perspectives of the kind proposed by Tugendhat can solve the philosophical problem of self-consciousness. He points out that Tugendhat cannot simply be claiming that the condition for the truth of an '"I $\phi$" sentence' is that it be translatable into a corresponding true sentence in the third person. In this case, we could interpret the regular whistling of a locomotive, as it is about to enter the station, as an expression of its conscious intention to stop and pick up passengers.[27] In other words, if the attribution of a psychological predicate from the third-person perspective is also to imply an attribution of self-consciousness, a specific knowledge on the part of the 'I'-speaker must be presupposed. This is the knowledge that his or her self-description *can* be taken up in the third person (recall that for Tugendhat, the entity referred to by 'I' is not identified, but is *'meant'* as identifiable). For, as Tugendhat himself admits: 'from the start and quite generally it is essential to the use of "I" that whoever uses it does so in such a way that he knows that someone else can take up his speech so as to refer to the same person with "he" that the original speaker refers to with "I"'[28] However, Henrich argues, this knowledge on the part of the speaker must involve a knowledge of what it *means* for his proposition to be taken up as the attribution of a conscious state. And – as we have already seen – what this taking up means is that precisely such knowledge of what taking up means must be attributed to the speaker. In other words, the he-speaker must attribute to the I-speaker the knowledge that the he-speaker attributes this very same knowledge to the I-speaker. Indeed, since the I-speaker must be able to anticipate the third-person attribution when ascribing a predicate to himself, whether it actually occurs or not, one can allow the external reference to drop, and simply state that the I-speaker must be in possession of a form of knowledge, part of whose *content* is this form of knowledge itself.[29]

By this point it will be clear that Tugendhat's 'semantic' explanation of self-consciousness is far from dissolving – indeed, simply reproduces via a circuitous 'intersubjective' route – the classic paradoxes of self-referentiality which are central to explorations of self-consciousness in the tradition of German Idealism, and which Henrich insists must be confronted without facile evasions. To name only the most obvious: if there is a form of knowledge whose content includes itself, then – prior to the act of knowing – no such content is available to be known. But if there is nothing for the act of cognition to latch on to, until it has *already* latched on, how does this self-knowing ever begin at all? Thus, the profoundly damaging implication of Henrich's critique is that the shift to an intersubjective paradigm does not dissolve the problems generated by an erroneous philosophical model, but simply reproduces them in a different, more convoluted form. Interaction cannot *generate* but, rather, presupposes the primary self-acquaintance at the core of self-consciousness.

At this point, however, a defender of Habermas might object that the Critical Theorist's views diverge from those of Tugendhat specifically with respect to the cognitive status of self-awareness. Despite his philosophical sympathy, Habermas argues that Tugendhat's position transforms the experiences which 'ego' expresses into *'states of affairs* to which there is privileged access or inner episodes . . . and thus *assimilates them to entities in the world'*.[30] Against this, Habermas argues that mental states cannot be identified independently from the processes of their linguistic articulation and disclosure. He therefore suggests that the semantic approach to self-consciousness must be expanded in a pragmatic direction, taking into account the performative function of the term 'I' which is revealed in expressive uses of language.[31] In this respect, Habermas can be seen as steering a middle course between Tugendhat and Wittgenstein: utterances concerning my own inner states are not knowledge claims, as Tugendhat suggests; yet – contrary to Wittgenstein's view – they are not simply equivalent to exclamations, but raise a distinct validity-claim – that of authenticity.

Yet even if this correction of Tugendhat is accepted, the fact remains that the speaker must be aware that the authenticity-claim is about him- or herself, and this cognitive core still requires explanation. Significantly, Mead acknowledged that his account of the formation of the self through the internalization of the attitudes and responses of others could not be the full answer to the problem of self-consciousness. In his thought, the socially constituted self, or 'Me', is counterposed to what he terms the 'I', the spontaneous source of innovation and awareness which cannot be grasped reflectively, since as soon as it is reflected on it is transformed into the 'Me'. This distinction is necessary in order to prevent the self from being no more than a passive internalization of social relations, but also poses a problem which – as Mead is fully aware – cannot be solved at the level of 'social behaviourism'. In *Mind, Self and Society* he writes: 'I do not mean to raise the metaphysical question of how a person can be both "I" and "me", but to ask for the significance of this distinction from the point of view of conduct itself.'[32] To put this 'metaphysical' issue in elementary terms: the capacity to identify the other's reaction as directed towards *me* already presupposes an awareness of myself. Without this, I would not be able to distinguish such reactions from those towards third parties: the object 'Me' could not even be constituted as an indifferent object among others.

In a more recent text Habermas has in effect acknowledged this difficulty, stating that 'a rudimentary self-relation must already develop along with the primitive [i.e. pre-linguistic] consciousness of rules'.[33] In connection with this, one should also remember that Henrich in no sense contests the necessary (but not sufficient) role of the intersubjective, communicative context in the emergence of a linguistically competent, fully self-reflective subject. Thus, it might appear that the philosophical gulf between Henrich and Habermas is in fact merely a matter of terminological preferences and the evaluations they convey. Unlike Henrich, Habermas simply refuses to confer on a rudimentary, pre-linguistic self-awareness the dignity implied by the concept of the subject. He affirms:

> No pre-linguistic subjectivity needs to precede the self-relations which are posited through linguisitic intersubjectivity and via the reciprocal relations of Ego, Alter and Neuter, because everything which merits the name of subjectivity, even the most preliminary self-acquaintance [*Mit-sich-Vertrautsein*], is due to the stubbornly individuating force of the linguistic medium of personality-forming processes.[34]

## The Status and Role of Metaphysics

Such doubts about the philosophical import of the initial Habermas/Henrich clash are quickly dispelled, however, when one considers the wide-ranging metaphilosophical dispute to which it has subsequently given rise. This began with Habermas's polemical response to a book of Henrich's which was published in 1982. *Fluchtlinien* (*Baselines* – but also 'lines of flight') consists of five sparsely annotated essays in which Henrich seeks to speak plainly and directly in his own voice, rather than as an outstanding analyst of the intricacies of German Idealism. The concern of the book is to outline what Henrich takes to be the central tasks and responsibilities of philosophy in the current phase of the modern era. In particular, he aims to combat the tendency towards 'reductionism in theory and the renunciation of an understanding which would reach out to comprehend the world'.[35] In Henrich's view, philosophy can and should still be orientated towards the elaboration of what he calls a '*Lebensdeutung*', an interpretation by conscious life of its own place and significance within reality as a whole.

Henrich is only too aware that such a claim may sound absurdly over-ambitious in view of the far more modest, if not deflationary, projects of most contemporary thinking. His first task, therefore, is to show that philosophical thinking of a kind which strives towards a comprehensive account of human existence cannot be durably repressed or eliminated, because the need for such an account arises spontaneously from the self-conscious life which we lead as human beings. *Fluchtlinien* begins with the proposition: 'Every human being philosophizes' [*Jeder Mensch philoso-phiert*]. Ultimately, Henrich contends, it is the barely articulable questions that oppress every human being which give explicit, conceptually elabo-rated traditions of thinking, such as that which begins with the Greeks, their force and legitimacy.[36] However, if philosophical questions are intrin-sic to human existence, then this can only be because conscious life itself is characterized by fundamental, intractable tensions, and is thus experi-enced as inherently problematic. Henrich's first task, therefore, is to explain the nature of such basic conflicts and tensions.

These arise, Henrich suggests, from the division of the self-conscious human being between what he calls the 'subject' and the 'person'. The person is the psychophysical individual, who distinguishes him- or herself from others in a common world, and who understands him- or herself as a living being with a place among all other mundane things. The subject, by contrast, consists in that self-consciousness which cannot be derived from or explained in terms of any specific feature of the world, and finds everything thinkable and experienceable related to the 'one' which it is, in so far as it is aware of itself at all. As persons, we are in the world; as subjects, we transcend it as a whole.[37]

Stated in this way, the conflict between 'subject' and 'person' may sound rather abstract – a philosophical contrivance, rather than a felt diremption which marks every conscious human life. In Henrich's view, however, these two dimensions of our existence are revealed through fundamental human experiences which stand in an exclusive relation to each other. In *Fluchtlinien*, and in an earlier essay entitled 'Glück und Not', Henrich explores the significance of 'happiness' [*Glück*] and 'distress' [*Not*], which he views not simply as states of mind, but as two fundamental ways of experiencing the relation between oneself and the world in general. In happiness, we feel that consciousness can reach fulfilment, that it can be in harmony with the fundamental conditions of everything which it knows; in distress we feel the unjustifiable character of the course of the world, and the groundlessness of conscious life.[38] In Henrich's view, each of these con-ditions – in contrast to mere sensations and moods – raises a claim to be a true interpretation of the world, and therefore enters into logical conflict with its contrary: 'Such claims cannot be entirely suspended without con-scious life losing its relation to meaning and truth altogether.'[39]

Furthermore, since human beings, in order to preserve a coherent sense of self, cannot simply reject past experiences, but must integrate them into the continuity of a life history, the contradictory claims of happiness and distress, and the more specific modes of experience anchored in them, must be synthesized – the task of what Henrich terms a '*Lebensdeutung*'.

Henrich's central term for the contradictory relation between 'subject' and 'person', self and world, is '*Grundverhältnis*', or fundamental relation.[40] In *Fluchtlinien* he argues that the effort to reconcile the conflicting tendencies of this relation can be seen as one of the deepest motivations of human culture, and in particular of the great religions, which can be separated into two groups roughly along an East–West axis. Monotheistic religion collapses the distinction between subjectivity and personhood in the idea of a supreme Person who posits an independently existing world out of his own fullness, rather than being confronted with an irreducible contingency. The tensions of the *Grundverhältnis* of finite conscious life can then be overcome through participation in the divine personal life. Conversely, Oriental conceptions of a transpersonal consciousness encourage us to transcend our mundane individuality towards an anonymous universality. In the latter case, as Henrich writes:

> The human being can grasp that what is in itself unlimited is also at work in him. He himself is only a site or a moment, where the impersonal ground of the world or anonymous universal consciousness becomes conscious of itself. But in this sense the human being is also in truth something unlimited. His distress arises from a conciousness which is unable to leave his finite life as a person behind.[41]

Henrich is clear, however, that the great religions were bound to 'symbolic interpretations of the world' which can no longer be sustained in the current phase of modernity. The contemporary world, he suggests, is characterized by a 'double reflection': we have learned not only to separate ourselves from the world as thinking subjects, but also to adopt a detached observer stance over against the dynamic of our own consciousness and will-to-interpret. The traditional world-pictures have been unable to withstand the corrosive force of this suspicion,[42] yet this intensified reflection cannot in itself dispel the need for a *Lebensdeutung*. For it still remains the case that the two basic dimensions of self-conscious existence generate a contradiction between 'self-centring' and 'self-relativization'.[43] On the one hand, we are capable of distancing ourselves from all that we are, as entities in the world, and of regarding this as contingent. On the other, pure self-consciousness, which supposedly constitutes the vantage point from which this contingency appears, itself appears as empty and illusory in comparison with our concrete life in the world. Thus we can orientate ourselves exclusively neither towards a self-contained subjective life nor towards living merely as one individual entity among others in the world.

This is the context in which Henrich's specific conception of the task of what he terms 'metaphysics' arises. For Henrich, metaphysics inherits the role of religion at the stage of 'double reflection' – it has the task of providing an interpretation of conscious life which can, as far as possible, hold together the contradictory tendencies of the *Grundverhältnis* through insight into the unity which underlies them. Henrich stresses that this is a specifically 'post-Kantian' conception of metaphysics. Such thinking does not aim to capture the ultimate objective structure of the world, since 'no supramundane ontology is accessible by means of some kind of intellectual intuition'.[44] Rather:

> revisionary metaphysics is *interpretation* of conscious life on the part of conscious life. It is by no means the disclosure of a supramundane realm which we could conceive as the domain into which we have to transform ourselves. What undergoes transformation is our *understanding* of ourselves and our condition. Thus the very world in which we live appears in a new light once it has become subject to a new description.[45]

In this way Henrich seeks to deny the ultimate incompatibility – indeed, to affirm the possibility of an integration – of existential and speculative forms of conceptual exploration. Since there will always remain something unfathomable [*unausdenkbar*] about the fact of self-consciousness, which generates the impulse to philosophical thought, given that no self-relation as such can explain it, metaphysics – in Henrich's sense – will also always remain attached to its pre-theoretical origins in a way which it cannot make fully perspicuous to itself.[46] Accordingly, it is not in terms of the capacity to provide an entirely self-contained and self-grounded world-orientation that a *Lebensdeutung* can be assessed as to its truth but, rather, in terms of its capacity for integrating conflicting tendencies, each of which has a compelling immanent rationale. As Henrich writes:

> 'Truth' does not mean in this context scientifically guaranteed knowledge. The human being recognizes as true what has the most comprehensive self-evidence and opens up the most illuminating perspectives. And this is not a truth 'as if', with the reservation that we cannot help but think like that, but the strongest affirmation in actual conscious life of which a human being is capable. In this sense the great interpretations of life were certainly true.[47]

## Habermas's Critique of Henrich

In his review of a group of publications including *Fluchtlinien*, published in 1984, Habermas sharply criticized Henrich's attempt at the rehabilitation of metaphysics, bluntly associating it with the recent conservative

*Tendenzwende* in German politics. His objections, as one might expect, are inseparable from the differing positions which he and Henrich take on the question of the relation between subjectivity and communicative intersubjectivity. Recapitulating the arguments of volume one of *The Theory of Communicative Action*, Habermas contends that Henrich simply insists on the intuitive experience of self-consciousness as a 'discourse-free presence of ultimate grounds'. It is only Henrich's refusal to accept the logic of the philosophical shift to an intersubjective or communicative model which allows him to insist on the paradoxical character of the *Grundverhältnis*. Here, for the first time, Habermas invokes Foucault's *The Order of Things* as a bolster for his argument that the inescapability of the 'dilemma of self-objectification' is tied historically to the specific paradigm of the philosophy of subjectivity.[48]

Habermas goes on to argue that it is only Henrich's retention of the starting point of self-consciousness, his conviction that '"conscious life" has an extramundane root, transcends the world', which allows him to make claims for the privileged status of metaphysics, over against the procedurally secured forms of 'research' [*Forschung*] and objectifying science. Henrich, his rival claims:

> endows philosophy or *thought* with the inherited rights of a metaphysical self-enlightenment of conscious life. Dialectical thought is considered to reach beyond research, which is condemned to partiality. Unconcerned by demands for scientific rationality, thought reigns in its primordial domain – the self-relation of a being endowed with consciousness, which describes itself as a person and understands itself as a subject.[49]

As these formulations make clear, Habermas's critique of the philosophy of the subject is intimately bound up with his deep suspicion of claims for an illumination of existence which evades 'the standards of a fallible knowledge orientated towards universal validity-claims'.[50] The privileged status attributed to such a doctrine is simply incompatible with modern consciousness, and Henrich's attempt to revalidate metaphysics as *Lebensdeutung* must therefore be dismissed as inflated and pretentious.[51]

As we have already seen, Habermas believes that the obstinate illusion of the 'extramundane root' of the self can be dissipated once we adopt a communicative account of the genesis of self-consciousness, inspired by Mead. In identifying with the dialogic other, the subject turns back on itself in a *performative* attitude:

> The transcendental-empirical doubling of the relation to self is only unavoidable so long as there is no alternative to this observer perspective; only then does the subject have to view itself as the dominating counterpart to the world as a whole or as an entity appearing within it. No mediation is possible between the extramundane stance of the transcendental I and the intramundane stance of

the empirical I. As soon as linguistically-generated intersubjectivity gains primacy, this alternative no longer applies. Then ego stands within an inter-personal relationship that allows him to relate to himself as a participant in an interaction from the perspective of alter. And indeed this reflection undertaken from the perspective of the participant escapes the kind of objectification inevitable from the reflexively applied perspective of the observer.[52]

Broadly paraphrased, Habermas's contention is that if the reflexivity of the self is simply the internalized form of concrete interactions, the appar-ently ineradicable philosophical temptation to assume an extramundane dimension of the self loses its compulsion. However, we have also seen that even Habermas's performative inflection of Tugendhat's argument fails to demonstrate that the core self-awareness of the subject is generated entirely from communicative interactions. His loosely formulated talk of a self-relation which would be 'produced' by the speaker's taking over of the listener's perspective towards him or her fudges the distinction between a social identity, which is evidently a product of symbolic interactions, and the essential reflexivity of the subject, which is not. Only thus can he deny the metaphysical basis for a distinction between all particular psychologi-cal features of the person and the underlying awareness of possessing these features. This distinction does not require that everything empirical be objectified, merely that – as Henrich puts it – 'The world is for [the subject] the totality of everything which can be thought and encountered.'[53]

Even if Habermas's communicative account of the genesis of self-consciousness were acceptable in its broad outlines, however, his troubles would not be over. For it would still be plausible to argue that the funda-mental tensions of *Bewußtseinsphilosophie* simply emerge in another form within the new communicative paradigm. And if this is the case, the force of Habermas's advocacy of the shift to a communicative paradigm would be much weakened in one important sense.

## The Status of the Paradigm Shift

In a generic form, this objection has been put by Herbert Schnädelbach in his essay for the Habermas *Festschrift*, 'The Face in the Sand: Foucault and the Anthropological Slumber'.[54] Schnädelbach argues that the scope of Foucault's analysis of the empirico-transcendental oscillation which char-acterizes the modern philosophical *episteme* is culturally restricted; Foucault is implicitly equating post-Kantian philosophy *in toto* with the Left Hegelian–Marxist tradition which was such a powerful influence in postwar France. Other currents of post-Kantian philosophy (e.g. Husserl's transcendentalism or analytical anti-psychologism) are in fact directed towards an overcoming of the confusions of the anthropological paradigm.

Nevertheless, Schnädelbach suggests, Foucault's analysis does accurately capture the diffuse pragmatic outlook which characterizes modern scientific consciousness, but is not usually thought through with sufficient reflexive rigour to generate the dilemmas which Foucault identifies. Modern consciousness is dominated by a '*practical pragmatism* . . . an attitude of doing science that abstains from transcendental questions of principle and is content to take the plausibility of those anthropocentric couplings at face value and otherwise to proceed pragmatically. One can at some point be quite justified in taking the positive fundamentally, whereas in other contexts this is not recommended.'[55]

Schnädelbach goes on to argue that Habermas's 'grand theory' is a prime contemporary example of this pragmatic syndrome, which constitutes the heart of modern anthropocentrism. By translating the Kantian *a priori* into the terms of a reconstructive–fallibilistic, formal–pragmatic analysis of structures of communication, Habermas himself becomes involved in the oscillations of the empirico–transcendental doublet described by Foucault. Furthermore, the fact that Habermas's theory operates with categories of communication rather than those of consciousness does not materially affect the philosophical problems raised. Even setting aside its lax equation of the philosophy of consciousness with the philosophy of the subject, 'Linguistic formal–pragmatic philosophy of intersubjectivity does not in any case get beyond the anthropocentrism Foucault has in mind. It too remains in the realm of the empirical–transcendental *clair obscur* that shines forth as the stronger theory only as long as one renounces a totalizing theoretical self-closure and is content with a pragmatic approach.'[56]

In making this criticism, Schnädelbach refers to an essay by the Austrian philosopher Ludwig Nagl, which systematically dissects Habermas's claims for the achievements of the paradigm shift. *The Philosophical Discourse of Modernity* contends that a communicative paradigm can overcome the aporia in each of the three dimensions of the anthropocentric *episteme* which Foucault analyses: the oscillation between the empirical and the transcendental, the conflict between the *cogito* and the unthought, and the retreat and return of the origin. Firstly, Habermas suggests, the perpetual ambiguous doubling of the subject into empirical and transcendental dimensions can be obviated, since adopting the performative attitude of the other towards oneself in communication is the internalization of an intramundane relation, and cannot be equated with the reflective self-objectification of an isolated consciousness. Secondly, the perpetual retreat of the unconscious from the grasp of the *cogito* need no longer represent an impasse, since although the lifeworld as an encompassing context cannot be retrieved as a whole from the standpoint of a participant, its formal infrastructures can be described by a theory of communicative action, and this theory can in turn be connected with individual processes of self-reflection. Finally, the perpetual retreat into the past, or advance into the future, of the ground of our own self-conscious activity need no longer present us with the unacceptable choice between history as an arbitrary 'sending' (the Heideggerian *Geschick*) or history as the conscious product of the human species, if we view the life-world as reproduced through the ongoing assessment of the *criticizable* validity claims raised by participants.[57]

On all three of these points, Nagl contests Habermas's claims. As far as the empirical–transcendental doubling is concerned, he suggests, we still need to be able to account for the 'ideality' of practical reason which is apparent in the subject's capacity to respond to the intersubjective validity of moral claims in abstraction from all considerations of self-interest. Similarly, with regard to the tension between the conscious and the unconscious, Habermas's thought is directed towards reflecting upon and eliminating the unconscious social processes which obscure and hamper the rationality of communication, while being aware that this can never be definitively achieved. Finally, the question of the genesis of linguistic intersubjectivity itself, and in general of the historical transition from nature to culture, is no less of a problem for Habermas than for any more subject-centred philosopher. There remains the question of whether the potentialities of culture are already implicitly contained in nature, and thus – we could add – of whether the final achievements of communicative rationality would simply be the fulfilment of a tendency present in nature from the very beginning, or whether a certain opacity of natural compulsion will always remain opposed to, and capable of thwarting, the struggle for rational transparency.[58] Summarizing Nagl's objections, one could say that the 'quasi-transcendental' status of the linguistically mediated lifeworld, which Habermas himself emphasizes, inevitably generates philosophical difficulties, since it appears to be the 'condition of possibility' for the natural world on which it is in turn dependent. Similarly, the moment of transcendence which characterizes linguistically conveyed validity-claims makes discourse, in Habermas's own paradoxical phrase, 'the condition of the unconditioned'.[59] These difficulties are clearly analogous to the classic problems of modern philosophy raised by the conflict between subjective and objective perspectives, or by the lack of a location for the conscious self in a nature understood in physicalist terms.[60]

In one sense, this objection seems so obvious that one wonders how Habermas could continue to assert so blithely that his own philosophical position is 'postmetaphysical'. Indeed, on closer inspection it becomes apparent that his thought has left metaphysics behind only in the pragmatic sense which Schnädelbach evokes: namely by avoiding or ruling out of court the metaphysical issues which its own internal structure raises.

These evasions emerge clearly in a recent text by Habermas where he attempts to characterize, from a historical perspective, the general character of metaphysics, and the nature of postmetaphysical thinking.

In 'Themes in Postmetaphysical Thinking', Habermas outlines with broad strokes what he takes to be the basic features of metaphysical thought: firstly, the attempt to grasp the unity of the world by means of a derivation from an ultimate ground; secondly, the assumption of the ultimate identity of thought and being, which in fact establishes the idealistic primacy of the unitary, universal and necessary over the temporal and contingent; and lastly, the 'strong concept of theory' which is taken to embody a possibility of purification, and even salvation, superior to any worldly practice.[61] Since the beginning of the modern period, Habermas suggests, this conception of metaphysics has been undermined by a counter-movement of thought ultimately rooted in social and historical experiences. In the wake of the rise of the natural sciences, a procedural conception of rationality has replaced a conception of reason as the substantive content of the world as a totality, and undermined the cognitive privilege of philosophy. The ensuing rise of the historical and social sciences has forced a 'de-transcendentalization' of basic philosophical categories, and deprived the subject of its 'transmundane' position. And a shift of focus to language, and everyday pragmatic contexts of action and communication, has revealed the implicit anchoring of theory in practice, and deprived philosophy of its claim to be in contact with a transcendent reality.[62]

It can readily be seen that all these arguments ultimately involve the relativization of philosophical claims to the context of the lifeworld, and of communicative relations within it. Procedural reason is concerned with the intersubjective validation of specific forms of knowledge; the transcendental functions of the subject are now taken over by the background structures of the lifeworld; and theory itself is embedded in the lifeworld, although – against contemporary forms of contextualism – Habermas maintains that the lifeworld itself is essentially patterned by the operations of communicative reason. Yet this line of argument, of course, leaves open the question of how lifeworlds structured by a reason which raises context-transcendent claims, and the subjectively experienced meanings which crystallize within them, can be accommodated within a naturalistic account of reality of the kind to which Habermas appears to be committed. Habermas himself stresses that in the modern period 'inner' and 'outer' become divided between culture and nature, the domains of the human and natural sciences respectively. Nature, it appears, has no 'interiority', blocks all hermeneutical access, while the human world can be adequately grasped only interpretatively.[63] The question which then emerges once again is: in what sense is this 'splitting apart of object domains', as Habermas terms it, any less philosophically problematic than the classic difficulties raised by the apparent incompatibility between subjective and objective perspectives on the world?

This question can perhaps be sharpened by considering more thoroughly one of the claims which Habermas makes in 'Themes in Postmetaphysical Thinking' – the by now familiar contention that the 'de-transcendentalization' of the subject initiated by post-Husserlian phenomenology can be completed only by the move to an intersubjective and communicative paradigm. Habermas suggests that in *Being and Time* – as in Husserl's fifth *Cartesian Meditation*, or Sartre's *Being and Nothingness* – the problem of how individual, world-projecting subjects can establish a common intersubjective world remains insoluble because of a residual allegiance to the paradigm of *Bewußtseinsphilosophie*. These difficulties encourage Heidegger, in his later work, to dissolve altogether the world-projecting power of the subject, who is left without recourse against the arbitrary, world-disclosing power of Being itself. By contrast, Habermas claims, the notion of the reproduction of a shared lifeworld via the communicative action of its participants allows the dialectic of dependency and rational innovation in the transformation of the disclosed world to be thought in a non-contradictory way. Yet this proposal also presents us with a new version of the original difficulty. For either there is a plurality of lifeworlds – in which case the problem of co-ordination and harmonization of perspectives to produce a *single world* merely reappears at a higher level – or we assume that *all* human subjects participate in and help to reproduce *one* lifeworld. But in this second case, where the concept of the lifeworld is no longer treated quasi-sociologically, the dialectical cycle between 'the lifeworld as the resource, from which communicative action draws, and the lifeworld as the product of this action'[64] begins to look remarkably close in its structure to the speculative categories of German Idealism such as Hegel's concept of a *Geist*, which can realize itself *only* as the co-belonging of a plurality of interacting subjects. Certainly, it would seem incumbent on Habermas, were he explicitly to choose this second option, to explain how such a conception is compatible with his commitment to naturalism, since it apparently results in the collapse of the distinction between the lifeworld and the world *tout court*.

It should be noted that this type of objection to Habermas does not entail that his diagnosis of the crisis of traditional metaphysics is entirely unconvincing. Rather as Volker Gerhardt has suggested, the weakness of Habermas's position is that it equates the critique of no longer plausible answers with a demonstration of the obsolescence of an entire domain of problems.[65] But since this equation undermines Habermas's own parallel with paradigm shifts in the history of the natural sciences, we might conclude that metaphysical problems cannot be dissolved by a shift of paradigm, and that an important task of contemporary philosophy would be to elaborate a viable conception of what metaphysical reflection can and cannot achieve. In fact, an examination of Henrich's work, both in *Fluchtlinien* and in his polemical response to Habermas's polemics, suggests that Henrich's account of metaphysics does not ultimately violate the constraints which Habermas establishes.

Henrich denies, for example, that the concept of metaphysics implies infallibility: metaphysical theories need not claim exemption from criticism and correction. Thus, it would appear that on Henrich's definition metaphysical thinking would be perfectly compatible with Habermas's insistence that all forms of knowledge must respect the requirements of 'procedural rationality', since this respect ultimately boils down to no more than a willingness to engage in discussion. The ensuing susceptibility to correction and refutation cannot delegitimate metaphysics for Henrich, because – as we have already seen – he considers such inquiry, as indeed did Kant, to be an inescapable impulse of human thinking: 'Metaphysics is formed in the spontaneous thinking of every human being, prior to any possible formulation in the language of theory.'[66] For Henrich, to be beyond conclusive demonstration is not equivalent to being beyond challenge and criticism:

> understanding and interpretation, beyond anything which can be ascertained with proofs, belong just as much to our sense of reason as proof and criticism. Only when it is exempted from criticism, and from a comprehensive evaluation of every pro and contra, does the discussion of conceptions of ultimate resolution [*Abschlußgedanken*, i.e. ways of reconciling the conflicting tendencies of conscious life without any one-sided reduction of complexity] become an undertaking characterized by arbitrariness and presumption.[67]

Habermas's further contentions that modern thought must acknowledge historicity and contingency, and the primacy of practice over theory, are, of course, accommodated by Henrich's distinctively post-Kantian conception of metaphysics, which we have already examined. In this conception, metaphysical thinking does not raise foundational claims, or deduce from first principles, or seek to trump the knowledge of the natural sciences with their own means. Rather, metaphysics is a self-explication of conscious life which remains bound to the standpoint of the experiencing consciousness. Such a metaphysics does not claim to decipher the 'objective meaning in being', to employ a phrase of Habermas's.[68] Rather, Henrich argues, 'The authentic world of modern metaphysicians was neither a *Hinterwelt* [i.e. a world behind the world] nor a world of objectivities which was left standing uninterpreted over against knowledge itself.'[69] Furthermore, in Henrich's view, it is only Habermas's harmonistic conception of the lifeworld which makes it possible for him to ignore those 'inner discrepancies in our primary concept of the world and primary self-descriptions'[70] which give rise to existential conflict and the consequent need for ultimate, synthesizing concepts.

Henrich's powerful response inevitably raises the question of what remains of Habermas's claims for the achievements of the paradigm shift. Are we to conclude that there is no plausibility at all in the broad historical narrative, which Habermas recounts, of a shift from an ontological to an epistemological, and then to a linguistic paradigm in philosophy, the last of these being fully achieved only when accompanied by an intersubjective turn? The disillusionment need not be quite so drastic, but two important lessons do seem to have emerged. Firstly, rather than exemplifying a series of clean paradigm breaks which leave the old problems behind, the history of philosophy consists of overlaps, reversions, spiralling movements. Herbert Schnädelbach, for example, has suggested an alternative analysis of the history of philosophy in terms of an oscillation between 'metaphysical discourse' and 'critical discourse', the former being concerned with securing the intersubjective relation through the relation to the object, the latter with anchoring the relation to the object in intersubjectivity.[71] In Schnädelbach's account, the oscillation between these modes of discourse overlays the linearity of the paradigm shifts between being, consciousness and language. Thus, metaphysical thinking can easily emerge within the linguistic paradigm, just as the ontological paradigm need not exclude issues of epistemic validity and meaning. Secondly, and in consequence, although the emphasis on intersubjectivity which has been important in nineteenth-century philosophy, and even more so in the twentieth century, has opened up new areas of inquiry, and enabled major advances in our understanding of questions of moral and epistemological grounding, this shift cannot definitively settle the status and role of metaphysics. For in contrast with specific domains of philosophical inquiry, such as the moral or epistemological, metaphysics expresses our need for a general orientation, our concern with how the various dimensions of our knowledge and experience, and the world in which these emerge, cohere. In retrospect, it seems difficult to understand how the drive to pose these ultimate questions could be quelled by a paradigm shift, albeit both linguistic and intersubjective, of the kind Habermas advocates. For just as Habermas rightly criticizes his opponents for confusing the critique of a particular (instrumentalized) model of reason with the demolition of reason as such, so – it would seem – his own conception of postmetaphysical thinking makes sense only against the background of a restricted characterization of the nature and dynamic of metaphysical thought. Once this restriction has been exposed, there seems no good reason why fears of extravagant claims to privileged insight and their possible political consequences – claims which are, in fact, more typical of a certain 'postmetaphysical' discourse – should outweigh our legitimate dismay at the confinement of thought within the functionalized routines of contemporary life.

## Notes

1. Jürgen Habermas, *The Philosophical Discourse of Modernity*, trans. Frederick Lawrence, Cambridge, MA: MIT Press 1987, p. 296

2. Ibid., p. 294.

3. Ibid., p. 295.

4. Fred Dallmayr, 'The Discourse of Modernity: Hegel, Nietzsche, Heidegger (and Habermas)', *Praxis International*, vol. 8, no. 4, January 1989, pp. 397–8.

5. J.M. Bernstein, 'The Causality of Fate: Modernity and Modernism in Habermas', in ibid., p. 420.

6. Jürgen Habermas, 'Metaphysik nach Kant', in *Nachmetaphysisches Denken*, Frankfurt am Main: Suhrkamp 1988, p. 32/ 'Metaphysics after Kant', in *Postmetaphysical Thinking: Philosophical Essays*, trans. William Hohengarten, Cambridge: Polity Press 1992, p. 24.

7. Dieter Henrich, 'The Origins of the Theory of the Subject', in Axel Honneth *et al.*, eds, *Philosophical Interventions in the Unfinished Project of Modernity*, Cambridge, MA: MIT Press 1992, p. 31.

8. Dieter Henrich, 'Die Grundstruktur der modernen Philosophie', in *Selbstverhältnisse*, Stuttgart: Reclam 1982, p. 95.

9. Ibid., p. 97.

10. Ibid., p. 98.

11. See ibid., pp. 89–93.

12. Ibid., p. 101.

13. Ibid., p. 102.

14. Ibid., p. 103–4.

15. See Dieter Henrich, 'Fichte's Original Insight', in Darrel Christensen *et al.*, eds, *Contemporary German Philosophy*, vol. 1, 1982, pp. 15–54; 'Selbstbewußtsein. Kritische Einleitung in eine Theorie', in R. Bubner *et al.*, eds, *Hermeneutik und Dialektik* (Festschrift für Hans-Georg Gadamer), Tübingen: J.C.B. Mohr 1970/'Self-Consciousness: A Critical Introduction to a Theory', *Man and World*, vol. 4, 1971.

16. See 'Fichte's Original Insight', p. 20.

17. See ibid., p. 21, and 'Selbstbewußtsein. Kritische Einleitung in eine Theorie', p. 226/ 'Self-Consciousness: A Critical Introduction to a Theory', p. 12.

18. 'Selbstbewußtsein', p. 279/p. 24.

19. Jürgen Habermas, *Theorie des kommunikative Handelns*, vol. 1, Frankfurt am Main: Suhrkamp 1981, p. 529/*The Theory of Communicative Action*, vol. 1, trans. T. McCarthy, London: Heinemann 1984, p. 395.

20. Habermas claims here that Mead retrieves Hegel's insight into the constitution of the identity of the 'I' through reciprocal recognition 'under the naturalistic presuppositions of pragmatism': 'Arbeit und Interaktion. Bemerkungen zu Hegels Jenenser "Philosophie des Geistes"', in *Technik und Wissenschaft als Ideologie*, Frankfurt am Main: Suhrkamp 1968, p. 19n./'Labour and Interaction: Remarks on Hegel's Jena "Philosophy of Spirit"', in *Theory and Practice*, trans. John Viertel, Cambridge: Polity Press 1989, p. 279n.

21. George Herbert Mead, *Mind, Self and Society*, Chicago: University of Chicago Press 1962, p. 138.

22. Ibid., p. 140.

23. Ernst Tugendhat, *Selbstbewußtsein und Selbstbestimmung*, Frankfurt am Main: Suhrkamp 1979, ch. 3/*Self-Consciousness and Self-Determination*, trans. Paul Stern, Cambridge, MA: MIT Press 1986, ch. 3.

24. Ernst Tugendhat, *Vorlesungen zur Einführung in die sprachanalytische Philosophie*, Frankfurt am Main: Suhrkamp 1976, p. 102/*Traditional and Analytical Philosophy: Lectures*

*on the Philosophy of Language*, trans. P.A. Gower, Cambridge: Cambridge University Press 1982, p. 73.
25. *Selbstbewußtsein und Selbstbestimmung*, p. 84/*Self-Consciousness and Self-Determination*, p. 71.
26. See Manfred Frank, *Die Unhintergehbarkeit der Individualität*, Frankfurt am Main: Suhrkamp 1986, pp. 64–92; Gianfranco Soldati, 'Selbstbewußtsein und unmittelbares Wissen bei Tugendhat', in M. Frank, G. Raulet and W. van Reijen, eds, *Die Frage nach dem Subjekt*, Frankfurt am Main: Suhrkamp 1988, pp. 85–100. Both Frank and Soldati highlight the contradiction between Tugendhat's insistence that self-consciousness is a form of 'empirical knowledge', and his conceding that this knowledge is non-inductive and not perceptually based.
27. Dieter Henrich, 'Noch einmal in Zirkeln: Eine Kritik von Ernst Tugendhats semantischer Erklärung von Selbstbewußtsein', in Clemens Bellut and Ulrich Müller-Scholl, eds, *Mensch und Moderne. Beiträge zur philosophischen Anthropologie und Gesellschaftskritik*, Würzburg: Königshausen & Neuman 1989, pp. 102–3.
28. *Selbstbewußtsein und Selbstbestimmung*, p. 84/*Self-Consciousness and Self-Determination*, p. 70.
29. See 'Noch einmal in Zirkeln', pp. 102–10.
30. *Theorie des kommunikative Handelns*, vol. 1, p. 531/*The Theory of Communicative Action*, vol. 1, p. 397.
31. See *Theorie des Kommunikative Handelns*, vol. 2, Frankfurt am Main: Suhrkamp 1981, p. 159/*The Theory of Communicative Action*, vol. 2, p. 104.
32. *Mind, Self and Society*, p. 173.
33. 'Metaphysik nach Kant' p. 34n./'Metaphysics after Kant', p. 27n.
34. Ibid.
35. Dieter Henrich, *Fluchtlinien*, Frankfurt am Main: Suhrkamp 1982, p. 9.
36. Ibid., p. 7.
37. Ibid., p. 21.
38. Dieter Henrich, 'Glück und Not', in *Selbstverhältnisse*, p. 135.
39. *Fluchtlinien*, p. 22.
40. In a text composed in English, 'Philosophy and the Conflict between Tendencies of Life', Henrich speaks of a 'basic constitution', and this term can therefore be considered as his own translation of '*Grundverhältnis*'. See Dieter Henrich, *Konzepte*, Frankfurt am Main: Suhrkamp 1987, pp. 117–27.
41. *Fluchtlinien*, p. 24.
42. Ibid., p. 30.
43. Ibid., p. 114.
44. 'Philosophy and the Conflict between Tendencies of Life', p. 122.
45. Ibid.
46. In *Fluchtlinien*, Henrich points out: 'If I did not already have the capacity to relate to myself, no study of any self-relations in the world, not even those which (seen from a third-person perspective) are my own, could lead me to the conclusion that I exist, and that I necessarily find myself in such a relation' (p. 148).
47. *Fluchtlinien*, p. 31. One could perhaps compare this account with Charles Taylor's view that human life must – 'existentially' speaking – be guided by a system of values organized around and polarized by a 'hyper-good'. Like Henrich, Taylor contends that we have no other criterion for the truth of such a system, and the reality of the moral sources to which it gives us access, than that it is the 'Best Account' of human life of which we are capable at any given time. See Charles Taylor, *Sources of the Self*, Cambridge: Cambridge University Press 1989, pp. 62–75.
48. Jürgen Habermas, 'Rückkehr zur Metaphysik? – eine Sammelrezension', in *Nachmetaphysiches Denken. Philosophische Aufsätze*, Frankfurt am Main: Suhrkamp 1988, pp. 275–6.
49. Ibid., p. 273.
50. Ibid., p. 274.
51. For a critical discussion of the conception of metaphysics and its cognitive status which Habermas assumes in his attack on Henrich, see Volker Gerhardt, 'Metaphysik und ihre Kritik: Zur Metaphysikdebatte zwischen Jürgen Habermas und Dieter Henrich', *Zeitschrift*

*für Philosophische Forschung*, vol. 42, no. 1, 1988. Unfortunately, despite its subtitle, this interesting essay contains no discussion of Henrich's alternative position.

52. *The Philosophical Discourse of Modernity*, p. 297.

53. *Fluchtlinien*, p. 21.

54. Herbert Schnädelbach, 'The Face in the Sand: Foucault and the Anthropological Slumber', in *Philosophical Interventions in the Unfinished Process of Enlightenment*.

55. Ibid., p. 324.

56. Ibid., p. 333.

57. See *The Philosophical Discourse of Modernity*, pp. 297–301, 316–21.

58. See Ludwig Nagl, 'Zeigt die Habermassche Kommunikationstheorie einen "Ausweg aus der Subjektphilosophie"? Erwägungen zur Studie "Der philosophische Diskurs der Moderne"', in *Die Frage nach dem Subjekt*.

59. Jürgen Habermas, 'Einleitung zur Neuausgabe', in *Theorie und Praxis*, Frankfurt am Main: Suhrkamp 1972, p. 25.

60. For a restatement of these problems by a contemporary philosopher, see Thomas Nagel, 'The Subjective and the Objective', in *Mortal Questions*, Cambridge: Cambridge University Press 1979; and for a wide-ranging meditation on them, idem, *The View from Nowhere*, New York: Oxford University Press 1986.

61. See Jürgen Habermas, 'Motive nachmetaphysischen Denkens', in *Nachmetaphysisches Denken*, pp. 35–42/'Themes in Postmetaphysical Thinking', in *Postmetaphysical Thinking*, pp. 28–34.

62. Ibid., pp. 52–7/pp. 44–8.

63. Ibid., p. 43/p. 36.

64. Ibid., p. 51/p. 43.

65. 'Metaphysik und ihre Kritik', p. 64.

66. Dieter Henrich, 'Was ist Metaphysik – was Moderne? Zwölf Thesen gegen Jürgen Habermas', in *Konzepte*, p. 14.

67. Ibid., p. 13.

68. 'Rückkehr zur Metaphysik', p. 271.

69. 'Was ist Metaphysik – was Moderne?', p. 27.

70. Ibid.

71. See Herbert Schnädelbach, 'Zum Verhältnis von Diskurswandel und Paradigmenwechsel in der Geschichte der Philosophie', in *Zur Rehabilitierung des* animal rationale. *Vorträge und Abhandlungen 2*, Frankfurt am Main: Suhrkamp 1992.

# Facticity, Validity and
# the Public Sphere

On the 9th of November 1992, the anniversary of *Kristallnacht*, the philosopher Manfred Frank was invited to give the principal address at the memorial service which is held annually in the Paulskirche in Frankfurt. The Paulskirche was the home of the first democratically elected German national assembly, which flourished briefly amid the revolutions of 1848–9, and Frank, in keeping with this setting, refused to limit himself to a 'retrospective ritual of mourning'. Rather, he used the occasion to consider contemporary events in Germany, in particular the rise of a violently xenophobic right-wing element, which had already claimed seventeen lives in the course of the year, and the reaction of the established parties to this situation. Central to this reaction was the attempt to limit the right of political asylum enshrined in article 16 of the Grundgesetz, the German Constitution. The provisional agreement reached between the main political parties on 6 December 1992 was aimed at abolishing this right for applicants arriving from an EU country or from a 'safe third country' deemed to have satisfactory asylum procedures of its own. Since Poland and the Czech Republic were declared to fall into this category, these measures were intended effectively to cut off the flow of asylum applicants, the vast majority of whom reach Germany by land.[1]

Frank suggested that in Germany an ethnic rather than a political definition of the nation, and an excessive concern with national unity and security, had repeatedly overridden the protection of individual freedoms, and hindered the development of an appropriate conception of democracy: 'The predominant conception of the essence of democracy is expressed in the demand that politics should bow to pressure from the streets.' Frank illustrated this view with quotations from leading protagonists in the *Asyldebatte* from both Right and Left. He then reached for a shocking comparison: 'Goebbels's populism invented a fitting jingle for what happens when one adapts to the unqualified feelings of the populace: "Our thinking was simple, because the people are simple. Our thinking was primitive, because the people are primitive."' At this point many members of the audience, including the entire Christian Democrat contingent, walked out. Subsequently, all the parties in the Frankfurt Parliament (including the Greens) repudiated the speaker, and the furore occupied the local press for a fortnight afterwards.

These events illustrate the drawback of one possible interpretation of *Faktizität und Geltung*, Jürgen Habermas's recent book on the philosophy of law and the theory of the constitutional state. Under the headline 'Jürgen Habermas makes peace with the constitutional state', a pre-publication review in *Der Spiegel* (18 October 1992) sought to present the book as an old Leftist's recantation in response to the collapse of Communism, and his belated return to the fold of liberal democracy. But one of the deepest motivations of Habermas's work has been an anxiety that the institutions and practices of the modern democratic state may not be sufficiently firmly anchored in the traditions of German thought and politics. He is convinced that the emancipatory potential of such a state needs to be defended against the powerful current in German philosophy and culture which views democratic ideals as – at best – helpless before, and – at worst – a positive symptom of, the spiritual desolation of modernity. It is not surprising, therefore, that Habermas should have sprung to Manfred Frank's defence. In a highly combative article in *Die Zeit* (11 December 1992) he denounced the German government's increasing tendency to contemplate altering, or even simply bypassing, the Constitution, for the sake of Germany's self-assertion as a 'normal' nation-state. This 'D-Mark patriotism' is, in Habermas's view, an attempt to compensate for the 'normative deficits' of a bungled reunification process, with its disastrous social consequences, particularly in the East. He repeated the argument he has made before: instead of what amounted to an administrative incorporation, through provisions contained in the Grundgesetz of the old Bundesrepublik, the reunited German nation should have had the opportunity to conclude a new 'social contract' in the form of a new constitution.

The ambitious, multidimensional argument of *Faktizität und Geltung* (*Facticity and Validity*) provides the philosophical background to these political arguments. The book's title already indicates the main direction in which Habermas's thinking has moved in the last decade, since he began to work more intensively on the universalist foundation of morality in the tradition of Kant. Ever since the 1960s, he has contended that human communication is necessarily framed by 'relations of recognition' between language-users, and that such recognition always involves – implicitly, at least – commitment to a search for consensus. Naturally, Habermas does not deny that it is always possible for individuals to use language 'strategically', in order to mislead, intimidate, or exclude others. But even in this case the expectation that linguistic communication will convey verifiable truths and justifiable imperatives is being obliquely exploited. The require-ment that speakers provide grounds for their claims and assertions, when these do not initially appear convincing, is ultimately not culturally deter-mined, but is built into the necessary conditions of communication, and provides the basis for a conception of the rightness of moral norms. Such norms are objectively 'right' when they result from a consensus attained through free and equal discussion by all concerned in the light of their respective interests (this is the principle of what has come to be known as 'discourse ethics').

Since he began to formulate this approach in the 1970s, Habermas has often been accused, from various directions, of confusing a principle of political democracy with a principle of morality. It has been argued – by his colleague Albrecht Wellmer, for example – that moral convictions are anchored in the personality at a level which blocks their being readily altered, even in the light of discussion, whereas collectively agreed norms, though the obligation to obey them may have 'weak' moral force, can change in the light of shifting opinions or circumstances. In Kantian terms, immoral actions are those which we, as rational agents, cannot even coher-ently will, let alone fail consensually to agree upon.[2] It has also been argued (by feminist critics inspired by Carol Gilligan's *In a Different Voice*) that moral awareness involves an attentiveness to individuals in their uniqueness, and a concern with the sustaining of interpersonal relation-ships, which are not susceptible to universal regulation. The conclusion of both these lines of argument is often that Habermas, sympathetically interpreted, has failed to capture philosophically the core of our sense of morality, while offering a compelling basis for the regulation of public issues through discussion and collective decision-making.

In *Faktizität und Geltung* Habermas takes the major step of accept-ing – albeit in a qualified form – the force of this criticism. He begins from the historical consideration that in modern societies a morality based on universal principles progressively separates itself from those forms of ethical practice which are bound to specific social roles and expectations. As a result, what has been referred to, since Hegel, as *Sittlichkeit* degener-ates into mere convention. Habermas still insists on this, despite the objections of his critics – communitarian in the United States, Neo-Aristotelian in Germany – that even modern morality ultimately derives what force it has from communally shared convictions. But while Habermas has resisted this move, and continues to defend the formal pri-ority of a universalistic point of view, he now also stresses its corresponding weaknesses. First, the complexity of the situations that moral agents need to adjudge generates a 'cognitive indeterminacy' which can make excessive demands on the individual. Second, to be effective this morality must be transformed from a form of social knowledge into the driving force of the individual conscience. (An additional difficulty here is that the moral agent is disadvantaged if others do not follow the same norm, as he or she is entitled to expect.) Third, the level of social organization required if some moral duties are to be fulfilled – for example, aid for disaster-struck regions of the world – often lies far beyond the range of individual initiative.[3]

On these grounds, Habermas argues, it is clear that a post-conventional morality requires the complementary form of law. Law enables a society to regulate interactions without having to rely directly on the motivations of its members; indeed, it vastly increases the scope for strategic action, yet in a manner still ultimately anchored in the principle of a communicative consensus. In other words, law generates a higher-level reflexive social facticity, which compensates for the increasing risks posed by those conflicts which arise when traditional lifeworlds splinter, and the space for the pursuit of individual interests expands.

Habermas wants to emphasize, however, that law must also satisfy expectations of legitimacy: if it is to fulfil its socially integrative role, it must be generated through a democratic procedure in which all concerned can, in principle, take part.[4] From this he draws the conclusion that his general principle of 'discursive grounding' ('Those norms of action are valid, which all those who may be concerned could accept in a rational discourse') separates into two distinct principles: a 'principle of morality' (which specifies the aim of consensus in the light of all relevant interests) and a new 'principle of democracy'. This second principle is contrasted with the first:

> Whereas the moral principle operates at the level of the *internal* constitution of a particular form of argumentation, the principle of democracy relates to the level of the *external* (effective) institutionalization enabling equal participation in the discursive formation of will and opinion, which in its turn takes place within legally guaranteed forms of communication.[5]

In Habermas's view, this 'principle of democracy' provides a means of resolving the dispute represented paradigmatically by Kant and Rousseau: does the autonomy of the private individual come before the 'public autonomy' of the citizen, or are the subjective freedoms central to liberal political thought themselves bestowed by an act of collective self-definition? Habermas proposes a 'logical genesis' for the system of rights – a more modest version of the dizzying feats of deduction of his German Idealist predecessors – in which the subjective right to the greatest possible freedom of action compatible with equal freedom for others is understood as a condition of participation in a law-governed polity. Since such a polity must also define a status for its associates, offer guarantees of this status, and legitimate its content collectively, a spiralling movement of internalization generates further basic rights: of recognized membership of the community; of protection and redress; of political expression and participation. Underpinnning all these are rights to the preservation of the social, technical and ecological bases of life itself. All such a derivation presupposes, according to Habermas, is 'an intuitive understanding of the discourse principle, and the concept of the form of law'.[6]

Even during his most abstract excursions, Habermas remains aware that a purely normative conception of law is likely to fall prey to idealist illusions, misconceiving an institution essentially torn between facticity and validity. He therefore seeks to bring into his picture the sceptical results of that 'sociological disenchantment' which sees law as a self-contained system, interacting with other social systems, or simply as an implement of unequally shared power. Habermas's social theory as a whole is based on a fundamental distinction between a 'lifeworld', organized primarily through tacit consensus, and the systems of state administration and the market economy, which use money and power to co-ordinate actions without the need to gain agreement. In *The Theory of Communicative Action*, he analysed contemporary developments in terms of a distinction between law as 'institution', ultimately anchored in the moral expectations of the lifeworld, and law as 'steering medium', or an administrative mechanism intermeshed with those processes of bureaucratization and monetarization which 'colonize' the lifeworld. From such a standpoint the crucial question is how the legislative process can be brought under the democratic control which, according to Habermas, the modern concept of law intrinsically implies. *The Theory of Communicative Action* bequeathed us the problem of how the lifeworld can 'steer' such systems, and limit their intrusions, without disrupting their functioning.

To address this problem, Habermas has recourse here to the category of the 'public sphere' [*Öffentlichkeit*]. This concept, first developed in *Struckturwandel der Öffentlichkeit* (*The Structural Transformation of the Public Sphere*), provides a sketch-map of Habermas's entire intellectual itinerary, and is the key to his conception of the continuing emancipatory content of democratic ideals. The public sphere consists of both the direct and the mediated discussions of 'critically reasoning' individuals, who thereby form public opinion, and are thus able to exert pressure on the political system, without being formally part of it. Already in the early 1960s, Habermas had appreciated that, under contemporary conditions, only groups and organizations providing internal forums for discussion could hope to withstand the blizzard of advertising, public relations and the mass media – an insight seemingly confirmed by more recent developments, such as the emergence of the 'new social movements'. Accordingly, in *Faktizität und Geltung*, he intertwines the concept of the 'public sphere' with that of 'civil society', a more recent term for those spontaneous movements and associations beyond the reach of the state which bring new problems and perspectives to political attention. He emphasizes the 'dual politics' characteristic of such movements, which do not aim simply to influence the political system, as traditional interest groups do, but also to hold open new spaces of communication.[7]

In this way Habermas seeks to span the gulf between the 'anarchistic' core of communicative action, which leaves no truth-claim in principle unchallenged, and the remote, inflexible mechanisms of the modern state. Is this conception convincing? He does not conceal the mass of evidence suggesting the extent to which the manipulated, media-saturated public sphere destroys the potential for an effective democratic opinion to form. Statistics such as those indicating that the average length of the 'sound bites' of presidential candidates speaking on American television has declined from 42.3 seconds in 1968 to 9.8 seconds in 1988 seem to confirm the worst apprehensions of *Structural Transformation*. One could also argue that Habermas's enthusiasm for the 'post-Marxist' category of 'civil society', already tarnished by the latest developments in Eastern Europe, seriously underplays the continuing role of social class as a factor in determining access to channels of political influence. In *Faktizität und Geltung* he is obliged to appeal, rather weakly, to the 'normative self-understanding of the mass media', as informing and facilitating public discussion, in order to convince his readers that issues of sufficient common concern will eventually obtain a hearing. Even then, however, he stresses that only crises are capable of mobilizing people successfully. Can such sporadic movements really be said to constitute 'communicative practices of self-determination'?[8] And how are the democratic impulses of civil society to be distinguished effectively from that pressure from the streets whose role in German politics, as we have seen, Habermas so fears?

To these political concerns can be added reservations about the philosophical bases of Habermas's conception of a *Rechtsgemeinschaft*. He believes his theory can help to resolve the problem of the oscillation between the goals of formal equality and of compensatory intervention, which has become explicit in more recent legal discussion, and which he illustrates by discussing recent feminist debates. The problem highlighted by feminist critics is that welfare-state legal intervention simply assumes what the needs of specific groups are, and makes allowance for these as 'deviations' in the light of a norm which is not itself neutral. The solution, Habermas suggests, cannot be the return to a 'formal' liberalism, which has irretrievably lost its innocence, but, rather, a move to a 'proceduralist' paradigm, where social groups themselves can bring forward the relevant interpretations of their needs and aspirations. In the light of this move: 'a programme of law proves to be discriminatory when it is insensitive to the freedom-limiting side-effects of actual inequality, and paternalistic when insensitive to the freedom-limiting side-effects of the state-organized compensation for these inequalities'.[9]

There is no critique here of law as such. Yet ten years ago, in *The Theory of Communicative Action*, Habermas described the increasing intrusion of law into the lifeworld as 'de-worlding', or as isolating and antagonizing individuals, and disrupting a social integration essentially grounded in values, norms, and processes of understanding. He now renounces this conception of an unavoidable dilemma whereby a simultaneous process of emancipation and colonization is the result of encroaching 'juridification' [*Verrechtlichung*]. Yet it is fair to ask whether his earlier insights may not have been suppressed by his current, more positive evaluation of law.

In *The Struggle for Recognition*, Axel Honneth, a younger representative of the Frankfurt School tradition, suggests that the recognition of individuals as subjects of universal legal rights is not sufficient if they are to achieve an undistorted sense of selfhood. Individuals also require acknowledgement of their contribution to the general welfare if they are to be able to value as well as respect themselves, and it is only this reciprocally endowed sense of worth which makes forms of social solidarity possible.[10] From such a standpoint, the intrusion of law must have a damaging effect, because what is at stake is not merely the maximization of freedom, in terms of individual autonomy and political participation, as Habermas's formulation suggests. One can see this from the feminist critiques of state intervention which Habermas himself discusses. What is at issue here is not simply whether such intervention restricts the freedom of women but, rather, that it treats women as anomalies, and does not reflect an appropriate, non-androcentric valuing of their specific contributions to society. What is ultimately required, therefore, is not merely further legal reform but a change in the values which organize the possibilities of social solidarity.

Habermas suggests at several points in this book that in contemporary societies the resources most urgently in need of protection are not economic or administrative but, rather, those of a 'social solidarity which is currently disintegrating'. It is doubtful, however, whether the 'project of the realization of law' alone, whatever content it is imbued with, is sufficient to combat this distintegration. Indeed, Habermas himself has recently made it clear that a concern with rights, which enable self-determination, must be balanced by sentiments of solidarity, which enable self-realization: '*Justice* is connected with the equal freedoms of unique and self-determining individuals, whereas *solidarity* is connected with the well-being of one's fellows, who are bound together in an intersubjectively shared form of life – and thus also with the sustaining of the integrity of this form of life itself.'[11]

Habermas goes on to emphasize, of course, that solidarity cannot be restricted to the internal relations of one social group, closing itself against others, but must be construed in a universalist spirit. In this case, however, a philosophical space appears to be opened up by his own argument for an inquiry into the fundamental structures of the human form of life, as the locus of the 'archaic, binding energies' which drive even this expanded, cosmopolitan solidarity. The need for such an investigation is perhaps suggested by Habermas's blunt declaration, in a recent interview, that 'emancipation – if the word is given an unambiguous interpretation – makes human beings more independent, but not automatically happier'.[12] Against the background of German history, his reluctance to provide even an outline of how the striving for solidarity might be fulfilled is understandable, but this very reluctance risks discouraging and dampening emancipatory impulses. An attempt to explore what is essential to the integrity of human life-forms in general might enable more to be said about the goals which could inspire collective self-determination, without damaging that steadfast, subtle universalism which has been the hallmark of Habermas's massive contribution to contemporary philosophical debate.

## Notes

1. Reviewing Jürgen Habermas, *Faktizität und Geltung. Beiträge zur Diskurstheorie des Rechts und des demokratischen Rechtsstaats*, Frankfurt am Main: Suhrkamp 1992.

2. See Albrecht Wellmer, *Ethik und Dialog*, Frankfurt am Main: Suhrkamp 1986, pp. 67–8/'Ethics and Dialogue: Elements of Judgement in Kant and Discourse Ethics', in *The Persistence of Modernity*, trans. David Midgley, Cambridge: Polity Press 1991, pp. 58–9.

3. *Faktizität und Geltung*, pp. 147–9.

4. Ibid., p. 111.

5. Ibid., p. 142.

6. Ibid., p. 163.

7. Ibid., p. 447.

8. Ibid., p. 536.

9. Ibid., p. 503.

10. See Axel Honneth, *The Struggle for Recognition: The Moral Grammar of Social Conflicts*, Cambridge: Polity Press 1995.

11. Jürgen Habermas, 'Gerechtigkeit und Solidarität', in *Erläuterungen zur Diskursethik*, Frankfurt am Main: Suhrkamp 1991, p. 70.

12. Jürgen Habermas, *Vergangenheit als Zukunft*, Zurich: Pendo Verlag 1991, p. 141/*The Past as Future*, trans. and ed. Max Pensky, Lincoln, NB: University of Nebraska Press 1994, p. 107.

# Morality, Ethics and
# 'Postmetaphysical Thinking'

At a time when a 'postmodern' thinker such as Michel Foucault can be valued precisely for the fragmented – even inconsistent – character of his *œuvre*, there might seem to be something almost touchingly antique about the stubbornness with which Jürgen Habermas has struggled to articulate his key philosophical intuitions throughout a long and distinguished career. In rereading Habermas, one is often surprised to find that concepts (such as 'communicative action') which became prominent only at a relatively late stage in his work in fact have a complex prehistory, in which they played a subsidiary but nevertheless significant role. At the same time, however, Habermas's thinking is far from being inflexible and dogmatic (qualities which are sometimes fashionably assumed to be the only alternatives to a happy-go-lucky dispersion). Rather, over the years it has undergone major transformations of emphasis and conceptual articulation, usually in response to debate and criticism, while nevertheless constituting a powerful diagnosis of modernity and its problems, unified around a cluster of central insights.[1]

It is doubtless these qualities which have enabled even Habermas's early work to acquire new relevance in the context of current debates. There are many cases of this. One could cite, for example, the way in which Habermas's concern at the political implications of Heidegger's philosophy, first expressed in his shocked newspaper review of *Introduction to Metaphysics* in 1953, has resurfaced as a dimension of the latest round of the Heidegger controversy, sparked by the books of Farias and Ott.[2] But perhaps the most striking and significant instance is the widespread influence which Habermas's classic early book on *The Structural Transformation of the Public Sphere* (1962) is currently exerting on historians, sociologists, political scientists, as well as feminist and cultural theorists, in the English-speaking world, since the appearance of its long overdue English translation in 1989.

The basic philosophical insight underlying *Structural Transformation* concerns the crucial role of public discussion and debate in the formation of the needs, interests and aspirations of individuals. Even now, there are some critics of Habermas who cannot conceive of 'discourse' in his technical sense (egalitarian discussion aimed at resolving practical disputes through consensus) as anything other than a means of discovering the interests which each participant already has, although perhaps he or she is not aware of the fact. For Habermas, however, needs and interests are not an irreducible given, natural bedrock beneath a cultural topsoil, as it were, but exist only as shaped by traditions of interpretation. This is not to say that individuals' understandings of their own interests may not be 'inauthentic' – rather, that the path to a true understanding of individual and collective needs and aspirations can pass only via democratic debate in which these are articulated and, thereby, transformed and clarified.

The corresponding historical thesis of *Structural Transformation* is that such a 'public sphere' of discussion, sandwiched between the private sphere and the state, did emerge in West European countries such as Britain, France and Germany during the eighteenth century, supported by a culture of coffee-houses and salons, newspapers and novel-reading. However, this public sphere was necessarily restricted in its social scope, suppressing class tensions and inequalities through its equation of 'citizen' and 'bourgeois'. At the level of political theory, Habermas's account traces how this inherent contradiction of the liberal public sphere was reflected in the changing conceptions of it, from Locke, via Kant, to Marx and de Tocqueville. But the book also seeks to show, historically and sociologically, how the development of capitalism itself has hollowed out the public sphere [*Öffentlichkeit*], reducing the reasoning and communicating public to atomized consumers, subject to the manipulative ministrations of politicians, advertisers and public-relations experts. In this respect *Structural Transformation* has remained a beacon of interdisciplinarity.

Habermas now admits that his original account confused the historical and normative dimensions of the public sphere, tending to evoke a utopian moment of earlier capitalist society when conditions for the rational formation of public opinion, albeit restricted by social class and gender, obtained. Nevertheless, the centrality of the notion of the public sphere to his thought is attested by its re-emergence in his recent major work on the philosophy of law, *Faktizität und Geltung* (1992), where it combines with more recent theories of 'civil society' to provide an account of how the 'lifeworld' can exercise control through legislation over markets and bureaucracies. Habermas still affirms that in a complex modern society the quality of democracy ultimately depends not on formal political mechanisms but on 'a free political culture and an enlightened political socialization, above all on the initiatives of opinion-forming associations . . . which constitute and regenerate themselves to a large extent spontaneously'.[3] Indeed, what seems primarily to have changed since

*Structural Transformation* is Habermas's evaluation of the power of the mass media. Abandoning his earlier Adornian pessimism, he now believes that the role of the media in relation to the formation of effective public opinion can, at the very least, be qualified as 'ambivalent'.[4]

In this respect some suspicion must remain that it is Habermas's philosophical commitment to the principle of dialogue, rather than hard sociological evidence, which has obliged him to revise his formerly gloomy prognoses concerning the survival of rational political debate in a consumerized society. But even if these worries are set aside, the very transformative role which Habermas allots to discussion, and which enables him – plausibly, in many ways – to locate himself philosophically between liberal individualism and communitarianism, also raises problems for his assumption that the immanent *telos* of all discussion is consensus. This is another philosophical motif which has been central to Habermas's work from the very beginning. It is manifested in *Structural Transformation*, for example, in the contention that John Stuart Mill's 'perspectivist epistemology' is no more than a tacit capitulation in the face of irreconcilable social interests.[5]

As Thomas McCarthy has argued, however, Habermas's emphasis on the culturally saturated character of needs, which underlies his notion of an emphatically 'public' opinion, can be seen as problematizing the expectation of consensus which is an equally important aspect of his work. For if needs are always-already interpreted within specific cultural frameworks, why should we be confident, especially in an increasingly multicultural society, that a 'common', even 'universal', style of discourse will be found, which can harmonize divergent interpretations? As McCarthy puts it: 'consensus could be achieved only if all participants could come to agree on the authentic interpretation of each's needs, and they would have to do so from the very different hermeneutic starting points afforded by a pluralistic and individualistic culture'.[6] From this argument McCarthy draws the conclusion that compromise must play a far more important role in political discussion and negotiation than Habermas is willing to allow. We should not expect the force of the better argument alone to be the determinant of the outcome of public discussion, merely that 'the force of the better argument can contribute to the final shape of whatever type of agreement is reached'.[7] Throughout his more recent writings, however, Habermas has refused to alter his conception of normative grounding in the light of this objection.

## Distinguishing Morality and Ethics

In general, Habermas's work can be divided into two phases, with reference to the basic type of normative background on which he relies. Right from the beginning, he sought to add a missing dimension to the Marxist theory of history, and remove an ambiguity in Marx's theory of emancipation, by stressing that communicative relations cannot be reduced to the instrumentality of material production. Up until *Knowledge and Human Interests*, however, Habermas had assumed that the historical realization of freedom could be understood in terms of a reflective dissolution of distorted communicative relations, driven by an 'emancipatory interest', without the need to spell out philosophically the criteria for this distortion. From the early 1970s onwards, however, an account of the normative structure of communication becomes his central concern, and is intended to provide a basis for the critique of the colonizing 'functional reason' of social systems, such as markets and bureaucracies, as well as for a validity of moral norms transcending the diversity of cultural contexts.

Habermas's strategy for the grounding of moral norms is set out in the central essay of *Moral Consciousness and Communicative Action*, 'Discourse Ethics: Notes on a Program of Philosophical Justification', dating from the early 1980s. The idea from which he begins is that communicative action aimed at the resolution of practical disagreements involves implicit commitment to a set of norms of discussion which entail the equal participatory rights of all concerned, along with an obligation to provide grounds for challenged assertions and claims. Indeed, these principles *have to be* regarded by participants as instantiated to an adequate degree in order for discussion to have any sense at all. Given the constitutive normativity of these presuppositions, Habermas argues, a moral rule could be regarded as 'right' – i.e. objectively valid – if it were agreed on as the result of discussion conducted in the 'ideal speech situation' which we necessarily anticipate whenever we discuss at all. Under such circumstances: '*All* affected can accept the consequences and the side effects [which the norm's] *general* observance can be anticipated to have for the satisfaction of *everyone's* interests.'[8] (This is the rule of argumentation for moral discourse which Habermas calls 'U'.)

Even if Habermas is correct to argue that we can give a genuine sense to the notion of moral objectivity, he still has to explain how this notion might have any purchase in the tough world of actual moral and political discussion. Here an important part of his strategy in recent writings has been to distinguish between 'moral' and 'ethical' questions: the former are concerned with what is right or just for everybody, without restriction; the latter are concerned with how I as an individual – or we as a particular community – can live lives which authentically express who we are. Thus ethical questions can be answered only with reference to the content of specific cultural traditions. Having insisted on this distinction, Habermas now allows that, besides moral discourses, there can be 'ethical discourses', whose results are valid only for a specific person or group, rather than for humanity as a whole.

This contrast allows Habermas to make a disarmingly simple move in relation to many of the criticisms which have been put to him. In the long central essay of *Justification and Application*, where he parries a wide range of objections raised by leading contemporaries, he is able to admit that in a multicultural society the number of issues which can be resolved on a universalistic basis is likely to shrink. In response to McCarthy, however, he maintains that:

> finding a solution to these few more sharply focused questions becomes all the more critical to coexistence, and even survival, in a more populous world. It remains an empirical question how far the sphere of strictly generalizable interests extends. Only if it could be shown in principle that moral discourses must prove unfruitful despite the growing consensus concerning human rights and democracy – for example, because common interests can no longer even be identified in incommensurable languages – would the deontological endeavour to uncouple questions of justice from the context-dependent questions of the good life have failed.[9]

Accordingly, Habermas also argues that in cases where it proves impossible to find a universalizable interest, such as the debate over abortion, we may be forced to conclude that the best that can be achieved is a balance between different *ethical* conceptions:

> In other cases it is possible to deduce from the inconclusive outcome of practical discourses that the problems under consideration and the issues in need of regulation do not involve generalizable interests at all; then one should not look for moral solutions but instead for fair compromises.[10]

The problem with this defensive manoeuvre, however, apart from its drastic narrowing of the scope of morality, is that its account of the distinction between moral and ethical issues looks circular. According to Habermas, we may conclude that an issue is not a moral one if it proves impossible to settle through the identification of universalizable interests. But then his claim for the existence of a universalistic moral viewpoint no longer functions as a *counter* to relativist views of morality, since it abolishes moral issues resistant to universal regulation by definitional fiat, and relegates them to a domain called ethics, which lacks the categorical character of the moral. Furthermore, it is clearly problematic, in his own terms, for Habermas to claim that how far the domain of universalizable interests extends is an 'empirical issue'. For since the criterion of moral validity is consensus under *ideal* conditions, it would always remain open for some of those concerned to claim that a generalizable interest *could* ultimately be discovered, given the indefinite length of time required to strip the veils of inauthentic need-interpretation.

A couple of examples may clarify this issue. In the political realm, many people regard a voting system based on proportional representation as a matter of justice, since without it not everyone's vote has the same weight in deciding the political outcome, and a basic democratic right is violated. Others might argue, however, that a non-proportional system is more in keeping with the political traditions and self-understanding of a particular national community, and indeed may also have pragmatic advantages. How is the decision whether this is a moral or an ethical issue to be made? Similarly, a strong moral conception of human equality may come into conflict with the refusal of certain churches to admit the ordination of women, yet even the female members of such churches may deny that they have an 'interest' in equality that overrides the forms of religious fulfilment which the current gender-specific practices within their community make possible. More generally, it is clear that potential moral principles, in Habermas's sense, are not neutral between different ethical conceptions, and may therefore meet with ethical resistance. How, then, are we to decide whether they are genuinely moral, in Habermas's sense of universalizable, or not?

These problems come to a head in Habermas's discussion – in *Justification and Application* – of cases in which adherence to a moral norm 'cannot be reasonably expected from an existential point of view', because the norm clashes too drastically with an individual's self-conception and project of self-fulfilment.[11] In a situation such as this it is hard to avoid the question: in what sense is the norm concerned moral (i.e. strictly universalizable), since its consequences are not compatible with the 'ideal' interest of at least one individual concerned in sustaining a basic sense of identity? This question inevitably stirs the suspicion that when Habermas includes the reference to 'interests' in 'U' (rather than simply referring to what all can agree on, for whatever reason), he is trying to smuggle in a naturalistic anthropological baseline which will make the goal of consensus appear more plausible.

These are only some of the difficulties faced by Habermas's attempt to draw a sharp distinction between the 'ethical' and the 'moral'. In considering them, it seems natural to raise the following issue: given his fundamental antipathy to relativism, why does Habermas not at least try to solve his difficulties by admitting that ethical conceptions can *also* claim universal validity? In this way the constant clash in his work between the universality of the moral and the particularity of the ethical would be resolved. This strategy is not just an abstract possibility, since it informs the work of a contemporary thinker such as Charles Taylor, who argues against Habermas that moral principles have no culture-neutral justification, and are always anchored in a specific ethical conception of human life, but – at the same time – does not simply abandon the domain of the ethical to relativism. In Taylor's view, it *is* possible to give arguments for why one ethical conception is superior to another – not in a decontextual-ized way, by appealing to general principles, but in the same way that, through transformative encounters and experiences, we may come to appreciate that we formerly had an inadequate grasp of what we really felt and aspired to, and thus of who we truly were and what the best way to live our lives might be.[12]

In relation to such positions, Habermas's response is a curious one. On the one hand, he stresses repeatedly in *Justification and Application* that we live in a period when no conception of the world and of the human good can dogmatically claim supremacy: 'Modern worldviews must accept the conditions of postmetaphysical thought to the extent that they recognize that they are competing with other interpretations of the world within the same universe of validity claims.'[13] In Habermas's account the irreducible plurality of ethical views, as we have already seen, is cited precisely as a reason for defending an abstract but universalistic morality. Yet, given Habermas's own analysis of communication, and of validity-claims such as truth and rightness, which he sees as consensually resolvable in principle (under ideal conditions), this plurality of competing claims cannot be seen as logically irreducible. Accordingly, he writes: 'The idea of "reasonable disagreement" permits us to leave truth claims undecided while simulta-neously upholding their unconditional character.'[14] However, if the plurality of world-views and associated ethical views is contingent, not essential, then it seems that, ultimately, ethical universals could be identi-fied, and the distinction between morality and ethics would once again collapse. The correlative of this, of course, would be a global culture, but such a thing is not logically inconceivable; moreover, were it to be instan-tiated, we would be entitled to ask whether a definitive 'metaphysical' interpretation of the place and purpose of human life had not also been attained. This possibility also highlights the issue of whether the basis for Habermas's constant assertion that we are living in a 'postmetaphysical' age is historical or philosophical.

## The 'Extraordinary'

The metaphilosophical assumptions which underpin Habermas's current writing, and inform his distinctions between the cognitive, moral and eth-ical domains, are more directly discussed in the essays collected in *Postmetaphysical Thinking*. It is doubtful, however, whether Habermas can be said to have harmonized the complex and contradictory impulses to which these assumptions give voice. One of his most significant moves in this book, reminiscent of Feuerbach, is to suggest that the world as a meaningfully organized totality, the traditional 'object' of metaphysical thinking, was always in fact a mystified projection of the totality of particular lifeworld. Accordingly, Habermas now claims that the successor activity to metaphysics, which he calls 'interpretation', limits itself to the hermeneutical excavation of the deep intuitions and assumptions of a particular lifeworld, and cannot make claims about the world as a whole. In this way, Habermas seeks to acknowledge the continuing validity of philosophy's totalizing scope, while undermining the notion of philosophy as access to the absolute or the 'unconditioned'. Since the only totality available is that of the pre-reflective lifeworld in which we are immersed, and this can never be fully objectified by thinking, interpretation always remains bound in opaque ways to a finite context.

The difficulty with this conception, of course, is that it embodies what Charles Taylor has criticized as 'sophisticated naturalism'.[15] In order to 'reduce' metaphysical thinking in this way to the conceptual articulation of a specific lifeworld, Habermas must commit himself to the philosophical vision of a variety of lifeworlds coexisting within the space of a world which is essentially value-neutral, and to which none of the world-interpretations anchored in specific lifeworlds can therefore ultimately correspond. Yet what entitles Habermas to this vision? Could one not argue that his background assumption of a 'disenchanted' world overlaid with a variety of totalizing interpretations itself betrays a residual metaphysical objectivism? Hilary Putnam has made a similar point, in his essay collection *Realism with a Human Face*, in criticizing both realism and relativism: 'One kind of philosopher views [the world] as a product from a raw material: Unconceptualized Reality. The other views it as a creation ex nihilo. But the world isn't a product. It's just the world.'[16]

What these difficulties suggest is that Habermas's current position depends on a somewhat precarious division of labour, in which the distinction between morality and ethics is supported by a contextualizing move which renders philosophical claims relative to a lifeworld (apart from the reflexive arguments grounding the 'moral point of view'), and thereby supposedly overcomes 'metaphysics' definitively. For very sound reasons Habermas believes that being 'post-Enlightenment' involves overcoming the illusion that our conception of the good could be based on the 'objective meaning in being' once deciphered by metaphysics. Therefore, from *The Structural Transformation of the Public Sphere* onwards, he has concentrated his philosophical efforts on showing the priority of the discursively achieved agreement of citizens over all speculative elucidations of human purpose.

Yet Habermas is still too much of a dialectician not to be aware that the suppression of democratic potentials is not the only cause for concern in an instrumentalized modern society. For meaning, too, as he often puts it, is a resource which is becoming ever more scarce, and without such a resource, once conserved by myth and religion, we have nothing in the light of which we can discuss and decide collectively about our lives. This is a problem which Habermas has only once addressed at length, in an essay on Walter Benjamin,[17] but its pressure is always felt just beneath the surface of his work, since the meaningfulness of decisions cannot be guaranteed merely by the decision procedure itself, however democratic.

One indication of this 'subterranean' preoccupation can be found in the remarks scattered through *Postmetaphysical Thinking* which suggest a more conciliatory attitude towards religion than was expressed in some of Habermas's earlier writings. Aware that only 'contact with the extraordinary' [*das Außeralltägliche*] can ultimately renew the sources of meaning, Habermas describes a division of labour in which philosophy cannot entirely supplant religion:

> Philosophy, even in its postmetaphysical form, will be able neither to replace nor to suppress religion as long as religious language is the bearer of a semantic content which is inspiring, and even indispensable . . . and continues to resist translation into reasoning discourses.[18]

Yet since he has made this concession – and, indeed, argued that one of the tasks of philosophy is to appropriate critically the content of religious traditions – one wonders whether it can be anything but political caution which prevents Habermas from admitting that philosophy, too, may have a certain autonomous contact with the 'extraordinary', and tap into the ultimate sources of meaning. Today, of course, this could be achieved only in a self-denying, 'negative' form, through an oblique approach to what Wittgenstein called 'the mystical', Heidegger 'Being', and Adorno 'the non-identical'.[19] Yet such an approach would not be equivalent to that total renunciation of the unconditioned in favour of 'procedural reason' which Habermas urges in *Postmetaphysical Thinking*.

Over the years Habermas has constructed an imposing, multifaceted and, indeed, tension-laden philosophical edifice, whose basis is a strict distinction between different theoretical tasks. But by piecing together the elements which Habermas himself provides in a different way, we can see that the interdependencies between science, morality, ethics, and 'metaphysical' (albeit fallible and non-objectivistic) reflection concerning the ultimate meaning of our knowledge and action are far more intimate than he is usually willing to admit.

# Notes

1. Reviewing Jürgen Habermas, *The Structural Transformation of the Public Sphere: An Enquiry into a Category of Bourgeois Society*, trans. Thomas Burger, Cambridge: Polity Press 1989; *Moral Consciousness and Communicative Action*, trans. Christian Lenhardt and Shierry Weber Nicholsen, Cambridge: Polity Press 1992; *Postmetaphysical Thinking: Philosophical Essays*, trans. William Hohengarten, Cambridge: Polity Press 1992; *Justification and Application: Remarks on Discourse Ethics*, trans. Ciaran Cronin, Cambridge: Polity Press 1993.

2. See Jürgen Habermas, 'Martin Heidegger: On the Publication of the Lectures of 1935' (1953), in Richard Wolin, ed., *The Heidegger Controversy: A Critical Reader*, Cambridge, MA: MIT Press 1993; Victor Farias, *Heidegger and Nazism*, trans. Paul Burrell, Philadelphia: Temple University Press 1989; Hugo Ott, *Martin Heidegger: A Political Life*, trans. Allan Blunden, London: HarperCollins 1993.

3. Jürgen Habermas, *Faktizität und Geltung*, Frankfurt am Main: Suhrkamp 1992, p. 366.

4. See Jürgen Habermas, 'Further Reflections on the Public Sphere', in Craig Calhoun, ed., *Habermas and the Public Sphere*, Cambridge, MA: MIT Press 1992, pp. 436–9.

5. *The Structural Transformation of the Public Sphere*, p. 135.

6. Thomas McCarthy, 'Practical Discourse: On the Relation of Morality to Politics', in *Habermas and the Public Sphere*, p. 61.

7. Ibid., p. 67.

8. *Moral Consciousness and Communicative Action*, p. 65.

9. 'Remarks on Discourse Ethics', in *Justification and Application*, p. 91.

10. Ibid., p. 60.

11. Ibid., p. 87.

12. See Charles Taylor, *Sources of the Self*, Cambridge: Cambridge University Press 1989, esp. part 1.

13. 'Remarks on Discourse Ethics' in *Justification and Application*, p. 94.

14. Ibid.

15. *Sources of the Self*, p. 67.

16. Hilary Putnam, 'Realism with a Human Face', in *Realism with a Human Face*, Cambridge, MA: Harvard University Press 1992, p. 28.

17. See Jürgen Habermas, 'Walter Benjamin. Bewußtmachende oder rettende Kritik', in *Philosophisch-politische Profile*, Frankfurt am Main: Suhrkamp (2nd expanded edition) 1981/'Consciousness-raising or Pure Critique: The Contemporaneity of Walter Benjamin', *New German Critique*, no. 17, 1979.

18. 'Themes in Postmetaphysical Thinking', in *Postmetaphysical Thinking*, p. 51 (translation altered).

19. See Herbert Schnädelbach, 'Metaphysik und Religion heute', in *Zur Rehabilitierung des animal rationale. Vorträge und Abhandlungen 2*, Frankfurt am Main: Suhrkamp 1992, p. 155.

# PART IV

# Psychoanalysis

# The Crisis of Oedipal Identity:
# The Early Lacan and the
# Frankfurt School

Perhaps we do not find it surprising enough that the thought of Jacques Lacan should have come to function as a major point of reference for feminist theory in the English-speaking world. Lacan's best-known work, dating from the inception of his *Seminar* in 1953, is characterized by an almost obsessive concern with the relation between language and subjectivity, but Lacan shies away from connecting his formal conception of language to any historical, let alone ideological, dimension of meaning. Rather, in his reformulation, psychoanalysis is focused on the simultaneous relation of dependency and non-identity between the subject and language *as such*: Lacan is unequivocal that in psychoanalysis 'it is not a question of the relation of man to language as a social phenomenon'.[1] To this extent, the appeal of his work for feminists derives not from its historical or sociological insights, but purely from its emphasis on the symbolically structured character of subjectivity in its gendered dimension, an emphasis which undermines any naturalistic conception of the opposition between the psychology of the two sexes.

At the same time, however, the political advantage which this emphasis might be considered to bring is profoundly elusive, since – in his later work, at least – Lacan gives little reason to assume that such symbolic structuring might be alterable. Even those feminists most sympathetic to Lacan have found themselves struggling with the dilemma that his thought appears to establish an intrinsic relation between phallic primacy and the symbolic order. Thus, Jacqueline Rose has written:

> For Lacan, to say that difference is 'phallic' difference is to expose the symbolic and arbitrary nature of its division as such. It is crucial . . . that refusal of the phallic term brings with it an attempt to reconstitute a form of subjectivity free of division, and hence a refusal of the notion of symbolization itself.[2]

If, however, refusal of the phallic term is equivalent to the absolute refusal of symbolization, then the role of the phallus can hardly be considered 'arbitrary'. Rose recognizes this, for she goes on to defend her position by suggesting:

> While the objection to . . . [the] dominant term [i.e. the phallus] must be recognized, it cannot be answered by an account which returns to a concept of the feminine as pre-given, nor by a mandatory appeal to an androcentrism in the symbolic which the phallus would simply reflect. The former relegates women outside language and history, the latter simply subordinates them to both.[3]

It is difficult to understand, however, why the grounding of phallocentrism in androcentrism should subordinate women to language and history, unless this androcentrism itself is considered to be immutable. Conversely, if the symbolic role of the phallus in the unconscious formation of gender identity is entirely detached from the question of the actual relations, including power relations, between men and women, it is hard to perceive where the interest of psychoanalysis for feminists might lie.

In the light of these difficulties, it might appear that other intellectual traditions, both psychoanalytically informed and committed to social critique, might offer better starting points for a feminist theorization of sexual difference. The tradition which inevitably springs to mind here is that of the Frankfurt School, which has in general been much more sensitive than Lacanian approaches to the intersections between psychoanalysis and social theory. The earlier Frankfurt School, in particular, appreciated the need to introduce a dimension of historicity into even the most fundamental psychoanalytic categories, arguing – against Freud himself – that there can be no purely timeless unconscious, since 'concrete historical components already enter early childhood experience.'[4] Until recently, however, this tradition has had little to say about the specific question of women's oppression – indeed, the issue is more present, though scarcely prominent, in the work of the earlier Frankfurt School than in the contemporary critical theory of Habermas. Furthermore, although there are now the beginnings of a feminist reception of Critical Theory, particularly in North America, this reception has not – on the whole – been particularly sensitive to the psychoanalytic dimension of earlier Critical Theory, or tried to make use of it to any significant extent. Rather, its principal aim has been to modify the gender-insensitive universalism of Habermasian social and moral theory.[5]

On the one hand, therefore, we find the powerful influence of a form of *psychoanalytic* theory within Anglo-American feminism which appears remote from sociological and historical concerns; on the other, a tradition of *critical* theory, now being adapted and developed by feminists, which has lost the psychoanalytic emphasis on the complex internal structure of subjectivity, in its shift to an investigation of the normative structures of *inter*subjectivity. However, a consideration of the early – now almost forgotten – phases of Lacan's thinking opens up possibilities of at least modifying this dichotomy. For Lacan's first forays in psychoanalytic theory, prior to the inception of the *Seminar*, were by no means as hostile to historical and sociological perspectives as his later thought appears to be. Furthermore, the account of the crisis of the modern family which Lacan developed during the 1930s – and which is most fully presented in a lengthy encyclopaedia article of 1938, *Les complexes familiaux* – evinces many striking similarities with the contemporaneous work of the Frankfurt School on the same issue. Against the background of these affinities, the question of why Lacan's work evolved as it did can be posed in a new way. Indeed, as we shall see, the later Lacan's apparently 'transcendental' model of a phallocentric symbolic order can itself be understood as a response to a specific *historical* crisis. Simultaneously, the possibility opens up of comparing Lacan's later work, as a response to the familial and social crisis which he diagnoses, with recent developments in psychoanalysis which attempt both to build on and to respond to the earlier thought of the Frankfurt School from a critical, feminist perspective – most notably the work of Jessica Benjamin.

## Lacan on the Oedipus Complex

Perhaps the most striking feature of *Les complexes familiaux* is the manner in which Lacan insists, against Freud himself, that the Oedipus complex is at the centre of a historically specific type of identity-formation, which emerges within the context of the patriarchal family. Lacan makes it clear that marriage and the family are two distinct social institutions, and argues that the modern form of the family, centred on the 'matrimonial' relation between the parents, should not be confused in its psychological effects with earlier familial structures, even where these seem to overlap in terms of personnel. Indeed, he specifically criticizes Freud, on the grounds that he 'presents this psychological element [of the Oedipus complex] as the specific form of the human family and subordinates to it all the social variations of the family.'[6] By contrast, Lacan claims, 'The methodological order proposed here, both in the consideration of mental structures and of the social facts, will lead to a revision of the complex which will allow us to situate contemporary neurosis in the history of the paternalistic family, and to cast further light on it.'[7]

In the account which Lacan then develops, the specific virtue of Oedipal identity-formation consists in the extreme psychological tension which is generated by the role of the father, as both 'the agent of prohibition and the example of its transgression'.[8] As Lacan writes:

It is . . . because it is invested with the power of repression that the paternal imago projects its original force into the very sublimations which are to surmount it; it is from binding together the progress of its functions in such an antinomy that the Oedipus complex derives its fecundity.[9]

In other terms, the paradoxical paternal injunction 'Be and do not be like me', which confronts the child in the Oedipal situation, makes possible a form of identification which fuses emulation and difference in an advanced form of individuation. As Lacan states:

If, as a result of their experience, both the psychoanalyst and the sociologist can recognize in the prohibition of the mother the concrete form of primordial obligation, they can also demonstrate a real 'opening up' of the social bond in paternalist authority and affirm that, through the functional conflict of the Oedipal situation, this authority introduces into repression a promissory ideal.[10]

Elaborating this general characterization, Lacan gives three principal reasons for the superiority of Oedipal identity-formation over other corresponding processes. Firstly, because authority is incarnated in a familiar form by the nearest generation, it is more readily open to creative subversion. Secondly, because the psyche is formed not simply by the constraint of the adult but by his positive image (Lacan considers the father–son relationship the pre-eminent example here), there occurs a 'positive selection of tendencies and gifts, and a progressive realization of the ideal in the character'.[11] Thirdly, the evidence of sexual life on the part of those imposing moral constraints 'raises the tension of the libido to the highest degree, and increases the scope of sublimation'.[12] On these grounds, Lacan has only the highest praise for the achievements of the modern family (by which he means the type of family, based on the free choice of partners, which began to emerge in Europe from the fifteenth century onwards):

It is by realizing in the most human form the conflict of man with his most archaic anxiety, it is by offering the most loyal closed domain where he can measure himself against the profoundest figures of his destiny, it is by putting the most complete triumph over his original servitude within his grasp, that the complex of the conjugal family creates superior successes of character, happiness and creation.[13]

By contrast with this view, Lacan is unequivocal about the 'stagnation' which is implied by non-patriarchal patterns of socialization. In such forms the repressive social instance and the social ideal are separated: Lacan cites Malinowski's accounts of societies in which the first of these roles is played by the maternal uncle, while the father has a more companionate relationship to the child. Because of this separation, such forms are unable to rival the dialectical, sublimatory tension generated by the Oedipal model. Commenting caustically on the Melanesian idylls evoked by Malinowski, Lacan remarks: 'the harmony of these societies contrasts with the stereotypical quality which marks the creations of the personality, and of art and morality in such cultures'.[14]

Despite his paeans to the patriarchal family, however, Lacan is extremely sensitive to the fact that this social form is caught up in a fateful historical dialectic. Up to a certain point, a positive cycle occurs in which the 'normative ideals, juridical statutes and creative inspirations' made possible by Oedipal identity-formation react back on to the family, thereby helping to concentrate even further within it the conditions of the Oedipal conflict, and 'reintegrating into psychological progress the social dialectic engendered by this conflict'.[15] However, this self-reinforcing cycle eventually reaches a crisis point, where the level of individuation achieved begins to undermine the now highly compacted conditions of Oedipal identity-formation itself. According to Lacan, the progress of culture is manifested in the increasing demands which are imposed on the ego with regard to 'coherence and creative *élan*', with the result that 'the accidents and caprices of this [Oedipal] regulation increase step by step with this same social progress which, in making the family evolve towards the conjugal form, submits it more and more to individual variations'. And Lacan concludes:

> This 'anomie', which made possible the discovery of the complex, gives rise to the degenerated form in which the analyst recognizes it: a form which we could define in terms of an incomplete repression of the desire for the mother, with a reactivation of the anxiety and curiosity inherent in the birth relation; and a narcissistic debasement of the idealization of the father, which causes the emergence, in Oedipal identification, of the aggressive ambivalence immanent in the primordial relation to the counterpart.[16]

Against the background of this deeply historical account of structures of subjectivity, Lacan's later thought appears in a new light. On one plausible interpretation, proposed by Mikkel Borch-Jacobsen, the later Lacan attempts to shore up the Oedipus complex by transforming it into a 'transcendental' structure constitutive of subjectivity as such, while haunted by the awareness that the Oedipal norm no longer corresponds to the socially predominant processes of identity-formation. Indeed, Lacan himself suggests in *Les complexes familiaux* that the emergence of psychoanalysis itself – in the melting-pot of turn-of-the-century Vienna, with its chaotic multiplicity of family forms, from the most traditional to the most irregular – can be explained in terms of the incipient crisis of Oedipal identity-formation. The 'true' Oedipus complex, one might say, can be recognized only privatively, through the psychoanalytic inventory of the effects of its distorted and degenerating forms.

## Horkheimer on the Family

Before examining Lacan's own later response to this situation in more detail, however, I would like to highlight further the distinctive features of Lacan's account of the crisis of the bourgeois family by comparing it with the approach of the Frankfurt School at the same period. Significantly, Max Horkheimer's classic essay on 'Authority and the Family' was written only two years before *Les complexes familiaux*, in 1936. Unlike Lacan, however, Horkheimer grounds his analysis from the normative standpoint of an anticipated society devoid of institutionalized relations of force and their internalized equivalents. From this point of view, the psychic apparatus is understood as serving primarily to 'interiorize, or at least to rationalize and supplement physical coercion'.[17] Horkheimer does not deny the historical advance represented by the modern patriarchal family, whose emergence he dates – as does Lacan – from the fifteenth century:

> At the beginning of the bourgeois age the father's control of his household was doubtless an indispensable condition of progress. The self-control of the individual, the disposition for work and discipline, the ability to hold firmly to certain ideas, consistency in practical life, application of reason, perseverance and pleasure in constructive activity could all be developed, in the circumstances, only under the dictation and guidance of the father whose own education had been won in the school of life.[18]

However, Horkheimer argues, the function of authority can change from being progressive to regressive, relative to the goals of 'self-development and happiness' which are internal to his normative standpoint.[19] As the capitalist organization of society is consolidated, the role of the family increasingly becomes that of inculcating an adaptive and submissive attitude to authority, which is now reified and depersonalized in the form of the economic system itself. Within the family, the authority of the father, based on superior physical strength and economic power, comes to embody that irrational facticity of the social in the face of which individuals would be 'irrational' to do anything other than submit.

In Horkheimer's account, the dialectic thus set in motion eventually leads to the undermining of the role of the father. He argues:

> The education of authority-oriented personalities, for which the family is suited because of its own authority structure, is not a passing phenomenon but part of a relatively permanent state of affairs. Of course, the more this society enters a critical phase because of its own immanent laws, the less will the family be able to exercise its educational function . . . The means of protecting the cultural totality and developing it further have increasingly come into conflict with the cultural content itself. The father as an arbitrary power no longer offers possibilities of identification, and the child instead identifies with repressive social instances.[20]

The result of this direct identification with social power is the spread of the malleable narcissistic personality type, lacking those inner capacities for self-direction which the buffer of paternal authority once provided, ostensibly well-adapted but inwardly cold and emotionless, inclined to power-worship and masochistic submission.

In considering the validity of this analysis, and its political consequences, it is instructive to compare the reasons which Lacan and Horkheimer supply for the fateful dialectic of the bourgeois family. In Horkheimer the essential mediating role is played by the capitalist economy, on the assumption that 'The idealization of paternal authority, the pretense that it comes from a divine decision or the nature of things or reason, proves on closer examination to be the glorification of an economically conditioned institution.'[21] However, as the development of the economy moves beyond its private, entrepreneurial phase into an era characterized by increasing monopolization and bureaucratic intervention, the individual becomes increasingly dependent on processes which lie beyond his or her control, and capacities for personal initiative become ever more redundant. In this context, the father is no longer able to provide a model of authority in the traditional sense, with its inextricable interweaving of rational and irrational dimensions. Rather: 'The fullest possible adaptation of the subject to the reified authority of the economy is the form which reason really takes in bourgeois society.'[22] The family, while not being abolished, is hollowed out, instrumentalized: the dialectic of the universal (society), the particular (the family), and the individual, as envisaged by Hegel, begins to split apart.[23]

Against the background of Horkheimer's views, it becomes apparent that there are two strands of diagnosis in Lacan's text. Lacan, too, lays considerable emphasis on the failure of the father as the crucial factor in contemporary character disorders. In his view, these disorders find their 'principal determination in the personality of the father, who is always lacking in some way, absent, humiliated, divided, or fake'.[24] Furthermore, his description of the results of this failure converges strikingly with the Frankfurt School account of the narcissistic personality:

> Like sinister godmothers installed at the cradle of the neurotic, impotence and utopianism enclose his ambition, so that he either smothers within himself the creations awaited by the world in which he appears, or misrecognizes his own impulse in the object against which he revolts.[25]

Lacan also admits that the decay of the paternal imago is in part, at least, the result of social and economic factors. It is a

> decline conditioned by the rebounding against the individual of the extreme effects of social progress, a decline which in our time is most pronounced in the

collectivities which have been most tested by the effects of such progress: namely, the concentration of economic power and political catastrophes.[26]

Horkheimer makes the comparable claim that 'The cell of society is no longer the family but the social atom, the solitary individual. The struggle for existence consists in the resolution of the individual, in a world of apparatuses, machinery and manipulation, not to be annihilated at any moment.'[27] Unlike Horkheimer, however, Lacan detects another – perhaps deeper – reason for this decline, which he connects not with the lack of genuine individuality in mass society but, rather, with the dialectic of individuation as such. In his view, Oedipal socialization requires what he calls a 'typical quality in the psychological relation between the parents',[28] – in other words, relatively well-defined maternal and paternal roles. However, in the ever more predominant 'conjugal marriage', dominated by the personal choice and interaction of the partners, this typical quality tends to disappear. What Lacan terms the 'matrimonial demands' of the modern conjugal family, generated by the very conception of marriage as a relationship between equals, one might say, leads to the 'social decline of the paternal imago'.[29] At this level, Lacan's diagnosis could be said to run in the opposite direction to that of Horkheimer. For the latter, the crisis of individualization occurs at the point at which the tendencies towards concentration and bureaucratization of the capitalist economy begin to eliminate the need for individual creativity, judgement and conscience. For Lacan, however, working in an intellectual tradition profoundly influenced by Durkheim, it is individualization as such which poses the fundamental problem. The very 'coherence and creative *élan*' which modern culture demands of individuals produces a degree of anomie which destroys the minimum of typicality in the relation between the parents necessary for the functioning of the Oedipus complex. Once this historical turning point is reached, then personalities characterized by a 'narcissistic subduction of the libido' will begin to be formed.

## A Critical Response to Lacan

As I have already indicated, a thought-provoking interpretation of the shift from the Lacan of *Les complexes familiaux* to the later, and better-known, Lacan has been provided by Mikkel Borch-Jacobsen. In his book *Lacan: The Absolute Master*, and in a paper on 'The Oedipus Problem in Freud and Lacan', Borch-Jacobsen suggests that in *Les complexes familiaux* Lacan sets out to resolve a difficulty which had already troubled Freud: how can the identificatory rivalry of the Oedipus complex be resolved precisely through a *further* identification with the rival? Borch-

Jacobsen argues that Lacan attempts to resolve this problem by drawing a much more rigorous distinction than Freud between the superego and the ego-ideal – the former forbidding rivalrous identification, the latter encouraging a sublimatory identification.[30] As we have already seen, for the Lacan of *Les complexes familiaux* the contemporary crisis of Oedipal identity-formation consists in the fact that this distinction is breaking down: both the 'lacking' father and the arbitrarily authoritarian father fail to sustain the delicate equilibrium between idealizing identification and repression.

On Borch-Jacobsen's reading, Lacan's later work, with its strict distinction between imaginary and symbolic registers, represents an attempt to shore up a form of identity-formation which has already fallen into decay. The Lacanian concept of the 'Name-of-the-Father', equivalent to the totem of 'primitive' societies in its function as the pole of identification which allows a symbolic resolution of the Oedipal crisis, and the concomitant distinction between the 'imaginary' and the 'symbolic' phallus, are in fact *normative* concepts and distinctions, vain attempts to sustain an ideal of subjectivity which no longer maps on to the actual social processes of identity-formation. As Borch-Jacobsen writes:

> how is it possible to prevent the identification with the symbolic father-phallus from being confounded with the rivalrous and homosexualizing imaginary father-phallus? . . . it does absolutely no good whatsoever to invoke the *rightful* difference between the two identifications, since that difference, far from being a fundamental, *a priori* structure of every society, turns out actually to be bound solely to the 'elementary structures of kinship'. Our societies, on the other hand, are defined by a general crisis of symbolic identifications – 'deficiency of the paternal function', 'foreclosure of the name of the father', perpetual questioning of the symbolic 'law' and 'pact', confusion of lineage and general competition of generations, battle of the sexes, and loss of family landmarks.[31]

Borch-Jacobsen's own attitude to these social developments, however, is curiously insouciant. He believes it is possible simply to 'stop treating the Oedipus complex as a *problem*', and accept the accelerating symbolic breakdown of our societies.[32] But this response seems far too sanguine: Lacan was among the first twentieth-century thinkers to grasp the significance of the rise of what he calls, in *Les complexes familiaux*, 'an introversion of the personality through a narcissistic subduction of the libido';[33] and in his diagnosis of the social consequences of this introversion he concurs to a considerable extent with other traditions of social critique. As a number of commentators have argued, the 'postmodern' dismantlers of subjectivity and celebrators of symbolic fragmentation, who view themselves as transcending such a standpoint of critique, in fact often end up espousing an even more exaggerated form of subjectivist voluntarism.[34] Unless one simply brushes aside Lacan's claim that 'the promotion of the ego, consistent with the utilitiarian conception of man which reinforces it, culminates today in an ever more advanced realization of man as individual, that is to say, in an isolation of the soul ever more akin to its original dereliction',[35] the question must be raised of possible alternative patterns of identity-formation, which would be opposed to the 'deregulation' to which Borch-Jacobsen seems resigned, but would also bridge the impossible gulf between the *pays réel* and the *pays légal* which appears to open up in later Lacanian theory.

Understandably, it is above all feminist psychoanalysts, and psychoanalytically informed feminist theorists, who have tried to address the issue of possibilities of post-Oedipal identity-formation. For such identity-formation, even if it is accepted as having been relatively 'successful' during a certain historical phase, suffers from an intrinsic gender disequilibrium and distortion. Indeed, it is fascinating to observe that in the final pages of *Les complexes familiaux* Lacan himself describes the crisis of Oedipal identity-formation as inevitably arising from the historical suppression of the feminine principle. In a further dialectical twist, the progressive individualization which Oedipal socialization promotes leads to the rejection by women of their predetermined familial role. Thus, Lacan suggests, 'One may perceive in the virile protest of woman the ultimate consequence of the Oedipus complex.'[36]. He fully admits that 'The origins of our culture are too connected to what we willingly describe as the adventure of the paternalist family, for it not to impose, upon all the forms whose psychic development it has enriched, a prevalence of the male principle . . .',[37] and he is aware that, in the long historical run, this social and cultural bias must generate an unstable situation. The occultation of the feminine principle by the masculine ideal, as he calls it, has resulted, in contemporary society, in an 'imaginary impasse of sexual polarisation', in which are 'invisibly engaged' the 'forms of culture, morals and the arts, struggle and thought'.[38] Significantly, it is with this thought that *Les complexes familiaux* – somewhat abruptly – concludes: contemporary feminist theoreticians working within a psychoanalytic framework can be seen to be addressing precisely that 'social antinomy' which Lacan had presciently described, and found himself unable to circumvent, in 1938.

## Feminist Theory and the Oedipus Complex

In the concluding part of this discussion, I shall take the work of Jessica Benjamin as the primary example of an attempt to address the issues raised in *Les complexes familiaux* from a feminist perspective. Benjamin's work is of special interest in the present context because it seeks to build on and transform the heritage of the earlier Frankfurt School, which – in her view –leads to the same 'social antinomy' which we have just found evoked in Lacan. She considers that Horkheimer's view of individual capacities for nonconformity and critical resistance as grounded in the internalization of paternal authority fails to acknowledge the distorted form of identity produced by Oedipal socialization, which is based on an autarkic separation of the self from others and an instrumental relation to objects, at the cost of capacities for reciprocity and empathetic communication.[39]

The core of Benjamin's argument consists in the contention that the symbolic *exclusivity* of the phallus, although not its *primacy* as the unconscious embodiment of agency and desire, is the result of an androcentric social structure.[40] Identifying with the father as bearer of the phallus allows the male child to separate from the mother, although to an excessive extent which involves a *repudiation* of femininity; while this identification is not adequately available to the female child, who nevertheless has no alternative route to independence. Benjamin's contention is that a more nurturing father and a more socially autonomous mother could provide *two* poles of idealizing identification, replacing the classical counterposition of progressive, individuating father against regressive mother.

Benjamin notes that theorists who lament the decline of the paternal imago rarely foreground the ambivalence of the father figure. Drawing on Freud's tracing of the genesis of the incest taboo to the overthrowing of the father of the primal horde in *Totem and Taboo*, Benjamin argues:

> Paternal authority . . . is a far more complex emotional web than its defenders admit: it is not merely rooted in the rational law that forbids incest and patricide, but also in the erotics of ideal love, the guilty identification with power that undermines the son's desire for freedom.[41]

She suggests that it is not possible to make a hard-and-fast distinction between Oedipal and pre-Oedipal figures, and that it is misleading to do so in order to defend the notion of the rational, progressive father. To this extent, her account seems to focus on the crucial problem for Lacan highlighted by Borch-Jacobsen: Oedipal identity-formation can be defended as an ideal only on the normative assumption that ego-ideal and superego can and should be held apart, even though they are embodied in the same person. In Borch-Jacobsen's account, this has *never* been possible:

> For what mysterious reason should the hate identification with the rival *necessarily* be transformed into a respectful identification with the bearer of authority? Identification *is* precisely the reason for the rivalry and, even more essentially, for 'affective ambivalence', so there is every reason to believe that the post-Oedipal identification should, instead, perpetuate that ambivalence.[42]

In response to this problem, Benjamin contends that the pre-Oedipal identificatory love for the father cannot simply be equated with a rivalrous
homosexual identification. Rather:

> To explain what Freud called the 'short step from love to hypnotism', from ordi-
> nary identificatory love to bondage, we must look not merely to the distinction
> between oedipal and pre-oedipal, but to the fate of the child's love for the father
> in each phase . . . the idealization of the pre-oedipal father is closely associated
> with submission when it is thwarted, unrecognized.[43]

The importance of this argument is that, in Lacan's account, there is no
equivalent *idealizing* identificatory love. Lacan, prior to the entry into the
symbolic order brought about by the Oedipus complex, knows only the
jealousy and rivalry of narcissistic identification, which – in *Les complexes
familiaux* – he theorizes in terms of the child's relationship to the intruding
sibling. It is this rivalry which is ultimately broken by the identification
with the paternal ego-ideal. Thus Lacan states:

> The identification, which was formerly mimetic, has become propitiatory: the
> object of sado-masochistic participation detaches itself from the subject,
> becomes distant from it in the new ambiguity of fear and love. But, in this step
> towards reality, the primitive object of desire [i.e. the mother] seems to vanish.[44]

If one distinguishes from this process an initial idealizing paternal identification, however, then a reinterpretation of the roles of the sexes also
becomes possible. Benjamin stresses that the result of the Oedipus complex is that the male child must abandon not only his incestuous but also
his identificatory love for the mother. This is because, even more than in
the case of the father, such identificatory love is taken to be regressive.
In Lacan's early theory, for example, the maternal imago is described
as embodying the 'the metaphysical mirage of universal harmony, the
mystical abyss of affective fusion, the social utopia of a totalitarian
guardianship, all emerging from the haunting sense of the lost paradise
before birth, and the more obscure aspiration towards death'.[45] Lacan is
undoubtedly justified in pointing out that the interference of 'primordial
identifications' will mark the maternal ego-ideal, and perhaps also in contending that the father presents the ego-ideal in its purest form, but he
provides no explanation for his assertion that the maternal ideal must
'fail', leading to a feeling of repulsion of the part of the female child,
and – presumably by extension – in the case of the negative male Oedipus
complex.[46] One might conclude that this failure, as in the paternal case,
which Lacan himself – in part, at least – attributes to the pressure of
social and economic factors, derives from the general lack of recognition
of the autonomy of the mother. Benjamin herself is far from suggesting
that the role of the father – and, indeed, of the phallus – in the process of

separation and individuation can be superseded, but she nevertheless argues that the possibility for separation without exaggerated rupture would be opened up by a different relationship to the mother. In this case, the father might also be able more readily to accept the female child's phallic identification, since this identification would not be driven by the desperation of the need to break away from an engulfing mother.

It will be apparent that the key to Benjamin's revision of the Oedipus complex, which she wishes to view as 'only a step in mental life, one that leaves room for earlier and later levels of integration',[47] consists in her conception of the identificatory love which she associates with the pre-Oedipal *rapprochement* phase, in which the child seeks an initial balance between unity and separation. It is significant, therefore, that the French psychoanalyst Julia Kristeva should also be concerned with this type of love in her attempt to break down the rigidities of the Lacanian conception of Oedipal identity-formation. Like Benjamin, Kristeva is engaged in a re-evaluation of narcissism, in an attempt to circumvent the aporia which she formulates in the observation: '[T]o seek to maintain, against the winds and tides of our modern civilization, the requirement of a severe father who, through his name, bestows on us separation, judgement and identity is a necessity, a more or less pious wish.'[48] Kristeva's more detailed investigations of the character of pre-Oedipal identificatory love may therefore provide a useful corroboration and substantiation of the perspective Jessica Benjamin seeks to propose.

Kristeva's essay 'Freud and Love: Treatment and its Discontents', in her book *Tales of Love*, is fundamentally an attempt to retheorize the notion of narcissism, so that narcissism no longer appears as constituting an inevitable block to the achievement of individuation. Kristeva seeks to show, contrary to Lacan's account, that the emergence of the subject cannot be connected exclusively with the Oedipal crisis, with the breaking apart of the mother–child dyad through the intervention of the father. In Kristeva's account, narcissism already represents an advance over an undifferentiated autoeroticism; it implies an initial gap between self and other, before the intervention of the symbolic order – or rather, before its intervention in its purely signifying aspect. Kristeva does not deny that the symbolic order is always-already in place, but she suggests that there are diverse 'modalities of access' to the symbolic function. In imitating and, at the same time, libidinally investing the speech of the mother, the child is already entering into an identification which constitutes an elementary form of subjectivity. However, the Other with whom the child identifies is not the purely symbolic Other of Lacanian doctrine:

> Finally, by virtue of being the pole of a loving identification, the *Other* appears not as a 'pure signifier', but as the space of metaphorical movement itself: as the

condensation of semic traits as well as the unrepresentable heterogeneity of the drives which subtends them, exceeds them and escapes them . . . Lacan situates idealization in the field of signifiers and of desire alone, and has detached it clearly – even brutally – both from narcissism and from the heterogeneity of the drives and their hold on the maternal container.[49]

For Kristeva, however, this initial identification does not take place with the mother figure alone. Here she agrees with Benjamin, who suggests that during the *rapprochement* phase the distinction between male and female identifications has not yet consolidated. Developing a suggestion of Freud, Kristeva describes an 'imaginary father', a 'coagulation of the mother and her desire', which allows the mother to function as lack and plenitude simultaneously, thereby making possible an initial distanciation *prior to* the entry into the Oedipal situation. The immediacy of the relation to this 'father–mother conglomerate', Kristeva suggests, has an important consequence: 'the term "object", like that of "identification", becomes *inappropriate* in this logic. A not-yet-identity [of the child] is transferred, or rather is displaced, to the locus of an Other who is not yet libidinally invested as an object, but remains an Ego Ideal.'[50]

It is fascinating to observe how the concerns of Benjamin, emerging from and reacting to the Frankfurt School, and those of Kristeva, similarly related to Lacanian thought, converge in this respect. This convergence should not, however, be taken to imply a strict parallelism between the traditions which they oppose. For if one looks more closely at Horkheimer's position, it appears that Horkheimer did not attribute individuation and a capacity for resistance solely to the role of the father, as Jessica Benjamin frequently claims. In his 1960 essay 'Autorität und Familie in der Gegenwart', he writes:

> Earlier, the mother provided the child with a sense of security, which made it possible for it to develop a certain degree of independence. The child felt that the mother returned its love, and in a certain way drew on this fund of feeling throughout its life. The mother, who was cut off from the company of men and forced into a dependent situation, represented, despite her idealization, another principle than the reality principle. . . .[51]

Horkheimer goes on explicitly to affirm that the sustaining of the child's relationship to the mother can help to prevent too rapid an adaptation to reality, at the cost of individuation.

This conception might appear to be nostalgic, despite the fact that in its emphasis it coincides with, rather than contradicting, the tenor of Jessica Benjamin's account. The difference of orientation – bourgeois past rather than feminist future – derives from Horkheimer's conviction that, with the increasing incorporation of women into the rationalized extrafamilial world, the distinctive structure and emotional quality of the family is being destroyed: 'The equality of women, their professional activity, the much quicker emancipation of the children, alters the atmosphere of the home. . . . Like existence in general, marriage is tending to become more rational, more purposive, more sober.'[52] Nevertheless, Horkheimer is in general critical of the separation between the sensual and the ideal in the traditional image of the mother, and in the father's attitude towards her. He argues: 'under the pressure of such a family situation the individual does not learn to understand and respect his mother in her concrete existence, that is, as this particular social and sexual being . . . the suppressed inclination towards the mother reappears as a fanciful and sentimental susceptibility to all symbols of the dark, maternal and protective powers'.[53] Thus, against Lacan's view, Horkheimer suggests that it is precisely the *repression* of identificatory love which would tend to transform the imago of the mother into a focus for the longing for regressive fusion. Furthermore, he does not assume that, on logical grounds, a different orientation of social development might not be possible in which, instead of rationalization transforming the mother into a mere relay of social authority, the specific positive capacities which women have developed because of their historical exclusion from the public realm might contribute to the transformation of the instrumentalized structures of society: '[The woman's] whole position in the family results in an inhibiting of important psychic energies which might have been effective in shaping the world.'[54]

## Facticity, Normativity and Trauma

At this point, however, it might appear plausible to object, from a Lacanian standpoint, that Horkheimer misunderstands the fundamental concepts of psychoanalytic theory, in so far as he equates 'repression' with a putative suppression of the corporeal, a renunciation of drive-satisfaction [*Triebverzicht*]. It is striking, for example, that at the beginning of 'Authority and the Family' Horkheimer quotes not Freud, but Nietzsche's *On the Genealogy of Morals*, in order to substantiate his view that 'the whole psychic apparatus of members of a class society, in so far as they do not belong to the nucleus of the privileged group, serves in large measure only to interiorize or at least to rationalize and supplement physical coercion'.[55] Psychoanalysis, on this view, explores the effects within the individual psyche of the general structures of social power. However, one could argue, this direct articulation of society and the psyche elides the complex relation between anxiety and phantasy in the formation of the '*Urverdrängt*', the pre-social core of the repressed.

Lacan, by contrast, begins from the assumption that the process of

weaning, the traumatic series of breaks with the mother which is the precondition of independent subjectivity, is always culturally structured, and
that the subject can transcend this trauma only by internalizing and repeat-
ing it. In this interpretation, castration is not a threat in which real paternal
authority is embodied; rather, it is a phantasy by means of which the subject both masters through repetition the anxiety of separation from the
mother, and sets up a barrier against the regressive – indeed, deathly – tendencies which the maternal imago embodies. The phantasy of castration,
Lacan suggests:

> represents the defence which the narcissistic ego, identified with its specular
> double, opposes to the resurgence of anxiety which tends to overwhelm it, in the
> first stage of the Oedipus complex: a crisis which is caused not so much by the
> irruption of genital desire in the subject, as by the object which it reactualizes,
> namely the mother. The subject responds to the anxiety awakened by this object
> by reproducing the masochistic rejection through which it overcame its pri-
> mordial loss, but it does so according to the structure which it has acquired, that
> is through an imaginary localization of the tendency.[56]

Thus from his early work onwards it was Lacan's view that the prohibiting
father functions as the *support* of the phantasy of castration, which allows
the child to master the trauma of separation from the mother.
Furthermore, he suggests that in order for the child to achieve a measure
of psychic independence, to come to *be* as a subject at all, the father's status must appear inexplicable and ungrounded, a sheer *social fact* to be
accepted, like the facts of birth and weaning themselves. Such an account
seems to entail that the need for authority finds an ultimate anchoring
point in the unconscious, and – as such – is ineradicable.

There can be little doubt that Lacan's position corresponds more closely
to the mature insights of Freud, as expressed, for example, in *Inhibitions,
Symptoms and Anxiety* (1926). Here Freud definitively abandons the view,
recurrent throughout his earlier work, that repression is a form of defence
against impulses which are incompatible with the social and ethical norms
which have shaped the personality, and that it is the cathexis of the
repressed idea which is transformed into anxiety. He now argues: 'It was
anxiety which produced repression and not, as I formerly believed, repression which produced anxiety.'[57] In other words, it is the attempt to escape
the feelings of helplessness arising from separation – first unavoidably
experienced at birth, and later focused on the threat of castration – which
becomes the core motive for the formation of neurotic symptoms, of whatever kind. At the same time however, Freud also emphasizes that the ego
learns to use modified 'doses' of anxiety – which he defines as 'a reaction
to the danger of a loss of an object'[58] – in order both to master the emotion
and to signal the need to ward off unwanted impulses. The only major

alteration which Lacan introduces into this account is to deny Freud's assumption that the threat of castration which emerges in response to the impulse is in any sense 'real'.[59] On the contrary, as we have seen, the phantasy of castration, supported by the imputed authority of the father, protects the subject against the dangers of symbolic de-differentiation and merger. At the same time, however, the subject refuses this acknowledgement of radical insufficiency at the level of consciousness, falling victim to the narcissistic illusion of autonomy which is the core of the ego. Lacan summarizes this process, in *Les complexes familiaux*, with his reference to 'these inherent properties of the human subject, the miming of its own mutilation, and the seeing of itself as other than it is'.[60]

It is important to note, however, that by the time he came to co-author *Dialectic of Enlightenment* in 1944, Horkheimer has developed a conception of the 'primal history of subjectivity' far more complex than that of 'Authority and the Family' and, indeed, far more 'psychoanalytic' in its interweaving of the themes of traumatic separation, law and sacrifice. In the Odysseus chapter of *Dialectic of Enlightenment*, the violence of the break between self and nature, which cannot help but take place in the interests of self-preservation, gives rise to a demand for restitution: 'The self wrests itself free from dissolution in blind nature, whose claim is always re-asserted by sacrifice.'[61] However, the more the self attempts to evade this demand, as Odysseus does through trickery in his repeated encounters with the mythic powers, the more the very form of its subjectivity becomes sacrifice. The denial of the superiority of nature leads merely to an illusion of independence from nature: 'The self-identical self, which originates in the overcoming of sacrifice, is indeed once again an unyielding, rigidified sacrificial ritual that men and women celebrate upon themselves by setting consciousness in opposition to the nexus of nature.'[62] In contrast to the assumptions of 'Authority and the Family', this opposition, and its disastrous consequences, seem to follow inevitably from the emergence of the self as such, suggesting a convergence with Lacan's conception of irreducible trauma and illusion. There remains, however, one important distinction between the two accounts. Despite their lack of any coherent alternative, non-repressive model of the self, Horkheimer and Adorno seek to suggest that the trauma of separation and its sacrificial repetition are not necessary preconditions of subjectivity – that 'the institution of sacrifice is the scar of an *historical* catastrophe, an act of force that befalls humanity and nature alike'.[63] Only in this way can they defend the validity of the 'urge for total, universal and undiminished happiness',[64] despite the evidently deathly features of the imago of nature-as-mother, which emerge – for example – in their commentary on the Sirens episode.

The comparison with Lacan makes it clear that Horkheimer and Adorno can cling to their extravagant ideal of reconciliation only because of a primordial lack of differentiation between mother and father figures. It is the power of nature which is 'mythically objectified' in the form of legal relationships, of the archaic contracts which Odysseus seeks to evade, so that the 'remembrance of nature in the subject' which the book famously invokes would presumably also bring about the dissolution of legal form. In *Dialectic of Enlightenment* this form is no more than a normative cosmetic for the brute facticity of superior power. By contrast, Lacan's conception of submission to a symbolic Law which originates elsewhere than from the mother, and which is essential to the subject as the precondition of its existence as lack or desire, undermines any antinomian utopia. It does so, however, at the cost of instating an essentially 'alienated' subject, capable of sustaining its being only by bowing to an authority whose prototype is that of the father, and which must ultimately remain inscrutable.

Is there any way out of this impasse? I would suggest that at least the direction in which a solution could be sought may emerge if we read a certain response to Horkheimer and Adorno, within the Frankfurt School tradition, *against the grain* of its own intentions. It is well known that Jürgen Habermas has criticized *Dialectic of Enlightenment* for continuing the type of totalizing critique initiated by Nietzsche, which strives for an ultimate revelation of the intertwining of genesis and validity, power and reason, rather than accepting that their disintrication can only be an ongoing, dialogical process.[65] At the same time, however, it could be argued that Habermas himself seeks to play down the traumatic features of the separation between genesis and validity which his own account of the quasi-transcendental norms of dialogue presupposes. Thus, on the one hand, he repeatedly refers to the 'Janus-face' of validity-claims, to the fact that they are torn between particularity and universality, immanence and transcendence, and he describes their effectivity in violent terms as a force which 'bursts every provinciality asunder' – indeed, '"blots out" space and time'.[66] Yet on the other hand, Habermas wishes to deny that his position implies any problematic tension or split between empirical and transcendental, factual and normative dimensions, which would endanger the general project of a reconciliatory 'de-sublimation' or naturalization of reason.[67]

Yet perhaps we should read Habermas against himself. Such a reading might make it apparent that entry into the normative dimension of human communication and social regulation does indeed involve a traumatic break with the bond we can think of as maternal. But at the same time an acceptance that the *normative* as such – the symbolic Law, in Lacan's terms – emanates neither from one subject nor from a collectivity of subjects, should not be equated with submission to specific, contingent social norms. There is indeed a painful de-centring and wounding of narcissism contained in the realization that – as Habermas puts it – 'we are exposed to the movement of a transcendence from within which is no more at our disposal than the actuality of the spoken word makes us masters of the structure of language (or logos)'.[68] Yet this realization need not entail the acceptance of an authority which is ultimately exempt from requirements of legitimation, as Lacan's notion of the paternal function as support of the 'Law' often seems to imply. At the same time, however, it is clear that feminist attempts to think beyond the impasse of Oedipal identity cannot simply shift the emphasis to the continuities between the emerging self and its environment, in order to combat the traditional 'masculine' stress on forms of rupture and radical division. Such attempts must also explore new ways of figuring the inevitable anguish of loss and self-dispossession. Significantly, whereas Lacan insists that 'castration anxiety is like a thread which runs through all the stages of development',[69] Freud himself was more circumspect, sometimes allowing that the castration complex was merely one of a series of encounters with 'the danger of psychical help-lessness'.[70] Thus the founding texts of psychoanalysis leave open the space for a rethinking of individuation and autonomy, one which could acknowledge an irreducible core of dependency while relativizing the gender-skewed images of separation as mutilation which are still so centrally embedded in our culture.

## Notes

1. Jacques Lacan, 'La signification du phallus', in *Écrits*, Paris: Seuil 1966, p. 688/'The Signification of the Phallus', in *Écrits: A Selection*, trans. A. Sheridan, London: Tavistock 1977, p. 285. It is worth noting that this claim is explicitly directed against what Lacan takes to be the 'culturalist' standpoint of feminism, and against any theory of 'ideological psychogenesis'.

2. Jacqueline Rose, 'Feminine Sexuality – Jacques Lacan and the *école freudienne*', in *Sexuality in the Field of Vision*, London: Verso 1986, p. 80.

3. Ibid., p. 81. Other feminist defences of Lacan's theory of sexual difference are even less reflective. Ellie Ragland-Sullivan, for example, simply asserts that 'culture paradoxically crowns the male with the empty signifier of difference itself as standing in for limit or law', without offering any account of why this 'paradox' should arise. See 'The Sexual Masquerade', in Ellie Ragland-Sullivan and Mark Bracher, eds, *Lacan and the Subject of Language*, London: Routledge 1991, p. 75. It should be added that Rose's more recent shift from Lacan towards Klein has not altered her somewhat simplifying conviction that feminist revisions of traditional psychoanalytic doctrine are based on 'the idyll of an early fusion with the mother'. See 'Negativity in the Work of Melanie Klein', in Jacqueline Rose, *Why War?*, Oxford: Blackwell 1993, p. 140.

4. Theodor Adorno, 'Psychology and Sociology', *New Left Review* 47, January–February 1967, p. 90.

5. See, for example, the essays by Nancy Fraser, Iris Marion Young and Seyla Benhabib in Seyla Benhabib and Drucilla Cornell, eds, *Feminism as Critique*, Cambridge: Polity Press 1987.

6. Jacques Lacan, *Les complexes familiaux*, Paris: Navarin 1984, p. 49.

7. Ibid.

8. Ibid., p. 50.

9. Ibid., pp. 66–7.

10. Ibid., p. 68.

11. Ibid., p. 70.

12. Ibid., p. 71.

13. Ibid.

14. Ibid., p. 66.

15. Ibid., p. 67.

16. Ibid., pp. 95–6.

17. Max Horkheimer, 'Authority and the Family', in *Critical Theory: Selected Essays*, New York: Continuum 1972, p. 56.

18. Ibid., p. 101.

19. Ibid., p. 71.

20. Ibid., p. 127.

21. Ibid., p. 123.

22. Ibid., p. 83.

23. Ibid., p. 128.

24. *Les complexes familiaux*, p. 73.

25. Ibid.

26. Ibid., p. 72.

27. Max Horkheimer, 'Vernunft und Selbsterhaltung' (1942), in *Traditionelle und kritische Theorie*, Frankfurt am Main: Fischer Verlag 1992, p. 288.

28. *Les complexes familiaux*, p. 103.

29. Ibid, p. 72.

30. See Mikkel Borch-Jacobsen, 'The Oedipus Problem in Freud and Lacan', *Critical Inquiry*, vol. 20, no. 2, Winter 1994.

31. Ibid., p. 282.

32. Ibid. See also the comparable discussion in Mikkel Borch-Jacobsen, *Lacan: The Absolute Master*, Stanford, CA: Stanford University Press 1991, ch. 1. As we shall see, Borch-Jacobsen's suggestion, in both texts, that Lacan is merely nostalgic for 'good old traditional societies, where one still knew *who* one was' (*The Absolute Master*, p. 41) fails to consider his awareness of the basic instability of patriarchal structures.

33. *Les complexes familiaux*, p. 107.

34. See, for example, Charles Taylor, 'Logics of Disintegration', *New Left Review* 170, July–August 1988.

35. Jacques Lacan, 'Aggressivity in Psychoanalysis', in *Écrits: A Selection*, p. 27.

36. *Les complexes familiaux*, pp. 110–11.

37. Ibid.

38. Ibid., p. 112.

39. See Jessica Benjamin, 'Authority and the Family Revisited: or, A World without Fathers', *New German Critique*, no. 13, 1978.

40. In fact, this is Jessica Benjamin's implicit rather than explicitly stated position. At a number of points in *The Bonds of Love* (London: Virago 1990), she makes the argument against the Lacanian position that 'In the pre-oedipal world, the father and his phallus are powerful because of their ability to stand for separation from the mother' (p. 95). At the same time, however, she also admits that 'the . . . problem is that the symbolic level of the psyche already seems to be occupied by the phallus' (p. 124). Her solution is to propose a symbolization of woman's desire in terms of Winnicott's notion of 'holding space', which would seek not to rival or supplant the symbolism of the phallus but, rather, to coexist with it. See *The Bonds of Love*, pp. 123–32.

41. *The Bonds of Love*, p. 143.

42. 'The Oedipus Problem', pp. 273–4.

43. *The Bonds of Love*, pp. 145–6.

44. *Les complexes familiaux*, p. 63.

45. Ibid., p. 35.

46. See ibid., pp. 64–5.

47. *The Bonds of Love*, p. 177. Benjamin has recently pushed this revision further by emphasizing the potential 'post-Oedipal' role of early cross-gender *identifications* in helping to

overcome the rigidity of Oedipal *identity*. See 'Sameness and Difference: Toward an "Over-inclusive" Model of Gender Development', in Anthony Elliott and Stephen Frosh, eds, *Psychoanalysis in Contexts*, London: Routledge 1995.

48. Julia Kristeva, 'Freud et l'amour: le malaise dans la cure', in *Histoires d'amour*, Paris: Éditions Denoël (paperback edn) 1983, p. 62/'Freud and Love: Treatment and its Discontents', in *Tales of Love*, trans. Leon S. Roudiez, New York: Columbia University Press 1987, p. 46.

49. Ibid., p. 53/p. 38.

50. Ibid., p. 56/p. 41.

51. Max Horkheimer, 'Autorität und Familie in der Gegenwart', in *Zur Kritik der instru-mentellen Vernunft*, Frankfurt am Main: Fischer Verlag 1985, p. 278.

52. Max Horkheimer, 'Die Zukunft der Ehe', in ibid., p. 298/'The Future of Marriage', in *Critique of Instrumental Reason*, trans. Matthew J. Connell, New York: Seabury Press 1974, p. 97.

53. 'Authority and the Family', p. 121.

54. Ibid., p. 120. For a further critical response to Benjamin's critique of Horkheimer, see Pauline Johnson, 'Feminism and Images of Autonomy', *Radical Philosophy*, no. 50, Autumn 1988.

55. 'Authority and the Family', p. 56.

56. *Les complexes familiaux*, p. 61.

57. *Inhibitions, Symptoms and Anxiety*, in Sigmund Freud, *On Psychopathology*, Pelican Freud Library vol. 10, Harmondsworth: Pelican 1979, p. 263.

58. Ibid., p. 329.

59. Freud persists bizarrely, throughout this text, in speaking as though castration were a genuine danger. For example: 'We have also come to the conclusion that an instinctual demand often only becomes an (internal) danger because its satisfaction would bring on an external danger – that is, because the internal danger represents an external one' (p. 328). .

60. *Les complexes familiaux*, pp. 93–4.

61. Theodor Adorno and Max Horkheimer, 'Odysseus or Myth and Enlightenment' (new translation by Robert Hullot-Kentnor), *New German Critique*, no. 56, Spring/Summer 1992, p. 118.

62. Ibid., pp. 118–19.

63. Ibid., p. 116 (emphasis added).

64. Ibid., p. 122.

65. Jürgen Habermas, *The Philosophical Discourse of Modernity*, trans. Frederick Lawrence, Cambridge, MA: MIT Press 1988, p. 130.

66. Ibid., pp. 322, 323.

67. Herbert Schnädelbach has skilfully highlighted the incompatibility between the Kantian structures of Habermas's theory and his attachment to a naturalistic version of re-conciliation motifs inherited from Hegel and the Left Hegelians. See 'The Face in the Sand: Foucault and the Anthropological Slumber', in Axel Honneth *et al.*, eds, *Philosophical Interventions in the Unfinished Process of Enlightenment*, Cambridge, MA: MIT Press 1992.

68. Jürgen Habermas, 'Transzendenz von innen, Transzendenz ins Diesseits', in *Texte und Kontexte*, Frankfurt am Main: Suhrkamp 1991, p. 142.

69. Jacques Lacan, *Le Séminaire livre XI: Les quatres concepts fondamentaux de la psych-analyse*, Paris: Seuil 1973, p. 62/*The Four Fundamental Concepts of Psychoanalysis*, trans. A. Sheridan, Harmondsworth: Peregrine 1986, p. 64.

70. See *Inhibitions, Symptoms and Anxiety*, pp. 299–301; and the commentary in Jean Laplanche, *Problématiques II: Castration. Symbolisations*, Paris: PUF 1980, pp. 154–61.

# The Tremor of Reflection:
# Slavoj Žižek's Lacanian
# Dialectics

*In memory of Hinrich Fink-Eitel (1946–95)*

At first glance, the work of the Slovenian philosopher Slavoj Žižek seems to offer an irresistible range of attractions for theorists wishing to engage with contemporary culture, without accepting the flimsy postmodernist *doxa* which is often the only available gloss on it. Žižek's thought is still strongly coloured by his Althusserian background, and he is therefore rightly sceptical of the anti-Enlightenment sloganizing, and revivals of the 'end of ideology', which are the staple of so much cultural commentary today. At the same time, far from being dourly Marxist, his writings are informed by a vivid and sophisticated grasp of Lacanian psychoanalytic theory, and enlivened by constant reference to works of fiction, cinema, classical music and opera. They also cheerfully disregard ingrained oppositions between high and mass culture, without proclaiming a pseudo-populist levelling of aesthetic distinctions. Finally, Žižek's East European provenance provides a quirkily original perspective on the questions of subjectivity, phantasy and desire, and the problem of the resurgence of collectivist identities, which are so high on the agenda of the Left in Western Europe and North America today.

The very existence of this already sizeable body of work raises many intriguing questions. Why, for example, should the notoriously obscure and rebarbative thought of Lacan be of political interest not just to Žižek, but to a whole circle of Slovenian intellectuals? And why should Žižek be interested in using Lacan not simply to elaborate a new theory of ideology, but also to develop an extensive rereading and defence of Hegel – the supposedly totalizing enemy of most contemporary theory? In short, why should a combination of German Idealism and psychoanalysis be seen as the most appropriate way to develop a critical social philosophy amid the current upheavals and conflicts of Eastern Europe, and of the Balkans in particular?

The historical and political answer to these questions is to be found in the development of philosophy in ex-Yugoslavia between Tito's revolution and the break-up of the country, which began in 1991 with the secession of Slovenia. For Yugoslavian philosophical life was far from being dominated by the creaking orthodoxies of Soviet-style dialectical materialism, and included the far more plausible and congenial positions of what came to be known as the Praxis School.[1] The Marxism of the Praxis School was in fact a counterpart to the philosophical current known in the other half of Europe as 'Western Marxism'. But whereas in Western Europe the thought of Lukács, of Gramsci, of Adorno or Lefebvre could scarcely be taken to represent anything other than an oppositional and critical stance, the specific difficulty faced by the Praxis School was that their 'humanist' version of Marxism, inspired by the 1844 manuscripts of Marx, became – albeit unwittingly – supportive of the dominant ideology of the Yugoslavian regime – namely, the representation of the Yugoslav social and economic system as a form of 'self-managing socialism'.

This, at least, is the view of Žižek and his fellow thinkers. In their account, the problem facing Slovenian intellectuals in the early 1980s was how to criticize the oppressive and manipulative character of a system which was itself based on the denunciation of bureaucratic manipulation. As Žižek puts it:

> not until the emergence of Yugoslav self-management did Stalinism effectively reach the level of deception in its strictly human dimension. In Stalinism, the deception is basically still a simple one: The power (Party-and-State bureacracy) feigns to rule in the name of the people while everybody knows that it rules in its own interest . . . in Yugoslav self-management, however, the Party-and-State bureacracy reigns, but it reigns in the name of an ideology whose basic thesis is that the greatest obstacle to the full development of self-management consists in the 'alienated' Party-and-State bureacracy.[2]

Pre-empted, as it were, by the opacity of a system based on the ideal of the transparency of a democratic and social control of production, younger Slovenian philosophers, in the 1980s, were looking for a theoretical approach which could function critically in their specific social context. When the ideal of transparency congeals into an obfuscating ideology, then perhaps the only way to preserve a certain aspiration to transparency is by acknowledging, rather than suppressing, an irreducible element of opacity in all social relationships.

At the same time, Žižek and his fellow thinkers did not wish to abandon the critical and dialectical tradition altogether, like intellectuals in other parts of Central and Eastern Europe, who have turned towards Hayekian celebrations of the free market, or the bleak accounts of modernity to be found in Heidegger or Foucault. And it is this determination, a reminder of the uniquely autochthonous features of Yugoslav socialism, which explains the unexpected arrival of Lacan in Ljubljana. For Lacan, as Žižek tirelessly reminds his readers, is no Nietzschean or post-Nietzschean.[3] He is a theorist influenced above all by Freud and Hegel, two thinkers who – in their very different ways – can be viewed as seeking to preserve the essential impulse of critical, enlightening thought from the reductive and self-destructive simplifications of the Enlightenment itself. Indeed, Žižek formulates the aim of one of his books in the following terms: 'against the distorted picture of Lacan as belonging to the field of "post-structuralism"; against the distorted picture of Lacan's obscurantism, it locates him in the lineage of rationalism. Lacanian theory is perhaps the most radical contemporary version of Enlightenment.'[4]

It is thus the political context which in large part explains the intellectual investment of Žižek and his colleagues in a Lacanian reading of Hegel. Against the Left Hegelianism of the Praxis School, Žižek wants an account of Hegel which will bring out the intricate balance in his work between a profound adherence to the Enlightenment goals of freedom and autonomy, and the acknowledgement of a pervasive non-transparency of social life, which is rendered unavoidable by modern individualism and the complex state mechanisms which seek to compensate for it. Correlatively, this reading of Hegel may then serve, by a kind of feedback effect, to rescue Lacanian theory, as a source of insights into the subjective dimension of ideology, from poststructuralist appropriations. Of course, this project of reconciling Lacan and Hegel also helps to explain why Žižek's work is of more general relevance in the context of contemporary philosophical and political debates. In Western Europe and North America a disillusionment with the Marxist tradition has led to types of theorizing which, at the end of their deconstructive contortions, often boil down to little more than the endorsement of an existing culture of liberal pluralism. In Slovenia – and elsewhere in Eastern Europe – however, this pluralism cannot be taken for granted, for painfully obvious reasons. The idea that the 'Enlightenment project' is the source of all our ills can scarcely look other than callow to left intellectuals in Ljubljana, not to mention Belgrade or Sarajevo. Accordingly, once one penetrates behind Žižek's skittish mode of presentation, it becomes clear that there is far more than simply philosophical coherence at stake in the assessment of his Lacanian–Hegelian enterprise.

## The Lacanian Subject

One of the most powerful aspects of Žižek's work is its defence of the category of the subject against poststructuralist depredations. In his critiques of deconstruction, for example, Žižek shows that even this most sophisticated form of poststructuralist theory attempts to define the concept of the subject with the aid of an inappropriate model of self-presence, to which the movement of *différance* can then be counterposed. Taking the work of Rodolphe Gasché as his exemplar of such a view, Žižek shows that deconstructive theorists cannot ultimately avoid positing some substrate (characterized by Gasché in terms of 'infrastructures') which resists the reflective self-presence of the subject. Even if this substrate is given its minimal Derridean characterization as *'différance'*, it must nevertheless still be presupposed as logically prior to, and as the condition of possibility for, the constitution of an identity which is thus revealed as ultimately factitious.[5] Žižek therefore argues:

> In a paradoxical way, Derrida remains prisoner of the – ultimately 'commonsensical' – conception which aims at freeing heterogeneity from the constraints of identity; of a conception which is obliged to presuppose a constituted field of identity (the 'metaphysics of presence') in order to be able to set to the unending work of its subversion.[6]

Against this construction, in which the reflective self-identity of the subject is seen as excluding the 'tain of the mirror' which makes this reflection possible, Žižek argues that the identity of the subject consists in nothing other than the continual failure of self-reflection. In other words, there is no 'space of inscription' independent of and prior to the emergence of the supplement or the 're-mark', which vainly attempts to encapsulate the text by means of a self-referential twist:

> Reflection, to be sure, ultimately always fails – any positive mark included in the series could never successfully represent/reflect the empty space of the inscription of marks. It is, however, this very failure as such which 'constitutes' the space of inscription. . . . In other words, there is no infrastructural space of the inscription of marks without the re-mark. Re-mark does not 'represent'/reflect some previously constituted infrastructural network – the very act of reflection as failed constitutes retroactively that which eludes it.[7]

The Lacanian inspiration of this argument is clear. Žižek thinks of the subject not in terms of the imaginary self-coincidence of what Lacan calls the 'ego' but, rather, in terms of the lack or gap which is the correlative of the signifier's incapacity to signify the subject *as* signifying. In Lacanian theory, Žižek asserts, 'the subject is nothing but the impossibility of its own signifying representation – the empty place opened up in the big Other [of the symbolic order] by the failure of this representation'.[8] According to Lacan, this subject does encounter itself at the level of phantasy in the forms of the *'objet petit a'*, the object-cause of desire. But it encounters itself not in the sense of identifying itself reflectively, as in the mirror, but, rather, in the sense of confronting its own ungraspability. As Žižek writes: 'The spot of the mirror-picture is thus strictly constitutive of the subject; the subject qua subject of the look "is" only in so far as the mirror-picture he is looking at is inherently "incomplete" – in so far, that is, as it contains a "pathological" stain – the subject is correlative to this stain.'[9] Deconstruction, and other disruptions of the supposed 'self-identity' of the subject, are thus based on a 'metaphysical' misreading of the subject, since they fail to realize that *différance*, non-self-coincidence, does not disrupt a subject essentially defined by its self-coincidence but is, rather, the fundamental structure of subjectivity as such.

So far, this Lacanian riposte to deconstruction, plausible though it is in its own terms, is not particularly surprising. The plot thickens, however, when Žižek claims that an account of reflection as implying an intrinsic 'failure', an insufficiency which defines the subject, is already to be found in Hegel's *Logic*.

## Hegel's Logic of Reflection

The theory of reflection which Hegel provides in the first chapter of the 'Doctrine of Essence', the second book of the first volume of the *Science of Logic*, is one of the constant touchstones of Žižek's analyses. The 'Doctrine of Essence' as a whole is Hegel's exploration of the structure of what could be termed 'theoretical consciousness' – the epistemic stance of any attempt, whether scientific or metaphysical, to explain reality in terms of underlying principles and processes. It follows on from Book One, the 'Doctrine of Being', where Hegel demonstrates the internal inconsistency of the unreflective categories of our common-sense encounters with the world ('one' and 'many', 'quality' and 'quantity', 'magnitude, 'measure', and so on), and leads on to the second volume, the 'Doctrine of the Notion', where the problematic dualism of theoretical consciousness, with its splits between 'essence' and 'appearance', 'matter' and 'form', 'necessity' and 'contingency', is itself intended to be resolved. The opening chapter of the 'Doctrine of Essence' is of particular interest to Žižek because it is here that Hegel describes the fundamental processes of 'reflection', of abstraction and determination, which are the means by which the subject of theoretical consciousness gets a grip on its object. Since subjectivity, as it is understood in the modern period, seems to presuppose the capacity to turn inward on oneself, to divert attention from the immediate being of the object to the relation between the object 'in-itself' and the forms of awareness in which it is revealed, the logic of reflection – so Žižek seems to assume – must give a vital clue to what Hegel takes the subject to be.

Throughout his work, Žižek employs many examples to illustrate the stages of reflection explored by Hegel – 'positing', 'presupposing', 'external', and 'determinate' (or 'absolute'). But one of the most accessible accounts is still to be found in the final chapter of his first book in English, *The Sublime Object of Ideology*. Here Žižek employs the example of literary interpretation in order to illustrate the relation between the different forms of reflection. Thus, the initial standpoint of 'positing reflection' [*setzende Reflexion*] would be that from which we naively assume that the manner in which we interpret a work of literature gives us direct access to that work's true meaning. But this in turn requires us to presuppose the existence of a meaning which is objectively 'out there', to be identified and grasped. Hence positing and presupposing [*voraussetzende*] reflection are intimately interrelated – indeed, are simply two sides of the same process. Awareness of the unavoidability of presuppositions in all positing thus leads to the standpoint which Hegel terms 'external reflection'. Žižek describes this as the perspective from which the true meaning of the text is viewed as an 'in-itself', to which any specific, historically determined interpretation can only approximate. However, it could equally be the view that the text is merely the material 'support' for a variety of interpretations, each valid in its own terms. The tension between these two dimensions of external reflection (one positing, one presupposing) is finally resolved in 'determinate reflection', which Žižek compares with the standpoint of Gadamerian hermeneutics; here successive interpretations are viewed as the temporal unfolding of the intrinsic meaning or essence of the work itself.[10]

But this comparison with Gadamer, helpful though it is, may still give rise to misunderstanding, according to Žižek. He suggests:

> if we grasp the plurality of phenomenal determinations [i.e. interpretations] which at first sight blocked our approach to the 'essence' as so many self-determinations of this very 'essence' [or ways in which the true meaning reveals itself], it could still be said that in this way – through 'determinate reflection' – the appearance is ultimately reduced to the self-determination of the essence, 'sublated' in its self-movement, internalized, conceived as a subordinate moment of self-mediation of the essence.[11]

To counter this misunderstanding, Žižek goes on to affirm: 'it is not only that appearance, the fissure between appearance and essence, is a fissure internal to the essence itself; the crucial point is that, inversely, "essence itself is nothing but the self-rupture, the self-fissure of the appearance".'

In order to clarify what he means by this, Žižek takes up the case of Feuerbach's critique of Christianity. He explains that from the standpoint of external reflection, the essence must be understood as something radically outside and opposed to the reflecting subject. In Feuerbach's account, this would be the relationship between the human being and God, understood theologically; and of course, it is precisely this standpoint which he characterizes as that of religious alienation. The aim of Feuerbach's 'Philosophy of the Future' is to overcome this situation by reappropriating the divine powers as in truth the powers of the reflecting subject, the embodied human being.[12] Žižek, however, criticizes this Feuerbachian recipe for the overcoming of alienation – a powerful influence on the young Marx – arguing that, in Hegel's view, such a remainderless reappropriation of hypostatized powers is not possible:

> The Feuerbachian gesture of recognizing that God as an alien essence is nothing but the alienated image of man's creative potential does not take into account the necessity for this reflexive relationship between God and man to reflect itself into God himself. . . . It is not enough for the subject to recognize-reflect himself in this Entity as in his inverse image; the crucial point is that this substantial Entity must itself split and 'engender' the subject (that is, 'God himself must become man').[13]

More formally, Žižek argues that 'we pass from external to determinate reflection simply by experiencing the relationship between these two moments – essence as movement of self-mediation, self-referential negativity; essence as substantial positive entity excluded from the tremor of reflection – as that of reflection: by experiencing how this image of the substantial-immediate, positively given essence is nothing but the inverse-alienated reflection of the essence as pure movement of self-referential negativity.'[14]

Žižek is certainly correct to suggest that the arrival at 'determinate reflection' represents the achievement of a certain plateau of stability within the overall development of Hegel's *Logic*. What he does not emphasize, however, is that the principal reason for this stability is the emergence of a proto-intersubjective structure, in which the interiority of the subject finds its balancing counterpart in the interiority of the object. For up until this point, as Hinrich Fink-Eitel has shown in his fine commentary,[15] the movement of reflection has been determined by a tension between 'negativity' and 'otherness' which betrays the basic instability of the structure of 'essence' itself. To the extent that the 'object' of reflection was merely posited, and therefore merely 'negative' (non-self-sufficient), its lack of inner determinacy reacted back on the reflecting subject: to decipher only the meanings one has oneself projected into things is ultimately to confront one's own vapidity. Correlatively, the elusive 'otherness' of the object presupposed by external reflection also threatened to reduce the subject to a helpless state of negativity, of epistemic exile from being, since if the object is entirely outside of our doings and sayings, then nothing can count as our responding to or being in touch with it.

By contrast, determinate reflection resolves this dilemma through the relation to an 'object' which is 'reflected into itself' (which has a determinant 'interior'), so that its otherness is no longer cancelled by its negativity, and its negativity by its otherness.[16] In seeking to define this interior, however, determinate reflection breaks apart into what Hegel calls '*Wesenheiten*' ('essentialities') or '*Reflexionsbestimmungen*' ('determinations of reflection'/'reflexive determinations'), such as 'identity', 'difference', and 'diversity', which can be thus considered as the basic structuring principles of any theoretically constituted object-domain. In this sense, as Fink-Eitel points out, 'The determination of reflection is a relation of relations ("reflections-into-self").'[17] Formerly the distinction between the 'inside' and the 'outside' of the object was itself directly drawn by the reflective activity of the subject, and was therefore radically other, a merely 'related relation', with respect to the subject as 'relating relation'. But now this relation internal to the object is negated in its otherness, because it turns out to be the same relating relation (or 'reflection-into-self') which characterizes the subject also. In terms of the development of the *Logic*, we have thus reached not only an equilibrium between subject and object, but an adumbration of what Fink-Eitel terms an 'intersubjective conceptual constellation'.[18] As Hegel himself puts it: 'The determination of reflection . . . has for . . . [its] ground reflectedness-into-self. Positedness [i.e. the fact of being 'opposed' *to* the subject *by* the subject] fixes itself into a determination precisely because reflection is equality-with-self in its negatedness; its negatedness is consequently itself a reflection-into-self.'[19]

## The Logic of Intersubjectivity

It is important to remember, however, that this 'equality of reflection with itself' can offer only a temporary respite. For the 'Doctrine of Essence' as a whole is concerned with working through the consequences of the fundamental contradiction or lopsidedness in the concept of essence: the fact that 'essence' refers both to the distinguishing and relating of a 'surface' and an 'interior' which Hegel regards as central to the structuring of reality in scientific and metaphysical thinking, and to one side of this relation – the 'interior' side – which is given ontological and explanatory primacy. It is this asymmetry which resurfaces after the achievement of the standpoint of determinate reflection, producing a movement through a series of 'determinations of reflection', from identity to difference, and thence to diversity and on to contradiction. It re-emerges because the determinations of reflection are not themselves understood as relational, as the pattern of the self-articulation of essence. They appear as equally valid (and hence as equally 'arbitrary') characterizations of an otherness which ultimately remains external to them.

Thus the logic of the determinations of reflection replays the logic of reflection from the opposite side of the contradictory structure of essence, as it were. Since the other of reflection is in fact the relation of reflection itself, the determinations of reflection will also be the externalized or 'posited' forms of the modes of reflection. Thus to positing reflection there corresponds the other as the empty negativity of self-identity; to presupposing reflection, the abstract other as presupposed difference; to external reflection, the other as diversity; and to determinate reflection, the other as negative but reflected into itself, and thus as opposed.[20] But because of the basic asymmetry – or inclusive/exclusive structure – of essence, the more the other is specified as opposed to the reflecting subject, the more the reflecting subject will find itself opposed to itself. To adapt a well-known formula of Lacan's: reflection receives back from the other of reflection its own message in an inverted form.[21]

In Hegel's account, this process culminates in a crisis: 'The self-subsistent determination of reflection that contains the opposite determination, and is self-subsistent in virtue of this inclusion, at the same time also excludes it; in its self-subsistence, therefore, it excludes itself from its own self-subsistence. . . . It is thus contradiction.'[22] As an intersubjective constellation, this relation can be characterized as a process of 'excluding reflection' in which each subject shuts out the other subject through whom she is constituted, and thus shuts out herself.[23] A temporary, proleptic resolution is provided by the shift to the final determination of reflection, 'ground'. For 'ground' refers to that which accounts for the relation between the other, apparently conflicting determinations, and thus, in intersubjective terms, to an acknowledgement of commonality beyond our singular perspectives.[24] But the 'logic of inner contingency' which permeates essence, as Fink-Eitel terms it, can be definitively overcome only with the transition to the concept in the second volume of the *Logic*, the 'Doctrine of the Notion'.

Hegel's theory of the concept[25] can be understood in this perspective as characterizing a reciprocal relation of recognition, which overcomes the abstracting and subsuming *modus operandi* of reflective cognition. The vicious circularity of the structure of essence cannot be broken open by a further act of knowing, but only when the reflecting subject no longer seeks to ground its own identity by abstracting from its relation to the other. Only by acknowledging this relation as constitutive of its identity, just as this identity enters into the relation, can it finally resolve the conflict between necessity and contingency, the ground and that which is grounded.[26] At first sight, it may appear far-fetched to interpret the structure of the Hegelian concept in terms of reciprocal recognition; inversely, it may not be clear why Hegel would designate what we now term 'inter-subjectivity' as 'the concept' (i.e. conceptuality). But this proposal can perhaps be made more plausible if we consider that the conceptuality of language, which is fundamental to human sociality, establishes a permanent possibility of reconciling conflicting subjective perspectives. Clashes of immediate viewpoint typically give rise to hermeneutically reflective conflicts, while a continuing discrepancy between interpretative schemata will eventually push us back to the basic shared question of what it means to grasp something conceptually at all, however different our orientations may be. Indeed, it could be argued that for Hegel the 'life of the concept' consists in nothing other than this constant process of rupture and nego-tiation.[27]

Thus Hegel's account of the concept does not imply a seamless, non-conflictual – perhaps even repressive – identity of self and other. In the *Encyclopaedia* Hegel himself characterizes the intersubjective relation which is 'the Idea that has developed into self-consciousness' as 'the violent diremption of mind or spirit into different selves which are both in and for themselves and for one another, are independent, absolutely impene-trable, resistant, and yet at the same time identical with one another. . . .'[28] As Fink-Eitel stresses, contingency is not eliminated by Hegel in this account. It is precisely as contingent, self-reflective individuals that sub-jects must come to accept and affirm the commonality which binds them. This acceptance (which we could call 'love') does not cancel the acknowl-edgement of difference (which we could call 'recognition'). For if identification simply abolished the relation of exclusion, then the result would be an undifferentiated tautology. In this sense: 'The fundamental conflict of speculative logic as a whole, the conflict between immediacy and mediation, being oneself [*Selbstsein*] and otherness [*Andersheit*], is at the same time the basic conflict of Hegel's practical philosophy, that between being oneself through love and being oneself through recogni-tion.'[29] Nevertheless, this conflict is very different from the ruinous contradiction of the subjective standpoint of reflection, in which the sub-ject struggles to objectify the intersubjective context in which she finds herself, and continually transforms this context in the very process. For the conflict between subjectivity and intersubjectivity is itself constantly under negotiation. It cannot, therefore, be equated with Žižek's opaque, irre-movable stain at the core of the every subject.

## Reason and Contingency: Hegel's Monarch

In his resistance to such a reading of Hegel, Žižek frequently invokes the account of the monarchy in *The Philosophy of Right*. Indeed, Hegel's theory of the monarchy functions in Žižek's work as a crucial demonstration of the fact that Hegel fully acknowledges a blind spot at the very heart of his system, one which is itself a systematic requirement. For Žižek, the fact that Hegel installs at the summit of his constitution an individual selected by the natural contingency of birth clearly shows his grasp of the fact that 'rational totality clings to an inert "piece of the real" precisely insofar as it is caught in a vicious circle',[30] and that the political community therefore needs a point of transsymbolic condensation, where it can confront the opacity of its own identity.

Serious difficulties are raised, however, by Žižek's elevation of the Hegelian monarch to paradigmatic status. First, as commentators have long pointed out, the deduction of the monarchy in the *Philosophy of Right* violates Hegel's own procedure, inverting the usual dialectical movement – from the universal, via the particular, to the individual – between paragraphs 273 and 275. In the former, Hegel divides the 'state as political entity' into 'legislature' (universal), 'executive' (application to particular) and 'crown' (individual power of ultimate decision), whereas in the latter he begins with the 'power of the crown', and argues that it 'contains in itself the three moments of the whole . . . viz. (a) the universality of the constitution and the laws; (b) counsel, which refers the particular to the universal; and (c) the moment of ultimate decision, as the self-determination to which everything else reverts and from which everything else derives the beginning of its actuality'.[31]

As Vittorio Hösle has suggested, the departure from Hegel's own method which his option for the monarchy requires can be seen only as a regressive irruption of a monological *Subjektmetaphysik* at the summit of a system whose deepest intuitions derive from the dynamics of intersubjectivity.[32] This is made starkly apparent by the fact that Hegel earlier argues – in line with contemporary conceptions – that sovereignty can belong only to the system of powers within the state as a whole – that 'sovereignty depends on the fact that the particular functions and powers of the state are not self-subsistent or firmly grounded either on their own account or in the particular will of the individual functionaries, but have their roots ultimately in the unity of the state as their single self'.[33] As Hösle indicates, this view is hard to square with the claim that the will of the community must ultimately be entrusted to the subjectivity of a single individual. Furthermore, Hegel's argument that the natural immediacy of the head of state as an individual requires that he be selected by the accident of birth is laughable, as Marx – following Ruge – pointed out: 'Hegel has demonstrated that the monarch must be born, a truth no one has questioned, but he has not proved that birth makes the monarch.'[34] It should also be noted that the role of the Hegelian monarch is not always limited to 'dotting the i's', as Žižek likes to suggest. In fact, in the main text of *The Philosophy of Right* the monarch is described as having more extensive powers: he can appoint the government, can reject laws as well as endorse them, and is responsible for foreign affairs. Indeed, Hegel stresses that no ground can be required for the king's decisions.[35] But, as Hösle also argues, there are no reasons *internal* to Hegel's system why the ultimate power of decision should not be vested in an elected president, or even in a collective leadership, rather than being allotted by parentage.[36]

## Lacan's Critique of Hegel

The dubiousness of Žižek's use of the Hegelian monarch as a test case for his account of the relation between rational system and contingency suggests that his Lacanian reading of Hegel does not do justice to the complexity of Hegel's thought. For Žižek persistently jams the dialectical movement prior to the point where the 'inner contingency' of essence is overcome through the move from essence to concept.[37] It is only this truncation of Hegel's thought which enables him not only to assert the compatibility of Hegel and Lacan, but even to claim that Lacan's own critique of Hegel is in fact an unwitting confirmation of Hegel.[38] At the same time, however, a strong case can be made that Lacan's resistance to healing the rift between universality and particularity is justified, since the Hegelian concept – despite its intersubjective traits – is ultimately the embodiment of a domineering, subsumptive universality. To read Hegel in this way would in fact mean endorsing Lacan's criticisms of Hegel, whereas Žižek himself consistently suggests that these criticisms are misguided and misplaced. So what is the basis of Lacan's critique of Hegel? Is it true to claim, as Žižek does, that it is no more than naively 'deconstructivist' *avant la lettre*?

Lacan's divergence from Hegel begins in the early 1950s. Up until this point, he had been profoundly influenced by the notion of a dialectic of recognition derived from Kojève's and Hyppolite's interpretations of the *Phenomenology*. But from the second *Seminar* (1954–5) onwards, he begins to ask: how can recognition itself be recognized? How can I ever be sure that the sign or gesture which the other offers me is indeed an expression of recognition? What this means, in Hegel's own terminology, is that the disjunction between (subjective) certainty and (intersubjective) truth, which drives the *Phenomenology of Spirit*, can no longer be resolved in absolute knowing, any more than the opposition of 'being' and 'essence' can be overcome in the 'concept'. According to Lacan: 'Truth – for Hegel – is nothing other than that which knowledge can apprehend as knowledge only by putting its ignorance to work. A real crisis in which the imaginary is resolved, through the engendering of a new symbolic form, to use my own categories.' However, Lacan continues:

This dialectic is convergent and attains the conjuncture defined as absolute knowledge. In the form in which it is deduced, it can only be the conjunction of the symbolic with a real of which there is nothing more to be expected. What is this real, if not a subject fulfilled in his identity to himself? From which one can conclude that this subject is already perfect in this regard, and is the fundamental hypothesis of this whole process.[39]

What Lacan opposes, therefore, is what he takes to be the Hegelian presupposition of the identity of subject and Other, the assumption that the real is ultimately construable in terms of the reflexive structure of self-consciousness. Indeed, if truth in the emphatic sense revealed by psychoanalysis is marked by the unpredictability and unmanageability of the real, then it can be said that 'the ideal which Hegel promises us as absolute knowledge' would be the 'perfect instrument' for 'shutting the bolt on truth [verrouiller la vérité]'.[40]

In the light of this Lacanian critique of Hegel, it is interesting to observe how Žižek attempts to reconcile Hegel's account of 'absolute knowledge' with his Lacanian convictions. He writes:

usually Absolute Knowledge is understood as the phantasy of a discourse which is full, without rupture or discord, the phantasy of an Identity which includes all divisions, whereas our interpretation, by bringing out, in absolute knowledge, the dimension of the traversal of phantasy perceives exactly the opposite. . . . Far from filling the lack felt by finite consciousness, separated from the absolute, Absolute Knowledge displaces the lack into the Other itself. The turning introduced by Absolute Knowledge concerns the status of lack: finite or alienated consciousness suffers the loss of the object, and 'disalienation' consists simply in the experience of the fact that this object was lost from the very beginning, and that any given object merely fills the empty place of this loss.[41]

Here Žižek interprets the subject's confrontation with the gap-filling function of the object of desire as the 'loss of loss', and equates this with the Hegelian 'negation of the negation'. The loss of loss, Žižek writes, 'is the moment when loss ceases to be the loss *of* something and becomes the opening of the empty space where the object is located'.[42] Yet the differences between this account and that of Hegel are not hard to discern. For, as Fink-Eitel suggests, the negation of the negation in Hegel can be understood as the self-destruction of the negative relation between consciousnesses whose relation to themselves (and thus to each other) is negative or abstract (polarized between empirical plenitude and reflective vacancy, or vice versa), with the result that the other ceases to be a *limit* of the self.[43] In Žižek's intepretation of Lacan, however, the loss of loss does not involve the cancellation, or even relativization, of a limit or lack but, rather, an acceptance of the fact that what appeared to be a *reparable* loss is in fact a *constitutive* lack. The resulting conclusion – that 'subject is the nonsubstance, he exists only as a nonsubstantial self-relating which maintains its distance from inner-worldly objects'[44] – is surely incompatible with Hegel's claim that 'everything turns on grasping and expressing the True, not only as S*ubstance*, but equally as S*ubject*'.[45] Indeed, the confrontation between a subject reduced to empty reflexivity and an ontologically distinct world of objects, which Žižek here evokes as the definitive Hegelian view, constitutes precisely what Hegel considers to be the contradictory standpoint of 'external reflection'.

## Reflection and Being: The Hegelian Equation

So far we have found that the Lacanian theory of the subject is not compatible with Hegel's philosophy, as Žižek repeatedly claims – with an insistence one is tempted to interpret psychoanalytically. At the same time, Hegel's speculative logic of the concept [*Begriff*] has been presented not as the theory of an abstractly dominating universal but, rather, as *modelling* an intersubjectivity which overcomes the one-sidedness of reflection – tracing a structure which renders it hermeneutically accessible. At least to this extent it appears to converge with Lacan's fundamental aim: to overcome the reified, reflective structure of the ego through the subject's acceptance of its position within the order of symbolic exchange. In consequence, might we not be driven to conclude that Lacan is indeed compatible with Hegel, although in a different perspective from that which Žižek adopts? Here it is fascinating to observe the convergence between Lacan's Hegel-critique and the discussion of the problems of Hegel's theory of reflection to be found in the work of contemporary German philosophers such as Dieter Henrich and Manfred Frank.

As we have already seen, Hegel's logic of reflection concludes with determinate reflection: the structure in which the relation between essence and appearance *within* the object of reflection is no more than an externalized mirroring of the relation *between* the reflecting subject and this object itself. In such a perspective, essence has proved itself to be the 'truth of being',[46] transforming the latter into illusory being or *Schein*. In the terms of Dieter Henrich's classic account, the 'autonomous' or self-related negation which defines 'essence', and which he considers the fundamental operation [*Grundoperation*] of Hegel's philosophy in general, has negated itself, giving rise to the immediacy of being. Yet since this immediacy is the result of the self-application of negation, it loses its self-sufficiency, becoming no more than the negative pole in the self-relation of essence.[47] However, as Henrich points out, this argument relies on a questionable shift of meaning [*Bedeutungsverschiebung*] of the term 'immediacy' between the 'Doctrine of Being' and the 'Doctrine of Essence'. In the former, immediacy is indifferently opposed to mediation, whereas in the latter it becomes a feature of self-sufficient mediation, of the negative self-relation.[48] Henrich himself suspends judgement on whether this shift in meaning is theoretically justified or justifiable. But Frank, developing his argument, is unequivocal: Hegel's logic of reflection falsely assumes that the result of the self-cancellation of autonomous negation can still be seen as the shadow of such negation, even after it has cancelled itself, or that the relation between reflection and the *other* of reflection can be construed in terms of the reciprocal implication of positing and presupposing within reflection itself.[49] In other words, Hegel elides the notion that positing might be what *defines* immediacy as negative, without being its *originator*.[50]

This insistence on the irreducibility of being to reflection is clearly in harmony with Lacan's fundamental intuitions. Yet at the same time it also seems to block the emergence of those patterns of dialectical interaction (whether purely reciprocal or not) with which both Hegel and Lacan are so centrally concerned. It is important to remember here, however, that current 'intersubjective' readings of the *Logic*, inspired by the pathbreaking work of Michael Theunissen, do not claim that Hegel delivers a speculative *deduction* of intersubjectivity.[51] Indeed, according to Theunissen, Hegel's account of the concept tends to reinstate precisely the dominating metaphysics of reflection it was intended to overcome, as when he claims that the concept has '*subjugated* [*sich unterworfen*] being and essence, which from other starting points include also feeling and intuition and representation, and which appeared as its antecedent conditions, and has proved itself to be their unconditioned ground'.[52] But in contrast with this, as Theunissen also indicates, other passages in the *Logic* portray the experiential content of the concept in terms of Hegel's youthful terminology of 'love', thus implying that the concept lies beyond the limits of theory (and so of reflection).[53] Thus, as Fink-Eitel has suggested, the intersubjective reading of Hegel's famous 'negation of the negation' as the self-abolition of the negative relation between negatively self-related individuals

> avoids becoming an indeterminate tautology only because the determinate distinction between recognition and what is recognized is presupposed by the relation of recognition, whose introduction is thus external to the *Logic*. Self-determined negation [Henrich's 'autonomous negation'] is the premiss of the logic of the concept, because its premiss is the intersubjective relation of recognition.[54]

In other words, the logic of the concept is tied hermeneutically to its practical context: 'The medium of intersubjective recognition is the ground of speculative logic.'[55]

## A Lacanian Politics?

On the one side, therefore, we have critiques of Hegelian 'absolute reflection', such as that of Manfred Frank, which block the absorption of being into reflection, but thereby risk perpetuating an unmasterable contingency of being, against which reflection breaks. On the other, we have readings of Hegel which seek to overcome this risk by stressing that his work is inspired by experiences – such as that of love – which transfigure and transcend such contingency, although it also betrays them through its tendency to deny the limits of philosophical theory and to reinstate a metaphysics of reflection. Paradoxically, Žižek belongs in the first camp, while believing himself to be offering an exegesis and a defence of the unsurpassability of 'absolute reflection'. Žižek's Lacanianism is thus not Hegelian; it cannot acknowledge and incorporate the complexity and ambivalence highlighted by the second interpretative tradition. But if Žižek does not in fact succeed in fusing Lacan and Hegel, there are grounds for scrutinizing the success with which he reconciles the Enlightenment and counter-Enlightenment impulses of his political thinking in general.

In his article on 'Eastern European Liberalism and its Discontents', for example, Žižek argues that liberal universalism secretes an irrational attachment to particularity as its necessary counterpart:

> The Rawlsian liberal-democratic idea of distributive justice ultimately relies on a 'rational' individual who is able to abstract a particular position of enunciation, to look upon himself or herself and all others from a neutral place of pure 'metalanguage' and thus to perceive all their 'true interests.' This individual is the supposed subject of the social contract that establishes the coordinates of justice. What is thereby *a priori* left out of consideration is the realm of fantasy in which a community organizes its 'way of life' (its mode of enjoyment).[56]

More generally, Žižek claims that 'every "enlightened" political action legitimized by reference to some form of "true interests" encounters sooner or later the resistance of a particular fantasy space: in the guise of the logic of "envy", or the "theft of enjoyment"'.[57] In consequence: 'the supposedly neutral liberal democratic framework produces nationalist closure as its inherent opposite'.[58] These political claims follow directly from Žižek's conception of the subject as the counterpart of the traumatic contingency of the real, which remains excluded from the regulated exchanges of the symbolic order.

It is true that Žižek sometimes presents the subject's attachment to the contingent 'Thing' which embodies enjoyment as dissoluble. In the essay on Eastern European liberalism he argues that 'the way to break out of the vicious circle is not to fight "irrational" ethnic particularism but to invent forms of political practice that contain a dimension of universality beyond capital'.[59] He suggests that the ecological movement may embody such a dimension. However, since Žižek portrays the subject as *essentially* split between universality and particularity, it is not clear how the *type* of universality invoked can resolve this ontological dilemma. Similarly, when he attempts to give his position a critical edge by suggesting that we may bring ourselves to experience 'the collapse of the big Other' – in other words, of the symbolic order – or 'consummate the act of assuming fully the "nonexistence of the Other"',[60] he ignores the fact, which he stresses elsewhere, that the Other is a transcendental function for Lacan.[61] Of course, no particular holder of power can be equated in his or her function with the 'Master Signifier', which sustains the Other of the symbolic order as such. But at the same time, the tendency towards this conflation is viewed by Žižek and his school as a profound and ineradicable feature of human sociality.

These consequences of Žižek's position could be summarized in the suggestion that Žižek is ultimately a 'Right Hegelian' masquerading – albeit unwittingly – as a 'Left Hegelian'. He views the modern individual as caught in the dichotomy between his or her universal status as a member of civil society, and the particularistic attachments of ethnicity, nation and tradition, and this duality is reflected in his own ambiguous political profile – *marxisant* cultural critic on the international stage, member of a neo-liberal and nationalistically inclined governing party back home. Indeed, in some respects Žižek's stance can be compared with that of the followers of Joachim Ritter, who powerfully reasserted the Right-Hegelian tradition in his classic essay on 'Hegel and the French Revolution'. For Ritter: 'Hegel conceives the dichotomy of historical existence into subjectivity and objectivity as the form in which its unity maintains itself and in which the modern world finds its corresponding shape.'[62] The abstract and ahistorical principle of modern civil society, as the sphere of interactions between individuals pursuing their private, naturally determined interests, paradoxically 'sets free . . . the life relationships which are not reducible to it' – namely, the corresponding sphere of tradition in which 'the right of subjectivity's particularity and freedom are preserved'.[63] Consequently, Ritter argues, 'it becomes clear to Hegel that the dichotomy not only does not have to lead to the destruction of world-historical continuity, but is precisely the condition which makes it possible and can secure the continuance of the substantial order of tradition within the realm of the modern world'.[64]

Ritter's interpretation of Hegel's politics is clearly contentious, and the members of his school have regularly been attacked by the Left in Germany for their political disingenuousness. Under the conditions of contemporary capitalism, it is argued, Ritter's 'tradition' could only take the form of ideological planning – the provision of a cushion of 'fake substantiality', in Habermas's phrase, against the harshness of an increasingly instrumentalized world. At the same time, Ritter's account of *Entzweiung* has a venerable history: it is a version of the conservative view of Hegelian 'reconciliation' as insight into the inevitability of diremption which is as old as Hegel's philosophy itself.

Significantly, Žižek takes a similar line. '"Reconciliation"', he claims, 'does not convey any kind of miraculous healing of the wound of scission, it consists solely in a reversal of perspective by means of which we perceive how the scission is in itself already reconciliation. . . .'[65] Indeed, while Ritter's position remains true to Hegel's intentions in so far as it seeks to strike a balance between universality and particularity, ahistorical form and historical content, Žižek's account of ideological closure explicitly *prioritizes* particularity over universality, contingency over necessity, in a way which denatures the Hegelian dichotomy, however it is understood, and transforms all reason into 'rationalization', in the Freudian sense: 'A system reaches its equilibrium, i.e. it establishes itself as a synchronous totality, when – in Hegelese – it "posits" its external presuppositions as its inherent moments and thus obliterates the traces of its traumatic origins.'[66] Thus if the bad faith of Ritter's conservatism consists in the refusal to acknowledge that, under modern conditions, 'tradition' inevitably degenerates into ideological fabrication, the *méconnaissance* of Žižek's leftism lies in his apparent innocence of the fact that his theory ultimately endorses the covert cynicism of the Ritter school.

## Love and Law: Tracking the *objet a*

It was suggested above – and, I hope, has been established by this point – that Žižek's Lacanianism is not Hegelian. But I now want to ask: is it even Lacanian? Might it not be the case that Lacan's own position is closer, in its aspirations and oscillations, to the second reading of Hegel (that of Theunissen and his followers) than to Manfred Frank's critique of Hegel's theory of reflection?

Žižek never ceases to emphasize that the subject must be seen as the correlative of the opaque stain which Lacan describes as the *objet a*. The introduction of the *objet a* at the end of the 1950s was indeed the result of Lacan's growing realization that something fundamental to the subject cannot be expressed by the collectively shared, and thus universal, 'treasure of the signifier'. As Lacan's thought developed, however, he increasingly came to appreciate that the status of the *objet a* cannot be reduced to brute contingency, but derives from the fact that it is the object of the *desire* of the Other. Thus, in a certain sense, the mediation between subject and Other is restored by the *objet a*, for this object is phantasized as securing the being of the subject by embodying that mysterious part of the subject which is desired by the Other.[67] Of course this relationship, in which the *objet a* serves to connect desire to desire, still leaves a fundamental elusiveness on both sides – the unknowability of the desire of the Other corresponds to the unknowability of the self. But it is nevertheless misleading to suggest, as Žižek frequently does, that the subject must either accept its own lack (as in earlier Lacan), or come to terms with the lack in the Other (the Other's incapacity to return full recognition). For the lack in the Other *is* its own lack, and in this sense at least the subject and the Other are one. According to Žižek, the 'impossibility' of absolute reflection derives from the 'dark spot' in the mirror which is said to be 'strictly constitutive of the subject'[68] – but this means that, strictly speaking, he has no account of intersubjectivity at all. By contrast, for Hegel and – I would argue – for Lacan, this impossibility stems from the foreclosure by reflection of its own intersubjective (which does not mean transparent) ground.

Thus, ultimately, Lacan's thought can be seen as directed towards that 'communicative freedom' which is also the focus of Theunissen's reading of Hegel.[69] Lacan translates the conflict between love and recognition (between being with *oneself* in the Other, and being with oneself in the *Other*) into the tension between love and law, which is generated by the simultaneity of the *non-identity* between subject and Other, and the *identity* implied by the non-identity between *both* self and Other and the symbolically mediated relation between them.[70] Lacan faces the question of love when he asks: what happens when the subject comes face to face with the object of desire – when it ceases to be the unconscious object of phantasy? In accepting the contingency of its own desire, may not the subject be able to pass beyond it? And at the end of his seminar on *The Four Fundamental Concepts of Psychoanalysis*, he concludes: 'The analyst's desire is not a pure desire. It is a desire to obtain absolute difference, a desire which intervenes when, confronted with the primary signifier, the subject is, for the first time, in a position to subject himself to it. There only may the signification of a limitless love emerge, because it is outside the limits of the law, where alone it may live.'[71]

It is important to note that Lacan speaks of a signification of love 'outside the limits of the law'. For there is a tendency in the work of Žižek and his school to view love as merely a compensatory mirage generated by law. It is assumed that an 'inherent impossibility of attaining the object' is concealed by the apparent hindrances to love; that 'it is the constraint (of discourse, of the social symbolic structure) that actually produces love' as a 'dissimulation which covers the subject's own radical lack'.[72] But when Lacan suggests that 'what is aimed at in love is the subject, the subject as such, insofar as it is presupposed behind an articulated phrase, which is organized, or can be organized, in terms of a life as a whole', he does not claim that this integrity of the subject – however difficult – is downright unattainable.[73] For all his pessimism, Lacan was far too astute not to know that an ontology of 'inner contingency', of the foreclosure of trauma, and thus of insuperable irrationality and domination, would be no less suspect than one of eirenic consensus. Indeed, one could claim that in stressing the status of love as the 'failure of the unconscious' (in other words, the paradoxical breakdown of the constitutive inaccessibility of subjects to each other),[74] the final stage of Lacan's work confirms Žižek's hypothesis of the ultimate convergence of Lacanian and Hegelian thought. For both Lacan and Hegel can be seen as grappling with the problem of the relation between love and law, and thus between ethical life and morality, which is surely one of the most desperate political questions posed to us by the modern world. But at the same time Žižek's 'Lacanian' reading of Hegel – which takes the 'tremor of reflection' as Hegel's final word on subjectivity, and thus condemns the subject to a perpetual alienation – renders this question, the true focus of the convergence, impossible even to frame.

## Notes

1. For a representative sample of the work of the Praxis School, see Mihailo Marković and Gajo Petrović, eds, *Praxis: Yugoslav Essays in the Philosophy and Methodology of the Social Sciences* (Boston Studies in the Philosophy of Science, vol. XXXVI), Dordrecht: Riedel 1979. See also the journals *Praxis*, 1965–74; and *Praxis International*, 1980–93.

2. Slavoj Žižek, *The Sublime Object of Ideology* (hereafter SOI), London: Verso 1989, p. 198.

3. '. . . Lacan's work makes almost no references to Nietzsche. Lacan always insists on psychoanalysis as a truth-experience: his thesis that truth is structured like a fiction has nothing to do with the post-structuralist reduction of the truth-dimension to a textual "truth-effect".' (SOI, p. 154)

4. SOI, p. 7.

5. 'Cette alterité est même la condition de la présence . . .' Jacques Derrida, *La voix et le phénomène*, Paris: PUF 1968, p. 73/*Speech and Phenomena*, trans. David B. Allison, Evanston, IL: Northwestern University Press 1973, p. 65.

6. Slavoj Žižek, *For They Know Not What They Do: Enjoyment as a Political Factor* (hereafter FTKN), London: Verso 1991, p. 88.

7. FTKN, p. 86.

8. SOI, p. 208.

9. FTKN, p. 89.

10. See SOI, pp. 213–14.

11. Ibid., p. 214.

12. See Ludwig Feuerbach, *Principles of the Philosophy of the Future*, Indianapolis: Hackett 1986, esp. pp. 52–73.

13. SOI, p. 228.

14. Ibid., pp. 227–8.

15. See Hinrich Fink-Eitel, *Dialektik und Sozialethik: Kommentierende Untersuchungen zu Hegels 'Logik'*, Meisenheim: Anton Hain 1978.

16. See ibid, pp. 94–5.

17. Ibid., p. 95.

18. Ibid., p. 94.

19. G.W.F. Hegel, *The Science of Logic*, trans. A.V. Miller, Atlantic Highlands, NJ: Humanities Press 1989, p. 407.

20. See *Dialektik und Sozialethik*, p. 114.

21. 'Human Language . . . constitutes a communication in which the sender receives back his own messsage from the receiver in an inverted form.' (Jacques Lacan, 'The Function and Field of Speech and Language in Psychoanalysis', in *Écrits: A Selection*, trans. A. Sheridan, London: Tavistock 1977, p. 85.)

22. *Science of Logic*, p. 431.

23. See ibid., p. 432. Miller translates 'ausschließende Reflexion' more weakly as 'exclusive reflection'.

24. As Charles Lewis points out in his pioneering, Lacan-inflected reading of the *Logic*, 'ground' – as the determination of the other determinations – can thus 'represent the totality of "Reflexionsbestimmungen" while being one member of the totality: by ceaselessly circulating through all the "Wesenheiten" it creates the totality (and therefore itself) in the act of circulation.' It therefore inscribes the ambivalent position of the subject within the intersubjective field of language. See Charles Lewis, *Hegel's Critique of Reason*, PhD thesis, University of Cambridge 1978, p. 175.

25. 'Concept' seems preferable as a translation of '*Begriff*' to Miller's use of the traditional English equivalent 'Notion', with its numinous overtones. 'Theory', rather than 'doctrine', is often the most idiomatic rendition of '*Lehre*'.

26. See *Dialektik als Sozialethik*, pp. 193–201.

27. See Christoph Menke, 'Der "Wendepunkt" des Erkennens: Zu Begriff, Recht und Reichweite der Dialektik in Hegels *Logik*', in Christoph Demmerling and Friedrich Kambartel, eds, *Vernunftkritik nach Hegel*, Frankfurt am Main: Suhrkamp 1992, esp. pp. 50–51.

28. *Hegel's Philosophy of Mind. Part Three of the Encyclopaedia of the Philosophical Sciences*, trans. William Wallace and A.V. Miller, Oxford: Oxford University Press 1971, p. 177 (paras 436, *Zusatz* and 437, *Zusatz*).

29. *Dialektik und Sozialethik*, p. 116.

30. Slavoj Žižek, *Enjoy Your Symptom: Jacques Lacan in Hollywood and Out*, London: Routledge 1992, p. 88.

31. *Hegel's Philosophy of Right*, trans. T.M. Knox, Oxford: Oxford University Press 1967, p. 179. This methodological discrepancy was noted at an early date. In 1821 Nikolaus von Thaden, who had corresponded with Hegel for many years, sent him a letter in which he inquired why the logical order introduced in para. 273 had been dropped, and why 'out of zeal for the princes – when the only thing at issue is the deduction of the Idea – a dogmatic constitution has been preferred to an actual one?' As far we know, the hapless disciple never received a reply. See Nikolaus von Thaden, 'Brief an Hegel (1821)', in Manfred Riedel, ed., *Materialien zu Hegels Rechtsphilosophie*, vol. 1, Frankfurt am Main: Suhrkamp 1975, pp. 76–80; Vittorio Hösle, *Hegels System: Band 2: Philosophie der Natur und des Geistes*, Hamburg: Felix Meiner Verlag 1988, p. 568.

32. See *Hegels System: Band 2*, p. 570.

33. *Hegel's Philosophy of Right*, pp. 179–80 (para. 278).

34. Karl Marx, 'Critique of Hegel's Doctrine of the State', in *Early Writings*, Harmondsworth: Penguin 1975, p. 91.

35. 'The personal majesty of the monarch . . . as the final *subjectivity* of decision, is above all answerability for acts of government' (*Hegel's Philosophy of Right*, p. 187).

36. See *Hegels System: Band 2*, p. 570n.

37. Another glaring example of this abuse of Hegel's thought is Žižek's repeated citation of the phrase 'Spirit is a bone', from the phrenology chapter of the *Phenomenology of Spirit*, as if this were Hegel's definitive statement on Spirit (See SOI, pp. 207–9; FTKN, p. 119, etc.). The claim that Žižek arbitrarily arrests the movement of Hegel's thought is, of course, the basis of Rodolphe Gasché's reply to the critique of his position in FTKN, pp. 72–80. Unfortunately, the issues here are almost hopelessly tangled. Gasché is certainly right to complain that Žižek creates 'the deceptive impression that Hegel's concept of identity is

always already bereft of its absolute telos' (See Gasché, 'Yes Absolutely', in *Inventions of Difference: On Jacques Derrida*, Cambridge, MA: Harvard University Press 1994, p. 213 and n. 14, pp. 278–9). However, Gasché wants to claim *both* that Hegel moves beyond the antinomies of reflection with his concept of 'absolute identity', *and* that deconstruction can unpick absolute identity without becoming re-entangled in those antinomies. It is these claims which Žižek rightly rejects as implausible. In developing a deconstruction of absolute identity (as being constituted through its relation to an unmasterable other, etc.), Gasché simply reproduces Hegel's own critical 'logic of reflection'. Furthermore, in so far as he tries to place deconstruction beyond this logic by appealing to an Otherness which would not be 'an Otherness *in opposition* to identity' (ibid., p. 279), he sets up a non-relation between identity and Otherness which immediately replays the paradoxes of reflection (e.g. Gasché's 'infrastructures' must be without relation to identity, yet they cannot be because they are 'quasi-transcendentally' constitutive of it, and thus inevitably contaminated by it). But this does not mean that Žižek's view is ultimately to be preferred because it stresses the unsurpassability of these paradoxes. Rather, the move beyond reflection which Gasché terms 'philosophical thinking' (ibid.) needs to be understood not in terms of a self-defeatingly theoreticist version of deconstruction, but in terms of the opening of thought towards the tension of love and recognition.

38. See FTKN, pp. 94–5n.

39. Both quotations are from *Écrits: A Selection*, p. 296.

40. Jacques Lacan, 'Réponses à des étudiants en philosophie sur l'objet de la psychanalyse', *Cahiers pour l'analyse*, no. 3, May–June 1966, p. 6.

41. Slavoj Žižek, *Le plus sublime des hystériques – Hegel passe*, Paris: Point Hors Ligne 1988, p. 159.

42. Ibid., p. 154.

43. See *Dialektik und Sozialethik*, p. 203.

44. *Enjoy Your Symptom*, p. 137.

45. *Hegel's Phenomenology of Spirit*, trans. A.V. Miller, Oxford: Oxford University Press 1977, p. 10.

46. 'The truth of *being* is *essence*' is the the first sentence of the 'Doctrine of Essence'.

47. See Dieter Henrich, 'Hegels Logik der Reflexion', in *Hegel im Kontext*, Frankfurt am Main: Suhrkamp 1975, p. 109. See also Henrich, 'Hegels Grundoperation', in U. Guzzoni *et al.*, eds, *Der Idealismus und seine Gegenwart*, Hamburg: Felix Meiner Verlag 1976.

48. See ibid., p. 111.

49. See Manfred Frank, *Der unendliche Mangel an Sein: Schellings Hegelkritik und die Anfänge der marxschen Dialektik*, Frankfurt am Main: Suhrkamp 1975, p. 57.

50. See ibid., p. 50.

51. For a sample of Theunissen's approach in English, see 'The Repressed Intersubjectivity in Hegel's Philosophy of Right', in Drucilla Cornell *et al.*, eds, *Hegel and Legal Theory*, London: Routledge 1991. Prospective readers should be warned that the translation is seriously garbled.

52. *Science of Logic*, p. 591. See Michael Theunissen, *Sein und Schein: Die kritische Funktion der Hegelschen Logik*, Frankfurt am Main: Suhrkamp 1980, p. 332.

53. '. . . the universal is, in its other, in peaceful communion with itself. We have called it free power, but it could also be called free love and boundless blessedness, for it bears itself towards its other as towards its own self; in it, it has returned to itself' (*Science of Logic*, p. 603).

54. *Dialektik und Sozialethik*, p. 205.

55. Ibid., p. 142.

56. Slavoj Žižek, 'Eastern European Liberalism and its Discontents', *New German Critique*, no. 57, Fall 1992, p. 44.

57. Ibid., p. 45.

58. Ibid., p. 47.

59. Ibid., pp. 46–7.

60. Slavoj Žižek, *Tarrying with the Negative*, Durham, NC: Duke University Press 1993, p. 237.

61. *Enjoy Your Symptom*, p. 103.

62. Joachim Ritter, 'Hegel and the French Revolution', in *Hegel and the French Revolution: Essays on the Philosophy of Right*, Cambridge, MA: MIT Press 1984, p. 65.

63. Ibid., pp. 77, 79.

64. Ibid., p. 78.

65. FTKN, p. 78.

66. *Tarrying with the Negative*, p. 227. For Žižek's formal argument that 'Necessity arises out of contingency', and is thus inherently ideological, see 'Why Should a Dialectician Learn to Count to Four?', *Radical Philosophy*, no. 58, Summer 1991.

67. Žižek ignores this 'return' to intersubjective mediation when he writes: 'in his Seminar on *Transference* (1960–1961), Lacan renounced the motif of intersubjectivity: what is lost in it is the fact that, to a subject, another subject is first and foremost an *objet (a)*, that which prevents him from fully realizing himself . . .' (*Enjoy Your Symptom*, p. 139). For the development of Lacan's theory of the *objet a*, see Catherine Millot, *Nobodaddy: L'hystérie dans le siècle*, Paris: Point Hors Ligne 1988, pp. 87–113.

68. FTKN, p. 88.

69. See *Sein und Schein*, pp. 37 ff.

70. This structure could thus be termed the 'difference of identity and difference'; its fundamental signifier in Lacan's work is, of course, the phallus. In a Lacanian reading of the *Logic* which differs strikingly from that of Žižek, Charles Lewis has suggested that the category of ground, which 'circulates' between the two poles of essence and thus resolves its antinomy, inscribes this function of the phallus. See *Hegel's Critique of Reason*, p. 175n and Note 24 above. Whether Lacan is justified in describing this function as essentially phallic is, of course, a highly contested issue to which I intend to return elsewhere.

71. Jacques Lacan, *The Four Fundamental Concepts of Psychoanalysis*, trans. A. Sheridan, Harmondsworth: Peregrine 1986, p. 276.

72. See Slavoj Žižek, *The Metastases of Enjoyment: Six Essays on Woman and Causality*, London: Verso 1994, p. 94; and Renata Salecl, 'Love: Providence or Despair', *New Formations*, no. 23, Summer 1994 (Special Issue on 'Lacan and Love'), pp. 22, 24.

73. Jacques Lacan, *Le Séminaire livre XX: Encore*. Paris: Seuil 1975, p. 48.

74. See the deliriously punning title of one of Lacan's last seminars: *L'insu-que-sait de l'Une-bévue s'aile à mourre* ('L'insuccès de l'Unbewußt, c'est l'amour'). For this late thematics of love in Lacan, see Serge André, *Que veut une femme?*, Paris: Navarin 1986, ch. 14.

# The Truth of the Subject:
# Language, Validity and
# Transcendence in Lacan and
# Habermas

In a recent conversation with Jacques Derrida, Jean-Luc Nancy suggested that, throughout the period when structuralism and poststructuralism were the predominant philosophical forces in France, Lacan was perhaps the only thinker to insist on keeping the 'name' of the subject.[1] Given the climate of the times, in which the concept of the 'subject' was dismissively associated with discredited, supposedly 'Sartrean' reveries of autonomy and self-transparency, this was indeed a significant act of intellectual resistance on Lacan's part, in any perspective. Covering his own tracks a little, one might suspect, Derrida responded to Nancy's remark by insisting that other thinkers of the 1960s and 1970s continued to work on the theory of the subject. Althusser, for example, 'seeks to discredit a certain authority of the subject only by acknowledging for the instance of the "subject" an irreducible place in a theory of ideology'; while in Foucault's case: 'we would appear to have a history of subjectivity that, in spite of certain massive declarations about the effacement of the figure of man, certainly never consisted in "liquidating" the Subject'.[2] Derrida's retrospective, however, tends to smooth out the awkward fact of Lacan's uniqueness. For in Lacan's thought, from a very early date, the concept of the 'subject' and the concept of 'truth' are intimately linked, whereas for the other prominent thinkers of the period the influence of Marx, Nietzsche and, indeed, Freud encouraged a view of the subject as the primary locus of (metaphysical) illusion. Althusser insisted, in his famous essay on the theory of ideology, that 'all scientific discourse is a subject-less discourse, there is no "Subject of science" except in an ideology of science'.[3] Similarly Foucault suggested, in his inaugural lecture at the Collège de France: 'It may well be that the theme of the founding subject permits one to elide the reality of discourse',[4] while declining to balance this critique with an alternative account of the 'non-founding' subject until much later in his work. The following remarks from the opening of Lacan's first *Seminar* form a striking contrast to such views:

I insist on the fact that Freud was exploring a line of research which is not characterized by the same style as other sciences. Its domain is that of the truth of
the subject. The quest for truth is not entirely reducible to the objective, and
indeed objectifying, research of the normal scientific method. It is a matter of
the realization of the truth of the subject, as a specific dimension which must be
detached in its originality from the notion of reality.[5]

But what is this truth of the subject for Lacan?

## Lacan on Language and Truth

In an essay dating from 1946, Lacan remarks: 'no linguist or philosopher
could in fact any longer defend a theory of language as a system of signs
doubling a system of realities, the latter defined by the common accord of
sound minds in sound bodies'.[6] His reasons for making this claim are similar to those which motivated Wittgenstein's well-known critique of the
notion of ostensive definition. Elsewhere Lacan suggests: 'there is only one
gesture, known since Saint Augustine, which corresponds to nomination:
that of the index-finger which shows, but in itself this gesture is not even
sufficient to designate what is named in the object indicated'.[7] Ostensive
definition is inadequate to establish reference, since without commentary
it can never determine which *aspect* or *feature* of the ostended context is
being isolated, and therefore presupposes the very capacity of language to
connect with the world which it is intended to explain. Lacan's conclusion
is that 'no signification can be sustained other than by reference to another
signification: in its extreme form this amounts to the proposition that
there is no language [*langue*] in existence for which there is any question of
its inability to cover the whole field of the signified, it being an effect of its
existence as language that it necessarily answers to all needs'.[8] Thus, for
Lacan there are no privileged points where language abuts directly on to
the real: rather, reference is inherent in the functioning of a language –
however minimal – as a whole.

However, Lacan does not draw from this insight the conclusion which
was popularized by the earlier Derrida – that the very distinction between
'signifier' and 'signified', or between language and the reality to which it
refers, must ultimately be regarded as betraying the 'metaphysical appur-
tenance' of the idea of the sign, an idea which 'falls into decay' when the
'exteriority of writing in general' is appreciated.[9] Rather, he takes the view
that the disclosure of the world involves an indissoluble tension between
the pre-reflexive, linguistic constitution of object-domains, and the reflexive assessment of beliefs about the contents of these domains. From such
a perspective, as Lacan emphasizes, 'the object is not without reference to
speech. It is from the very beginning partially given in the objectal, or

objective, system, in which must be included the sum of prejudices which constitute a cultural community. . . .'[10] This does not entail that the distinction between language and the reality to which it refers is ultimately untenable, as Derrida's notion of the 'general text' suggests, since what particular terms are taken to mean cannot be *entirely* separated from the pragmatic success of the beliefs which a linguistic community holds. In other words, there is a continuous interaction between knowledge and meaning, in which new discoveries – although never unmediated encounters with the real – can destabilize existing interpretations: we are not simply trapped within a specific 'disclosure' of the world until some arbitrary shift of perspective occurs. This, no doubt, is what Lacan is intimating when he claims that the network of the signified 'reacts historically' upon the network of the signifier, 'just as the structure of the latter commands the pathways of the former'.[11]

Lacan's account of this dialectic between signifier and signified suggests a divergence from more extreme hermeneutical positions, which are reluctant to admit that the failure of a truth-claim could effect a shift in the linguistic disclosure of the world which framed and made possible the formulation of the claim. But at the same time, Lacan equally opposes a pragmatic reduction of truth to an indicator of instrumental success. In his middle-period writings Lacan often illustrates the intertwining of language and truth, and the sense in which it cannot be instrumentally reduced, by counterposing animal behaviour and human communication. He defines a code in terms of 'the fixed correlation of its signs with the reality they signify', using as an example the 'language of the bees', in which different dance-patterns indicate the direction and distance of pollen-bearing flowers.[12] Although such forms of information-transmission cannot simply be reduced to sequences of stimulus and response, we are operating here only at the level of behavioural reactions to perceived patterns and *Gestalten*, a level which Lacan characterizes as the 'Imaginary'.

The reasons for this choice of term become clear when Lacan refers, as he frequently does in his middle-period writings, to the rituals of rivalry and courtship, and the accompanying forms of parade and display, to be found in the animal world. Lacan does not deny that it may be possible, in this sphere, to find forms of misleading behaviour and deception. Animals can lure and intimidate each other, and even fool each other as to their intentions, by creating a disjunction between appearance and reality. (In the human world, an equivalent to such behaviour can be found – as he suggests – in the use of diversionary tactics during a battle, or a feint during a boxing match.) But being captivated by an image is not equivalent to being misled by a falsehood – and this is Lacan's crucial point.

The lures of the Imaginary cannot be described as *mendacious*, since lying involves an unjustified claim to truth, and the question of truth does not arise in the domain of disjunctions between (physical) appearance and (psychological) reality. Although animals can produce deceptive *signs*, they cannot – to employ Lacan's contrast – produce deceptive *signifiers*, whose misleading character depends on the expectations of the recipient, and thus on the manner in which they will be interpreted in a specific situation. As Lacan suggests, an animal

> can succeed in throwing its pursuers off the trail by making a false start. This can go so far as to suggest that the game animal is honouring the element of display implied by the hunt. But an animal cannot pretend to pretend. It cannot make tracks whose deception consists in being taken for false, when they are true, in fact indicating the right trail.[13]

In other words, the animal cannot detach the question of truth and falsehood, which depends on intersubjective expectations, from the practice of accurate or inaccurate representation.

Lacan describes this detachment as the passage from 'the field of exactitude to the register of truth'.[14] He often illustrates it by means of a venerable Jewish joke about an exchange between two passengers on a Polish train: 'Why are you lying to me, why do you tell me you are going to Krakow, so that I will believe you are going to Lemberg, when all the time you are going to Krakow?'[15] Superficially, this story suggests that whether a statement functions as a lie is relative to the backdrop of expectations against which it is made, regardless of its 'representational' accuracy or inaccuracy. On further reflection, however, it also makes plain that a social world in which the majority of participants habitually lie is impossible on transcendental grounds: the universal expectation of mendacity would simply dissolve into a revision of interpretative schemata aimed at maximizing truth. Thus Lacan is here highlighting a fundamental asymmetry between truth and falsehood: the fact that a lie can function as such only within an intersubjective relation structured by the normative background assumption that the purpose of linguistic communication is to tell the truth. For if a statement considered true at a given time is a statement whose *claim* to truth has been (provisionally) accepted or upheld, a lie is not a claim to falsehood which has been similarly validated but, rather, a statement made with the intention of raising an unjustifiable claim to truth. Thus the possibility of the lie presupposes a 'convention' that the purpose of language is to tell the truth, whereas no such convention is required for the success of a feint or decoy. In Lacan's words: 'it is clear that Speech begins only with the passage from pretence to the order of the signifier, and that the signifier requires another locus – the locus of the Other, the Other witness, the witness Other than any of the partners – for the speech that it supports to be capable of lying, that is to say, of presenting itself as Truth'.[16]

This insight sharply demarcates Lacan's position from the Nietzsche-influenced dismantlings of truth which have been central to post-structuralist thinking, and continue to play a role in many contemporary 'postmodernist' debates. To confirm this, one need only recall the early Nietzsche's account of the origin of the prohibition on lying in 'On Truth and Lies in an Extra-Moral Sense'. Here Nietzsche suggests that human beings, 'out of necessity and boredom', eventually decided to do away with the most glaring manifestations of the *bellum omnium contra omnes:*

> This peace treaty brings with it something which appears to be the first step towards the achievement of that mysterious truth-drive [*Wahrheitstrieb*]. Specifically, what is from now on to count as 'truth' is fixed at this moment, in other words a regular, valid, and binding denomination of things is invented, and the legislating act of language also gives the first laws of truth: for at this point there arises for the first time the contrast of truth and falsehood.[17]

Thus, for Nietzsche, the prohibition on lying is a historically established moral prohibition, motivated by fear of the socially damaging conse-quences of the practice. He goes on to suggest that it is matched by a parallel prohibition on the utterance of dangerous and disruptive truths.[18]

By contrast, for Lacan the norm of truth-telling has a non-empirical, *a priori* status. It is not the result of an accord between the partners involved in communication, since for such an accord to be established the truth-telling function of language would have already to be presupposed. The norm of truth-telling is a condition of possibility of any meaningful dis-cussion and, therefore, of the conclusion of any peace treaty. As Lacan states:

> . . . I can deceive my adversary by a movement which is contrary to my battle plan, but this movement does not have its deceptive effect unless I produce it in reality and for my adversary. But in the proposals by means of which I open peace negotiations with him, it is in a third locus, which is neither my speech nor that of my interlocutor, that what it proposes is situated.[19]

This locus is described by Lacan, from the mid 1950s onwards, simply as the 'Other'.

## Habermas's Consensus Theory of Truth

If the above provides a fair sketch of Lacan's account of the relation between language and truth, it suggests that there may be unexpected par-allels between his thought and the philosophical approach to these issues which is currently defended by Jürgen Habermas. For one thing,

Habermas, like Lacan, has always resisted a naturalistic or pragmatist reduction of truth-claims. In a 1968 essay on Nietzsche's epistemology, for example, he objected to the Nietzschean version of instrumentalism:

> The meaning of the empirical accuracy of statements can be explicated with reference to the possibility of transforming them into technical recommendations. But the success of the operations to which these recommendations give rise is not for this reason identical with the truth of the propositions from which these recommendations are deduced, with the aim of achieving certain goals.[20]

Thus, from very early on, Habermas was convinced that truth possesses what he has more recently termed a 'context-exploding' force, although it took a long time before he was able to formulate this intuition theoretically.

Because of this conviction, Habermas has also argued that the question of truth cannot even be raised at the level of the perception of objects. In Lacan's account of the Imaginary, as we have seen, individuals can react to feints and deceptions with *appropriate* or *inappropriate* behaviour, but such actions and reactions cannot be characterized in terms of their truth or falsehood. Similarly, in 'Wahrheitstheorien', the founding presentation of his conception of truth, Habermas draws a distinction – even within the domain of language-use – between forms of action-related cognition, which are concerned with the adequacy of information about objects of experience, and the dimension of truth. 'In an action context', he suggests, 'the assertion has the role of information about an experience of objects, but in discourse it has the role of a statement with a problematized validity-claim. The same speech act can be in one case the expression of an experience, which is either objective or merely subjective, and in another, the expression of a thought, which is true or false.'[21] But despite these convergences between Lacan and Habermas, which constitute a somewhat surprising alliance against contemporary forms of contextualism and relativism, it is clear that the transcendental irreducibility of truth is construed rather differently in the two cases.

Habermas's approach gives rise to a 'discourse theory of truth', guided by the idea that agreement is the immanent *telos* of language. For Habermas it is part of the pragmatic meaning of making an assertion that the speaker commits him- or herself to the provision of grounds for what has been asserted, should the validity of the truth-claim raised be questioned. Such a process of questioning and resolving the validity of disputed claims takes place through the form of argumentation, relieved from the immediate pressure of action, which Habermas terms 'discourse' [*Diskurs*]. According to this conception, speakers of a language necessarily presuppose that it is possible to resolve, and possess an intuitive knowledge of how to resolve consensually, disputed validity-claims, since otherwise language would be unable to fulfil what Habermas takes to be its central function of co-ordinating action through agreement.

As is well known, this line of inquiry then leads Habermas to the notion of an 'ideal speech situation' – of those conditions under which truth-claims could be resolved in a way which would guarantee the objective validity of the outcome. In Habermas's view this notion is not simply an arbitrary construction, since our capacity to engage in discussion orientated towards the resolution of disputes over validity-claims presupposes an (at least tacit) awareness that conditions of equality and reciprocity between participants in a *Diskurs* must obtain if the consensus attained is to be veridical. Otherwise participants would not identify coercion, manipulation, and other structural inequalities as detrimental to the dialogical discovery of truth. The 'ideal speech situation' should thus not be understood either merely regulatively, by analogy with Kant's 'Ideas of reason', nor as a piece of 'existing reason' in Hegel's sense. Rather, Habermas suggests, when we engage in discussion, we cannot help but suppose, usually – possibly always – counterfactually, that the conditions of the ideal speech situation have already been at least approximately fulfilled. Thus, the ideal speech situation is neither an empirical phenomenon nor a rationalistic construction, but a 'fiction which is operatively effective in processes of communication'.[22] In behaving as though it were actual, we help to make it actual, although there can never be any conclusive proof of success, since it is impossible simultaneously to enter into discourse and to thematize reflectively the structure of this same discourse.

In Lacan, by contrast, there is no attempt to capture the context-transcending force of the claim to truth embodied in our utterances in the nets of an ideal structure of communication. This force is, rather, revealed by the unavoidability of the presupposition of the witness of an Other who cannot be equated with any possible empirical partner in dialogue. Thus Lacan writes that the 'register of truth' is 'situated entirely elsewhere [than the field of exactitude], properly speaking at the foundation of intersubjectivity. It is located where the subject can seize nothing except the very subjectivity which constitutes an Other as absolute.'[23] It is true that there appears to be an oscillation between an individual and a transindividual characterization of the 'Other' in Lacan's thought, for at times he characterizes the Other more impersonally as the 'third locus' or the 'locus of the signifying convention'.[24] However, this oscillation can perhaps be rendered more intelligible by considering the implications of the approach to truth of Karl-Otto Apel, a close colleague and interlocutor of Habermas over many years, who has developed a more explicitly 'transcendental' version of the consensus theory.

Apel replies to the 'convergence of the poststructuralist, hermeneutic, and pragmatist critique of transcendental philosophy' by arguing that the individual subject must be 'more than a point of intersection of historically contingent and structurally anonymous determinations', since as a thinking and reflecting subject he or she participates in an 'unlimited community of argumentation' [*unbegrenzte Argumentationsgemeinschaft*] which has the status of a 'transcendental subject of redeemable truth-claims'.[25] On the one hand, the rules which are discovered by reflection on universal communicative competences are not the *product* of consensus but the necessary preconditions of any attempt to reach consensus. They cannot, therefore, be equated with any empirically existing discursive conventions, which may in fact be distorted in various ways. In this sense, as Lacan says, the Other is the 'locus of the signifying convention' which cannot be equated with any of the participants in communication. But at the same time, the reconstruction of the transcendental–pragmatic rules makes possible the delineation of an 'ideal' – perfectly honest and perfectly sincere – 'witness to the truth', comparable to Apel's 'transcendental subject of redeemable truth-claims', to whom the incoherences and self-deceptions of my speech would become transparent. Indeed, if I could detect all the errors and self-deceptions in the Other's response, I could transform my 'real' into an 'ideal' partner, in confrontation with whom the illusions of my own speech would be definitively revealed. However, since in order to achieve this I would already myself have to be that ideal partner for another, the true structure of our interaction, and therefore of our stance as subjects constituted by this interaction, is destined to remain 'unconscious' – implicit in the dynamic of intersubjectivity but reflectively irretrievable from it.[26]

## Truthfulness and Authenticity

But even given these parallels between Lacan's views and 'transcendental' or 'universal' pragmatics, is not Lacan's conception of truth radically different from that of Habermas? One of Habermas's important innovations is to qualify the traditional centrality of 'truth' in philosophy by distinguishing between three 'validity-claims', which he categorizes as 'truth' [*Wahrheit*], 'rightness' [*Richtigkeit*] and 'truthfulness' [*Wahrhaftigkeit*]. The first of these terms describes the cognitive status of claims about the objective world, the second the normative status of the rules governing interpersonal relations within the social world, and the last the expressive status of claims concerning the subjective experiences of the individual.[27] In Lacan's vocabulary, however, what Habermas understands by truth is, rather, described as 'knowledge' [*savoir*], whereas what Habermas refers to as 'truthfulness' [*Wahrhaftigkeit*] – namely, the undistorted self-disclosure of subjectivity – seems at first glance to correspond more closely to what Lacan describes as the 'truth of the subject' [*la vérité du sujet*].

This is only the case 'at first glance', because a better suggestion might be that Lacan's *vérité* in fact corresponds to a category related to, but not identical with, that of truthfulness – namely, 'authenticity'.[28] Whereas truthfulness refers to the honest expression of a particular thought, experience, or feeling, authenticity can be said to concern whether this thought, experience, or feeling, as expressed in a particular context, is in turn a manifestation of what Alessandro Ferrara has termed 'the core of the actor's personality'.[29] The function of this concept can perhaps be illustrated by a critical procedure which is central to Charles Taylor's book *Sources of the Self*. Over and over again, Taylor shows that a particular philosophical conception was motivated by impulses and implicit convictions which it was incapable of articulating in terms of its own conceptual framework. Thus he writes of utilitarianism that it is:

> a very strange intellectual position. Built into its denunciation of religion and earlier philosophical views, built into its sense of rationality as an operating ideal, built into its background assumption that the general happiness, and above all the relief of suffering, crucially *matters*, and emerging in the sense that reason liberates us for universal and impartial benevolence, is a strong and at times impassioned commitment to the three goods which I enumerated above [self-responsible reason, the significance of natural fulfilments and benevolence]. But in the actual content of its tenets, as officially defined, none of this can be said; and most of it makes no sense.[30]

Another way of putting this claim would, of course, be to say that the utilitarian is 'inauthentic': although her expressions of belief and attitude may be truthful, these beliefs and attitudes do not in turn truly express the fundamental existential orientation of the person voicing them. Of course, the question of truthfulness may be said to shade into that of authenticity, since if many of a person's beliefs, albeit sincerely expressed at the conscious level, do not jell with other things we know of their history, behaviour and attitudes, we will be tempted to claim that they are not her *real* beliefs. Authenticity, in other words, concerns what might be termed the 'truthfulness of truthfulness'. But this definition in turn raises the question of how we could ever determine what a person's 'real' experience is, since inauthenticity can run very deep. It is perhaps because he sees this abyss about to open up that Habermas tends to define truthfulness rather perfunctorily in terms of the faithful expression of subjective experience, although he stresses that the inner world should not be understood objectivistically.[31]

## The Conflict of Knowledge and Truth

By contrast, Lacan, from an early date, identified a fundamental conflict between an existentially significant 'true speech' [*la vraie parole*], capable of disclosing the being of the subject, and 'veridical discourse' [*le discours vrai*], which might well be truthful. His fundamental thought is that it makes sense to distinguish an authentic self from a construction, however 'viable', only if this self exerts the force of a validity-claim. A conflict arises, however, because on the one hand the import of any vocabulary within which a subjective experience is identified and described itself depends on substantive assumptions about the world, including the relation between self and others, thus generating the regress of the 'truthfulness of truthfulness': 'true speech, in asking veridical discourse what it signifies, will find that a meaning always refers back to another meaning, since nothing can be shown except by means of a sign, and therefore it will make true discourse appear doomed to error'.[32] On the other hand, if veridical discourse seeks to extract a stable self-description from true speech, thereby detaching it from an evaluation of its context, it will find itself distorting the meaning of this speech:

> True discourse, in isolating in the proffered word what is given as a promise, will make it appear mendacious, since it commits itself to a future which, as they say, belongs to no one, and will also make the word appear ambiguous, to the extent that it transcends the being it concerns, in the dimension of alienation where the becoming of this being occurs.[33]

Lacan implies here that because subjective states are not susceptible to a punctual and definitive evaluation, but may always retrospectively acquire a different status and significance within the shifting perspectives of a continuing interaction with others, we are always liable to fall into an objectified construction of the subject's identity. Conversely, objective truth-claims – concerning the nature and significance of a specific event in an individual or collective history, for example – can scarcely be said to possess a timeless truth which would be independent of the conceptual framework which makes possible the historical interpretation, and which we can readily imagine being superseded in the future. Since the conceptual framework is ultimately an expression of our individual or collective self-understanding and orientation towards the world, the apparent stability of objective truth will be put in question by the intersubjective dynamic which true speech reveals.

In the third *Seminar*, given around the time of 'Variantes de la cure-type', the essay under discussion, Lacan returned to this clash between the claims of objectivity and subjectivity. He suggested that disinterested communication is ultimately nothing but failed testimony, or something about which everyone agrees. Everyone knows that this is the ideal of the transmission of knowledge. The entire thought of the scientific community is founded on the possibility of a communication whose limit is defined by an experiment which everyone can agree on. But the very establishment of the experiment is a function of testimony.[34]

Thus, for Lacan, scientific knowledge would be impossible without a certain 'forgetfulness' of the dimension of subjective experience out of which it emerges. Indeed, he goes so far as to suggest, at one point, that the antinomy arising from the clash between subjective and objective dimensions of truth is 'that of the meaning which Freud gave to the notion of the unconscious'.[35]

In contrast to Lacan, Habermas seeks to avoid the conflict between 'knowledge' and 'truth' by arguing that the process of rationalization characteristic of modernity has given rise to institutionally differentiated spheres dedicated to the articulation and resolution of the claims specific to one dimension of validity. Habermas admits that objectifying forms of knowledge can 'colonize' the lifeworld under the pressure of economic and bureaucratic imperatives, thereby inducing reifying distortions into our individual and collective self-understandings. But such colonization could, in principle, be avoided. The identities which locate us as subjects in the lifeworld are shaped by cultural traditions and inherited practices, and, given favourable political arrangements, these traditions could be drawn on in discussing how to control and orientate the development and application of scientific knowledge, including social-scientific knowledge, so as to foster who we (collectively) want to be. There is no hint in Habermas of the thought that the very fact of articulating such a shared self-understanding might be problematic, because of the intrinsic difficulties of defining what an adequate revelation of a subject's or community's existential orientation might consist in. These difficulties are, however, implicit in Habermas's account. For he has shifted towards a use of the term 'authenticity' to designate something like harmonious self-coincidence, or the redoubled claim to truthfulness 'all the way down' discussed above, and he now argues that there can be 'ethical-existential discourses' which thematize such individual and collective authenticity-claims.[36] But since the meaning of 'discourse' in Habermas is defined by the possibility (however remote) of consensus, this conflicts with his former view that claims to truthfulness cannot be discursively resolved, since their validity or non-validity affects the status of the very discourse in which they are assessed.[37]

## Beyond the Social Self

Despite this awkwardness, however, Habermas can feel basically comfortable with this view of authenticity because of his social account of the formation of the subject, an account derived from George Herbert Mead. The implication of this account is that the subject can never detach itself sufficiently from culture and tradition for the question of its relation to this context as a whole to become an issue. According to Mead, the capacity for self-reflection which is taken to be definitive of subjectivity emerges out of the process of identifying with the attitudes of others, a process which helps the individual successfully to negotiate the social environment. The advantage of this account, Habermas contends, is that it enables us to circumvent the 'poststructuralist' critique of the subject which understands self-reflection as implying an inevitable self-objectification: to respond to oneself as if from the standpoint of the other is not tantamount to objectifying oneself.[38] Self-reflection appears in this perspective as the internalized version of concrete social processes, not as an ability of the subject to abstract entirely from its empirical social context.

It seems questionable, however, whether Habermas's account of the social and interactive genesis of the self is fully able to account for the capacity for abstraction which is a precondition of the subject's ability to participate in discourses orientated towards the redemption of validity-claims. Habermas is quite clear that such participation requires subjects to take a hypothetical attitude towards their own specific interests – for example, in deciding what norm might be in the interests of all concerned. Similarly, in the discussion of the cognitive claims of the sciences, the participants must abstract from any interest they may have in the outcome, other than that it should be objectively valid. Admittedly, Habermas emphasizes that this capacity for reflection on specific problematic issues does not rest on an ability to abstract *entirely* from the lifeworld context which shapes our identity.[39] He also stresses, however, that the notion of rightness or truth towards which participants orientate their contributions to discussion is an ideal which transcends any empirical context – indeed, Habermas now uses the term 'transcendence from within' to describe this 'context-exploding' force of validity-claims.[40] And it seems clear that a subject which can orientate itself towards such a transcendence must itself transcend any given empirical context, at least in one dimension of its being. Certainly, Apel implies this when he stresses that there is a 'transcendental–pragmatic dimension of the self-reflection of the arguing subject' which 'cannot be objectivized and formalized', since it consists of insight into the *a priori* norms of argumentation which arises in the course of argumentation itself, and presupposes participation in a 'transcendental language game'.[41] For how could a subject which is merely a precipitate of empirical social interactions, however non-objectifying, participate in such a game? These considerations suggest, at the very least, the need for caution with regard to Habermas's Meadian attempts to reconstruct a purely social and evolutionary genesis of the self.

It can be argued that it is precisely his sensitivity to this non-empirical dimension of the subject which leads Lacan to suggest a conflict between what he terms knowledge and truth. For it is a remarkable feature of Lacan's work that despite his central emphasis on intersubjectivity, and his reinterpretation of the unconscious itself as an intersubjective phenomenon, he also suggests that there is an irreducible moment of 'Cartesian' transcendence which characterizes the subject. Indeed, Lacan draws a close connection between the emergence of modern science and the emergence of the reflexive subject. In his essay 'La science et la vérité', for example, he writes that the distinctive position of modern science can be characterized in terms of 'a radical change of style in the *tempo* of its progress, of the galloping speed of its involvement in our world, the chain reactions which characterize what we can call the expansion of its energetic. What seems to be at the root of all this is a modification of our position as subjects, in a double sense: it inaugurates this development, and science reinforces it more and more.'[42] Lacan goes on to argue that this modification can be traced to 'a historically defined moment which we should perhaps be aware can be strictly repeated in experience, that which is inaugurated by Descartes and which is called the *cogito*'.[43]

At first glance, Lacan's claim may seem rather surprising. After all, he begins his celebrated paper on the 'Mirror Stage' by suggesting that the experience of this stage 'makes us oppose any philosophy directly issuing from the *cogito*'.[44] Even here, however, the qualificatory adverb promises further complexities, and in later writings Lacan will stress that the isolation of the 'subject' which Descartes undertakes through the suspension of any cognitive relation to the world reveals something decisive about the subject, its 'transcendental–pragmatic' status (to use Apel's term) as an indubitable presupposition of all discourse. For Lacan, Descartes's mistake was merely to take the subject he had discovered for a substantial subject of consciousness. He argues that 'it is by taking place at the level of the utterance [*énonciation*]' that the *cogito* acquires its certainty, but this certainty cannot be translated into the form of a proposition [*énoncé*] expressing a specific self-interpretation: the *I think* is 'reduced to this punctuality of being certain only of the absolute doubt concerning all signification, its own included. . . .'[45] Viewed in this way, the Cartesian *cogito* 'denounces what is privileged in the moment on which it is based, and shows how fraudulent it is to extend this privilege to conscious phenomena, in order to establish their status'.[46] For Lacan, in other words, the subject is that moment of non-mundanity, of transcendence, which must be seen as both eluding and making possible the reflexive structure of self-consciousness, even when the emergence of that structure is understood in terms of intersubjective identifications.[47]

We have seen that Lacan argues for a fundamental distinction between 'knowledge' and 'truth', or between *le discours vrai* and *la vraie parole*. However, the recognition of a difference between the validity-status of truthfulness (or authenticity as a 'redoubled' form of truthfulness) and truth does not, taken by itself, imply a conflict between them. Habermas tries to avoid this conflict by suggesting that the reified self-understanding of *le discours vrai* is not inevitable. Within the sphere of the lifeworld individuals do not spontaneously relate to themselves and others in objectifying ways. This occurs only when the exclusive orientation to truth characteristic of the sciences is imported back into the sphere of intersubjective communication from the specialized institutional spheres where it legitimately holds sway, in the process which Habermas describes as the 'colonization of the lifeworld'. From such a perspective, it is the failure to respect the limits between different types of discourse and their appropriate domains which leads to a disabling of the capacity to ask who we truly are and what we really want, not to some intrinsic diremption of the modern self.

## Authenticity and Truth

It is significant, therefore, that another contemporary representative of the Critical Theory tradition, Martin Seel, has contested Habermas's view that different validity-claims can be thematized in distinct forms of discourse, each of which can be insulated from other dimensions of validity. Seel suggests that each specialized discourse will necessarily be infiltrated by 'assumptions and presuppositions which cannot themselves be thematized with regard to their validity in the current discourse'.[48] A moral discussion, for example, will often need to draw on aesthetic and therapeutic claims, just as aesthetic discussions cannot entirely dispense with questions of (cognitive) truth. In consequence, Seel suggests:

> The specialization of the expert consists merely in not allowing the different type of validity of the presuppositions to be expressed, and it is on this that his purely immanent, sovereign considerations are based. The *illusion* of specialization, whether it is theoretical, practical or aesthetic, is always the belief in an 'ultimate foundation' of one's own (superior) activity, which separates it from the opaquely determined activity of the dilettantes.[49]

If this argument is taken seriously, then it does indeed suggest that no 'truth' – no cognitive claim, in Habermas's sense – can be irrelative to the inextricable interplay of validity-dimensions which constitutes the disclosure of a specific lifeworld, and provides our 'ethical' orientation. The natural sciences may represent an exception in this respect, since here an independent criterion of instrumental success is operative, and may even have *replaced* considerations of cognitive truth.[50] But for most institutionalized domains of knowledge in the social and human sciences, 'truth' cannot be quarantined from the wider play and interfusion of validity-dimensions in this way.

Pushing a similar argument somewhat further than Seel would wish to go, Charles Taylor has tried to defuse the conflict between truth and authenticity in the opposite way to Habermas, precisely by not holding them apart. In an extensive series of writings, Taylor has powerfully criticized the representationalism of the predominant conceptions of language within modern analytical philosophy, suggesting that such views leave what he terms the 'expressive', 'disclosive' and 'constitutive' dimensions of language out of account. By 'expression' Taylor means the manner in which language displays the stance of the speaking subject towards a certain reality, or towards others with whom he or she is engaged in dialogue. By 'disclosure' he understands the way in which language is capable of 'articulating' an issue, and thereby first renders it available as a matter of (public) concern. Finally, language is 'constitutive' for Taylor because our linguistically articulated self-understandings are not simply a 'grid' through which we interpret our experiences and feelings, but enter into the moral texture which makes these experiences and feelings what they are.[51]

Taylor's argument is not simply a corrective to the *predominance* of the representationalist view of the self as a detached observer confronting an objective world. He makes the stronger argument that 'in some sense, the expressive dimension seems to be more fundamental: in that it appears we can never be without it, whereas it can function alone, in establishing public space, and grounding our sensitivity to the properly human concerns'.[52] Moreover, not only is the expressive dimension more fundamental for Taylor, it appears that even the stance of the disinterested observer is itself ultimately the 'expression' of a specific self-understanding, rooted in traditions which have acquired predominance in our culture: 'My claim is that the ideal of the modern free subject, capable of objectifying the world and reasoning about it in a detached, instrumental way, is a novel variant of [a] very old aspiration to spiritual freedom.'[53] The implication of this view is that even what is taken to be a cognitive 'point zero' – paradigmatically, the detached self of the Cartesian *cogito* – is in fact an expression of a particular value-orientation, so that its apparent value-neutrality is specious. Indeed, Taylor claims: 'What you get underlying our representations of the world – the kinds of things we formulate, for instance, in declarative sentences – is not further representations, but rather a certain grasp of the world that we have as agents in it. This shows the whole epistemological construal of knowledge to be mistaken.'[54] On similar grounds, he has also argued against Habermas's moral philosophy, suggesting that the commitment to the goal of rational consensus cannot be derived from the normative structure of the speech situation as such. The implication here is that Habermas's whole conception of a discourse ethics ultimately rests on specific, albeit culturally deep-rooted, commitments to freedom and autonomy.[55]

On closer consideration, however, it seems that Taylor is uncertain whether the modern 'disengaged' epistemological and moral standpoint is achievable but undesirable, or simply not possible at all. He states, for example: 'Even to find out about the world and formulate disinterested pictures, we have to come to grips with it, experiment, set ourselves to observe, control conditions. But in all this, which forms the indispensable basis of theory, we are engaged as agents coping with things.'[56] Here Taylor does not seem to dispute the human capacity to formulate 'disinterested pictures', merely to resist the over-generalizing of the ontology which they imply. But if this is the case, it would not be the belief in the possibility of detachment, but merely the belief that the 'monological observer's standpoint' is 'the way things really are with the subject' which would be 'catastrophically wrong'.[57] Indeed, on this construal, what Taylor terms the 'punctual view of the self' must capture at least *part* of 'the way things are with the subject', and it is this which he often appears reluctant to admit.

In the light both of these difficulties, and of the complementary difficulties faced by Habermas in distributing the detached and the situated subject between different socio-ontological domains, the philosophical power of Lacan's conception of the subject becomes clearer. For Lacan elaborates a performative, or 'transcendental–pragmatic', rereading of the Cartesian demonstration of the existence of the subject, but at the same time he does not consider this subject as a participant in a 'transcendental language game' whose distinctive structure can be identified (Apel), or – in Taylor's terms – as 'ideally disengaged, that is, free and rational to the extent that he has fully distinguished himself from his natural and social worlds. . . .'[58] Rather, the presupposition of a 'subject of the utterance' [*sujet de l'énoncé*], who is the non-empirical subject ultimately responsible for the production of the statement [*énonciation*], is made necessary by the fact that human communication essentially raises validity-claims which transcend all particular contexts. In other words, the subject's speech in its performative dimension raises a claim to 'truth' (as authenticity) whose normativity is not grounded in convention but, rather, has transcendental force.

Thus, while Lacan would agree with those critics of Habermas who deny that the ideal speech situation can be viewed as the final site of cognitive and moral truth, he would do so not because of a fashionably contextualist constriction of the scope of cognitive truth but, rather, because of a *de*-limitation of truth as 'authenticity' (the truth of the subject). Habermas has claimed: 'The individual gains reflexive distance from her own life history only within the horizon of forms of life which she shares with others, and which in turn form the context for different specific life projects.'[59] Accordingly, he also stresses that authenticity itself is a culturally specific ideal.[60] For Lacan, by contrast, once the Cartesian breakthrough has been made, the subject may always find itself confronted, at the unconscious level of enunciation, with the question of whether *any* construal of the predominant, culturally accepted ideals would make possible an authentic self-realization.

Undoubtedly, Habermas would be tempted to reject this question as meaningless. For him, the issue of the subject's identity, and thus of what its 'good' might be, becomes downright unposable once one abstracts from every social and cultural horizon. And here we reach the heart of the divergence between Habermas and Lacan. For Lacan contends that the experience of psychoanalysis reveals a subject who, at the level of the unconscious, obstinately questions her existence beyond any culturally specific horizon of meaning. The subject is engaged in a questioning 'not of the place of the subject in the world, but of his existence as subject, a questioning which beginning with himself, will extend to his in-the-world relation to objects, and to the existence of the world, insofar as it, too, may be questioned beyond its order'.[61] Lacan does not deny, of course, that this questioning will be formulated in terms of the symbolic repertoire of a specific culture, but his formulations imply that what is at issue is – in part, at least – the relation of the subject to *any* symbolic repertoire in general, and thus the problem of the finitude of its self-realization *as* subject.

Support for Lacan's conception can be found in many other currents of contemporary psychoanalysis. The Freudian Oedipus complex, for example, is increasingly coming to be understood by analysts in terms of the child's confrontation with the trauma of having to be *either* male *or* female, while perverse sexual scenarios are consequently viewed as the outcome of the failure to confront this trauma successfully. Thus Louise Kaplan writes in her recent book *Female Perversions*: 'The fundamental wish in perversion is to obliterate all knowledge of the differences between the child and adult generations. The perverse adolescent or adult will arrange his perverse scenario so that he may live forever in the never-never land where there are no real differences between the sexes and no difference between infantile sexuality and adult sexuality.'[62] And she concludes that it is 'The despair of having to be only one sex, the terror of the finitude of living only one life, ageing, and dying, the infantile anxieties of annihilation, abandonment, separation and castration' which are 'held in abeyance by a perverse enactment'.[63]

But paradoxically, only a being which is not entirely enclosed by its own finitude can experience the terror of being entirely enclosed by its own finitude. And if the modern subject is not to 'forget his own existence and his death, and at the same time to misconstrue the particular meaning of his life in false communication',[64] this acknowledgement of the limit of truth-as-authenticity must itself be included in the claim to truth-as-authenticity which the discourse of the subject necessarily raises. Recently, Richard Rorty has claimed of Freud that his *only* utility lies in his ability to turn us away from the universal to the concrete, from the attempt to find necessary truths, ineliminable beliefs, to the idiosyncratic contingencies of our individual pasts, to the blind impress all our behavings bear'.[65] But against this, and in the wake of Lacan, one could rather claim Freud's teaching to be that we experience ourselves as subjects stretched painfully *between* the concrete and the universal, between the idiosyncratic contingency of our pasts and ineluctable truths, indispensable beliefs. Indeed, perhaps it is psychoanalysis, running counter to the deflationist and contextualist trend which Rorty so vividly represents, which has inherited the ancient philosophical task of asking who we are, and what we ultimately desire.

# Notes

1. '"Eating Well," or the Calculation of the Subject: An Interview with Jacques Derrida', in Eduardo Cadava, Peter Connor and Jean-Luc Nancy, eds, *Who Comes after the Subject?*, London: Routledge 1991, p. 97.

2. Ibid.

3. Louis Althusser, 'Ideology and Ideological State Apparatuses', in *Lenin and Philosophy and Other Essays*, London: New Left Books 1971, p. 160.

4. Michel Foucault, *L'ordre du discours*, Paris: Gallimard 1971, p. 49/'The Order of Discourse', in Robert Young, ed., *Untying the Text: A Poststructuralist Reader*, London: Routledge 1981, p. 65.

5. Jacques Lacan, *Le Séminaire livre I: Les écrits techniques de Freud*, Paris: Seuil 1975, p. 29/*The Seminar of Jacques Lacan: Book 1: Freud's Papers on Technique*, trans. John Forrester, Cambridge: Cambridge University Press 1988, p. 20–21.

6. Jacques Lacan, 'Propos sur la causalité psychique', in *Écrits*, Paris: Seuil 1966, p. 166.

7. Jacques Lacan, *Maurice Merleau-Ponty* (pirate edition), Paris, no date, p. 13/'Merleau-Ponty', in Keith Hoeller, ed., *Merleau-Ponty and Psychology*, Atlantic Highlands, NJ: Humanities Press 1993, p. 78.

8. Jacques Lacan, 'L'instance de la lettre dans l'inconscient', in *Écrits*, p. 498/'The Agency of the Letter in the Unconscious', in *Écrits: A Selection*, trans. A. Sheridan, London: Tavistock 1977, p. 150.

9. Jacques Derrida, *Of Grammatology*, trans. Gayatri Chakravorty Spivak, Baltimore, MD and London: Johns Hopkins University Press 1976, p. 14.

10. Jacques Lacan, *Le Séminaire livre I*, p. 126/*The Seminar of Jacques Lacan: Book 1*, p. 108.

11. Jacques Lacan, 'La chose freudienne', in *Écrits*, p. 414/'The Freudian Thing', in *Écrits: A Selection*, p. 126.

12. Jacques Lacan, 'Fonction et champ de la parole et du langage en psychanalyse', in *Écrits*, p. 297/'The Function and Field of Speech and Language in Psychoanalysis', in *Écrits: A Selection*, p. 84.

13. Jacques Lacan, 'Subversion du sujet et dialectique du désir dans l'inconscient freudien', in *Écrits*, p. 807/'Subversion of the Subject and Dialectic of Desire in the Freudian Unconscious', in *Écrits: A Selection*, p. 305.

14. Jacques Lacan, 'Le séminaire sur "La Lettre volée"', in *Écrits*, p. 20/'The Seminar on the "Purloined Letter"', in John P. Muller and William J. Richardson, eds, *The Purloined Poe*, Baltimore: Johns Hopkins University Press, p. 35.

15. Ibid. See also *The Four Fundamental Concepts of Psychoanalysis*, Harmondsworth: Peregrine 1986, p. 139.

16. 'Fonction et champ de la parole et du langage', p. 252/'The Function and Field of Speech and Language in Psychoanalysis', p. 43. The complete quotation runs: 'Même s'il ne communique rien, le discours représente l'existence de la communication; même s'il nie l'évidence, il affirme que la parole constitue la vérité; même s'il est destinée à tromper, il spécule sur la foi dans le témoignage.' ('Even if it communicates nothing, discourse represents the existence of communication; even if it denies the evidence, it affirms that speech constitutes truth; even if it is intended to deceive, it speculates on the faith in testimony.') See also 'Position de l'inconscient', *Écrits*, p. 839, where Lacan states: 'L'Autre est la dimension exigée de ce que la parole s'affirme en vérité' ('The Other is the dimension required by the fact that speech is affirmed in truth'), and many other passages in Lacan's work.

17. 'Dieser Friedenschluß bringt etwas mit sich, was wie der erste Schritt zur Erlangung jenes rätselhaften Wahrheitstriebes aussieht. Jetzt wird nämlich das fixiert, was von nun an "Wahrheit" sein soll, das heißt es wird eine gleichmäßig gültige und verbindliche Bezeichnung der Dinge erfunden und die Gesetzgebung der Sprache gibt auch die ersten Gesetzte der Wahrheit: denn es entsteht hier zum ersten Male der Kontrast von Wahrheit und Luge.' Friedrich Nietzsche, 'Über Wahrheit und Luge im äussermoralischen Sinne', in Giorgio Colli and Mazzino Montinari, eds, *Sämtliche Werke: Kritische Studienausgabe*, Berlin and New York: de Gruyter 1967–77, vol. 1, p. 877/'On Truth and Lies in a Nonmoral Sense', in *Philosophy and Truth: Selections from Nietzsche's Notebooks of the Early 1870s*, trans. and ed. Daniel Breazeale, Sussex: Harvester Press 1979, p. 81.

18. 'Die Menschen fliehen dabei das Betrogenwerden nicht so sehr, als das Beschädigtwerden durch Betrug. . . . In einem ähnlichen beschränkten Sinne will der Mensch auch nur die Wahrheit: er begehrt die angenehmen, Leben erhaltenden Folgen der Wahrheit, gegen die reine folgenlose Erkenntnis ist er gleichgültig, gegen die vielleicht schädlichen und zerstörenden Wahrheiten sogar feindlich gestimmt.' ('Human beings take flight not so much from the possibility of being deceived as from that of being harmed by deception . . . It is in a similarly restricted sense also that human beings want the truth; they desire the pleasant, life-sustaining consequences of truth, but are indifferent towards pure knowledge without practical consequences, and indeed are even hostile towards truths which may be damaging or destructive.') (Ibid.)

19. 'L'instance de la lettre', p. 525/'The Agency of the Letter in the Unconscious', pp. 172–3.

20. Jürgen Habermas, 'Nietzsches Erkenntnistheorie', in *Kultur und Kritik: Verstreute Aufsätze*, Frankfurt am Main: Suhrkamp 1973, p. 255.

21. Jürgen Habermas, 'Wahrheitstheorien', in *Vorstudien und Ergänzungen zur Theorie des kommunikativen Handelns*, Frankfurt am Main: Suhrkamp 1984, p. 134.

22. Ibid., p. 180.

23. 'Le séminaire sur "La Lettre volée"', p. 20/'The Seminar on the "Purloined Letter"', p. 35.

24. 'L'instance de la lettre', p. 525/'The Agency of the Letter in the Unconscious', p. 173.

25. Karl-Otto Apel, 'Das Problem einer philosophischen Theorie der Rationalitätstypen', in Herbert Schnädelbach, ed., *Rationalität: Philosophische Beiträge*, Frankfurt am Main: Suhrkamp 1984, pp. 27–8.

26. An important consequence of this account, of course, is that for Lacan the unconscious is essentially an intersubjective phenomenon: 'The unconscious is that part of the concrete discourse, in so far as it is transindividual, that is not at the disposal of the subject in reestablishing the continuity of his conscious discourse.' ('The Function and Field of Speech and Language in Psychoanalysis', p. 490.)

27. See Jürgen Habermas, 'Handlungen, Sprechakte, sprachlich vermittelte Interaktionen

und Lebenswelt', in *Nachmetaphysisches Denken*, Frankfurt am Main: Suhrkamp 1988, pp. 63–104.

28. I realize that the equation between Lacan's 'truth of the subject' and the concept of authenticity will seem to many an 'existentialist' betrayal of Lacanian psychoanalytic insights. However, Lacan himself makes use of the category of the authentic up until the mid 1950s ('Each time that a man speaks to another in a full and authentic manner there is, in the proper sense, a transference, a symbolic transference . . .': *The Seminar of Jacques Lacan: Book 1*, p. 109.) And even after this date, the notion of passing beyond illusion to confront that which ultimately defines the being of subject, in the form of the *objet petit a*, remains central. What else can the result of this confrontation be but that acceptance of oneself we call authenticity?

29. See Alessandro Ferrara, 'Authenticity and the Project of Modernity', *European Journal of Philosophy*, vol. 2, no. 3, December 1994, p. 243.

30. Charles Taylor, *Sources of the Self: The Making of the Modernity Identity*, Cambridge: Cambridge University Press 1989, p. 332.

31. 'In acts of self-presentation I do not assert anything about inner episodes, I make no statement at all, but rather I express an experience.' See 'Wahrheitstheorien', p. 157.

32. Jacques Lacan, 'Variantes de la cure-type', in *Écrits*, p. 352.

33. Ibid., p. 351.

34. Jacques Lacan, *Le Séminaire livre III: Les psychoses*, Paris: Seuil 1981, p. 49/*The Seminar of Jacques Lacan: Book 3: The Psychoses*, trans. Russell Grigg, London: Routledge 1993, p. 38.

35. 'Variantes de la cure-type', p. 353.

36. See Jürgen Habermas, 'On the Pragmatic, the Ethical, and the Moral Employments of Practical Reason', in *Justification and Application*, trans. Ciaran Cronin, Cambridge: Polity Press 1993, pp. 1–17. In earlier writings Habermas reserved the term 'authenticity' primarily for the distinctive claim to expressive validity of the work of art. More recently, he has corrected this overly subjectivist account of the aesthetic and reimported the resulting concept of authenticity as the achieved metaphorical interplay of validity-claims back into the ethical-existential domain. Here it seems to connote an absence of aesthetic, moral or cognitive one-sidedness or 'reification'.

37. See 'Wahrheitstheorien', pp. 182–3.

38. See Jürgen Habermas, *The Philosophical Discourse of Modernity*, trans. Frederick Lawrence, Cambridge, MA: MIT Press 1988, ch. 11.

39. See Jürgen Habermas, 'Treffen Hegels Einwände gegen Kant auch auf die Diskursethik zu?', in *Erläuterungen zur Diskursethik*, Frankfurt am Main: Suhrkamp 1991, pp. 33–6/'Morality and Ethical Life: Does Hegel's Critique of Kant Apply to Discourse Ethics?', in *Moral Consciousness and Communicative Action*, trans. Christian Lenhardt and Shierry Weber Nicholsen, Cambridge: Polity Press 1992, pp. 201–3.

40. See Jürgen Habermas, 'Exkurs: Transzendenz von innen, Transzendenz ins Diesseits', in *Texte und Kontexte*, Frankfurt am Main: Suhrkamp 1991.

41. See Karl-Otto Apel, 'The Problem of Philosophical Foundations in Light of a Transcendental Pragmatics of Language', in K. Baynes, J. Bohman and T. McCarthy, eds, *After Philosophy: End or Transformation?*, Cambridge, MA: MIT Press 1987, pp. 272–83.

42. Jacques Lacan, 'La science et la vérité', in *Écrits*, pp. 856–7.

43. Ibid., p. 857.

44. Jacques Lacan, 'Le stade du miroir', in *Écrits*, p. 93/'The Mirror Stage', in *Écrits: A Selection*, p. 1.

45. *The Four Fundamental Concepts of Psychoanalysis*, pp. 140–41.

46. 'Position de l'inconscient', in *Écrits*, p. 831.

47. For further discussion of Lacan's relation to Descartes, see Bernard Baas and Armand Zaloszyc, *Descartes et les fondements de la psychanalyse*, Paris: Navarin 1988, esp. chs 1–3.

48. Martin Seel, 'Die zwei Bedeutungen "kommunikativer" Rationalität', in Axel Honneth and Hans Joas, eds, *Kommunikatives Handeln*, Frankfurt am Main: Suhrkamp 1986, p. 57/'The Two Meanings of Communicative Rationality', in Axel Honneth and Hans Joas, eds, *Communicative Action*, trans. A. Gaines and Doris L. Jones, Cambridge: Polity Press 1991, p. 39.

49. Ibid., p. 58.

50. In *Reason, Truth and History* (Cambridge: Cambridge University Press 1981), Hilary Putnam suggests that 'according to the watered-down operationism which seems to have become the working philosophy of most scientists, the content of the scientific theory consists in testable consequences, and these can be expressed in statements of the form *if we perform such and such actions, then we will get such and such observable results*' (p. 178).

51. See Charles Taylor, 'Theories of Meaning', in *Human Agency and Language: Philosophical Papers 1*, Cambridge: Cambridge University Press 1985.

52. Ibid., p. 269.

53. Charles Taylor, 'The Concept of a Person', in *Philosophical Papers 1*, pp. 112–31.

54. Charles Taylor, 'Overcoming Epistemology', in *After Philosophy*, p. 477.

55. See *Sources of the Self*, pp. 85–7.

56. 'Overcoming Epistemology', p. 476.

57. Charles Taylor, *Philosophy and the Human Sciences: Philosophical Papers 2*, Cambridge: Cambridge University Press 1985, p. 258.

58. 'Overcoming Epistemology', p. 471.

59. 'On the Pragmatic, the Ethical, and the Moral Employments of Practical Reason', p. 11.

60. 'My identity is only responsive to – even at the mercy of – the reflexive pressure of an altered self-understanding if it observes the same standards of authenticity as ethical-existential discourse itself. Such a discourse already presupposes, on the part of the addressee, a striving to live an authentic life – or the suffering of a patient who has become conscious of the "sickness unto death".' (Ibid., p. 12.)

61. Jacques Lacan, 'D'un question préliminaire à tout traitement possible de la psychose', in *Écrits*, p. 550/'On a Question Preliminary to any Possible Treatment of Psychosis', in *Écrits: A Selection*, pp. 194–5.

62. Louise Kaplan, *Female Perversions*, Harmondsworth: Penguin 1993, p. 128.

63. Ibid., p. 361.

64. 'Fonction et champ de la parole et du langage', p. 282/'The Function and Field of Speech and Language in Psychoanalysis', p. 70.

65. Richard Rorty, *Contingency, Irony and Solidarity*, Cambridge: Cambridge University Press 1989, p. 34.

# Sources and Acknowledgements

Chapter 1 was first published in *New Left Review* 157, May/June 1986. It was subsequently included in Andrew Benjamin, ed., *Problems of Modernity: Adorno and Benjamin*, London: Routledge 1989; in Jay Bernstein, ed., *The Frankfurt School: Critical Assessments*, London: Routledge 1994, vol. 4; and in Slavoj Žižek, ed., *Mapping Ideology*, London: Verso 1994.

Chapter 2 is an amended version of an essay which was first published in *History of European Ideas*, vol. 14, no. 3, 1992.

Chapter 3 was written under the title 'Die Historisierung der analytischen Philosophie', and was published in the *Philosophische Rundschau*, vol. 41, no. 1, March 1994. It is translated here by the author.

Chapter 4 was first published in David Krell and David Wood, eds, *Exceedingly Nietzsche*, London: Routledge 1988.

Chapter 5 is a considerably revised version of an essay which was first published under the title 'Writing in the Lifeworld: Deconstruction as Paradigm of a Transition from Modernity to Postmodernity', in Francis Barker, Peter Hulme and Margaret Iverson, eds, *Postmodernism and the Re-reading of Modernity*, Manchester: Manchester University Press 1992.

Chapter 6 is previously unpublished.

Chapter 7 is a slightly expanded version of an essay written under the title 'Lebenswelt, Metaphysik und Naturethik bei Habermas', and published in Dieter Steiner and Wolfgang Zierhofer, eds, *Vernunft angesichts der Umweltzerstörung*, Opladen: Westdeutscher Verlag 1994. It is translated here by the author.

Chapter 8 is previously unpublished.

Chapter 9 was first published under the title 'Agreeing what's Right' in the *London Review of Books*, vol. 15, no. 9, 13 May 1993. It has appeared in a

German translation in the *Deutsche Zeitschrift für Philosophie*, vol. 41, no. 2, 1993, under the title 'Faktizität, Geltung und Öffentlichkeit', and in a Norwegian translation in Torben Hviid Nielsen, ed., *Tidens verdier: Variasjoner over moral og samfunn*, Oslo: Universitetsvorlaget 1994, under the title 'Faktisitet og gyldighet'. It is also included under the title 'Agreeing What's Right: Jürgen Habermas's *Faktizität und Geltung*' in Jay Bernstein, ed., *The Frankfurt School: Critical Assessments*, London: Routledge 1994, vol. 4.

Chapter 10 was first published as a critical notice under the title 'Morality, Ethics and "Postmetaphysical Thinking": Recent Books by Jürgen Habermas', in the *International Journal of Philosophical Studies*, vol. 3, no. 1, March 1995.

Chapter 11 is a revised version of an essay which was first published in Harry Kunneman and Hent de Vries, eds, *Enlightenments: Encounters between Critical Theory and Contemporary French Thought*, Kampen, the Netherlands: Kok Pharos 1993. The present version was first published in Anthony Elliott and Stephen Frosh, eds, *Psychoanalysis in Contexts: Paths between Theory and Contemporary Culture*, London: Routledge 1995.

Chapter 12 was first published in *Radical Philosophy* 71, July–August 1995.

Chapter 13 also appears in Simon Critchley and Peter Dews, eds, *Deconstructive Subjectivities*, Albany, NY: SUNY Press 1996.

I would like to thank all copyright holders for permission to reprint copyright material here.

# Bibliography

Adorno, Theodor, 'Psychology and Sociology', *New Left Review* 47, January–February 1967.
—— *Zur Metakritik der Erkenntnistheorie*, Frankfurt am Main: Suhrkamp 1970/*Against Epistemology*, trans. Willis Domingo, Oxford: Blackwell 1982.
—— *Negative Dialectics*, trans. E.B. Ashton, New York: Continuum 1973.
—— and Max Horkheimer, 'Odysseus or Myth and Enlightenment' (new trans. by Robert Hullot-Kentnor), *New German Critique*, no. 56, Spring/Summer 1992.
Althusser, Louis, 'Ideology and Ideological State Apparatuses', in *Lenin and Philosophy and Other Essays*, London: New Left Books 1971.
André, Serge, *Que veut une femme?*, Paris: Navarin 1986.
Andreski, Stanislav, ed., *The Essential Comte*, London: Croom Helm 1974.
Apel, Karl-Otto, 'Das Problem einer philosophischen Theorie der Rationalitätstypen', in Herbert Schnädelbach, ed., *Rationalität: Philosophische Beiträge*, Frankfurt am Main: Suhrkamp 1984.
—— 'The Problem of Philosophical Foundations in Light of a Transcendental Pragmatics of Language', in K. Baynes, J. Bohman and T. McCarthy, eds, *After Philosophy: End or Transformation?*, Cambridge, MA: MIT Press 1987.
—— 'Verantwortung heute – nur noch Prinzip der Bewahrung und Selbstbeschränkung oder immer noch der Befreiung und Verwirklichung von Humanität?', in *Diskurs und Verantwortung*, Frankfurt am Main: Suhrkamp 1992.
Austin, J.L., *How to Do Things with Words*, Oxford: Oxford University Press 1962.
Baas, Bernard and Armand Zaloszyc, *Descartes et les fondements de la psychanalyse*, Paris: Navarin 1988.
Bachelard, Gaston, *L'activité rationaliste de la physique contemporaine*, Paris: PUF 1951.
—— 'L'actualité de l'histoire des sciences', in *L'engagement rationaliste*, Paris: PUF 1972.
—— *La philosophie du non*, Paris: PUF 1975/*The Philosophy of No*, trans. G.C. Waterston, New York: The Orion Press 1968.
—— *Le rationalisme appliqué*, Paris: Vrin 1975.
—— *La formation de l'esprit scientifique*, Paris: Vrin 1977.
—— *Le nouvel esprit scientifique*, Paris: PUF 1978/*The New Scientific Spirit*, trans. A. Goldhammer, Boston: Beacon Press 1984.
—— 'Discursive Idealism', *Graduate Faculty Philosophy Journal*, vol. 1, no. 2, Spring 1978.
—— *La poétique de la rêverie*, Paris: PUF 1978/*The Poetics of Reverie*, trans. Daniel Russell, Boston: Beacon Press 1971.

Baudrillard, Jean, *Simulacres et simulation*, Paris: Galilée 1981/*Simulacra and Simulation*, trans. Sheila Faria Glaser, Ann Arbor, MI: University of Michigan Press 1994.

Beiser, Frederick, *The Fate of Reason: German Philosophy from Kant to Fichte*, Cambridge, MA: Harvard University Press 1987.

Benhabib, Seyla and Drucilla Cornell, eds, *Feminism as Critique*, Cambridge: Polity Press 1987.

Benjamin, Jessica, 'Authority and the Family Revisited: or, A World without Fathers', *New German Critique*, no. 13, 1978.

—— *The Bonds of Love*, London: Virago 1990.

—— 'Sameness and Difference: Toward an "Over-inclusive" Model of Gender Development', in Anthony Elliott and Stephen Frosh, eds, *Psychoanalysis in Contexts*, London: Routledge 1995.

Bernasconi, Robert, 'Deconstruction and Scholarship', *Man and World*, vol. 21, 1988.

Bernstein, J. M., 'The Causality of Fate: Modernity and Modernism in Habermas', *Praxis International*, vol. 8, no. 4, January 1989.

Black, Max, 'Metaphor', in *Models and Metaphors*, Ithaca, NY: Cornell University Press 1962.

Borch-Jacobsen, Mikkel, *Lacan: The Absolute Master*, Stanford, CA: Stanford University Press 1991.

—— 'The Oedipus Problem in Freud and Lacan', *Critical Inquiry*, vol. 20, no. 2, Winter 1994.

Borges, Jorge Luis, 'The Fauna of Mirrors', in *The Book of Imaginary Beings*, Harmondsworth: Penguin 1974.

Bowie, Andrew, *Schelling and Modern European Philosophy: An Introduction*, London: Routledge 1993.

Brumlik, Micha, 'Über die Ansprüche Ungeborener und Unmündiger. Wie advokatorisch ist die Diskursethik?', in Wolfgang Kuhlmann, ed., *Moralität und Sittlichkeit*, Frankfurt am Main: Suhrkamp 1986.

Bubner, Rüdiger, 'Kant, Transcendental Arguments and the Problem of Deduction', *Review of Metaphysics*, vol. 28, no. 3, March 1975.

Canguilhem, Georges, *La formation du concept de réflexe aux XVII^e et XVIII^e siècles*, Paris: PUF 1955.

—— *La connaissance de la vie*, Paris: Vrin 1965.

—— *Le normal et le pathologique*, Paris: PUF 1966/*The Normal and the Pathological*, trans. Carolyn R. Fawcett and Robert S. Cohen, New York: Zone Books 1991.

—— 'L'objet de l'histoire des sciences', in *Études d'histoire et de philosophie des sciences*, Paris: Vrin 1968.

—— 'De la science et de la contre-science', in Suzanne Bachelard *et al.*, *Hommage à Jean Hyppolite*, Paris: PUF 1971.

—— *Idéologie et rationalité dans l'histoire des sciences de la vie*, Paris: Vrin 1977.

Caruso, Paolo, *Conversazione con Lévi-Strauss, Foucault, Lacan*, Milan: V. Murcia and Co. 1969

Cavell, Stanley, 'What Did Derrida Want of Austin?', in *Philosophical Passages: Wittgenstein, Emerson, Austin, Derrida* (The Bucknell Lectures in Literary Theory, vol. 12), Oxford: Blackwell 1994.

—— 'Seminar on "What Did Derrida Want of Austin"', in *Philosophical Passages*.

Chomsky, Noam and Michel Foucault, 'Human Nature: Justice versus Power', in Fons Elders, ed., *Reflexive Water*, London: Souvenir Press 1974.

Christ, Kurt, *Jacobi und Mendelssohn: Eine Analyse des Spinozastreits*, Würzburg: Königshausen & Neuman 1988.

Cousins, Mark and Athar Hussein, *Michel Foucault,* London: Macmillan 1984.

Dallmayr, Fred, 'The Discourse of Modernity: Hegel, Nietzsche, Heidegger (and Habermas)', *Praxis International,* vol. 8, no. 4, January 1989.

Davidson, Donald, 'What Metaphors Mean', in *Enquiries into Truth and Interpretation,* Oxford: Clarendon Press 1984.

Derrida, Jacques, *De la grammatologie,* Paris: Éditions de Minuit 1967/*Of Grammatology,* trans. Gayatri Chakravorty Spivak, Baltimore, MD and London: Johns Hopkins University Press 1976.

—— *La voix et le phénomène,* Paris: PUF 1967/ *Speech and Phenomena,* trans. D. Allison, Evanston, IL: Northwestern University Press 1973.

—— 'Hors Livre', in *Dissémination,* Paris: Seuil 1972/'Outwork', in *Dissemination,* trans. Barbara Johnson, London: Athlone Press 1981.

—— *Marges de la philosophie,* Paris: Éditions de Minuit 1972/*Margins of Philosophy,* trans. Alan Bass, Sussex: Harvester Press 1982.

—— 'La différance', in *Marges de la philosophie.*

—— 'Les fins de l'homme', in *Marges de la philosophie.*

—— 'La mythologie blanche', in *Marges de la philosophie.*

—— 'Ousia et grammē', in *Marges de la philosophie.*

—— 'Signature, évènement, contexte' in *Marges de la philosophie*/'Signature, Event, Context', in *Limited Inc.*, trans. S. Weber, Evanston, IL: Northwestern University Press 1988.

—— *Positions,* Paris: Éditions de Minuit 1972/*Positions,* trans. Alan Bass, London: Athlone Press 1981.

—— *La vérité en peinture,* Paris: Flammarion 1978/*The Truth in Painting,* trans. Geoff Bennington and Ian McLeod, Chicago: University of Chicago Press 1987.

—— *Edmund Husserl's Origin of Geometry: An Introduction,* Stony Brook, NY: N. Hays 1978.

—— *Writing and Difference,* trans. Alan Bass, London: Routledge 1978.

—— 'Cogito and the History of Madness', in *Writing and Difference.*

—— 'Structure, Sign and Play in the Discourse of the Human Sciences', in *Writing and Difference.*

—— *La carte postale,* Paris: Flammarion 1980/*The Post Card: From Socrates to Freud and Beyond,* trans. Alan Bass, Chicago: University of Chicago Press 1987.

—— 'An interview with Jacques Derrida', in David Wood and Robert Bernasconi, eds, *Derrida and Différance,* Warwick University: Parousia Press 1985.

—— *Psyché: inventions de l'autre,* Paris: Galilée 1987.

—— 'Comment ne pas parler', in *Psyché.*

—— 'Le retrait de la métaphore', in *Psyché*/'The *retrait* of metaphor', *Enclitic,* vol. 2, no. 2, Fall 1978.

—— 'The Politics of Friendship', *Journal of Philosophy,* vol. 45, 1988.

—— 'Afterword', in *Limited Inc.*

—— '"Eating Well," or the Calculation of the Subject: An Interview with Jacques Derrida', in Eduardo Cadava, Peter Connor and Jean-Luc Nancy, eds, *Who Comes after the Subject?,* London: Routledge 1991.

—— 'Force of Law: The "Mystical Foundation of Authority"', in Drucilla Cornell, Michel Rosenfeld and David Gray Carlson, eds, *Deconstruction and the Possibility of Justice,* London and New York: Routledge 1992.

—— 'Philosophy and Communication: Round-table Discussion between Ricoeur and Derrida', appendix to Leonard Lawlor, *Imagination and Chance: The Difference between the Thought of Ricoeur and Derrida,* Albany, NY: SUNY Press 1992.

Derrida, Jacques, *Spectres de Marx*, Paris: Galilée 1993/*Specters of Marx*, trans. Peggy Kamuf, New York: Routledge 1994.

Dews, Peter, *Logics of Disintegration*, London: Verso 1987.

—— ed., *Autonomy and Solidarity: Interviews with Jürgen Habermas*, London: Verso (revised edn) 1992.

Dummett, Michael, *The Origins of Analytic Philosophy*, London: Duckworth 1993.

Farias, Victor, *Heidegger and Nazism*, trans. Paul Burrell, Philadelphia, PA: Temple University Press 1989.

Ferrara, Alessandro, 'Authenticity and the Project of Modernity', *European Journal of Philosophy*, vol. 2, no. 3, December 1994.

Feuerbach, Ludwig, 'Über den "Anfang der Philosophie"', in Wilhelm Bolin and Friedrich Jodl, eds, *Sämtliche Werke*, 2nd edn, Stuttgart: Frommann-Holzboog 1956, vol. 2.

—— 'Grundsätze der Philosophie der Zukunft', in *Theorie Werkausgabe*, Frankfurt am Main: Suhrkamp 1975, vol. 3/*Principles of the Philosophy of the Future*, Indianapolis: Hackett 1986.

Fichte, Johann Gottlieb, 'Die Wissenschaftslehre in ihrem allgemeinen Umrisse (1810)', in I.H. Fichte, ed., *Fichtes Werke*, Berlin and New York: de Gruyter 1971, vol. 2/'The Science of Knowledge in General Outline (1810)', trans. Walter E. Wright, *Idealistic Studies*, no. 6, 1976.

—— 'Second Introduction to the Science of Knowledge', in Peter Heath and John Lachs, eds, *The Science of Knowledge*, Cambridge: Cambridge University Press 1982.

—— *Wissenschaftslehre nova methodo* (lecture transcript of K. Chr. Fr. Krause 1798/9), Hamburg: Felix Meiner Verlag 1982/*Foundations of Transcendental Philosophy (Wissenschaftslehre) nova methodo*, trans. Daniel Breazeale, Ithaca: Cornell University Press 1992.

Fink-Eitel, Hinrich, *Dialektik und Sozialethik: Kommentierende Untersuchungen zu Hegels 'Logik'*, Meisenheim: Anton Hain 1978.

Fish, Stanley, 'With the compliments of the author: reflections on Austin and Derrida', *Critical Enquiry*, no. 8, Summer 1982.

Förster, Eckhart, 'How are Transcendental Arguments Possible?', in Eva Schaper and Wilhelm Vossenkuhl, eds, *Reading Kant*, Oxford: Blackwell 1989.

Foucault, Michel, 'Préface', in *Histoire de la folie à l'âge classique,* Paris: Gallimard 1961.

—— 'La Pensée du dehors', *Critique*, no. 229, 1966/'Maurice Blanchot: The Thought from Outside', trans. Brian Massumi, in *Foucault/Blanchot*, New York: Zone Books 1987.

—— 'Réponse au cercle d'épistémologie', *Cahiers pour l'analyse*, no. 9, Summer 1968.

—— *L'ordre du discours,* Paris: Gallimard 1971/'The Order of Discourse', in Robert Young, ed., *Untying the Text: A Poststructuralist Reader*, London: Routledge 1981.

—— *The Archaeology of Knowledge*, trans. A. Sheridan, London: Tavistock 1972.

—— *The Birth of the Clinic*, trans. A. Sheridan, London: Tavistock 1973.

—— *The Order of Things,* trans. A. Sheridan, London: Tavistock 1974.

—— *Discipline and Punish*, trans. A. Sheridan, Harmondsworth: Peregrine 1977.

—— *Language, Counter-memory, Practice*, ed. Donald Bouchard, Oxford: Blackwell 1977.

—— 'Nietzsche, Genealogy, History', in *Language, Counter-memory, Practice.*

Foucault, Michel, 'Georges Canguilhem: Philosopher of Error', *Ideology and Consciousness*, no. 7, Autumn 1980.
—— *The History of Sexuality: Volume 1: An Introduction,* Harmondsworth: Pelican 1981.
—— 'Structuralism and Post-Structuralism: an Interview with Michel Foucault', *Telos*, no. 55, Spring 1983.
—— *L'usage des plaisirs*, Paris: Gallimard 1984/*The Use of Pleasure*, trans. Robert Hurley, New York: Pantheon 1985.
—— 'Un cours inédit', *Magazine littéraire*, no. 207, May 1984/'Kant on Enlightenment and Revolution', trans. Colin Gordon, *Economy and Society*, vol. 15, 1986.
Frank, Manfred, *Der unendliche Mangel an Sein: Schellings Hegelkritik und die Anfänge der marxschen Dialektik*, Frankfurt am Main: Suhrkamp 1975.
—— *Was ist Neo-Structuralismus?*, Frankfurt am Main: Suhrkamp 1984/*What is Neo-Structuralism?*, trans. Sabine Wilke and Richard Gray, Minneapolis: Minnesota University Press 1989.
—— *Die Unhintergehbarkeit der Individualität*, Frankfurt am Main: Suhrkamp 1986.
—— *Zeitbewußtsein*, Pfullingen: Neske 1990.
Freud, Sigmund, *Inhibitions, Symptoms and Anxiety*, in *On Psychopathology*, Pelican Freud Library vol. 10, Harmondsworth: Penguin 1979.
Gadamer, Hans-Georg, *Wahrheit und Methode*, Tübingen: J.C.B. Mohr 1960/*Truth and Method*, trans. William Glen-Doepel, London: Sheed & Ward 1979.
—— 'Anmerkungen zu dem Thema "Hegel und Heidegger"' in Hermann Braun and Manfred Riedel, eds, *Natur und Geschichte: Karl Löwith zum 70 Geburtstag*, Stuttgart, Berlin, Cologne, Mainz: W. Kohlhammer 1967.
Gasché, Rodolphe, *The Tain of the Mirror*, Cambridge, MA: Harvard University Press 1986.
—— 'Deconstruction as Criticism', in *Inventions of Difference: On Jacques Derrida*, Cambridge, MA: Harvard University Press 1994.
—— 'Yes Absolutely', in *Inventions of Difference.*
Gerhardt, Volker, 'Metaphysik und ihre kritik: Zur Metaphysikdebatte zwischen Jürgen Habermas und Dieter Henrich', *Zeitschrift für Philosophische Forschung*, vol. 2, no. 1, 1988.
Gutting, Gary, *Michel Foucault's Archaeology of Scientific Reason*, Cambridge: Cambridge University Press 1989.
Habermas, Jürgen, 'Arbeit und Interaktion. Bemerkungen zu Hegels Jenenser "Philosophie des Geistes"', in *Technik und Wissenschaft als Ideologie*, Frankfurt am Main: Suhrkamp 1968/'Labour and Interaction. Remarks on Hegel's Jena "Philosophy of Spirit"', in *Theory and Practice*, trans. J. Viertel, Cambridge: Polity Press 1989.
—— 'Nietzsches Erkenntnistheorie', in *Kultur und Kritik: Verstreute Aufsätze*, Frankfurt am Main: Suhrkamp 1973.
—— 'Walter Benjamin. Bewußtmachende oder rettende Kritik', in *Philosophisch-politische Profile*, Frankfurt am Main: Suhrkamp (2nd expanded edn) 1981/'Consciousness-raising or Pure Critique: The Contemporaneity of Walter Benjamin', *New German Critique*, no. 17, 1979.
—— *Theorie des kommunikativen Handelns*, vols 1 and 2, Frankfurt am Main: Suhrkamp 1981/*The Theory of Communicative Action, Volume 1*, trans. Thomas McCarthy, London: Heinemann 1984; *The Theory of Communicative Action, Volume 2*, trans. Thomas McCarthy, Cambridge: Polity Press 1987.

Habermas, Jürgen, 'A Reply to My Critics', in John B. Thompson and David Held, eds, *Habermas: Critical Debates*, London: Macmillan 1982.

—— *Moralbewußtsein und kommunikatives Handeln*, Frankfurt am Main: Suhrkamp 1983/*Moral Consciousness and Communicative Action*, trans. Christian Lenhardt and Shierry Weber, Cambridge: Polity Press 1992.

—— 'Treffen Hegels Einwände gegen Kant auch auf die Diskursethik zu?', in *Moralbewußtsein und kommunikatives Handeln*.

—— 'Wahrheitstheorien', in *Vorstudien und Ergänzungen zur Theorie des kommunikativen Handelns*, Frankfurt am Main: Suhrkamp 1984.

—— *Der Philosophische Diskurs der Moderne*, Frankfurt am Main: Suhrkamp 1985/*The Philosophical Discourse of Modernity*, trans. Frederick Lawrence, Cambridge, MA: MIT Press 1987.

—— *Nachmetaphysisches Denken*, Frankfurt am Main: Suhrkamp 1988/ *Postmetaphysical Thinking: Philosophical Essays*, trans. William Mark Hohengarten, Cambridge, MA: MIT Press 1992.

—— 'Handlungen, Sprechakte, sprachlich vermittelte Interaktionen und Lebenswelt', in *Nachmetaphysisches Denken*.

—— 'Metaphysik nach Kant', in *Nachmetaphysisches Denken*.

—— 'Rückkehr zur Metaphysik?' in *Nachmetaphysisches Denken*.

—— 'Motive nachmetaphysischen Denkens', in *Nachmetaphysisches Denken*.

—— *The Structural Transformation of the Public Sphere: An Enquiry into a Category of Bourgeois Society*, Cambridge: Polity Press 1989.

—— *Vergangenheit als Zukunft*, Zurich: Pendo Verlag 1990/*The Past as Future*, trans. and ed. Max Pensky, Lincoln, NB: University of Nebraska Press 1994.

—— *Erläuterungen zur Diskursethik*, Frankfurt am Main: Suhrkamp 1991/ *Justification and Application: Remarks on Discourse Ethics*, trans. Ciaran Cronin, Cambridge: Polity Press 1993.

—— 'Gerechtigkeit und Solidarität', in *Erläuterungen zur Diskursethik*.

—— 'On the Pragmatic, the Ethical, and the Moral Employments of Practical Reason', in *Justification and Application*.

—— 'To Seek to Salvage an Unconditional Meaning Without God is a Futile Undertaking: Reflections on a Remark of Max Horkheimer.' in *Justification and Application*.

—— 'Transzendenz von innen, Transzendenz ins Diesseits', in *Texte und Kontexte*, Frankfurt am Main: Suhrkamp 1991.

—— *Autonomy and Solidarity: Interviews,* ed. Peter Dews, London: Verso (revised edn) 1992.

—— 'Further Reflections on the Public Sphere', in Craig Calhoun, ed., *Habermas and the Public Sphere*, Cambridge, MA: MIT Press 1992.

—— *Faktizität und Geltung. Beiträge zur Diskurstheorie des Rechts und des demokratischen Rechtsstaats*, Frankfurt am Main: Suhrkamp 1992.

—— 'Martin Heidegger: On the Publication of the Lectures of 1935' (1953), in *The Heidegger Controversy: A Critical Reader*, ed. Richard Wolin, Cambridge, MA: MIT Press 1993.

Hegel, G. W. F., *Philosophy of Right*, trans. T.M. Knox, Oxford: Oxford University Press 1967.

—— *Philosophy of Mind. Part Three of the Encyclopaedia of the Philosophical Sciences*, trans. William Wallace and A.V. Miller, Oxford: Oxford University Press 1971.

—— *The Logic of Hegel* (the 'Encyclopaedia Logic'), trans. William Wallace, Oxford: Clarendon Press 1975.

Hegel, G.W.F., *Hegel's Lectures on the History of Philosophy*, trans. E.S. Haldane and Frances H. Simpson, Atlantic Highlands, NJ: Humanities Press 1975.
—— *Faith and Knowledge*, trans. Walter Cerf and H.S. Harris, Albany, NY: SUNY Press 1977.
—— *The Difference between Fichte's and Schelling's Systems of Philosophy*, trans. W. Cerf and H.S. Harris, Albany, NY: SUNY Press 1977.
—— *Phenomenology of Spirit*, trans. A.V. Miller, Oxford: Oxford University Press 1977.
—— *The Science of Logic*, trans. A.V. Miller, Atlantic Highlands, NJ: Humanities Press 1989.
Heidegger, Martin, *Sein und Zeit*, Tübingen: Niemeyer 1927/*Being and Time*, trans. John Macquarrie and Edward Robinson, Oxford: Blackwell 1978.
—— 'On the Way to Language', in *On the Way to Language*, New York: Harper & Row 1971.
—— 'Letter on Humanism', in *Basic Writings*, trans. and ed. David Krell, New York: Harper & Row 1977.
—— *The Principle of Reason*, trans. Reginald Lilly, Bloomington and Indianapolis: Indiana University Press 1991.
—— *Nietzsches Lehre vom Willen zur Macht als Erkenntnis, Gesamtausgabe*, vol. 47, Frankfurt am Main: Vittorio Klostermann 1989/*Nietzsche: Volume 3: The Will to Power as Knowledge and as Metaphysics*, trans. Frank A. Capuzzi, Joan Stambaugh and David Krell, San Francisco: Harper & Row 1979.
Henrich, Dieter, 'Selbstbewußtsein. Kritische Einleitung in eine Theorie', in R. Bubner *et al.*, eds, *Hermeneutik und Dialektik* (Festschrift für Hans-Georg Gadamer), Tübingen: J.C.B. Mohr 1970/'Self-consciousness: A Critical Introduction to a Theory', *Man and World*, vol. 4, 1971.
—— 'Hegel und Hölderlin', in *Hegel im Kontext*, Frankfurt am Main: Suhrkamp 1975.
—— 'Hegels Logik der Reflexion', in *Hegel im Kontext*.
—— 'Hegels Grundoperation', in U. Guzzoni *et al.*, eds, *Der Idealismus und seine Gegenwart*, Hamburg: Felix Meiner Verlag 1976.
—— 'Fichte's Original Insight', in Darrel Christensen *et al.*, eds, *Contemporary German Philosophy*, vol. 1, 1982.
—— 'Die Grundstruktur der modernen Philosophie', in *Selbstverhältnisse*, Stuttgart: Reclam 1982.
—— 'Glück und Not', in *Selbstverhältnisse*.
—— *Fluchtlinien*, Frankfurt am Main: Suhrkamp 1982.
—— 'Was ist Metaphysik – was Moderne? Zwölf Thesen gegen Jürgen Habermas', in *Konzepte*, Frankfurt am Main: Suhrkamp 1987.
—— 'Philosophy and the Conflict between Tendencies of Life', in *Konzepte*.
—— 'Noch einmal in Zirkeln: Eine Kritik von Ernst Tugendhats semantischer Erklärung von Selbstbewußtsein', in Clemens Bellut and Ulrich Müller-Scholl, eds, *Mensch und Moderne. Beiträge zur philosophischen Anthropologie und Gesellschaftskritik*, Würzburg: Königshausen & Neuman 1989.
—— 'The Origins of the Theory of the Subject', in Axel Honneth *et al.*, eds, *Philosophical Interventions in the Unfinished Project of Modernity*, Cambridge, MA: MIT Press 1992.
—— *Der Grund im Bewußtsein: Untersuchungen zu Hölderlins Denken*, Stuttgart: Klett-Cotta 1992.
Hogrebe, Wolfram, *Prädikation und Genesis. Metaphysik als Fundamentalheuristik im Ausgang von Schellings "Die Weltalter"*, Frankfurt am Main: Suhrkamp 1989.

Honneth, Axel, *Kritik der Macht*, Frankfurt am Main: Suhrkamp 1982/*The Critique of Power*, trans. Kenneth Baynes, Cambridge, MA: MIT Press 1991.

—— *The Struggle for Recognition: The Moral Grammar of Social Conflicts*, Cambridge: Polity Press 1995.

Hörisch, Jochen, 'Herrscherwort, Gott und geltende Sätze', in Burkhardt Lindner and W. Martin Lüdke, eds, *Materialien zur ästhetischen Theorie: Th. Adornos Konstruktion der Moderne*, Frankfurt am Main: Suhrkamp 1980.

Horkheimer, Max, 'Authority and the Family', in *Critical Theory: Selected Essays*, New York: Continuum 1972.

—— 'Autorität und Familie in der Gegenwart', in *Zur Kritik der instrumentellen Vernunft*, Frankfurt am Main: Fischer Verlag 1985.

—— 'Die Zukunft der Ehe', in *Zur Kritik der instrumentellen Vernunft*/'The Future of Marriage', in *Critique of Instrumental Reason*, trans. Matthew J. O'Connell, New York: Seabury Press 1974.

—— 'Vernunft und Selbsterhaltung' (1942), in *Traditionelle und kritische Theorie*, Frankfurt am Main: Fischer Verlag 1992.

Horstmann, Rolf-Peter, *Die Grenzen der Vernunft: Eine Untersuchung zu Zielen und Motiven des Deutschen Idealismus*, Frankfurt am Main: Anton Hain 1991.

Hösle, Vittorio, *Hegels System: Band 2: Philosophie der Natur und des Geistes*, Hamburg: Felix Meiner Verlag 1988.

Husserl, Edmund, *Die Krisis der europäischen Wissenschaften und die transzendentale Phänomenologie*, Husserliana VI, The Hague: Martinus Nijhoff 1962.

—— *Cartesian Meditations*, trans. Dorion Cairns, The Hague: Martinus Nijhoff 1973.

Hylton, Peter, *Russell, Idealism, and the Origins of Analytical Philosophy*, Oxford: Clarendon Press 1990.

Jacobi, Friedrich Heinrich, *Über die Lehre des Spinoza in Briefen an Herrn Moses Mendelssohn*, in F.H. Jacobi, *Werke* (reprographic reprint, Darmstadt: WBG 1980), vol. 4, parts 1 and 2.

—— 'Brief an Fichte', 3–21 March 1799, in Werner Röhr, ed., *Appellation an das Publikum: Dokumente zum Atheismusstreit Jena 1798/99*, Leipzig: Reclam 1991/'Open Letter to Fichte', in Ernst Behler, ed., *Philosophy of German Idealism*, New York: Continuum 1992.

Jameson, Fredric, 'Marx's Purloined Letter', *New Left Review* 209, January–February 1995.

Jay, Martin, *Adorno*, London: Fontana 1984.

Johnson, Pauline, 'Feminism and Images of Autonomy', *Radical Philosophy*, no. 50, Autumn 1988.

Jonas, Hans, *Materie, Geist und Schöpfung*, Frankfurt am Main: Suhrkamp 1988.

—— *Das Prinzip Verantworting*, Frankfurt am Main: Suhrkamp 1989/*The Imperative of Responsibility*, trans. Hans Jonas and David Herr, Chicago: University of Chicago Press 1984.

Kaplan, Louise, *Female Perversions*, Harmondsworth: Penguin 1993.

Kirschner, Gilbert, 'La conception de l'histoire de la philosophie de F.H. Jacobi', in Klaus Hammacher, ed., *Friedrich Heinrich Jacobi: Philosoph und Literat der Goethezeit*, Frankfurt am Main: Vittorio Klostermann 1971.

Kofman, Sarah, 'Un philosophe "unheimlich"', in Lucette Finas *et al.*, *Écarts: quatre essais à propos de Jacques Derrida*, Paris: Fayard 1973.

Krings, Hermann, 'Knowing and Thinking: On the Structure and History of the Transcendental Method in Philosophy', in Darrell E. Christensen *et al.*, eds, *Contemporary German Philosophy*, vol. 4, 1984.

Kristeva, Julia, 'Freud et l'amour: le malaise dans la cure', in *Histoires d'amour*, Paris: Éditions Denoël (paperback edn) 1983/'Freud and Love: Treatment and its Discontents', in *Tales of Love*, trans. Leon S. Roudiez, New York: Columbia University Press 1987.

Kuhn, Thomas, *The Structure of Scientific Revolutions,* Chicago: University of Chicago Press 1974.

Lacan, Jacques, *Écrits*, Paris: Seuil 1966/*Écrits: A Selection*, trans. A. Sheridan, London: Tavistock 1977.

—— 'La signification du phallus', in *Écrits.*

—— 'Propos sur la causalité psychique', in *Écrits.*

—— 'L'instance de la lettre dans l'inconscient', in *Écrits.*

—— 'La chose freudienne', in *Écrits.*

—— 'Fonction et champ de la parole et du langage en psychanalyse', in *Écrits.*

—— 'Subversion du sujet et dialectique du désir dans l'inconscient freudien', in *Écrits.*

—— 'Le séminaire sur "La Lettre volée"', in *Écrits*/'The seminar on "The Purloined Letter"', in J.P. Muller and W.J. Richardson, eds, *The Purloined Poe*, Baltimore, MD: Johns Hopkins University Press 1988.

—— 'La science et la vérité', in *Écrits.*

—— 'Le stade du miroir', in *Écrits.*

—— 'Position de l'inconscient', in *Écrits.*

—— 'D'un question préliminaire à tout traitement possible de la psychose', in *Écrits.*

—— 'Variantes de la cure-type', in *Écrits.*

—— 'Aggressivity in Psychoanalysis', in *Écrits: A Selection.*

—— 'Réponses à des étudiants en philosophie sur l'objet de la psychanalyse', *Cahiers pour l'analyse*, no. 3, May–June 1966.

—— *Le Séminaire livre XI: Les quatre concepts fondamentaux de la psychanalyse,* Paris: Seuil 1973/*The Four Fundamental Concepts of Psychoanalysis*, trans. A. Sheridan, Harmondsworth: Peregrine 1986.

—— *Le Séminaire livre XX: Encore*, Paris: Seuil 1975

—— *Le Séminaire livre I: Les écrits techniques de Freud*, Paris: Seuil 1975/*The Seminar of Jacques Lacan: Book 1: Freud's Papers on Technique*, trans. John Forrester, Cambridge: Cambridge University Press 1988.

—— *Le Séminaire livre III: Les psychoses*, Paris: Seuil 1981/*The Seminar of Jacques Lacan: Book 3: The Psychoses*, trans. Russell Grigg, London: Routledge 1993.

—— *Les complexes familiaux*, Paris: Navarin 1984.

—— *Maurice Merleau-Ponty* (pirate edn), Paris, no date/'Maurice Merleau-Ponty', in Keith Hoeller, ed., *Merleau-Ponty and Psychology*, Atlantic Highlands, NJ: Humanities Press 1993.

Lakatos, Imre, *The Methodology of Scientific Research Programmes: Philosophical Papers Volume 1*, Cambridge: Cambridge University Press 1978.

Laplanche, Jean, *Problématiques II: Castration. Symbolisations*, Paris: PUF 1980.

Lawlor, Leonard, *Imagination and Chance: The Difference between the Thought of Ricoeur and Derrida*, Albany, NY: SUNY Press 1992.

Lecourt, Dominique, *Pour une critique de l'épistémologie*, Paris: Maspero 1972.

Lévi-Strauss, Claude, *Structural Anthropology 2*, Harmondsworth: Penguin 1978.

Lewis, Charles, *Hegel's Critique of Reason*, PhD thesis, University of Cambridge 1978.

Lyotard, Jean-François, 'Contribution des tableaux de Jacques Monory', in Gérald Gassiot-Talabot *et al.*, *Figurations 1960/1973,* Paris: Union Générale d'Editions 1973.

Lyotard, Jean-François, *Économie libidinale,* Paris: Éditions de Minuit 1974/*Libidinal Economy*, trans. Iain Hamilton Grant, London: Athlone Press 1993.
—— *Instructions païennes*, Paris: Galilée 1977.
—— and Jean-Loup Thébaud, *Au Juste*, Paris: Christian Bourgois 1979/*Just Gaming*, trans. Wlad Godzich, Manchester: Manchester University Press 1985.
—— *La condition postmoderne*, Paris: Éditions de Minuit 1979/*The Postmodern Condition*, trans. Geoff Bennington and Brian Massumi, Manchester: Manchester University Press 1984.
—— *Le differénd*, Paris: Éditions de Minuit 1983/*The Differend*, trans. Georges Van Den Abbeele, Manchester: Manchester University Press 1988.
—— 'Presentations', in Alan Montefiore, ed., *Philosophy in France Today*, Cambridge: Cambridge University Press 1983.
Macann, Christopher, 'Jacques Derrida's Theory of Writing and the Concept of the Trace', *Journal of the British Society for Phenomenology*, vol. 3 no. 2, May 1972.
McCarthy, Thomas, 'Practical Discourse: On the Relation of Morality to Politics', in Craig Calhoun, ed., *Habermas and the Public Sphere*, Cambridge, MA: MIT Press 1992.
Marcuse, Herbert, *Counterrevolution and Revolt*, Boston: Beacon Press 1972.
Marković, Mihailo and Gajo Petrović, eds, *Praxis: Yugoslav Essays in the Philosophy and Methodology of the Social Sciences* (Boston Studies in the Philosophy of Science, vol. XXXVI), Dordrecht: Riedel 1979.
Marx, Karl, 'Critique of Hegel's Doctrine of the State', in *Early Writings*, Harmondsworth: Penguin 1975.
Mead, George Herbert, *Mind, Self and Society*, Chicago: University of Chicago Press 1962.
Menke, Christoph, 'Der "Wendepunkt" des Erkennens: Zu Begriff, Recht und Reichweite der Dialektik in Hegels *Logik*', in Christoph Demmerling and Friedrich Kambartel, eds, *Vernunftkritik nach Hegel*, Frankfurt am Main: Suhrkamp 1992.
Merleau-Ponty, Maurice, 'Le Philosophe et son Ombre', in *Éloge de la philosophie*, Paris: Gallimard 1960/'The Philosopher and his Shadow', in *Signs*, trans. Richard C. McCleary, Evanston, IL: Northwestern University Press 1964.
—— 'The Philosopher and Sociology', in John O'Neill, ed., *Phenomenology, Language and Sociology*, London: Heinemann Educational 1974.
Millot, Catherine, *Nobodaddy: L'hystérie dans le siècle*, Paris: Point Hors Ligne 1988.
Nagel, Thomas, 'The Subjective and the Objective', in *Mortal Questions*, Cambridge: Cambridge University Press 1979.
—— *The View from Nowhere*, New York: Oxford University Press 1986.
Nägele, Rainer, 'The Scene of the Other: Theodor W. Adorno's Negative Dialectic in the Context of Post-structuralism', *Boundary* 2, Fall – Winter 1982–3.
Nagl, Ludwig, 'Zeigt die Habermassche Kommunikationstheorie einen "Ausweg aus der Subjektphilosophie"? Erwägungen zur Studie "Der philosophische Diskurs der Moderne"' in M. Frank, G. Raulet and W. van Reijen, eds, *Die Frage nach dem Subjekt*, Frankfurt am Main: Suhrkamp 1988.
Nietzsche, Friedrich, *The Will to Power*, ed. Walter Kaufmann, New York: Vintage 1967.
—— 'Über Wahrheit und Lüge im aussermoralischen Sinne', in Giorgio Colli and Mazzino Montinari, eds, *Sämtliche Werke: Kritische Studienausgabe*, Berlin and New York: de Gruyter 1967–77, vol. 1/'On Truth and Lies in a Nonmoral Sense', in *Philosophy and Truth: Selections from Nietzsche's Notebooks of the Early 1870s*, trans. and ed. Daniel Breazeale, Sussex: Harvester Press 1979.

Nietzsche, Friedrich, *Die Geburt der Tragödie aus dem Geiste der Musik*, in *Sämtliche Werke: Kritische Studienausgabe*, vol. 1/*The Birth of Tragedy*, in *The Birth of Tragedy and The Case of Wagner*, trans. Walter Kaufmann, New York: Vintage 1967.

—— *Götzendämmerung*, in *Sämtliche Werke: Kritische Studienausgabe*, vol. 6/*The Twilight of the Idols*, trans. R.J. Hollingdale, Harmondsworth: Penguin 1968.

—— 'On the Uses and Disadvantages of History for Life', in *Untimely Meditations*, trans. R.J. Hollingdale, Cambridge: Cambridge University Press 1983.

Norris, Christopher, *Jacques Derrida*, London: Fontana 1987.

Ott, Hugo, *Martin Heidegger: A Political Life*, trans. Allan Blunden, London: HarperCollins 1993.

Pêcheux, Michel, 'Idéologie et l'histoire des sciences', in Michel Pêcheux and Michel Fichant, *Sur l'histoire des sciences*, Paris: Maspero 1971.

Putnam, Hilary, *Meaning and the Moral Sciences*, London: Routledge 1978.

—— *Reason, Truth and History*, Cambridge: Cambridge University Press 1981.

—— 'Vagueness and alternative logic', in *Realism and Reason: Philosophical Papers Volume 3*, Cambridge: Cambridge University Press 1983.

—— 'Realism with a Human Face', in *Realism with a Human Face*, Cambridge, MA: Harvard University Press 1992.

Ragland-Sullivan, Ellie, 'The Sexual Masquerade', in Ellie Ragland-Sullivan and Mark Bracher, eds, *Lacan and the Subject of Language*, London: Routledge 1991.

Richards, I. A. , *The Philosophy of Rhetoric*, New York: Oxford University Press 1965.

Ricoeur, Paul, *La métaphore vive*, Paris: Seuil 1975/*The Rule of Metaphor*, trans. Robert Czerny *et al.*, London: Routledge 1978.

—— 'Philosophy and Communication: Round-table Discussion between Ricoeur and Derrida', appendix to Leonard Lawlor, *Imagination and Chance: The Difference between the Thought of Ricoeur and Derrida*, Albany, NY: SUNY Press 1992.

Riedel, Manfred, ed., *Materialien zu Hegels Rechtsphilosophie*, vol 1, Frankfurt am Main: Suhrkamp 1975.

Ritter, Joachim, 'Hegel and the French Revolution', in *Hegel and the French Revolution: Essays on the Philosophy of Right*, Cambridge, MA: MIT Press 1984.

—— and Karlfried Gründer, eds, *Historisches Wörterbuch der Philosophie*, article on *Natura naturans/naturata*, Basel/Stuttgart: Schwabe 1984, vol. 6.

Rorty, Richard, *Consequences of Pragmatism*, Minneapolis: Minnesota University Press 1982.

—— 'The Historiography of Philosophy: Four Genres', in *Philosophy in History*, ed. Richard Rorty, J. B. Schneewind and Quentin Skinner, Cambridge: Cambridge University Press 1984.

—— *Contingency, Irony and Solidarity*, Cambridge: Cambridge University Press 1989.

—— *Philosophical Papers Volume 1: Objectivity, Relativism and Truth*, Cambridge: Cambridge University Press 1991.

—— *Philosophical Papers Volume 2: Essays on Heidegger and Others*, Cambridge: Cambridge University Press 1991.

—— 'Is Derrida a Transcendental Philosopher?', in *Philosophical Papers Volume 2*.

Rose, Jacqueline, 'Feminine Sexuality – Jacques Lacan and the *école freudienne*', in *Sexuality in the Field of Vision*, London: Verso 1986.
—— 'Negativity in the Work of Melanie Klein', in *Why War?*, Oxford: Blackwell 1993.
Ryan, Michael, *Marxism and Deconstruction,* Baltimore, MD: Johns Hopkins University Press 1982.
Sacks, Mark, 'Through a Glass Darkly: Vagueness in the Metaphysics of the Analytical Tradition', in David Bell and Neil Cooper, eds, *The Analytic Tradition*, Oxford: Blackwell 1990.
Salecl, Renata, 'Love: Providence or Despair', *New Formations*, no. 23, Summer 1994 (special issue on 'Lacan and Love').
Salomon, Jean-Jacques, 'Canguilhem et la modernité', *Revue de Métaphysique et de Morale*, vol. 90, no. 1, January–March 1985.
Schelling, Friedrich Wilhelm Joseph, *Sämmtliche Werke,* ed. K.F.A. Schelling, Stuttgart: Cotta 1856–61.
—— *Philosophical Inquiries into the Nature of Human Freedom*, trans. James Gutman, La Salle, IL: Open Court Classics 1936.
—— *The Ages of The World,* trans. Frederick de Wolfe Bolman Jr., New York: Columbia University Press 1942.
—— *Die Weltalter. Fragmente in den Urfassungen von 1811 und 1813*, ed. Manfred Schröter, Munich: Biederstein & Leibniz 1946.
—— 'Of the I as Principle of Philosophy', in Fritz Marti, trans. and ed., *The Unconditional in Human Knowledge*, Lewisburg, PA: Bucknell University Press 1980.
—— *System der gesammten Philosophie und der Naturphilosophie insbesondere*, in Manfred Frank, ed., *Ausgewählte Schriften*, Frankfurt am Main: Suhrkamp 1985, vol. 3/First part translated as 'System of Philosophy in General and of the Philosophy of Nature in Particular', in Thomas Pfau, ed., *Idealism and the Endgames of Theory: Three Essays by F.W.J. Schelling*, Albany, NY: SUNY Press 1994.
—— 'Die Weltalter. Erstes Buch. Die Vergangenheit. Druck I' (1811), in Manfred Frank, ed., *Ausgewählte Schriften*, vol. 4.
—— *On the History of Modern Philosophy*, trans. Andrew Bowie, Cambridge: Cambridge University Press 1994.
—— (possible attribution) 'The "Oldest System-Programme of German Idealism"', trans. Taylor Carman, *European Journal of Philosophy*, vol. 3, no. 2, August 1995.
Schmidt-Biggemann, Wilhelm, 'Sprung in die Metaphysik oder Fall ins Nichts: Eine Alternative im Pantheismusstreit', in *Theodizee und Tatsachen: Das Profil der Deutschen Auflärung*, Frankfurt am Main: Suhrkamp 1988.
Schnädelbach, Herbert, 'The Face in the Sand: Foucault and the Anthropological Slumber', in Axel Honneth *et al.*, eds, *Philosophical Interventions in the Unfinished Process of Enlightenment*, Cambridge, MA: MIT Press 1992.
—— 'Metaphysik und Religion heute', in *Zur Rehabilitierung des* animal rationale. *Vorträge und Abhandlungen 2*, Frankfurt am Main: Suhrkamp 1992.
Schulz, Walter, *Die Vollendung des Deutschen Idealismus in der Spätphilosophie Schellings*, Pfullingen: Neske 1955.
—— ed., *Fichte–Schelling: Briefwechsel*, Frankfurt am Main: Suhrkamp 1968.
—— 'Das Problem der absoluten Reflexion', in *Vernunft und Freiheit: Aufsätze und Vorträge*, Stuttgart: Reclam 1981.
Seel, Martin, 'Die zwei Bedeutungen "kommunikativer" Rationalität', in Axel

Honneth and Hans Joas, eds, *Kommunikatives Handeln*, Frankfurt am Main: Suhrkamp 1986/'The Two Meanings of Communicative Rationality', in Axel Honneth and Hans Joas, eds, *Communicative Action*, trans. A. Gaines and Doris L. Jones, Cambridge: Polity Press 1991.

—— *Eine Ästhetik der Natur*, Frankfurt am Main: Suhrkamp 1991.

Soldati, Gianfranco, 'Selbstbewußtsein und unmittelbares Wissen bei Tugendhat', in M. Frank, G. Raulet and W. van Reijen, eds, *Die Frage nach dem Subjekt*, Frankfurt am Main: Suhrkamp 1988.

Spinosa, Charles, 'Derrida and Heidegger: Iterability and *Ereignis*' in Hubert L. Dreyfus and Harrison Hall, eds, *Heidegger: A Critical Reader*, Oxford: Blackwell 1992.

Steinkamp, Fiona, 'Différance and Indifference', *Journal of the British Society for Phenomenology*, vol. 22, no. 3, October 1991.

Stern, Robert, 'British Hegelianism: A Non-Metaphysical View?', *European Journal of Philosophy*, vol. 2, no. 3, December 1994.

Taylor, Charles, 'The Validity of Transcendental Arguments', *Proceedings of the Aristotelian Society* 1979.

—— 'Philosophy and its History', in Richard Rorty, J.B. Schneewind and Quentin Skinner, eds, *Philosophy in History*, Cambridge: Cambridge University Press 1984.

—— 'Theories of Meaning', in *Human Agency and Language: Philosophical Papers 1*, Cambridge: Cambridge University Press 1985.

—— 'The Concept of a Person', in *Philosophical Papers 1*.

—— *Philosophy and the Human Sciences: Philosophical Papers 2*, Cambridge: Cambridge University Press 1985.

—— 'Overcoming Epistemology', in *After Philosophy: End or Transformation?*, ed. K. Baynes, J. Bohman and T. McCarthy, Cambridge, MA: MIT Press 1987.

—— 'Logics of Disintegration', *New Left Review* 170, July–August 1988.

—— *Sources of the Self*, Cambridge: Cambridge University Press 1989.

Teichert, Dieter, 'Anamnetische Solidarität? Zum Begriff historischer Erinnerung bei Benjamin, Habermas und Ricoeur', *Konstanzer Berichte*, 1993/1, Zentrum für Philosophie und Wissenschaftstheorie, University of Konstanz.

Theunissen, Michael, *Sein und Schein: Die kritische Funktion der Hegelschen Logik*, Frankfurt am Main: Suhrkamp 1980.

—— *Negative Theologie der Zeit*, Frankfurt am Main: Suhrkamp 1991.

—— 'The Repressed Intersubjectivity in Hegel's Philosophy of Right', in Drucilla Cornell *et al.*, eds., *Hegel and Legal Theory*, London: Routledge 1991.

Tugendhat, Ernst, *Vorlesungen zur Einführung in die sprachanalytische Philosophie*, Frankfurt am Main: Suhrkamp 1976/*Traditional and Analytic Philosophy: Lectures on the Philosophy of Language*, trans. P. A. Gorner, Cambridge: Cambridge University Press 1982.

—— *Selbstbewußtsein und Selbstbestimmung. Sprachanalytische Interpretationen*, Frankfurt am Main: Suhrkamp 1979/*Self-consciousness and Self-determination*, trans. Paul Stern, Cambridge, MA: MIT Press 1986.

Vattimo, Gianni, 'Nihilisme et postmoderne en philosophie', in *La fin de la modernité*, Paris: Seuil 1987/'Nihilism and Postmodern in Philosophy', in *The End of Modernity*, trans. John R. Snyder, Cambridge: Polity Press 1988.

Wahl, François, *Qu'est-ce que le structuralisme: Philosophie*, Paris: Seuil (Collection Points edn) 1973.

Warnock, Geoffrey, *J.L. Austin*, London: Routledge 1989.

Wellmer, Albrecht, *Zur Dialektik von Moderne und Postmoderne*, Frankfurt am Main: Suhrkamp 1985.

Wellmer, Albrecht, *Ethik und Dialog*, Frankfurt am Main: Suhrkamp 1986.
—— *The Persistence of Modernity*, trans. David Midgely, Cambridge: Polity Press 1991.
—— 'Wahrheit, Kontingenz, Moderne', in Harry Kunneman and Hent de Vries, eds, *Enlightenments: Encounters between Critical Theory and Contemporary French Thought*, Kampen (the Netherlands): Kok Pharos 1993.
Wieland, Wolfgang, *Schellings Lehre von der Zeit*, Heidelberg: Carl Winter – Universitätsverlag 1956.
—— 'Die Anfänge der Philosophie Schellings und die Frage nach der Natur', in Manfred Frank and Gerhard Kurz, eds, *Materialien zu Schellings philosophischen Anfängen,* Frankfurt am Main: Suhrkamp 1975.
Wood, David, 'Différance and the Problem of Strategy', in David Wood and Robert Bernasconi, eds, *Derrida and Différance*, Warwick University: Parousia Press 1985.
—— 'Beyond Deconstruction?', in A. Phillips Griffiths, ed., *Contemporary French Philosophy*, Cambridge: Cambridge University Press 1987.
—— *Philosophy at the Limit*, London: Hutchinson 1990.
—— 'Deconstruction and Criticism', in *Philosophy at the Limit*.
—— 'Metaphor and Metaphysics', in *Philosophy at the Limit*.
Žižek, Slavoj, *Le plus sublime des hystériques – Hegel passe*, Paris: Point Hors Ligne 1988.
—— *The Sublime Object of Ideology*, London: Verso 1989.
—— *For They Know Not What They Do: Enjoyment as a Political Factor*, London: Verso 1991.
—— 'Why Should a Dialectician Learn to Count to Four?', *Radical Philosophy*, no. 58, Summer 1991.
—— *Enjoy Your Symptom: Jacques Lacan in Hollywood and Out*, London: Routledge 1992.
—— 'Eastern European Liberalism and its Discontents', *New German Critique*, no. 57, Fall 1992.
—— *Tarrying with the Negative*, Durham, NC: Duke University Press 1993.
—— *The Metastases of Enjoyment: Six Essays on Woman and Causality*, London: Verso 1994.

# Index

Note: **Bold** figures indicate a chapter on the topic.